# THE ECONOMY OF MODERN INDIA

Second Edi…

Rapid economic growth has put Indi… debates about the future of the global ec… …vised and updated text, B. R. Tomlinson pro… …omprehensive and wide-ranging account of the Indian economy over the last 150 years. He sets arguments about growth, development and underdevelopment, and the impact of imperialism, against a detailed history of agriculture, trade and manufacture, and the relations between business, the economy and the state. The new edition extends the coverage right up to the present day, and explains how one of the largest countries in the world has sought to achieve economic progress and lasting development, despite institutional weaknesses, rigid structures of political and social hierarchy, and the legacy of colonialism.

B. R. TOMLINSON is Emeritus Professor of Economic History at the School of Oriental and African Studies, University of London.

# THE NEW CAMBRIDGE HISTORY OF INDIA

*Founding Editors*

GORDON JOHNSON
Professor Emeritus of Wolfson College, and Former Director, Centre of South Asian Studies, University of Cambridge

C. A. BAYLY
Vere Harmsworth Professor of Imperial and Naval History, Fellow of St Catharine's College and Director, Centre of South Asian Studies, University of Cambridge

*and* THE LATE JOHN F. RICHARDS
Professor of History, Duke University

Although the original *Cambridge History of India*, published between 1922 and 1937, did much to formulate a chronology for Indian history and describe the administrative structures of government in India, it has inevitably been overtaken by the mass of new research published over the last seventy-five years.

Designed to take full account of recent scholarship and changing conceptions of South India's historical development, *The New Cambridge History of India* was developed as a series of short, self-contained volumes, each dealing with a separate theme within an overall four-part structure. The first volume was published in 1987 and the publication of updated second editions is in progress.

The four parts are as follows:

I The Mughals and Their Contemporaries

II Indian States and the Transition to Colonialism

III The Indian Empire and the Beginnings of Modern Society

IV The Evolution of Contemporary South Asia

A list of individual titles will be found at the end of the volume.

# THE NEW CAMBRIDGE HISTORY OF INDIA

III · 3

*The Economy of Modern India*
*From 1860 to the Twenty-First Century*

*Second Edition*

B. R. TOMLINSON

SCHOOL OF ORIENTAL AND AFRICAN STUDIES,
UNIVERSITY OF LONDON

CAMBRIDGE
UNIVERSITY PRESS

CAMBRIDGE
UNIVERSITY PRESS

4381/4 Ansari Road, Daryaganj, Delhi 110002, India

Cambridge University Press is part of the University of Cambridge.

It furthers the University's mission by disseminating knowledge in the pursuit of education, learning and research at the highest international levels of excellence.

www.cambridge.org
Information on this title: www.cambridge.org/ 9781107605473



First published 2013
First South Asian edition 2014

This South Asian edition is based on B. R. Tomlinson/ The Economy of Modern India-2nd edition / 9781107605473 / 2013

Printed in India by Raj Press, R-3 Inderpuri, New Delhi 110012

ISBN 978-1-107-66030-4 paperback

# CONTENTS

# FIGURES



Figure 2.1 is taken from *Report of the Royal Commission on Agriculture in India* (1928), p. 69; figure 2.2 from Michelle McAlpin, 'Price Movements and Fluctuations in Economic Activity', *Cambridge Economic History of India, Volume* 2, graph 11.3; figure 4.1 from Walter C. Neale and John Adams, *India: The Search for Unity, Democracy and Progress*, 2nd edn, New York, 1976, figure 10; figures 5.1, 5.2 and 5.3 were calculated from data available from the World Bank, *World Development Indicators* at http://data.worldbank.org/indicator.

# MAPS



Maps, 1.1, 1.2(b), 2.1(i) and 2.4 are based on, or taken from, material in C. Collin Davies, *An Historical Atlas of the Indian Peninsula*, [Bombay], 1949; maps 1.2(a), 2.1(ii)–(iv), 2.5(a), 2.5(b) and 3.1 on O. H. K. Spate, *India and Pakistan: A General and Regional Geography*, London, 1957; map 2.3 on Davies, *Historical Atlas*, and David E. Sopher (ed.), *An Exploration of India: Geographical*

*Perspectives on Society and Culture*, London, 1980, fig. 9; map 4.1 on Walter Neale and John Adams, *India: The Search for Unity, Democracy and Progress*, 2nd edn, New York, 1976, figure 2; and maps 2.2 and 4.2 on Dharma Kumar, with Meghnad Desai (ed.), *Cambridge Economic History of India, Volume 2*, Cambridge, 1983, maps 3 and 12, which are based on Joseph E. Schwartzberg (ed.), *A Historical Atlas of South Asia*, Chicago, 1978; map 5.1 is taken from Census of India, 2011 at www.imaginmor.com/census-of-india-2011.html.

# TABLES

# PREFACE TO THE SECOND EDITION

In the twenty years since the first edition of this text was completed, many things have happened to the Indian economy, and to the writing of its history. The recent phenomenon of rapid and sustained economic growth has put India at the centre of current debates about the nature of development, and the future of the global economy. This, in turn, has stimulated considerable interest from economists, economic historians and others, who had previously seen India as a special case outside the conventional story of economic progress. The contemporary Indian economy is much discussed and widely taught; these changes have created the opportunity for a second, revised, edition of this economic history to connect recent events to their historical context. This edition contains new material which extends the account of recent history from 1970 to the present day. The sections of the text that deal with history before 1970 have also been reviewed: a small amount of new matter has been added, and the whole has been revised for clarity, and to sharpen the exposition and argument. A new supplementary bibliography highlights recent specialist literature that has opened up new perspectives on our subject.

A number of colleagues have played significant roles in encouraging me to revise and extend this work. Notable among these are Aditya Mukherjee, whose dedicated supervision of the Institute for Advanced Studies at Jawaharlal Nehru University in New Delhi provides an ideal base for research and discussion; Tirthankar Roy, whose own work plays such an important part in opening up new insights into our subject; and a number of Japanese scholars, especially Shigeru Akita, Shoichi Watanabe and Natsuko Kitani, who have helped to advance my interest in the history of modern India in an Asian context. Over the years the circle of connections has also contracted, and a number of the colleagues whose work provided the underpinnings of the original edition are no longer active. In particular we must mourn the loss of two of the founding figures of our subject – Dharma Kumar (1928–2001) and Morris David Morris (1921–2011), who brought wit, precision and imagination to the analysis of the Indian economy and its history. We all stand upon their shoulders, and this edition is dedicated to their memory.

B. R. Tomlinson

# PREFACE TO THE FIRST EDITION

The writing of this book has benefited enormously from the criticism, advice and companionship over the years of a large number of fellow scholars, many of whom have produced the work that is discussed in its pages – including Amiya Bagchi, Chris Baker, Crispin Bates, Chris Bayly, Sugata Bose, Raj Brown, Raj Chandavarkar, Neil Charlesworth, Robi Chatterji, Kirti Chaudhuri, Pramit Chaudhuri, Clive Dewey, Omkar Goswami, Partha Gupta, John Harriss, Dharma Kumar, Michelle McAlpin, Morris David Morris, Aditya Mukherjee, Terry Neale, Rajat Ray, Tapan Raychaudhuri, Peter Robb, Sunanda Sen, Colin Simmons, Burton Stein, Eric Stokes, Dwijendra Tripathi, Marika Vicziany and David Washbrook. I am also grateful for the tolerance and confidence of Gordon Johnson, who has waited for this part of the *New Cambridge History of India* with grace and patience.

The text was begun while I was a Visiting Senior Research Fellow in the Department of Economic History at the University of Melbourne during the antipodean winter and spring of 1990 – a visit which was made enjoyable, stimulating and productive by the efforts of many people, notably David Merrett, Boris Schedvin and Allan Thompson. My colleagues at Birmingham, especially Peter Cain, Rick Garside, Tony Hopkins, Leonard Schwarz, Henry Scott and Gerald Studdert-Kennedy, have provided constant encouragement and support, while Suzy Kennedy made learning word-processing easy. Above all, my family – Caroline, Sam, Charlie, Martha and Edward – made possible the effort that created this book, which I dedicate to them in return.

B. R. Tomlinson

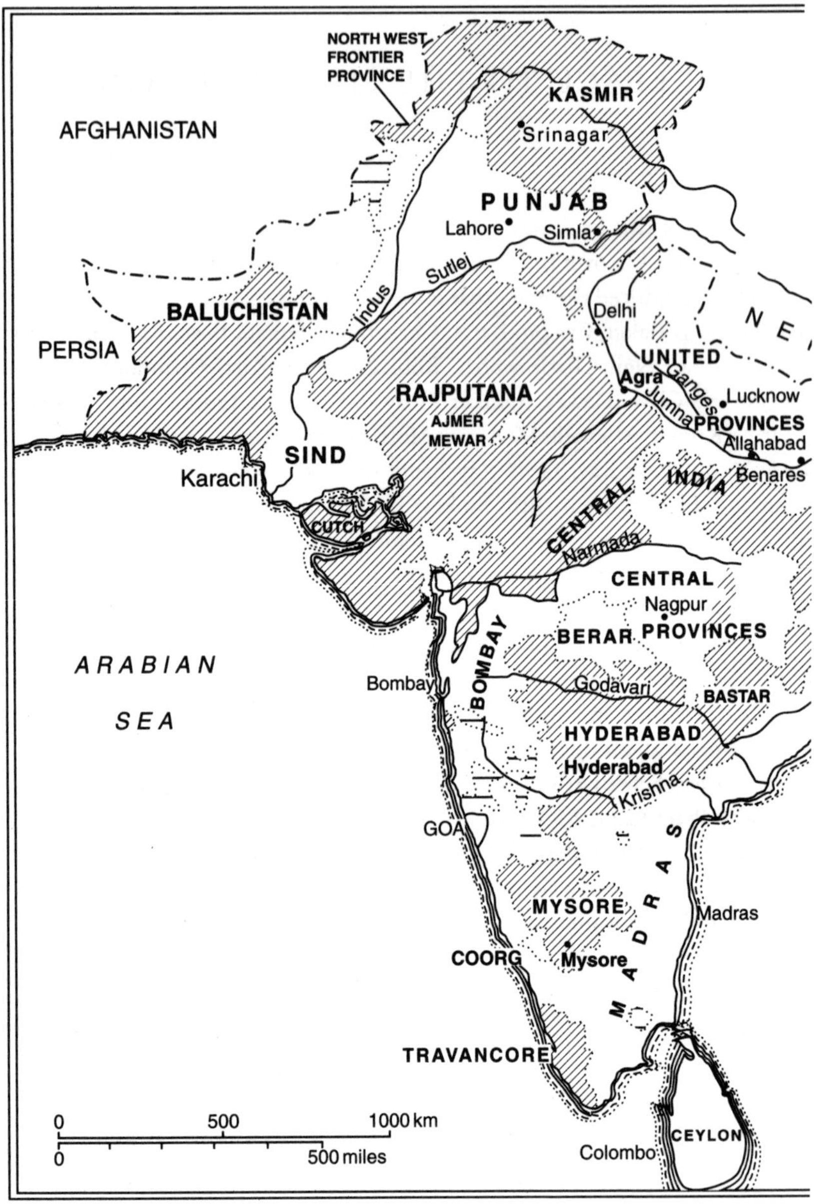


Map 1.1 India in 1938–1939

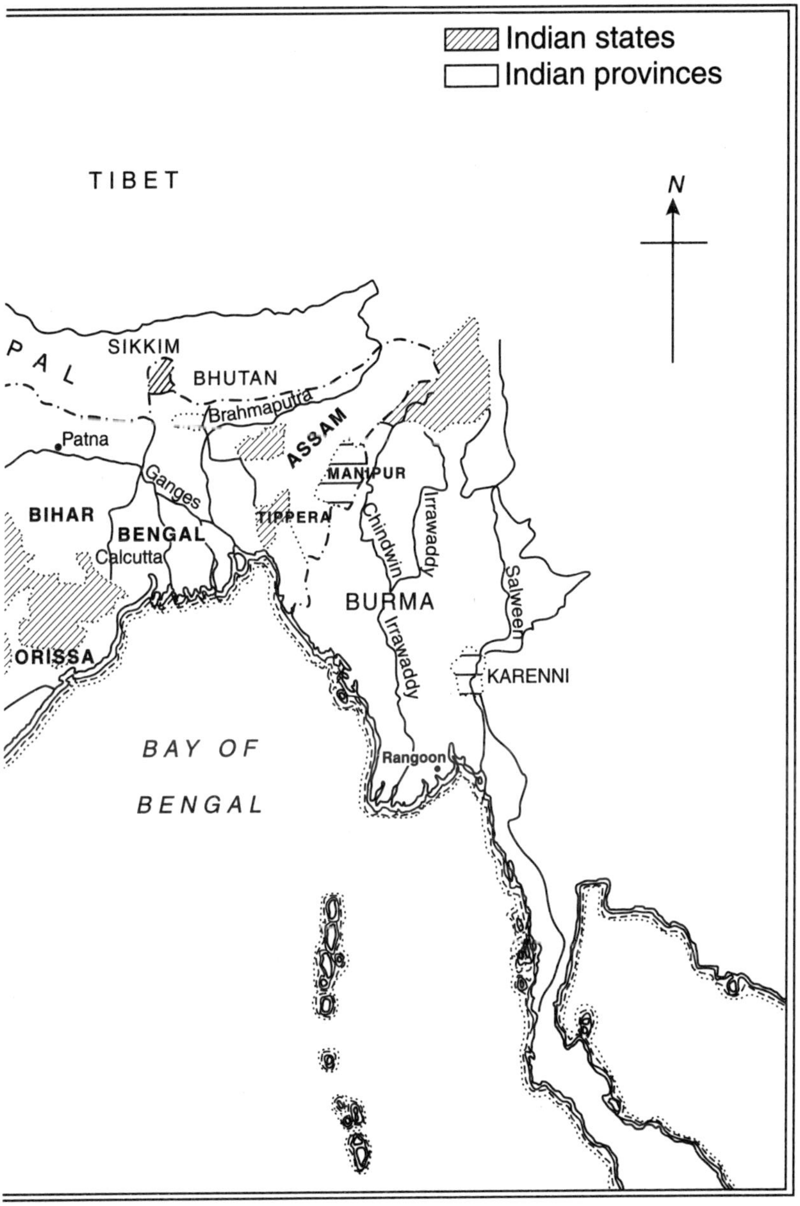

Indian states
Indian provinces
TIBET
N
PAL
SIKKIM
BHUTAN
Brahmaputra
ASSAM
Patna
MANIPUR
Ganges
BIHAR
BENGAL
TIPPERA
Chindwin
Irrawaddy
Calcutta
Salween
BURMA
Irrawaddy
ORISSA
KARENNI
BAY OF
BENGAL
Rangoon

CHAPTER 1

# INTRODUCTION: GROWTH AND DEVELOPMENT IN THE LONG RUN

## ECONOMICS AND INDIAN HISTORY

Modern India is a country where economic history is important: current issues and problems, and many of the institutions and systems that shape the contemporary economy, are closely linked to the legacy of the past.[1] Investigations of key issues in other disciplines – analyses of peasant society, political mobilisation, government policy, social relations of caste, class and community, hierarchies of power and subordination, and the persistence of poverty and inequality – all also depend on fundamental assumptions about the nature of economic structure and change over time, and the history of relations between producers, consumers and the state. Furthermore, the whole sub-discipline of development economics, at crucial stages in its evolution, has drawn heavily on the Indian example – in stressing the destructive effects of imperialism, for example, or the mechanisms by which government planning can mobilise savings in poor economies, or the importance of liberalisation in stimulating growth and broad-based economic change.

The wide spread of interest in our subject brings costs as well as benefits. Accounts of social relations among rural producers, for example, are usually based on very different theories of the nature of economic behaviour than are institutional studies of government tariff policy, or statistically generated estimates of changes in the composition of the gross national product. The most detailed studies of production and consumption at the village level often assume that economic phenomena in India exist only as a function of social and cultural relations. Indeed, many scholars who approach the larger discipline of economic history by way of the history of social and economic structures in South Asia have suspected that accounts of autonomous and self-contained processes of economic development, growth and change in other parts of the world are oversimplified corruptions of a complex reality that has been revealed more clearly in India than elsewhere. In return, those studying the history of

[1] As the World Bank acknowledged in 2005, 'economic development is deeply embedded in countries' history and structural conditions'. World Bank, *Economic Growth in the 1990s: Learning from a Decade of Reform*, Washington, DC, 2005, p. 59.

economic modernisation in the world as a whole have, until very recently, often concluded that South Asia is a special case best firmly shut out of their minds and excluded from their generalisations.

These methodological and conceptual problems are made worse because some of the standard techniques used by economic historians are of limited use in South Asia. Econometric analyses and accounts of the Indian economy can bring precision to some areas of discussion, but so much of the raw data available is misleading, deceptive or partial, with frequent and confusing changes in definitions and categories, that it cannot be used without great care and circumspection. The statistical accretions of the colonial administration often confuse more than they clarify; even where scholars have expended great time and effort in correcting, reclassifying and processing them into a more useful and trustworthy form, the results have often been disputed or ignored. Thus attempts to use a wide range of quantitative data and techniques to find definitive answers to old questions about fluctuations in national income in colonial India, about access to subsistence in famine conditions for different rural social groups, about the level of 'deindustrialisation' in the nineteenth century, about changes in the size and distribution of land-holdings, or about the incidence of poverty since Independence, have convinced few sceptics. One econometric skill well developed in all South Asianists is the ability to expose the fragility of data they wish to disbelieve. These problems are not confined to quantitative studies; much of the qualitative material collected by British administrators in India and other contemporaries is also based on misunderstandings, biased perceptions and limited perspectives. We cannot write an economic history of modern India by simply letting the data speak for themselves.

For these reasons it is hard to produce a convincing narrative account of what happened to the Indian economy in the nineteenth and twentieth centuries. Indeed, it is easy to assume that the Indian economy itself is a category that does not have much meaning. Scholars of all persuasions unite in drawing attention to our ignorance about how the economy of the subcontinent fitted together as a whole, especially what the extent and nature of wide-reaching capital and labour markets in the colonial period might be. Regional specialists often argue that the colonial South Asian economy should be seen as a weakly connected conglomeration of local networks, some of which have displayed considerable growth and dynamism, but which have been held back by transfers to less fortunate regions. At the local level, many economic systems seem self-contained, and to be regulated by social and cultural instruments that deny the very possibility of even a region-wide network of exchange and factor mobility. In addition, the definitions and expectations of market and institutional relations employed by individual historians are often determined by ideology, while the task of completing an aggregative analysis of a large number of local cases, each differing slightly in detail, makes patterns of change over time difficult to detect. The problems that Vera Anstey highlighted in 1929 in the preface to her book, *The Economic Development of India*, are still with us today:

> Much of the best work on Indian economic topics is, naturally, limited to the study of some particular problem or particular district, and, in addition, whether deservedly or not, has often been suspect, on account of its definitely official or anti-British origin, as the case may be.[2]

## GROWTH AND DEVELOPMENT UNDER COLONIALISM

Some indicators of the progress and performance of the Indian economy over the last 150 years are summarised in tables 1.1 and 1.2. These indicate that rates of population increase fluctuated considerably before 1921 (reflecting problems of enumeration, in part, but also the effect of famine and epidemic disease), and then began to rise consistently as a result of falling death rates. Levels of literacy, urbanisation and life expectancy were low in the late nineteenth century, and again increased slowly but steadily over the course of the twentieth century, especially after Indian Independence in 1947. Aggregate measures of welfare improved after 1950, slowly at first; since the 1980s there has been a more rapid improvement, a fall in the birth and death rates, and in the rate of increase of population. Population densities varied across different geographic regions and demographic zones of the subcontinent in the colonial period, as shown in map 1.2, with the heaviest concentrations in the great river deltas of eastern and south-eastern India, and along the alluvial plain watered by the Ganges and Jumna rivers in the north: this distribution has remained since 1950.

The performance of the economy in terms of national product and income levels is much more difficult to assess. Table 1.2a compares alternative estimates of national product between 1900 and 1946. Although these differ considerably in the relative shares of the total attributed to agriculture, manufacturing and services, and in the values assigned to each of these components, they do show a certain degree of convergence in identifying periods of growth and of stagnation.[3] Table 1.2b puts the colonial period into context by extending the

[2] Vera Anstey, *The Economic Development of India*, London, 1929, p. vii.

[3] The estimates used in table 1.2a are derived from S. Sivasubramonian, 'National Income of India, 1900–1 to 1946–7', Ph.D. dissertation, Delhi School of Economics, 1965, pp. 337–8; A. Maddison,

Table 1.1 *Demographic background, India 1871–2011*

| | Population (millions) | Population density (persons per km²) | Population growth rate (%)[a] | Birth rate (per '000)[a] | Death rate (per '000)[a] | Crude literacy rate (%) | | Urban population (%) | Life expectancy at birth (%)[a] | |
|---|---|---|---|---|---|---|---|---|---|---|
| | (1A) | (2A) | (3A) | (4A) | (5A) | (6A) | | (7A) | (8A) | |
| 1871 | 249.4 | | | | | | | 8.7[c] | | |
| 1881 | 254.5 | | 0.20 | | | | | 9.3[c] | | |
| 1891 | 276.7 | | 0.89 | | | (m) | (f) | 9.4 | (m) | (f) |
| 1901 | 280.9 | 77 | 0.11 | 51.4 | 50.1 | 9.8 | 0.6 | 10.0 | | |
| 1911 | 298.2 | 82 | 0.65 | 47.7 | 41.7 | 10.6 | 1.1 | 9.4 | 22.6 | 23.3 |
| 1921 | 299.6 | 81 | 0.09 | 49.1 | 48.6 | 12.2 | 1.8 | 10.2 | 19.4 | 20.9 |
| 1931 | 332.3 | 90 | 1.05 | 48.2 | 37.9 | 15.6 | 2.9 | 11.1 | 26.9 | 26.6 |
| 1941 | 382.6 | 103 | 1.41[b] | 45.2[b] | 31.0[b] | 24.9 | 7.3 | 12.8 | 32.1 | 31.4 |
| | (1B) | (2B) | (3B) | (4B) | (5B) | (6B) | | (7B) | (8B) | |
| 1951 | 361.1 | 117 | 1.25 | 39.9 | 27.4 | 25.0 | 7.9 | 17.3 | 32.4 | 31.7 |
| 1961 | 439.2 | 142 | 1.96 | 41.7 | 22.8 | 34.4 | 13.0 | 18.0 | 41.9 | 40.6 |
| 1971 | 548.2 | 177 | 2.20 | 41.2 | 19.0 | 39.5 | 18.7 | 19.9 | 46.4 | 44.7 |
| 1981 | 683.3 | 216 | 2.22 | 33.9 | 12.5 | 46.9 | 24.8 | 23.3 | 55.4 | 55.7 |
| 1991 | 846.4 | 267 | 2.16 | 29.5 | 9.8 | 52.7 | 32.2 | 25.7 | 60.9 | 59.7 |
| 2001 | 1028.7 | 325 | 1.97 | 25.4 | 8.4 | 63.2 | 45.2 | 27.8 | 63.3 | 63.9 |
| 2011[d] | 1210.2 | 382 | 1.64 | 22.5 | 7.3 | 71.2 | 57.0 | 31.2 | 68.8 | 66.9 |

Columns 1A, 3A–5A, 7A cover the Indian subcontinent, excluding Burma, Baluchistan and North-West Frontier Province; all other data is for Indian Union.

[a] Annual average for decade ending with year indicated; [b] source as Columns 4B and 5B; [c] includes Burma; [d] the data listed as 2011 are for the most recent year available in the source, some of the totals are provisional.

*Sources*: Columns 1A, 3A–5A, 7A, Leela Visaria and Pravin Visaria, 'Population (1975–1947)', *CEHI*, 2, tables 5.8, 5.13, 5.16 and 5.19. Other data from www.indiastat.com and *Census of India, 2011* on www.imaginmor.com, both accessed May 2011.

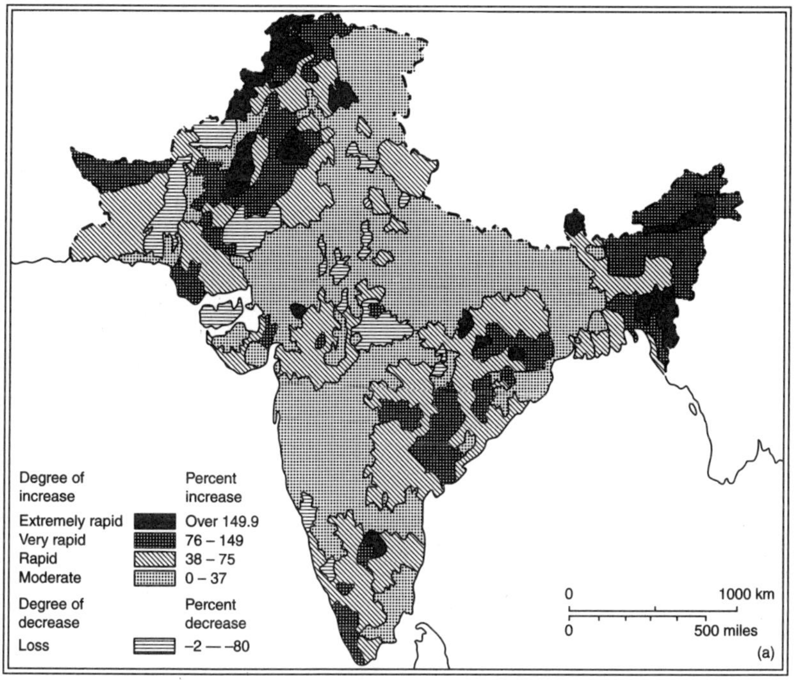


Map 1.2(a) Population, rates of increase by district, 1891–1941

analysis to the end of the twentieth century. These data clearly show how much the colonial economy suffered in the inter-war period from problems of agricultural productivity, strain on credit and labour markets, and the collapse of international trade during the Great Depression.

While precise comparisons are not possible, it would appear that crop yields, industrial productivity, and levels of human capital formation have been as low in India as anywhere in Asia over the last 150 years.[4] The bulk of the Indian

*Class Structure and Economic Growth: India and Pakistan Since the Moghuls*, London, 1971, pp. 167–8; A. Heston, 'National Income', in Dharma Kumar with Meghnad Desai (ed.), *Cambridge Economic History of India: Volume 2, c.1757–c.1970* (hereafter *CEHI*, 2) Cambridge, 1984, pp. 398–9. Both Sivasubramonian and Maddison have subsequently published revised estimates, but the broad picture they report remains unchanged: see S. Sivasubramonian, 'Revised Estimates of the National Income of India, 1900–1901 to 1946–47', *Indian Economic & Social History Review*, 34, 2, 1997, 113–68, and *The National Income of India in the Twentieth Century*, New Delhi, 2000, Ch. 9, and A. Maddison, 'Alternative Estimates of the Real Product of India, 1900–1946', *Indian Economic and Social History Review*, 22, 2, 1985, 201–10.

[4] R. P. Sinha, 'Competing Ideology and Agricultural Strategy: Current Agricultural Development in India and China Compared with Meiji Strategy', *World Development*, 1, 6, 1973, and Shigeru Ishikawa, *Essays on Technology, Employment and Institutions in Economic Development*, Tokyo, 1981, Ch. 1.

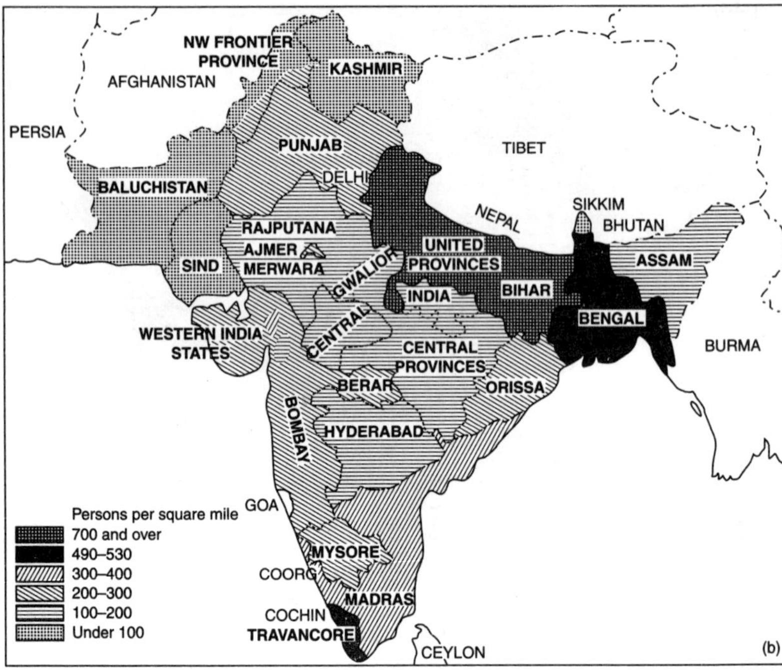


Map 1.2(b) Population densities by province, 1941

population was employed in agriculture throughout the late nineteenth and early twentieth century, although the sectoral contribution of agriculture to national product probably declined. The most widely used estimates are those made by George Blyn in his *Agricultural Trends in India, 1891–1947*, which suggest that productivity problems resulted in a clear fall of per capita agricultural output, especially for foodgrains, in the first half of the twentieth century. The basis of these calculations has often been disputed, but even the most optimistic account has concluded that aggregate agricultural productivity was static over the period from 1860 to 1950 as a whole, at the levels achieved in the early 1950s. On this assumption, per capita income rose by over 30 per cent between 1871 and 1911, and then stagnated for the rest of the colonial period. These data make it clear that at the close of the colonial period in 1947 the extent of development in India was still very limited: average per capita foodgrain availability was about 400 g; the literacy rate was 17 per cent of those over the age of 10, and life expectancy at birth only 32.5 years.[5]

[5] Heston, 'National Income', *CEHI*, 2, pp. 390, 397–9, 410–11.

Table 1.2 *Estimates of Indian national product and GDP, 1870–2001*

*(a) National product, 1900–1946*

| | Constant prices aggregate | | | Constant prices per head | | |
|---|---|---|---|---|---|---|
| | A | B | C | A | B | C |
| I. Indices (1913=100) | | | | | | |
| 1900 | 83 | 89 | 85 | 89 | 95 | 91 |
| 1913 | 100 | 100 | 100 | 100 | 100 | 100 |
| 1920 | 100 | 94 | 96 | 100 | 94 | 95 |
| 1929 | 127 | 110 | 126 | 116 | 100 | 115 |
| 1939 | 138 | 119 | 134 | 110 | 95 | 107 |
| 1946 | 149 | 127 | 142 | 109 | 93 | 104 |
| II. Rate of growth (%) | | | | | | |
| 1900–13 | 1.44 | 0.90 | 1.26 | 0.93 | 0.42 | 0.74 |
| 1914–20 | 0.03 | -0.86 | -0.58 | -0.05 | -0.88 | -0.70 |
| 1921–9 | 2.69 | 1.76 | 3.06 | 1.67 | 0.69 | 2.14 |
| 1930–9 | 0.82 | 0.79 | 0.59 | -0.54 | -0.51 | -0.72 |
| 1940–6 | 1.10 | 0.93 | 0.63 | -0.13 | -0.13 | -0.41 |

A: Sivasubramonian (national income at 1938–9 prices);
B: Maddison (net domestic product at 1938–9 prices);
C: Heston (net domestic product at 1946–7 prices).
*Source*: Goldsmith, *Financial Development of India*, table 1–2.

*(b) GDP and GDP per capita, 1870–2001*

| | GDP (in million 1990 US$) | GDP per capita |
|---|---|---|
| I. Indices (1913=100) | | |
| 1870 | 66 | 79 |
| 1913 | 100 | 100 |
| 1950 | 109 | 92 |
| 1973 | 242 | 127 |
| 2001 | 981 | 291 |
| II. Rate of growth (%) | | |
| 1870–1913 | 0.97 | 0.54 |
| 1913–1950 | 0.23 | -0.22 |
| 1950–1973 | 3.54 | 1.40 |
| 1973–2001 | 5.12 | 3.01 |

*Source:* Angus Maddison, *The World Economy, 1–2001 AD*, Volume 2, table 8b: OECD Development Centre Studies, 2003.

This evidence suggests that there was a distinct but slow-moving process of economic change at work in India over the colonial period as a whole, characterised by minimal improvements in rates of capital and labour productivity and resulting in fluctuating and uncertain patterns of growth. But this conclusion must be treated with care. The slight improvement in some indicators of living standards at various times in the nineteenth and early twentieth century is not evidence of the beneficial effects of British rule, while the evident poverty of large numbers of the Indian population in the 1940s does not prove conclusively that colonial rule alone caused the destitution of its subjects. More importantly, the bird's-eye view of the structure and characteristics of the Indian economy that can be derived from a very general interpretation of aggregate indicators should not lead us to the view that nineteenth-century India was a 'traditional' subsistence economy, awaiting the transforming touch of commercialisation and modernisation. Literacy, urbanisation, the growth of national product, improvements in productivity, and the spread of technical change, can only properly be understood in an ecological, social, economic and political context that pays due attention to local details as well as to national averages.

While the overall aggregate rate of growth was sluggish and unpredictable, this does not mean that nothing was happening in the Indian colonial economy. At certain times, in particular sectors and specific regions, there was quite considerable growth in output, associated with capital accumulation by peasants, landlords, merchants, bankers and industrialists, and some investment in productivity- and profit-enhancing production processes. Some agriculturalists were able to take advantage of increased world demand for crops such as jute, cotton and groundnuts, while Indian businessmen manufactured cotton yarn for export in the nineteenth century and a wide range of products for the domestic consumer market in the twentieth. Whatever the problems of agriculture, rural producers managed to just about sustain a steadily rising population, which increased at an average rate of 0.6 per cent per year between 1871 and 1941, and more rapidly since then. While all the best agricultural land was probably in use by 1900, some colonisation went on until the 1950s, and the area under irrigation almost doubled between 1900 and 1939, and rose sharply after 1947.

There was also considerable evidence of technical change in agriculture, in handicrafts, and in mechanised industry. The spread of new seeds and crop-strains aided output growth in cotton and groundnuts, for example, while techniques such as the transplantation of rice and the ginning of cotton increased yields and marketability. Indian workmen had few difficulties acquiring the skills needed to operate modern textile machinery, while the Tata Iron and Steel Company, the premier industrial enterprise of colonial India, set up a successful Technical Institute in 1921 and an Indian-staffed Research and Control Laboratory in 1937. In handicrafts, fly-shuttle looms and the use of rayon and other artificial fibres broadened the technological base of the handloom weavers in the inter-war years.

This evidence all suggests strongly that some growth, capital accumulation, technical change and innovation occurred in colonial South Asia, but despite these signs of dynamism, the Indian economy did not experience anything that can properly be called 'development' under British rule. Text-book definitions stress that development is a qualitatively distinctive phenomenon from the more limited process of output growth, characterised by intensive growth based on increased productivity and technical change, and raising incomes across the economy while not increasing inequality.[6] In the setting of densely populated agrarian economies such as those of South, South-East and East Asia, these conditions can only come about if, over time, labour achieves sustained increases in productivity, employment, and returns above subsistence. This definition of development also helps to bring its opposite, underdevelopment, into sharper focus. As Joseph Stiglitz has suggested, LDCs (less developed countries) are those in which fewer people than average have the capacity for full personal fulfilment, giving economists and economic historians the task of explaining the reasons for 'the dramatically different standards of living of those who happen to live in different countries and within different regions within the same country'.[7]

For colonial South Asia our problem is to explain an economic history in which technical change and capital accumulation took place, but in which productivity and welfare did not improve very much. Economic historians have found it difficult to explain the absence of development in the modern world, and, like Gershenkron and Schumpeter, have usually only managed to define 'backwardness' in terms of the absence of dynamic features seen in other countries or in the same country at a later date. Those such as Kuznets and Rostow, who have conceptualised the process of development as a series of preconditions or stages of growth, offer little help in understanding the history of economies which have failed to pass through the evolutionary processes laid down for them.

[6] Gerald M. Meier, *Leading Issues in Economic Development*, 5th edn, New York, 1989, p. 6.

[7] Joseph E. Stiglitz, 'Rational Peasants, Efficient Institutions, and a Theory of Rural Organization: Methodological Remarks for Development Economies', in Pranab Bardhan (ed.), *The Economic Theory of Agrarian Institutions*, Oxford, 1989, pp. 19–20.

## THE NATIONALIST CRITIQUE OF COLONIAL RULE

The descriptions and explanations of the apparent lack of growth and development in the Indian economy produced during the colonial period itself were dominated by the nationalist critique of British rule and the imperial response to it. This debate, which has continued to haunt the modern literature as well, was political in origin, revolving around the question of whether India had suffered or benefited from British rule. In economic terms, it focused attention on the evident poverty of the mass of the Indian people in the late nineteenth century, and the prevalence of famine in the 1870s and late 1890s, which seemed to suggest that agriculture could not support the population. The nationalist argument, put forward most forcefully by Dadabhai Naoroji, a Parsi businessman and founder of the Indian National Congress, who was elected to the House of Commons to speak for Indian interests in the 1890s, and by Romesh Chandra Dutt, who resigned from the Indian Civil Service to pursue his attacks on the revenue administration of Bengal, focused on the distortions to the Indian economy brought about by British rule, and the impoverishment of the mass of the population through the colonial 'drain of wealth' from India to Britain over the course of the nineteenth century.[8]

The central theme of the nationalist case was the way in which Indian resources were drained off to Britain by the mechanism of imperial rule. India had long appeared to be a major asset for Britain: yet as early as 1772, when a financial crisis in Bengal prevented the East India Company from paying a dividend and required it to ask the British Government for assistance, London was forced to face up to what became the great riddle of the Raj – whether India was Britain's foremost asset or its greatest liability. By the last quarter of the nineteenth century India was the largest purchaser of British exports, a major employer of British civil servants at high salaries, the provider of half of the Empire's military might, all paid for from local revenues, and a significant recipient of British capital.[9] The crucial point for the nationalists was that British rule brought about a 'drain of wealth' as India met a large deficit in goods and services with Britain, plus interest charges and capital repayments in London.

[8] Dadabhai Naoroji, *Poverty and Un-British Rule*, London, 1901; R. C. Dutt, *The Economic History of India in the Victorian Age*, London, 1906.

[9] According to the most complete direct estimates for British capital exports from 1860 and 1914, between £239 and £290 million raised in London was invested in India, more than half of it in the form of government loans. The Indian total represented about 20 per cent of all capital sent to the empire, and about 7 per cent of all capital exports from Britain. See Lance E. Davis and Robert A. Huttenback, *Mammon and the Pursuit of Empire: The Political Economy of British Imperialism, 1860–1912*, Cambridge, 1986, table 2.1.

The main lines of debate over the drain theory have long been established. Imperial apologists such as Theodore Morison and Vera Anstey argued that most of India's payments to Britain were made in return for services or capital that increased the wealth of the local economy. The size of the unrequited transfers, those needed to meet the 'Home Charges' (the administrative and military expenses of the Indian Government in Britain), was small, running at around Rs 20 million a year, less than 2 per cent of total export values at the end of the nineteenth century and less than 1 per cent by 1913.[10] Anstey herself claimed that if there had been no Home Charges and no loans in London, but India had provided for its own military and naval defence, then India would have come out the loser – 'it is surely obvious that the "saving" effected would be a negative quantity'.[11] Nationalists fiercely contested the assumptions on which such calculations were based, arguing in particular that India's defence establishment was designed to meet Britain's needs, and that the railways were an expensive military asset rather than an appropriate piece of developmental infrastructure. The classic nationalist case was that Britain's entire favourable balance of payments with its colony represented the size of the drain of wealth, with a convenient floor-figure set by India's export surplus in merchandise (representing the net total of Indian current payments to Britain less British capital exports to India). A recalculation on this basis has suggested that the drain in 1882 amounted to Rs 1,355 million (in 1946–7 prices), more than 4 per cent of national income in that year.[12]

Britain's balance-of-payments surplus with South Asia was an important element in the world pattern of settlements in the second half of the nineteenth century, enabling the United Kingdom to meet 30–40 per cent of its deficit with other industrialised nations, and helping to sustain its performance as an economy with a global balance-of-payments surplus long after its trading position in most parts of the world had declined.[13] From the Indian end, one notable feature of the balance-of-payments surplus was the volume of imports of gold and silver bullion. The Indian rupee was a silver currency on a bullion standard with open mints until 1893, and India was a major importer of silver in the late nineteenth century. About one-third of India's trade surplus in goods between 1872 and 1893 was financed by imports of specie,

[10] K. N. Chaudhuri, 'India's International Economy in the Nineteenth Century: An Historical Survey', *Modern Asian Studies*, 2, 1, 1968, p. 44.

[11] Anstey, *Economic Development of India*, p. 511.

[12] Irfan Habib, 'Studying a Colonial Economy – Without Perceiving Colonialism', *Modern Asian Studies*, 19, 3, 1985, p. 375–6.

[13] S. B. Saul, *Studies in British Overseas Trade, 1870–1914*, Liverpool, 1960, Ch. VIII.

mostly silver, the bulk of which was used either as transaction coinage or was saved in the form of hoarded coin, bullion and jewellery.[14] The main elements of India's balance of payments in this period are set out in table 1.3.

This analysis sets South Asia's traditional role in world trade as a 'sink' for precious metals, first noted by Pliny in ancient times, and used by J. M. Keynes in his *Indian Currency and Finance* (1913) to strengthen the case for a gold-exchange standard for India with a token currency, against the late-nineteenth-century theory of the colonial drain of wealth from India to Britain. Although the gold price of silver in the world economy fell by about 40 per cent in this period, it was not falling faster than any other gold price, so it is difficult to sustain the argument that the world was somehow acquiring India's exports cheap by paying for them with a devalued commodity. After 1900, when the rupee was linked to gold at a fixed rate through an exchange standard with sterling, the story told by continued bullion imports is less ambiguous. In the pre-war trade boom between 1909/10 and 1912/13, for example, India imported Rs 1,174 million worth of gold, including Rs 45 million worth of sovereigns which went into circulation, increased its gold reserves by Rs 294 million, and imported a further Rs 549 million worth of silver, only a third of which was used for coinage.[15]

Specie imports by themselves do not reveal anything about the pattern of distribution inside the colonial economy. It is possible to imagine a set of circumstances in which inequality increased along with bullion imports, and some modern historians working within the nationalist tradition have argued that capital did increase in India, but that it accumulated in the hands of 'parasitic' groups of landlords, usurers and native aristocrats. Certainly the availability of silver and gold for hoarding may well have discouraged the development of flexible savings instruments that could have helped finance more dynamic investment and more efficient provision of liquidity. What the inflow of specie does suggest, however, is that some Indians were increasing

[14] P. R. Brahmananda's monumental *Money, Income, Prices in 19th Century India: A Historical, Quantitative and Theoretical Study*, Delhi, 2001, estimates that bullion and jewellery hoards held an amount equivalent to 50 per cent of net domestic product (NDP) in the late nineteenth century, and grew by 50 per cent between 1861 and 1894 [Table 8.1a]: on the implications of this, see Meghnad Desai, 'Drains, Hoards and Foreigners: Does the Nineteenth Century Indian Economy Have Any Lessons for Twenty First Century India?', RBI Brahmananda Memorial Lecture, 2004, http://rbidocs.rbi.org.in/rdocs/Speeches/Pdfs/58008.pdf

[15] J. M. Keynes, *Indian Currency and Finance*, London, 1913, pp. 108–10, and G. Findlay Shirras, *Indian Finance and Banking*, London, 1920, p. 463. Goldsmith has estimated the net accumulation of gold and silver in India from 1896 to 1913 at 1.5 per cent of national income, 30–40 per cent of total domestic savings. Raymond W. Goldsmith, *The Financial Development of India, 1860–1977*, New Haven, 1983, pp. 21–2.

Table 1.3 *India, annual balance of payments on current account, 1869–1873 to 1894–1898 (£ millions, quinquennial averages)*

| | Balance of merchandise trade | Net treasure imports | Balance of visible trade (1+2) | Home charges | Other invisibles | All invisibles (4+5) | Balance of payments on current account (3-6) |
|---|---|---|---|---|---|---|---|
| | 1 | 2 | 3 | 4 | 5 | 6 | 7 |
| 1869–73 | +22.6 | -8.4 | +14.2 | - 8.8 | -15.6 | -24.4 | -10.6 |
| 1874–8 | +21.0 | -6.4 | +14.6 | - 9.3 | -18.0 | -17.3 | -12.7 |
| 1879–83 | +23.8 | -7.1 | +16.7 | -10.7 | -17.7 | -28.4 | -11.7 |
| 1884–8 | +23.8 | -9.2 | +14.6 | -12.3 | -18.0 | -30.3 | -15.7 |
| 1889–93 | +25.2 | -9.7 | +15.5 | -13.5 | -19.4 | -32.9 | -17.4 |
| 1894–8 | +20.7 | -5.6 | +15.1 | -13.9 | -18.9 | -32.8 | -17.7 |

*Note:* A plus sign (+) indicates net exports of goods; a minus sign (-) indicates net imports of goods and net exports of remittances, service charges and other invisibles.
The most thorough direct estimate of flows of long-term foreign capital into India from 1870 to 1899 gives a total of between £123.2 million and £144.8 million, most of which was in the form of sterling loans to the Secretary of State for India in London (see Lance E. Davis and Robert A. Huttenback, *Mammon and the Pursuit of Empire: The Political Economy of British Imperialism 1860–1912*, Cambridge, 1986, table 2.1).
*Source*: A. K. Banerji, *Aspects of Indo-British Economic Relations, 1858–98*, Bombay, 1982, tables 34A and 40A.

their assets during the colonial period. This is an important point, since the central contention of the drain theory in its original form was that the mechanisms of British rule removed any investible surplus above subsistence from India, and that therefore no growth at all was possible: as Naoroji put it, 'the drain prevents India from making any capital'.[16]

The imperial apologists who responded to this case argued that national income had increased somewhat in the late nineteenth century, but agreed that any process of economic growth was so slow as to be almost undetectable, being held back largely by social, cultural and religious barriers to material improvement. Despite the atavistic power of the debate over British rule and Indian 'improvement', this is the point at which the modern literature must

[16] Dadabhai Naoroji, 'Poverty of India', p. 38, in *Poverty and Un-British Rule.*

part company with its colonial ancestor, for almost all current accounts of the economic history of India are concerned with classifying a distinguishable process of economic change, however distorted or sluggish it may have been, and analysing its effect on classes and interests inside rather than outside South Asia. However, the slow rate of that growth, and its weak developmental effects, still require explanation.

## DEVELOPMENT AND UNDERDEVELOPMENT IN MODERN INDIA

In general, mainstream economic theory, in all its variants, has had little to say about the absence of development. In neo-classical analysis all economies tend towards equilibrium, but it is difficult to identify or explain what is happening to those in which an equilibrium is reached below maximum efficiency. In both classical and orthodox Marxist analyses, capitalism is usually seen as a uniquely progressive force in an economy, with capital accumulation and investment the only way to increase productivity, raise output and provide a surplus that can be redistributed to maintain returns to labour above subsistence.

Karl Marx, like almost all his contemporaries, saw the Asian economies of India and China as having no history, being the products of societies in which political and economic networks and institutional systems did not interact. In *Capital*, and elsewhere, Marx developed the concepts of 'primitive accumulation' and of an 'Asiatic mode of production' to explain the existence of large, static Eastern economies and societies that were not likely by themselves to progress through feudalism to capitalism. The self-sufficiency of the Indian economy was based on 'village republics' with 'cut and dried' patterns of community organisation, which encompassed communal property rights in a combination of agriculture and handicraft manufacture. Villages were entirely self-sustaining, containing within themselves all the conditions of production and surplus accumulation, while cities were mere military or princely camps, in which despotic rulers received tribute from the countryside in return for the maintenance of irrigation works.[17]

Marx thought that the coming of British rule was the greatest threat to this existing social and economic order, and argued that it would prepare the way for a capitalist economy dominated, eventually, by a domestic bourgeoisie.

[17] For a convenient, brief summary of Marx's views on India, see Daniel Thorner, *The Shaping of Modern India*, New Delhi, 1980, pp. 363 ff.

However, he was also highly critical of the disruptive effects of colonial administration in the 1830s, 1840s and 1850s, and saw the commercialisation of agriculture and the flooding of the Indian market with mass-produced Lancashire cotton goods as leading to the destruction of old social arrangements without any dynamic process of constructive change. Later theorists have followed these dual strands in Marx's own thinking by developing theories of imperialism that attribute the modes of production in the developing economies of the twentieth century directly to the impact of imperial systems and colonial states.

Central to many of these later accounts has been the concept of dependency, 'a situation in which the economy of certain countries is conditioned by the development and expansion of another economy to which the former is subjected'.[18] The notion of dependent development distinguishes between the role of capitalism as a progressive force in the core but a regressive one in the periphery, and gives a major role to imperialism in tightly circumscribing the extent of any development that peripheral capitalism can achieve. However, empirical studies of the pattern of growth in many developing countries since the 1960s have led to the revival of a more orthodox Marxist view of peripheral development, encapsulated in Geoffrey Kay's comment that 'capitalism created underdevelopment not because it exploited the underdeveloped world but because it did not exploit it enough'.[19] One striking revisionist account, Bill Warren's *Imperialism: Pioneer of Capitalism*,[20] explicitly took Marx's analysis of Britain's necessary role in transplanting capitalism in India as its starting-point. These 'menshevik' theories, as they have been called,[21] see capital as a progressive force, however exploitative, in Africa, Asia and Latin America. They are useful in disentangling capitalism from a functionalist relationship with imperialism, but they do not help much in analysing the inhibitory factors that prevented many economies subject to colonial rule from undergoing development. The notion of an underdeveloped world dominated by some sort of primitive economy in Marx's sense still lurks beneath their surface.

Nationalist interpretations of Indian economic history from the late nineteenth century onwards argued that India was far from being a primitive

[18] T. Dos Santos, 'The Structure of Dependence', *American Economic Review*, 40, 2, 1970, p. 231.

[19] G. B. Kay, *Development and Underdevelopment: A Marxist Analysis*, London, 1975, p. x.

[20] Bill Warren, *Imperialism: Pioneer of Capitalism*, London, 1980.

[21] Colin Leys, 'Conflict and Convergence in Development Theory', in Wolfgang J. Mommsen and Jürgen Osterhammel (eds.), *Imperialism and After: Continuities and Discontinuities*, German Historical Institute, London, 1986, pp. 321–2.

economy before the British. Colonial rule was thought to have removed or distorted the developmental base reached by domestic industry and agriculture in the eighteenth century, and then suppressed the entire economy in the nineteenth century by the mechanism of the drain of wealth. These ideas were sustained and refined in Indian Marxist analyses during the early twentieth century, notably in R. Palme Dutt, *India Today* (1940), and were then incorporated into dependency theory through the work of Paul Baran, who revived the notion that the coming of British rule in India had broken up pre-existing self-sufficient agricultural communities, and forced a shift to the production of export crops, which distorted the internal economy. In his *Political Economy of Growth* (1957), Baran took up the central insight of the nationalist analysis, suggesting that about 10 per cent of India's gross national product was transferred to Britain each year in the early decades of the twentieth century, asserting that had this sum been invested in South Asia, 'India's economic development to date would have borne little similarity to the actual sombre record'.[22] To Baran, the colonial drain was a mercantilist concept – India's loss of economic resources and their transfer to Britain was a consequence of its political subordination. Thus asymmetrical power and political relations, rather than natural endowments or comparative advantage, determined the economic history of underdeveloped countries.

The notion of colonial South Asia as host to a particular, regressive form of capitalism, leading to dependency, underdevelopment, or sustained backwardness, has been refined further, in the work of Amiya Bagchi and Hamza Alavi, for example, into the concept of a distinct colonial mode of production.[23] This argues that British rule brought about a process of economic change in South Asia which had some dynamic features, but that these were functionally determined to serve the needs of the metropolitan economy and so established a dependent form of underdevelopment. Colonial rule broke down the autonomous economy of independent handicraft workers and self-sufficient peasants, and directed domestic economic activity towards two main areas – export-oriented agriculture with very small returns to provide primary products for the West at bargain prices before Independence, and limited industrialisation dependent on alliances with foreign firms for technology since then. The laws, institutions and social structure of contemporary South Asia were thus a creation of Britain's requirement for cheap labour and cheap exports within

[22] Paul Baran, *The Political Economy of Growth*, New York, 1957, p. 148. It is worth noting that this estimate of the size of the drain is more than double that of Irfan Habib cited above.

[23] Amiya Kumar Bagchi, *The Political Economy of Underdevelopment*, Cambridge, 1982; Hamza Alavi *et al.*, *Capitalism and Colonial Production*, London, 1980.

the imperial system, and the dominant classes that have exercised control over agricultural and industrial capital for the last hundred years or so are identified as the product of this colonial transformation. By these means, Indian labour has been exploited indirectly but effectively for the sake of metropolitan capital, and successive forms of colonial and post-colonial capitalism have been created that did not need to increase productivity or wages.

The analysis of dependent underdevelopment contends, like the nationalist critique of the colonial economy before it, that the British conquest was the chief reason for India's development problems over the last 200 years. As we have already seen, such arguments put a heavy interpretative loading on the impact of British rule, and tend to overestimate the extent to which this destroyed either a self-sufficient 'primitive' economy, or a burgeoning state-capitalist developmental one. The British certainly altered the political economy and state structure of India fundamentally in the late eighteenth and early nineteenth centuries, and severely disrupted some established patterns of trade, of investment, and of agricultural and handicraft production, but the quantitative extent and qualitative significance of the consequences of this – in the form of deindustrialisation, forced commercialisation, and the transfer of land-holding to traders and moneylenders – is hard to assess. Studies of many different localities during the first century or so of British rule have stressed the extent of continuity rather than change in the holding and exercise of social and economic power. Local social structures, and the interaction between social power and economic opportunity, were often remarkably unaffected by the waxing and waning of imperial control; the chief reasons for economic stagnation were usually present before the British arrived, remained in place during their rule, and have stayed there after its ending.

## THE COLONIAL ECONOMY IN COMPARATIVE PERSPECTIVE

India before 1947 cannot be classified as a simple form of colonial economy, in which surplus extraction and functionally determined social organisation created a system of non-progressive economic activity. British imperialism had a very important impact on the economic history of modern South Asia, but it was not the only reason for the phenomenon of limited growth without development. The economic history of South Asia is not broadly dissimilar to that of other large and populous Asian economies such as China and Indonesia, which were not part of the British Empire. While these areas were exposed to European imperialism, formal or informal, in a broad sense, neither shared India's precise experience under foreign rule. The history of the

Indian economy since 1947 has revealed many of the same problems of low productivity and non-developmental social organisation that were apparent in the colonial period. India, like other developing economies, may have suffered from neglect by the liberal institutional structure of the post-war international economic system, and may have been subjected to neo-imperial ties through aid and direct private investment mechanisms, but such ties have been universal, affecting large numbers of countries in Asia, Africa and Latin America, and their impact in India cannot be attributed solely to its colonial past.

While Indian interests were clearly subordinated to British ones in important respects during the lifetime of the British Raj, Indian economic history was not simply that of a subaltern, subservient economy. As in other applications of subaltern studies to Indian history, the separate levels of dominance and subservience among different groups of Indians must be accounted for. The theme of inequality runs strongly through Indian colonial history, but economic relations were as unequal within colonial society as they were between the imperial power and its colonial subjects. Subaltern studies do not give much help in understanding the dominant agents in a subordinate economy. Some Indian professionals, businessmen, landlords and 'surplus peasants'[24] derived considerable benefits from the local power that was conferred on them by British rule; it is hard to see that these elites missed out on profits or advantages in the medium term because of India's subordinate position. Even those Indian businessmen who found their industrialising ambitions apparently thwarted by the colonial government's commitment to laissez-faire economic policies were eventually able to supplant their expatriate rivals as the dominant element in the private sector. There was no such thing as an entirely subordinate economy within the British Empire – every country's economy contained both dominant and subordinate groups. Subalterns certainly suffered in colonial India, and were more plentiful there than in imperial Britain, but they did exist in the core as well as at the periphery of the imperial system.

Like Marx, the classical economists of the late eighteenth and early nineteenth centuries were concerned to understand and explain processes of rapid and fundamental economic change. For the classical economists such change would inevitably be accompanied by the conventional measures of growth and development; the only alternative to a developing economy was a static one – a 'stationary state', in which there was no capital accumulation (profit) and

[24] 'Surplus' peasants are defined as those controlling family farms that could, in a normal year, grow and retain enough food and other produce to produce a surplus over their own subsistence requirements, without the need to seek off-farm employment.

no technical progress (investment or increased labour productivity). Thus, as Adam Smith commented on China (and by extension all Asian economies of the late eighteenth century):

China seems to have been long stationary, and had probably long ago acquired that full complement of riches that is consistent with the nature of its laws and institutions. But this complement may be much inferior to what, with other laws and institutions, the nature of its soil, climate and situation might admit of.[25]

In the event, Smith argued, 'the poverty of the lower ranks of the people far surpasses that of the most beggarly nations of Europe'.[26] Following Smith, later writers in the classical and neo-classical traditions have sought to explain economic backwardness in terms of inappropriate laws and institutions which prevent the dynamics of capitalism from unleashing the forces of growth. Such arguments stress that all economies can achieve development, providing that they expose themselves to the efficiencies generated by free markets and unfettered competition. In poor, densely settled regions, population pressures may make dynamic growth harder to achieve, but simple Malthusian traps can be avoided by foreign trade, by migration, and by technical progress to make land and labour more productive.

Scholars working within this broad framework have produced important alternative interpretations of the economic history of modern South Asia. One of the earliest of these was Gunnar Myrdal's portrayal in *Asian Drama* of the Indian economy as determined by social systems that bound it to a 'low-level equilibrium' characterised by low labour productivity, low per capita incomes, traditional and primitive production techniques and low levels of living. This interconnected causal relationship between productivity and incomes, levels of living, and labour inputs and productivity, could only be overcome by a positive programme of modernisation that would promote rationality, equality, planning, democracy, and appropriate values as well as economic efficiency. The only force that Myrdal saw as powerful enough to overcome the forces of stagnation, social stability and equilibrium that would perpetuate poverty and inequality was the nation state. Here, however, he thought the Indian government unequal to the task, categorising it as a 'soft' state, unable to impose the

[25] Adam Smith, *Wealth of Nations*, I, p. 106, quoted in H. W. Arndt, *The Rise and Fall of Economic Development*, Melbourne, 1978, p. 8.

[26] Smith, *Wealth of Nations*, I, p. 73, quoted in H. W. Arndt, 'Development Economics Before 1945', in Jagdish Bhagwati and Richard S. Eckaus (eds.), *Development and Planning: Essays in Honour of Paul Rosenstein Rodan*, London, 1972, p. 14.

social discipline needed to force economic, political and ideological change onto its unwilling subjects.[27]

Liberal critics of the activities of the Indian state since 1947 have identified the distortions caused by an inappropriate and ineffective regime of economic policies and planning as a crucial barrier to growth. From the 1970s onwards, bureaucratic controls in India were seen, in the work of Anne Kreuger and others, as an integral part of a 'rent-seeking society' in which the owners of scarce assets (land, capital) or privileges (such as import licences) were simply rewarded for this ownership, rather than being forced to earn a return on them by efficient working in an open market.[28] Thus productivity was not increased by competition; instead profits were maintained by limiting the number of rent-holders and closing off alternative routes for access to scarce assets. The result was political stability based on the interests of a narrow range of propertied and favoured groups, but accompanied by the economic irrationality of under-utilised industrial capacity, wasteful use of foreign exchange and industrial investment, inappropriate land reform, and a corrupt polity that made any genuine development almost impossible.

Generally speaking, accounts of South Asian development written within the neo-classical tradition identify Indian social and cultural arrangements as inhibitors of growth and change. However, such explanations bring special problems with them, and should not be used on their own without very significant qualification. The apparent non-material spirituality of Hindu life and beliefs that was so often stressed by colonial officials is not a very useful explanatory variable – indeed, many of the most successful Indian businessmen had strong links to religious charities and institutions. Fatalism is stronger when choice is limited, and local cultural systems have often had strong connections to interlinked social, political and economic relationships. As Eric Stokes argued forcefully, agrarian history shows that the demands of economics often overrode the constraints of morality and law in village cultivation arrangements; in some parts of north India, for example, Brahmins did their own ploughing, and Rajput *thakurs* discarded their stereotypical image of indolent rentier pride when economic circumstances provided incentives.[29]

[27] Gunnar Myrdal, *Asian Drama: An Inquiry into the Poverty of Nations*, Volume II, Harmondsworth, 1968, pp. 895 ff. There is a convenient summary of these points in B. L. C. Johnson, *Development in South Asia*, Harmondsworth, 1983, pp. 16–19.

[28] A. O. Kreuger, 'The Political Economy of a Rent-Seeking Society', *American Economic Review*, 64, 3, 1974.

[29] Eric Stokes, *The Peasant and the Raj: Studies in Agrarian Society and Peasant Rebellion in Colonial India*, Cambridge, 1978, pp. 234–6.

Such examples can be matched and multiplied from all other parts of the subcontinent. Culturalist explanations also require us to believe that a unique culture will determine a unique performance, and yet the economic consequences of Hinduism for the South Asian economy over the last 200 years or so have not been so singular. South Asia is not a solely Hindu region, yet its modern economic history has a certain unity, and also exhibits striking similarities to other areas, such as Indonesia and China, which have a different cultural base. Where variations do exist in the comparative histories of these regions they can be better explained by secular factors. Colonial India certainly exhibited an institutional rigidity in social and economic organisation, but this was not a uniquely Hindu, South Asian or colonial problem – indeed, much of the slow-down in Britain's own economic growth in the second half of the nineteenth century has often been attributed to the same cause.

Deepak Lal's analysis of a 'Hindu equilibrium' of cultural stability and economic stagnation provides a functional explanation of Indian social organisation and agricultural systems as a response to a specific environment.[30] Lal argued that traditional Hindu society, based around the caste system, was organised to facilitate decision-making under conditions of uncertainty, brought about by the four long-run constraints of labour shortage, political decentralisation in local warrior-states, climatic variability and ecological fragility, and a culture-based undervaluation of merchant activity. This identification of economic stagnation is so aggregated as to be highly misleading, however. Lal uses very general indicators that ignore regional diversity, and assumes changelessness over long periods and large areas, rather than self-cancelling fluctuations in time and space; he also assumes that the uniqueness of Hindu culture produces a unique economic situation in India, ignoring parallel work on labour utilisation in other rice-cultivating regions of Asia that suggests similarities to Indian cases at the local and regional levels.

Both Marxian and liberal approaches demonstrate the increasing unity of capital, commodity and labour markets across the Indian subcontinent, linking the subsistence sector and the commercial economy together. South Asian economic history was not dualistic – we cannot identify and distinguish separate 'modern' and 'traditional' sectors, each with its own institutions and sphere of operations. The linkages and interconnections between the markets for agricultural land, labour and capital, and between industrial organisation and the control of labour discipline and wages were elaborate, and often intermixed

[30] Deepak Lal, *The Hindu Equilibrium: Cultural Stability and Economic Stagnation, India 1500 BC-1980 AD*, Volume I, Oxford, 1984.

'modern' and 'traditional' forms in a complex and subtle way. The imperial economy of colonial South Asia took the form that it did because of the nature of the indigenous economy, while the indigenous economy was shaped, in turn, by the imperial economy. Market relations, in cash and kind, however imperfect, inefficient and often exploitative they may have been, suffused the South Asian economy as much as any other in the world throughout the eighteenth, nineteenth and twentieth centuries.

The extent of market penetration, the character of the markets that operate, and the involvement of various economic groups of producers and consumers in them provide a useful framework for understanding the modern economic history of colonial India as a whole.[31] Many of the capital, labour and commodity markets were interlinked, since the availability of land, credit and employment was often concentrated in the hands of the same small groups of agricultural managers and industrial entrepreneurs, although such interlinking was not constant, and could change in type and intensity over time. In some sectors of the economy, notably in parts of the rural labour market and in mechanised industry and export–import trade, markets were internalised into institutional structures such as customary (*jajmani*) service networks or vertically integrated firms. These institutions represented alternatives to market arrangements, and could replace them, or be replaced by them, under certain circumstances. Where transaction costs were particularly high, especially the costs of labour discipline and recruitment, or the diffusion of information and technological capacity, such internalising institutions were common. They could be created to distort or bypass existing market arrangements by substituting tied for free labour in agriculture, for example, or by integrating manufacturing, sales and distribution with the securing of raw material supply in industry. At times, however, these institutions could also collapse and fail, and by the end of the colonial period many had to be supported or replaced by state agencies.

The underlying characteristics of economic growth and development in colonial and post-colonial India were determined by the nature of the markets that decided how any surplus over subsistence was generated, and then divided it between capital, labour and the state. Imperfections in these markets led to the emergence of public and private economic institutions that altered, replaced and substituted for them over time, affected economic performance and decision-making profoundly, and magnified problems of risk

[31] On these issues in the rural economy, see Krishna Bharadwaj, *Production Conditions in Indian Agriculture*, Cambridge, 1974, reprinted in John Harriss (ed.), *Rural Development: Theories of Peasant Economy and Agrarian Change*, London, 1982, Ch. 12.

and risk management that were endemic in an underdeveloped economy with high levels of uncertainty. The process of creating economic institutions or markets was not entirely dominated by narrow classes or particular interest groups, but the arrangements that were made tended to favour the few rather than the many, and to reward the owners, or controllers, of scarce resources (land, capital, power) rather than the owners of the plentiful resource, labour. In addition, the colonial regime, which had its own peculiar priorities and purposes, played an important role in both shaping and directing the organisational framework of the economy. Thus the role of political and social power in economic relations was central, and the ideology and scope of the state also played an important role in shaping economic action. Both 'underconsumption' and 'rent-seeking' theories focus on important issues, but neither are enough, on their own, to fully analyse the interplay of development and underdevelopment in colonial South Asia. We need instead a historical context that can show the pattern of change and stasis over time. The chapters that follow will provide this by investigating the indigenous and external structures that determined the performance of agriculture, and trade and manufacture, and that shaped the relations between the colonial and post-colonial state and the economy of modern India.

## CHAPTER 2

# AGRICULTURE, 1860–1950: LAND, LABOUR AND CAPITAL

### AGRICULTURAL OUTPUT: YIELDS AND PRODUCTIVITY

Inadequate agricultural production lay at the heart of India's development problems in the colonial period. Agriculture, and ancillary activities such as animal husbandry, forestry and fishing, was the foundation of the economy: the rural sector employed about three-quarters of the workforce and produced well over half of national income between the 1860s and the 1940s. While the proportion of the workforce employed in agriculture increased very slightly between 1911 and 1951, the percentage of national income derived from the sector fell by 9 per cent over the same period.[1] Although several regions experienced some growth in agricultural output during the last quarter of the nineteenth century, a steady rate of population increase resulted in a subsistence crisis by the 1940s. Problems of labour utilisation, an endemic scarcity of capital and a lack of investment in irrigation and other capital inputs, created a shortage of productive land. In addition, low wages and other returns to labour in the rural economy limited demand for basic wage goods such as textiles, which in turn undermined wide-reaching economic growth based on mass consumption in the domestic market.

The classic work on Indian agricultural output and productivity in the colonial period, on which most general accounts of agrarian history have been based, remains that of George Blyn, first published in full in 1966.[2] Using the acreage and yield estimates collected by the colonial revenue administration, Blyn argued that there was a small expansion in per capita agricultural output

[1] While the percentage of the labour-force employed in agriculture rose from 74.8 per cent in 1911 to 75.7 per cent in 1951, the percentage of national income supplied by agriculture fell from 66.6 per cent in 1900–1/1904–5 to 57.6 per cent in 1942–3/1946–7. This gives a fall in the relative product (percentage of workforce divided by percentage of national income) from 0.89 to 0.76. The relative product of workers in manufacturing rose from 1.71 to 2.13 in the same period, and that of the workforce in services from 0.95 to 1.38. These estimates are based on Heston's figures for national income. See J. Krishnamurty, 'The Occupational Structure', in *Cambridge Economic History of India*, Volume 2, table 6.3.

[2] George Blyn, *Agricultural Trends in India, 1891–1947: Output, Availability and Productivity*, Philadelphia, 1966. It should be noted that this work substantially revised an earlier set of estimates by the same author (*The Agricultural Crops of India, 1893–1946: A Statistical Study of Output and Trends*, Philadelphia, 1951), which gave a significantly lower estimate for total yield increases.

in British India during the 1890s (a decade of minimal population growth), but a clear decline thereafter, so that although overall yields per acre rose very slightly over the first half of the twentieth century, per capita foodgrain availability fell by about 1 per cent per year between 1911 and 1947. Static overall yield figures do not mean that output everywhere was stagnant, but rather that progressive forces were always cancelled out by regressive ones, and that periods of dynamism were interspersed with periods of enervation. Market demand did stimulate significant increases in crop production and productivity, so that commercial crops with favourable market opportunities, such as cotton and sugar, achieved considerable yield increases, and had consistently higher average productivity per acre than did foodgrains. However, even export crops with favourable overseas demand performed less well in the difficult international trading conditions of 1926–41 than they had before 1914.[3]

Blyn's account of Indian agriculture is pessimistic, showing that foodgrain availability held up only at times of minimal population growth, and that cash-crop output was dependent on the unstable stimulus of international demand. His estimates have been subjected to minute scrutiny, and the fragility of their empirical base expounded at length, although direct estimates of agricultural output based on rigorous and wide-ranging crop-cutting experiments were not widely available until the 1940s. It is undeniable that much of the raw data for crop output and yields before that was gathered very casually as part of the fiscal system, and the linkage between land tax and output estimates may have encouraged under-reporting, especially as the British bureaucracy progressively gave up day-to-day supervision of rural administration after the political reforms of 1919. However, despite these distortions, the available data all suggest that aggregate agricultural yields were largely static in colonial India, especially for the subsistence crops that provided the basic needs of the rural population. Thus, while foodgrain and non-foodgrain output may both have risen faster than population from 1860 to 1920, even optimists accept that foodgrain output lagged behind population growth between 1920 and 1947.[4]

3 Extensive recalculations by S. Sivasubramonian have shown that the yields per acre of food crops probably fell by more than Blyn suggested after 1900. Sivasubramonian's totals include data for the Indian States, and suggest that the acreage of both food and non-food crops increased by more than Blyn estimated, but with lower productivity. S. Sivasubramonian, *The National Income of India in the Twentieth Century*, Delhi, 2000, pp. 63–75.

4 A. Heston, 'National Income', in Dharma Kumar with Meghnad Desai (ed.), *Cambridge Economic History of India: Volume 2, c.1757–c.1970* (hereafter *CEHI*, 2), Cambridge, 1984, p. 387. See also Michelle B. McAlpin, 'Famines, Epidemics and Population Growth: The Case of India', *Journal of Interdisciplinary History*, 14, 2, 1983, which shows that the expansion of foodgrain acreage lagged well behind the rate of increase in population between 1916 and 1941 (pp. 360 ff.).

All this does not mean that the rural economy lacked pockets of dynamism. In the Punjab, one of the most prominent areas of agricultural advance during the first half of the twentieth century, new investment, technology and enterprise led to considerable increases in the yields of some crops by expanding the acreage of irrigated land, and also by introducing new varieties of crop and changes in the cropping pattern. However, while yields of sugarcane, cotton and wheat increased, those of other foodgrains declined, especially that of gram (a staple 'inferior' foodgrain used by poorer consumers), which was hit by fungal disease and adverse weather conditions in the 1930s and 1940s. Thus the annual growth rate of total foodgrain output overall was no more than 1 per cent, which was less than the growth in provincial population during the period.[5]

The Punjab was not the only area where there was some agricultural growth during the late nineteenth and early twentieth centuries, underpinned by technological change and capital investment. Parts of the western United Provinces experienced a Punjab-style canal-based output boom between 1880 and 1920, and new cash crops for export, such as cotton and groundnuts, brought considerable advance in dry regions of Maharashtra and Madras in the decade after 1900. In the same period expanding acreage in both Gujarat and parts of Bengal led to output growth, while the arrival of the 'wheat frontier' in the Narmada valley in central India after 1880 caused extensive changes in economic activity and social relations. However, these patches of growth were rarely sustained, nor did they usually transform the locality through a process of long-term social or economic change; rather they ended, in Christopher Baker's graphic description, with 'the usual range of rural predators – the rentier, the usurer, the carpet-bagger and the State – fastening on like leeches to any red-blooded example of growth'.[6] The crucial issue for historians of Indian agricultural performance is not to explain the absence of growth, but to discover why such growth as did take place remained isolated, spasmodic and short-lived.

## THE RURAL ECONOMY BEFORE 1860

Between 1765 and 1820 the British East India Company created a regime that exercised political domination in most of peninsular South Asia, replacing the

[5] Carl E. Pray, 'Accuracy of official agricultural growth statistics and the sources of growth in the Punjab, 1907–1947', *Indian Economic and Social History Review*, 21, 3, 1984.

[6] Christopher J. Baker, 'Frogs and Farmers: The Green Revolution in India, and Its Murky Past', in Tim P. Bayliss-Smith and Sudhir Wanmali (eds.), *Understanding Green Revolutions: Agrarian Change and Development Planning in South Asia. Essays in honour of B. H. Farmer*, Cambridge, 1984, p. 41.

old Mughal empire and the autonomous and semi-autonomous successor states that it had spawned. The rural economy that the British now ruled was varied and complex, and it is clear that in the eighteenth century the Indian countryside was far from being the sort of 'stationary' society or economy, devoid of capital accumulation or technical advance, that classical political economists took it to be. In reality, agricultural colonisation and investment were widespread, although with many local variations and fluctuations, as new crops were produced for an extensive internal market. In some parts of north India considerable agricultural entrepreneurs had emerged to mobilise men and money to colonise new land for profit, while in the south the regime of Hyder Ali and Tipu Sultan in Mysore asserted dominance over the economy in return for direct investment in irrigation and cultivation. Elsewhere, peasant brotherhoods, or individual families, were capable of expanding extensive cultivation of dry land as physical security and economic opportunity allowed. The commercial economy was sufficiently widespread to allow regional specialisation in different crops and cultivation systems in many areas, bound together by networks of trade and credit that covered considerable distances and many levels of operation.

The agrarian commercial economy of the eighteenth century was largely organised on mercantilist principles, as the decentralisation of the Mughal empire led to the creation of independent or semi-independent subordinate fiefdoms, controlled by regional and local officials, military strongmen and political magnates. These states were driven by the requirements of 'military fiscalism', which determined the arrangements they made to secure revenue, supplies and support for their defence and expansion. Urban merchants and rural entrepreneurs who could supply cash, men or material to the state were rewarded with tax concessions and local power; market networks developed that met the needs of these internal patterns of demand, as well as serving the external requirements represented by the British East India Company and other foreign traders.

At the local level, agricultural production and rural social and political relations were determined by a complex mixture of ecological, customary and technological factors, as well as by the military and political superstructure imposed by the new regional states of the eighteenth and early nineteenth centuries. One consistent variation in the density and complexity of production and distribution systems was caused by the presence or absence of effective irrigation, between 'wet' and 'dry' lands, each of which had distinctive patterns of agrarian relations.[7] While this distinction should not be taken to imply

[7] For a convenient summary of this distinction, see David Ludden, 'Productive Power in Agriculture: A Survey of Work on the Local History of British India', in Meghnad Desai *et al.* (eds.), *Agrarian Power and Agricultural Productivity in South Asia*, Berkeley, 1984.

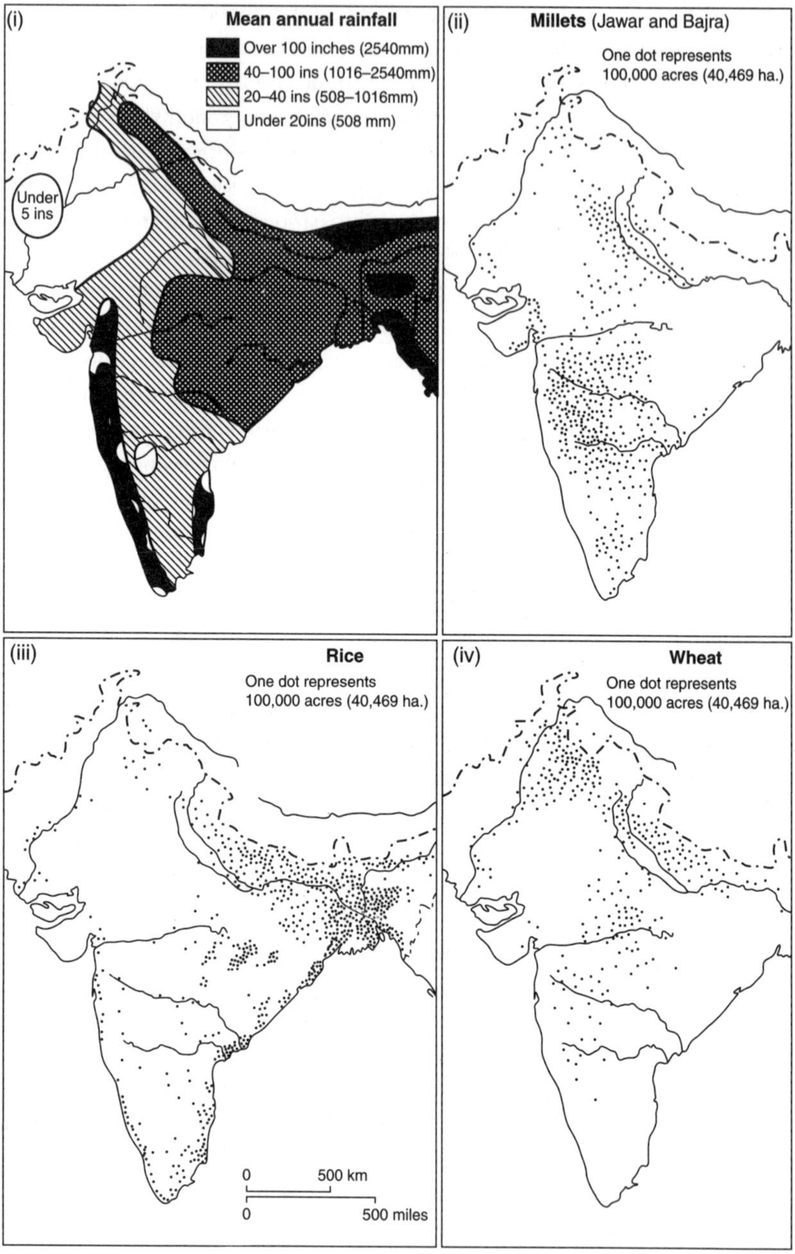


Map 2.1 Average annual rainfall and staple foodgrain production, 1938–1939

simple ecological determinism, it is possible to distinguish between 'wet' and 'dry' areas roughly by mapping the extent of irrigation and the spread of the main foodgrain crops. As shown in map 2.1, this distinction remained valid throughout the colonial period. The 'wet', well-watered rice-growing areas of the agricultural heartlands of the great river deltas sustained the hubs of traditional civilisation. Structured and hierarchical, with extensive urban and cultural centres, these areas depended on capital and labour-intensive rice cultivation, with rigid social distinction between the status of the landowners (high-caste, often Brahmin) and the labourers (low-caste, often untouchable). They were already supporting very high population densities by the eighteenth century, and could not easily expand further without exhausting the soil. By contrast, the 'dry' areas of upland India, notably in the Deccan, the Punjab and western Gangetic plain, were sparsely settled, semi-arid and grew millets and wheat irrigated by wells. Here agriculture was extensive, with long fallow periods, and was best organised by peasant families cropping their own lands. Free land, of a sort, was usually available, and the levers of productive and social power were more finely balanced, favouring decisively only those who could impose a monopoly on access to security, irrigation, or infrastructure – the keys to the successful development of such regions. In some 'dry' areas new crops, new irrigation and new transport links led to considerable expansion in the nineteenth century, especially where they allowed new frontiers to be opened up.

There was no substantial international market for Indian agricultural produce in the eighteenth century. Attempts to supplement exports of cloth to Britain with sugar, indigo and pepper were largely unsuccessful; indigo and sugar were unable to compete with main sources of European supply in the Caribbean, while the China market for raw cotton and opium was limited. Internal economic networks certainly existed, despite transport difficulties, financial constraints and political uncertainties. Transport costs inhibited long-distance trade in bulk items, notably foodgrains, except where military necessity demanded. Even on a well-established route, from Allahabad to Calcutta down the Ganges, river transport in the early nineteenth century took between twenty and sixty days to cover 860 miles.[8] However, viable long-distance transport was possible around the coasts and along the major rivers of north India, and overland elsewhere by carts, or as part of the *banjara* networks of cattle-drovers and nomadic traders. Overlapping networks of

[8] Tom G. Kessinger, 'Regional Economy 1757–1857: North India', *CEHI*, 2, p. 257.

internal markets connected often quite distant areas of the country, and linked monetary and market conditions in several regions. Jean-Baptiste Tavernier, one of the most quoted of European travellers in India in the seventeenth century, wrote of caravans of 10–12,000 pack oxen 'carrying rice to where only corn grows, and corn to where only rice grows, and salt to places where there is none'.[9]

Despite such observations, the impediments to commerce remained large in late-Mughal India. Financial services were relatively scarce, especially the provision of easy liquidity to conduct trade or finance military expenditure quickly. The ability to raise and direct investment for these purposes gave British officials, operating inside or outside the East India Company's institutions, a decisive advantage over their Indian rivals for trade and influence. Most important of all, perhaps, was the variable of military security. Trade and finance flourished best when sheltered and promoted by effective state power, which was another reason for British success, and for Indian merchants' desire to ally themselves with the East India Company. Furthermore, foreign invasion and local conflicts made agriculture insecure, especially in the 'shatter-zone' of the north-west, where rival armies marched and looted. Eighteenth-century India was not sunk in anarchy as the British later liked to claim, but it did often provide an unstable environment for agricultural production, in which the institutions of market integration and productive investment were only as secure as the state power and political influence on which they were based.

## COLONIAL SYSTEMS OF LAND REVENUE

Over the course of the nineteenth century the British changed and adapted the economic, political and social institutions of rural India fundamentally, with effects that were as often destructive of old development systems as they were creative in building new links. The most obvious impact of British institutions on the rural economy during the first century of colonial rule was through the imposition of new systems of land revenue and land ownership. Agricultural taxation provided an important source of revenue for any Indian government, and especially for the Company, which had to pay a dividend by using its surplus to purchase Indian goods for sale in Britain. The land-tax system also provided the focal point for the state's relations with the society it ruled, and Company officials believed that their Indian subjects would judge

[9] Quoted in Tapan Raychaudhuri, 'The Mid-eighteenth Century Background', *CEHI*, 2, p. 28.

them by the degree of continuity and security that they provided, for only thus could improvements in agricultural output and living standards be achieved.

Creating an adequate administrative system of this type caused particular problems in the Bengal Presidency, the first area of India to come under direct British control. The main difficulty here concerned the Company's relations with the large zamindars, rural magnates who had built up hereditary fiscal powers as agents and tax farmers for the Nawabs of Bengal. British officials generally agreed that the position of such men would have to be maintained since rural society required continuity and stability and a stable landlord class would promote social order. For these reasons it was decided in the 1790s that a permanent settlement should be made, giving rights in land to zamindars in perpetuity, provided that they continued to pay their revenue. Security of property rights was also intended to give landlords an incentive to improve their land, increasing the rent they could charge, and hence the profit they could make over the fixed land-revenue demand. Since the Bengal administration did not have the capacity for detailed assessments of agricultural output or value, it decided to fix the level of land revenue at the highest level previously imposed, that of 1789–90, resulting in a demand perhaps 20 per cent higher than that made before 1757.[10]

The sole check on landlord power under this system in its original form was the requirement to pay the land revenue in full. By this means the Company intended to ensure that only capable and efficient men would hold the title of zamindar. Those who could not make a profit on their estates would be sold up to make good any arrears, thus ensuring the survival of the fittest through the active market in land. As it turned out, many existing zamindars could not work the new system properly. Economic conditions were disturbed by depression and the aftermath of the great famine of 1769–70; furthermore, the effective power of many zamindars to extract rent from their tenants and to control their officials was often small. Between 1794 and 1807 the land on which 41 per cent of the government's revenue depended changed hands at fairly low prices, although within twenty years or so a stable landed interest had been established, and the 'rule of property' created in Bengal.

As an instrument for agricultural improvement the Permanent Settlement was a failure. The break-up of old estates put land and power into the hands of smaller landlords, mainly drawn from the rural gentry that had grown up

[10] This account of the Permanent Settlement and its consequences is based largely on P. J. Marshall, *Bengal: The British Bridgehead. Eastern India 1740–1828*, New Cambridge History of India, Volume II.2, Cambridge, 1987, Ch. 4.

around local administration, service industries and trade. While some zamindars did invest in agricultural improvements, and in promoting new crops such as indigo, the bulk of their income came from rents. Whereas the Bengal Government had thought that the level of land revenue assessment would leave a profit margin of about 10 per cent for efficient landlords, by the 1830s the profits on estates administered by the Court of Wards were often higher than the revenue demand.[11] Beneath the landlords a much larger number of substantial peasants and under-proprietors also profited from the control of agricultural output and the manipulation of social power. Yet by the 1830s, in many parts of eastern India, rural population levels were such that the bulk of cultivators were dependent on non-farm income to survive. The spread of high-value cash crops that required labour-intensive cultivation, such as sugar and mulberry and, to a lesser extent, indigo, opium and even rice for urban consumption, increased demand for labour in some areas, but the rewards of this enterprise were usually skewed towards those who controlled land, credit and employment. This was especially a problem in those areas where imports of textiles had displaced local handicraft workers, thus swelling the agricultural workforce.

Zamindari settlements, on the lines of the Permanent Settlement in Bengal, were imposed in other areas of central, northern and south-western India that the British acquired during the early nineteenth century. After 1820, however, the great settlements of most of north-western, western and southern India were conducted on a very different basis, that of a new *ryotwari* system of land settlement and taxation that vested control of the land in the hands of peasants *(ryots)*, eliminating 'parasitic' landlords and stimulating growth through direct assessments that were intended to reward careful husbandry. The ryotwari system required a direct, temporary settlement with the cultivator, or with a village-level intermediary responsible for paying rent in the past. In the large areas of northern and central India new tenurial arrangements, sometimes known as the *mahalwari* system, were made with village zamindars holding *pattidari* or *malguzari* rights, or with joint-owning brotherhoods (*bhaiachara*) that had had the right to raise revenue before British rule. Elsewhere, notably in western and southern India where such groups did not appear to exist, individual or joint settlements were made with peasant proprietors who claimed to have traditionally paid revenue and managed land rights in each village. Under these arrangements the state became the landlord and the cultivator or village proprietary body was designated the tenant, holding a lease granted

[11] *Ibid.*, p. 152.

for a fixed period at a fixed rent. Settlements were renewed, upon resurveying, at thirty-year intervals; in the meantime proprietary and cultivating rights in land were alienable, and proprietors could be sold up for failure to pay their rent.

In designing the ryotwari settlements of the 1820s, 1830s and 1840s officials drew directly on Ricardo's theory of rent, as adapted to Indian conditions by James Mill, Holt Mackenzie and John Stuart Mill, who were highly placed in the Company's London administration. Utilitarian doctrine held that rent was an 'unearned increment' which represented the advantages of productivity and fertility enjoyed by good lands over bad. Land revenue was the state's share of this rent, and could supposedly be fixed 'scientifically' by careful survey and settlement that would establish the product of each agricultural holding, enabling the state to leave the cultivator enough to meet the costs of production, subsistence and productive investment. The level of the revenue demand was initially fixed at nine-tenths of output before 1820, then modified to two-thirds in 1833. The declared aim of the ryotwari settlements was to revitalise the rural economy by setting cultivating peasant brotherhoods free from the depredations of corrupt state functionaries and greedy landlords. British officials believed that abolishing intermediaries, demanding payment of land revenue in cash, pitching these demands at a level high enough to ensure that only the competent survived, and creating a land market fuelled by the sale of the assets of defaulting ryots, were all essential parts of this programme. The purpose of radical reform was to overthrow an old elite seen as enervated and non-productive, and to encourage the emergence of enterprising farmers who would secure a proper return to capital within the limits of village corporate rights. This was not to be achieved simply by laissez-faire, however. The Utilitarians saw an important role for the state as the provider of social overhead capital and a redistributor of resources, and they remained ambivalent in their attitude to the development of rural capitalism in India. For these reasons, James Mill and his associates held out against giving private property rights in land, and insisted on trying to regulate the rental rates charged by occupancy ryots to those beneath them.

Direct revenue assessments of this type put tremendous strains on the administrative capacity of the Company and its British officials. Calculating the 'scientific' rent meant careful surveys of individual fields, and an accurate assessment of the market rental value of the land where no such market yet existed. Surveys and settlements that tried to impose Ricardian rent theory in any rigorous way ran into insuperable theoretical and practical difficulties, aggravated by the use of Indian subordinates who had their own preferences and contacts among the surveyed. Thus, by the 1840s, the Bombay Government, for one, had deliberately abandoned the rent doctrine in favour of precedent as the basis of settlement policy. Even so, revenue demands tended to be cripplingly high, and the export-oriented sectors of the agricultural economy suffered further from a major price depression in the late 1830s and early 1840s. In 1838 half of the arable land in the Bombay Deccan was reported to be waste, while elsewhere falling prices, collapsing trade and a series of financial crises led to a general depression, which frustrated hopes that agricultural development would follow the introduction of ryotwari principles. The early land settlements in northern and western India were later widely acknowledged to have been both onerous and inequitable. As the Administration Report of the North-Western Provinces (later the United Provinces, now Uttar Pradesh) for 1882–3 confessed,

> [i]t is now generally admitted that the proportion of the rental left to the proprietors by the old pre-1857 assessments in the N.W. Provinces was much less than was absolutely necessary to provide for the support of themselves and their families, bad debts, expenses of management, and vicissitudes of season.[12]

British administrators were becoming aware of the destructive effects of their new administrative system by the middle decades of the nineteenth century. Land settlements were now modified in pitch and methodology, with a statutory limitation of the revenue demand to half the rental assets laid down for the whole country in 1864. In the Bombay Deccan, in particular, new settlements in the 1840s based on more sensitive criteria and a lower tax, encouraged agricultural recovery directly. However, raising adequate amounts of revenue remained a major concern of British land policy, especially as the costs of administration rose after 1870. The main systems of land revenue that were to last for the rest of the colonial period were now in place; their geographical coverage, and the revenue burdens associated with them, are shown in map 2.2.

Even with a more pragmatic approach to revenue assessment, the ryotwari system had a disruptive impact on rural society. The village-level proprietors with whom the British were dealing in most parts of India were distinguished as holders of proprietary, rather than cultivating, rights. They represented the local elite with whom previous rulers had made agreements to farm revenues or collect taxes. Such groups often reinforced their local influence by acquiring a place in the local administrative hierarchy, usually as village headmen

[12] Quoted in Eric Stokes, *The English Utilitarians and India*, Oxford, 1959, p. 133.

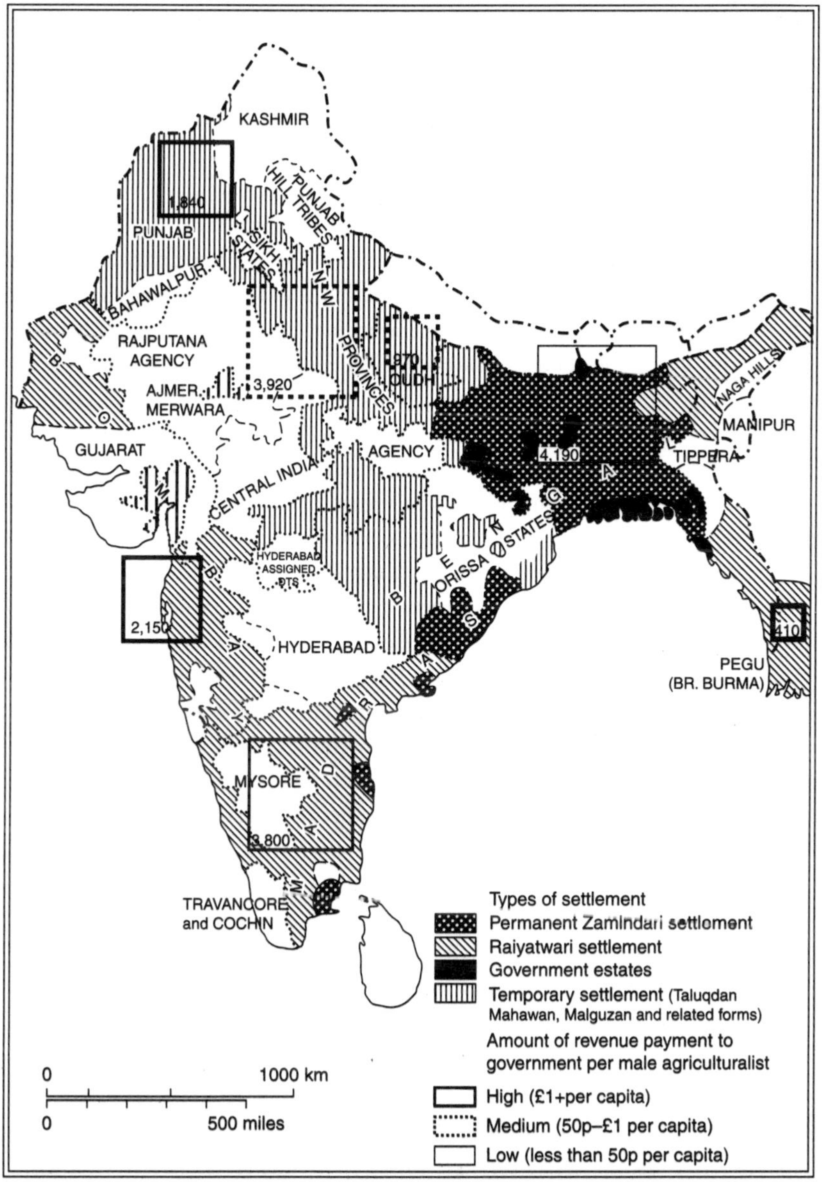


Map 2.2 Systems of land revenue settlement, 1872

or village accountants (who had the duty of registering land-holdings). These posts, in Bombay and Madras in particular, brought remuneration partly through dues in cash and kind and partly through rights to revenue-exempt *inam* land. Even in northern India many village proprietors lived largely on the profits of their role as local revenue and political managers for the state, rather than from direct rental income or agricultural production.

The creation of a land market in India in the first half of the nineteenth century was identified by nationalist historians as one of the most drastic effects of colonial rule that acted, especially in north India and Bengal, as a mechanism for transferring control of land out of traditional proprietors into the hands of merchants and moneylenders (*mahajans*). As demand for export crops such as sugar, indigo and cotton rose in the 1820s and 1830s, so the use of credit to finance agricultural trade and production increased. Cash revenue payers also borrowed extensively, especially since tax demands rarely coincided with harvest times. These developments certainly gave merchants and moneylenders a greatly enlarged function in the rural economy, and in some parts of northern India revenue rights in one-tenth of villages changed hands, although they usually came under the control of service gentry groups rather than traders.[13] However, the significance of these developments can be exaggerated. The largest volume of transfers of proprietary rights took place in the confused years before 1820. Where moneylenders and merchants did acquire proprietary rights in the 1830s it was usually in settlement of debts, or to secure an institutional link with village markets. Often such titles were leased back to their previous holders, in return for a tighter business connection. In poorer regions there were few rental profits to be had, and management could not be exercised without customary power. In the rural uprisings of 1857 the communities involved most extensively in the revolt were led by village brotherhoods that had succeeded in maintaining their independence from outside incursions.

Possession of government office was the key to economic superiority in the village in most of the ryotwari areas at the time of British conquest. Like the zamindars of Bengal, the village proprietors of northern, western and southern India had used an implicit licence from the state, backed up by military leadership, kinship ties, custom, and sometimes caste and ritual systems, to manage local society. But although this role had an economic function, and could secure economic rewards, it was not based solely, or mainly, on economic criteria. Only where man–land ratios were unusually high (as in the 'wet'

[13] Kessinger, 'North India', p. 264; Eric Stokes, *The Peasant and the Raj: Studies in Agrarian Society and Peasant Rebellion in Colonial India*, Cambridge, 1978, p. 86.

irrigated regions of the great river deltas) could local landlords exercise immediate command over agriculture by direct control of labour through dependent tenancies. Elsewhere, the less clear-cut and more delicately balanced systems of rural social, political and economic relations were submitted to great strains as a result of the imposition of British rule. Military service was no longer an option for most local elites and population increases diminished the shares of proprietary rights for each inheritor. The Company's demand for regular (and rather high) revenue payments was a considerable burden, especially in the 1830s when cash prices for agricultural produce fluctuated wildly. The village proprietors and superior ryots with whom the revenue settlements were made did not necessarily control either the marketing network inside or outside the locality, or have access to the liquid resources that were now so vital to meet fixed revenue payments that had to be paid in cash and could no longer be renegotiated annually. As a result the rate of attrition among such groups was quite high and there was a considerable volume of transfers of land titles, especially in north India.

## COMMERCIALISATION AND THE IMPACT OF FOREIGN TRADE, 1860–1930

The *Report of the Royal Commission on Agriculture in India* (1928) provides a convenient description of the principal crops of colonial South Asia in the early twentieth century:

> For the benefit of readers who may be unacquainted with Indian conditions, it may be explained that throughout northern India, the Central Provinces and the greater part of the Bombay Presidency, there are two well defined crop seasons, the rainy and the cold, yielding two distinct harvests, the autumn or *kharif* and the spring or *rabi*. In the south of the peninsula, the greater part of which gets the benefit of the north-east monsoon from October to January and in which the extremes of temperature are absent, the distinction between the sowings tends to disappear and there are merely early and late sowings of the same crops. As a general statement, both in the north and the south, the principal *karif* crops are rice, *juar*, *bajra* and sesamum, to which should be added cotton for northern, jute for north-eastern, and ground-nut and *ragi* for southern India. The principal *rabi* crops in northern India are wheat, gram, linseed, rape, mustard and barley; and in southern India, *juar*, rice, sesamum and gram. The season for cotton in the south of the peninsula varies with the type and the soil but it is throughout a much later crop than in other parts of India. Sugarcane is on the ground for at least ten months of the year ... Crops irrigated are, in the main, rice, wheat, barley, sugarcane, and garden crops. One-fifth of the total area under crops was irrigated in 1924–5.[14]

[14] *Report of the Royal Commission on Agriculture in India, 1928*, Cmd. 3132 of 1928, pp. 69–70. *Juar* [jowar], *bajra* and *ragi* are all varieties of millet, grown largely for subsistence on poorer and drier soils.

In 1900, if not before, Indian agricultural performance was closely linked to a network of external commodity markets, and remained so until the collapse of international demand in the 1930s. By the late 1920s 62 per cent of the cotton crop, 45 per cent of the jute crop and 20 per cent of the groundnut crop were exported, with a further percentage sold abroad in processed form. For foodgrains the story was more complicated, since a much smaller percentage was exported directly. Rice and jowar accounted for 66 per cent of the grain harvest in 1891 and 58 per cent in 1940: wheat (which in some market conditions could be a substitute for jowar) accounted for 13 per cent in 1891 and 18 per cent in 1940. The relative size of the cultivated area devoted to each major crop in India in this period is shown in figure 2.1.[15]

Whereas rice and millets were mostly consumed within the subsistence economy, a good deal of wheat was grown either for export or for sale in urban markets. In 1891–5, for example, about 17 per cent of the wheat harvest was exported, as against 8 per cent of the rice harvest. Before 1900, food prices in upland commercial centres were largely determined by direct trade with individual port-cities. By the first decade of the twentieth century, however, further improvements in transportation networks and infrastructure had increased direct shipments between the major regional centres considerably, creating a coherent internal national market for the major agricultural crops, marked by considerable convergence and integration of regional prices for bulk commodities.[16] International prices now influenced internal markets for foodgrains more profoundly because of the effect of imports of rice and wheat at the ports, while demand for 'inferior' foodgrains such as millets was influenced by the possibilities of substitution.

In the last decades of the nineteenth century the Indian rural economy experienced a significant expansion of overseas trade in primary produce that continued, with only minor fluctuations, until the late 1920s. Before 1860 India had exported indigo, opium, cotton (cloth and yarn, and raw cotton as well) and raw and manufactured silk. While all of these were traditional products, much of the new export-oriented enterprise (except for raw cotton, but including sugar which was tried in plantations in Bihar in the 1830s) depended at least initially on European enterprise and state support, and offered limited

[15] The acreage statistics on which this figure is based are flawed, especially as regards double-cropped and irrigated land. They are adequate for giving a general impression of the division of land among particular crops, but should not be used as evidence of major shifts in cultivation patterns.

[16] Michelle McAlpin, 'Price Movements and Fluctuations in Economic Activity (1960–1947)', *CEHI*, 2, Ch. XI. The output figures used in these calculations are taken from Blyn, *Agricultural Trends in India*, 1966.

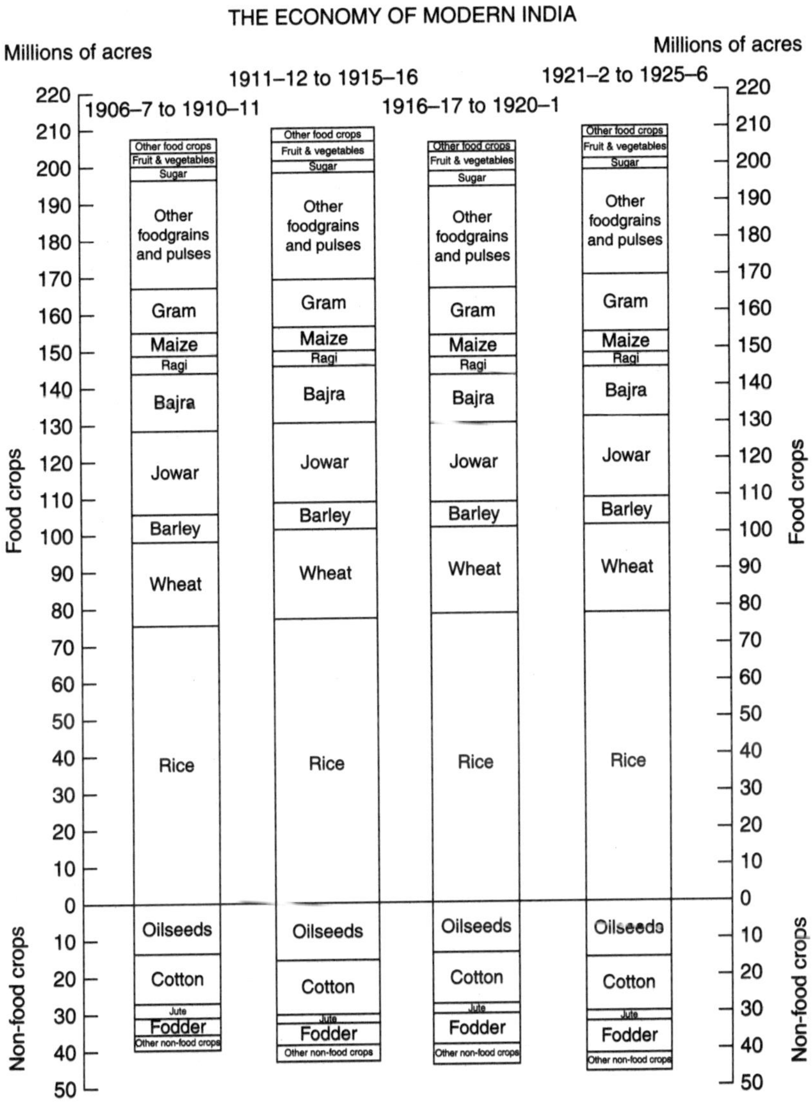


Figure 2.1 Gross area under main food and non-food crops, 1907–1925

opportunities to peasant cultivators. This was certainly the case with crops such as opium and, especially, indigo, over which collusive purchasers were able to exercise partial coercion by using their market power to secure monopsonistic control. By contrast, the new export staples of the later nineteenth century were much more firmly rooted in the peasant economy. While exports of indigo and opium fell away, their place was taken by raw jute, foodgrains (rice from Burma and wheat from India), oilseeds and tea, while raw cotton remained the largest single item of export by value in most years throughout the colonial period, as table 2.1 demonstrates. Of these products, tea was grown on plantations, but the remainder were produced as part of the peasant crop cycle. By the 1880s, wheat in north-western and central India, cotton in Bombay Presidency, groundnuts in Madras and jute in Bengal had become major staples of agricultural production.

Indian producers of export crops succeeded in breaking in to the world's major markets by virtue of the enterprise and adaptability of peasant farmers. The best example is that of cotton. Before 1830, India had exported substantial amounts of raw cotton, mostly to China as a complementary bulk cargo for the opium trade. Indian native cottons were short-staple varieties, and therefore largely unsuitable for Lancashire mills, which meant that exports to Britain were limited at first, until the opening up of new demand for Indian cotton in Continental Europe provided a re-export trade. Between 1840 and 1860 the British Government tried to teach the Indian peasant how to grow a better crop by importing American experts, setting up agricultural research stations, and creating a set of inducements recommended by British businessmen. This effort was largely unsuccessful, and the great boom in Indian cotton exports to Europe was delayed until the supply crisis in Lancashire caused by the American Civil War (1861–5), sustained by increased productivity resulting from the development of new hybrid cotton strains (notably the Dharwar-American), bred and diffused by the farmers themselves. The incentive for technical change in raw cotton production was economic: as one government official pointed out to the *Indian Famine Commission* in 1880, the spread of improved cotton gins in central India and elsewhere was chiefly the result of 'the first cotton merchant who offered a fraction of an anna more for clean than dirty cotton', who had done 'more for Wardha cotton than I, with all the resources of the Government at my back, ever accomplished'.[17] The boom of the 1860s proved unstable and short-lived, but from the 1870s, Indian cotton built up a substantial market in Continental Europe, where price-structures and mill technology were more favourable than in Lancashire, and after 1900, exports from Bombay became the chief source of supply for the Japanese cotton

[17] Quoted in D. R. Gadgil, *The Industrial Evolution of India in Recent Times, 1860–1939*, 5th edn, Bombay, 1971, p. 74.

Table 2.1 *Composition of Indian exports, 1860–1861 to 1935–1936 (percentage share in total export value)*

| | Raw cotton | Cotton goods | Indigo | Foodgrains | Raw jute | Manufactured jute goods | Hides and skins | Opium | Oilseeds | Tea |
|---|---|---|---|---|---|---|---|---|---|---|
| 1860–1 | 22.3 | 2.4 | 5.7 | 10.2 | 1.2 | 1.1 | 2.0 | 30.9 | 5.4 | 0.5 |
| 1870–1 | 35.2 | 2.5 | 5.8 | 8.1 | 4.7 | 0.6 | 3.7 | 19.5 | 6.4 | 2.1 |
| 1880–1 | 17.8 | 4.2 | 4.8 | 17.1 | 5.2 | 1.5 | 5.0 | 18.2 | 8.6 | 4.2 |
| 1890–1 | 16.5 | 9.5 | 3.1 | 19.5 | 7.6 | 2.5 | 4.7 | 9.2 | 9.3 | 5.5 |
| 1900–1 | 9.4 | 6.4 | 2.0 | 13.1 | 10.1 | 7.3 | 10.7 | 8.8 | 8.3 | 9.0 |
| 1910–1 | 17.2 | 6.0 | 0.2 | 18.4 | 7.4 | 8.1 | 6.2 | 6.1 | 12.0 | 5.9 |
| 1920–1 | 17.4 | 7.6 | - | 10.7 | 6.8 | 22.1 | 3.5 | - | 7.0 | 5.1 |
| 1930–1 | 21.0 | 1.6 | - | 13.5 | 5.8 | 14.5 | 5.3 | - | 8.1 | 10.7 |
| 1935–6 | 21.0 | 1.3 | - | - | 8.5 | 14.5 | - | - | - | 12.3 |

*Note:* These figures include exports from Burma, which explains the relatively high percentage of foodgrain exports.
*Source:* K. N. Chaudhuri, 'Foreign Trade and Balance of Payments (1757–1947)', *CEHI*, 2, table 10.11.

textile industry. The share of cotton in India's export values ran at between 10 and 20 per cent down to 1939.

The other great export staples – jute, wheat, oilseeds and tea – were also products of the last third of the nineteenth century, and, as table 2.2 shows, they allowed India to play a significant role in the emerging international primary commodity market made possible by improvements in global communication and transport networks. There were also significant rice exports from the British Indian empire, but these came mainly from the new frontier of cultivation being opened up in Burma. While much of this new land was served by Indian capital and worked by Indian labour, its development lies beyond the scope of this study. The opening of the Suez Canal in 1869 made bulk shipment of grain and other produce from Asia and Australasia to Europe cheaper and more practical. Indian wheat and oilseeds benefited from the transport improvements directly, while jute provided the bags in which most of the world's grain trade was carried. In addition, the steady depreciation of silver-based currencies such as the rupee against the gold-based currencies of Europe and North America kept Indian export prices competitive in the 1870s, 1880s and early 1890s, although the greatest boom in Indian exports occurred as a result of a surge in world demand from the mid 1900s to 1913, a period in which the rupee was fixed to sterling on a gold-exchange standard.

Raw and manufactured jute was India's largest single export by value in most years from 1900 to the late 1920s, although the development of substitutes and the mechanisation of grain handling was beginning to have an effect on demand even before the collapse of trade in primary produce in the Great Depression took its toll. International demand for Indian wheat was intermittent, especially as internal transport difficulties and other costs meant that its domestic price was usually above that on the world market; however, when harvests failed elsewhere in the world, India could be an important supplier, and provided nearly 18 per cent of Britain's total wheat imports between 1902 and 1913. The Government of India placed an embargo on wheat exports during the First World War because of worries about food availability, and the export trade did not revive in the glutted international market of the 1920s. Indian competitiveness in oilseeds was more assured, and by 1914 it was the world's largest supplier of rapeseed and groundnuts, much of which went to the expanding margarine industry of Continental Europe (notably France). Tea also benefited from transport improvements, and from a phenomenal growth in demand in Europe and North America, associated with rising real living standards for the mass of the population. By the early twentieth century, the effect of these changes had been to alter fundamentally many of the main lines

Table 2.2 *Geographical distribution of India's foreign trade, 1860–1861 to 1940–1941 (percentage share of each area in total value, excluding treasure)*

| | Britain | | China | | Malaya | | Continental Europe[a] | | Japan | | USA | |
|---|---|---|---|---|---|---|---|---|---|---|---|---|
| | Export | Import | Export | Import | Export | Import | Export | Import | Export | Import | Export | Import |
| | (%) | (%) | (%) | (%) | (%) | (%) | (%) | (%) | (%) | (%) | (%) | (%) |
| 1860–1 | 43.1 | 84.8 | 34.5 | 4.8 | 3.7 | 2.8 | 3.7 | 1.3 | - | - | - | - |
| 1870–1 | 54.6 | 84.4 | 22.3 | 4.6 | 2.8 | 2.3 | 3.6 | 1.0 | - | - | 3.1[b] | 0.5[b] |
| 1880–1 | 41.6 | 82.9 | 20.0 | 3.7 | 4.2 | 2.8 | 12.9 | 2.5 | - | - | 3.5 | 0.9 |
| 1890–1 | 32.7 | 76.4 | 14.4 | 3.4 | 5.8 | 3.2 | 15.8 | 4.2 | 1.2 | 0.1 | 4.0 | 2.1 |
| 1900–1 | 29.8 | 65.6 | 11.0 | 3.2 | 6.6 | 2.7 | 17.1 | 5.6 | 1.9 | 1.0 | 6.7 | 1.7 |
| 1910–1 | 24.9 | 62.2 | 9.2 | 1.8 | 3.7 | 2.3 | 20.8 | 6.6 | 6.4 | 2.5 | 6.4 | 2.6 |
| 1920–1 | 22.1 | 60.9 | 3.5 | 0.9 | 3.6 | 1.4 | 10.4 | 3.6 | 10.1 | 7.8 | 14.5 | 7.5 |
| 1930–1 | 23.5 | 37.2 | 6.0 | 2.0 | 2.8 | 2.4 | 15.1 | 11.9 | 10.8 | 8.8 | 9.4 | 9.2 |
| 1940–1 | 34.7 | 22.9 | 5.3 | 1.8 | 1.8 | 3.4 | 2.6 | 0.4 | 4.8 | 13.7 | 13.9 | 17.2 |

[a] France, 1870; France, Germany and Italy, 1880–1940.
[b] 1875–6.
*Source:* K. N. Chaudhuri, 'Foreign Trade and Balance of Payments (1757 – 1947)', *CEHI*, 2, table 10.21A.

of communication and economic exchange inside the subcontinent, creating a new pattern of agrarian activity focused on the port-cities of Calcutta, Bombay, Karachi and Madras, and their hinterlands, as shown in map 2.3.[18]

The expansion of Indian exports was assisted by the extension of domestic trade and transport networks, notably the building of railways after 1850. The first railway line was laid out of Bombay in 1853, followed by others from Calcutta (1854) and Madras (1856); then there was a patchwork process of construction, much of it initially for strategic purposes, culminating in the building of the main trunk-line network inland from the major port-cities in the 1880s. By 1910 India had the fourth-largest railway system in the world. In 1860 there were about 850 miles of track open in the subcontinent, 16,000 by 1890, 35,000 by 1920 and 40,000 by 1946, which meant that four-fifths of the total land area was no more than 20 miles from a railway line. Map 2.4 shows the full extent of the colonial railway network of the early 1930s. The quantity of freight carried increased from 3.6 million tonnes in 1871, to 42.6 million in 1901, to 116 million in 1929–30 and to 143.6 million in 1945–6.

Indian railways certainly provided quicker and cheaper transport than had been available hitherto. One estimate has suggested that freight-rates per tonne mile on the railways in 1930 were 94 per cent less than the charges for pack-bullocks in 1800–40, and 88 per cent less than those for bullock carts in 1840–60, creating a 'social saving' of about 9 per cent of national income.[19] Furthermore, the initial design of the network cut across existing trade routes, and gave significant advantages to commerce with the port-cities and the foreign trade sector. Even on the best routes neither the efficiency nor the costs of the service compared favourably with the railway systems of India's major international competitors. By the 1900s the system was severely under-capitalised, leading to delays in shipment, slow trains and obsolete rolling stock. The First World War put new strains on railway capacity, since India also supplied equipment for the military campaigns in Palestine and Iraq, and financial stringency and managerial weakness limited capital investment to solve the problems in the post-war years. By the 1920s the railway system was subjected to further fiscal controls, and in every year from 1926 to 1931

[18] The concept of the spatial reorganisation of India in the colonial period is taken from David E. Sopher, 'The Geographical Patterning of Culture in India', in David E. Sopher (ed.), *An Exploration of India: Geographical Perspectives on Society and Culture*, London, 1980, fig. 9.

[19] This saving does not represent the true developmental effect of Indian railways; for that the countervailing costs of state subsidies for capital and the weakness of the linkage effects between the railways and other transport networks in the economy must also be taken into account. John M. Hurd, 'Railways', *CEHI*, 2, pp. 740–1.

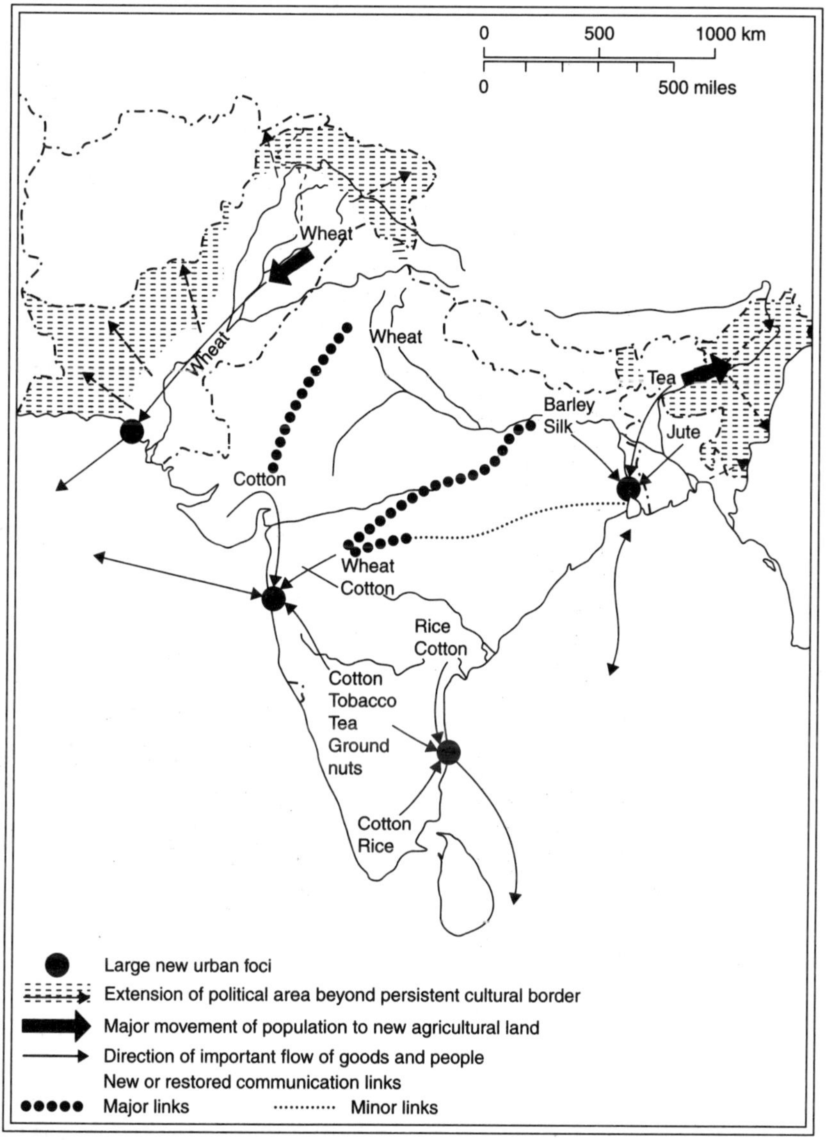


Map 2.3 Spatial reorganisation of colonial India

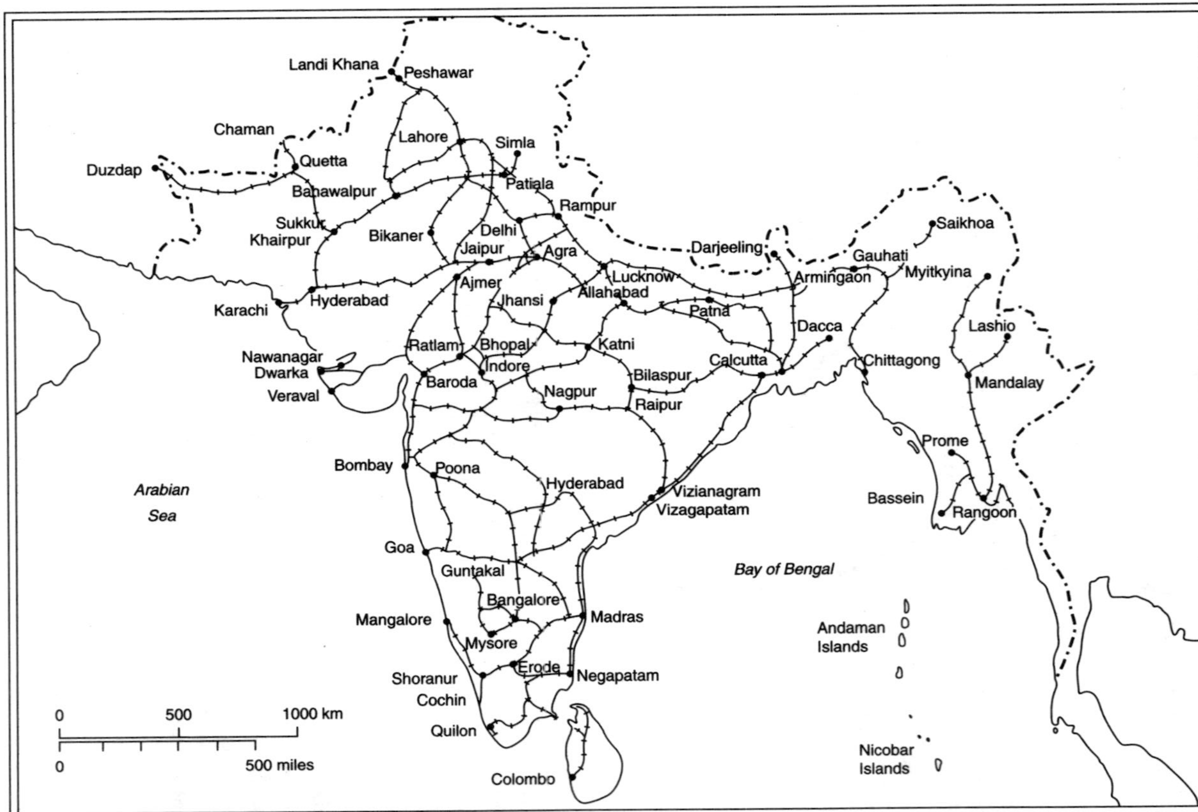


Map 2.4 Main-line railways, 1947

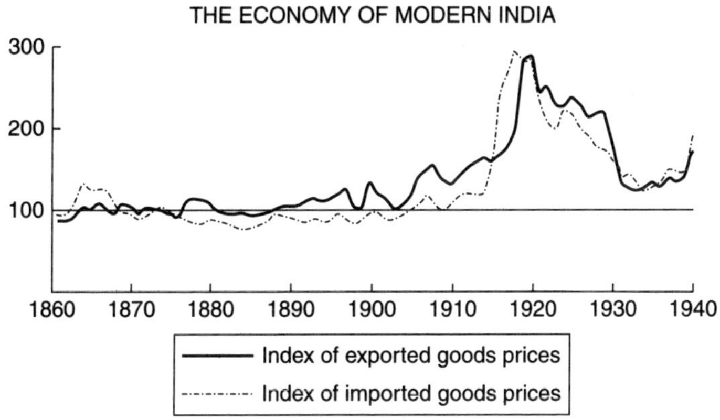


Figure 2.2 Indices of prices of exported and imported goods, 1860–1940

sharp increases in freight rates were accompanied by a decline in the volume of goods shipped.[20]

The price history of the fifty years from 1880 to 1929 shows that considerable profits could be made from the rural economy during periods of commercial expansion. The price data set out in figure 2.2 suggest that growing international demand and currency depreciation brought about rising internal prices for agricultural commodities from the 1880s to 1915, followed by a sharp increase during and immediately after the First World War. During the 1920s, agricultural prices fell back slightly, but remained well above their pre-war level, then almost halved in the depression at the end of the decade; export prices (representing commercially produced, non-edible cash crops such as cotton, tea and jute) fell more consistently during the 1920s, and slumped between 1929 and 1931.[21] The steady increases in prices for agricultural produce over most of the period were not linked to any clear rise in costs, at least before the 1920s; the terms of trade between agricultural and non-agricultural goods moved consistently in favour of the rural sector until 1929. At the same time, the incidence of taxation on agriculture was diminishing, and was never more than 5 per cent of the value of gross output.[22] Imports of gold, a preferred medium of savings

[20] *Ibid.*, pp. 756–8.

[21] The index-numbers for exported and imported goods were largely determined by cash-crop exports and manufactured consumer-goods imports. Price fluctuations for agricultural crops in the domestic market were a more uncertain indicator, especially before 1900, and sharp rises could be caused by falls in yields (resulting in shortages or famines) as well as by buoyant demand in the urban or external economy. McAlpin, 'Price Movements', *CEHI*, 2, pp. 883–4.

[22] Dharma Kumar, 'The Fiscal System', *CEHI*, 2, table 12.5. This calculation is based on Sivasubramonian's 1965 estimate of agricultural output.

in the rural economy, had become significant in the years before the First World War, and continued in the 1920s. These developments increased the volume and value of traded agricultural produce considerably. They also created new sources of wealth and sustenance within the rural economy, although they did nothing to guarantee that adequate returns would go to the cultivator.

There were profits for some in the agrarian economy, but the acceleration of commercialisation in the late nineteenth century was often seen as a malignant force. A series of devastating famines struck several parts of India in the 1860s and 1870s, centred in Orissa (1866–7), Rajasthan (1868–70), Bengal (1873–4), Madras (1876–8); and then later in western and central India in 1896–7 and 1899–1900. These famines had a high death toll – perhaps 16 million in all – and affected the lives of many millions of others. The immediate cause was crop failures and ineffectual relief policies, but these events have also often been interpreted as the consequence of larger structural shifts, including the creation of a nation-wide market for grain without adequate transportation systems for the interior, and problems of employment resulting from structural change in the rural economy. Agricultural labourers and village artisans were identified at the time as the two groups most likely to be put at risk by a severe disruption to agricultural production and the wages that were earned from this. A British official had argued that famines in India were 'rather famines of work than of food', as early as 1861, and this view was established as orthodoxy by the Government of India's Famine Commission report of 1880.[23] The official colonial view that famines were the result of failures of entitlement, rather than absolute shortages of foodgrains, has been generally borne out by later investigations, except for the famines of 1896–7 and 1899–1900, which occurred at a time of widespread major crop failures and severely diminished stocks.

The principles of political economy which some British administrators used to justify their rule in the mid nineteenth century saw little purpose in wasting resources on ineffective acts of philanthropy. Lord Lytton, the Viceroy during the period of severe famine in the 1870s, invoked the works of Malthus and Mill to justify non-intervention in famine districts, and reliance on the market to supply grain to the destitute.[24] This attitude softened over time,

[23] Jean Drèze, 'Famine Prevention in India', in Jean Drèze and Amartya Sen (eds.), *The Political Economy of Hunger*, 2, Oxford, 1990, p.17.

[24] The British state's policy towards its own poor citizens was similarly based on the doctrines of both Thomas Malthus and John Stuart Mill. However, as contemporary critics pointed out, colonial expenditure on Indian famine relief was a fraction of what the home government spent on sustaining the British poor.

and the 1880 Famine Commission took the view that the state had a duty to provide all practicable assistance at times of dearth; formal Famine Codes were then drawn up for each Province to guide the conduct of officials. Relief was now to be based on the creation of public works, close to the homes of those requiring assistance, for the employment of those strong enough to participate; and the provision of 'gratuitous' relief for those unable to work. However, the nineteenth-century colonial government remained convinced that the market, not the state, should supply food to famine districts, and refused to contemplate direct controls over food procurement or distribution, or any attempt to control prices or provide buffer stocks. Aware of the limitations of their power and timid in their commitment to public expenditure, the Victorian rulers of India could only hope that the gradual spread of the market, transport infrastructure and irrigation would bring about a solution to the endemic problems of famine in India. As one detailed account of their actions has concluded:

> If the available resources could not be allocated otherwise than through a free and uncluttered market mechanism, the only way out was to increase the supply of the available resources. It is then hardly surprising that all the suggested remedies for famine centred on measures to increase production, in other words, to achieve economic progress.[25]

The only way to achieve economic progress, it was widely believed, was through continued commercialisation, underpinned by whatever meagre safety-net of relief the colonial state could provide.

Bearing in mind these contrasts, the question of who benefited from commercialisation can only be answered by mapping changes in the systems of agricultural production with care. The imposition of the colonial land revenue and tenancy systems certainly caused major new problems for rentier landlords in the first half of the nineteenth century. Zamindars in permanently settled areas were given a legal right to collect rents, but did not necessarily have enough control of local resources to achieve this. Direct management of cultivation was made more difficult by the scattered nature of their holdings, which were often spread over quite a large area. As a result, few of the great estates consisted of properties that could be farmed as a coherent whole, and most zamindars had to confine direct supervision of cultivation to the portion of their holding they cultivated directly, usually known as the *sir* land.

By the 1860s, most landed proprietors had insufficient control over local resources to invest in agriculture. A few large landlords were still able to

[25] S. Ambirajan, 'Malthusian Population Theory and Indian Famine Policy in the Nineteenth Century', *Population Studies*, 30, 1, 1976, p. 13.

sustain their control of production by allying with or dominating crucial subordinates, and could back this position by improvements and investment in new agricultural opportunities, but this was becoming rare. Thus many zamindars retreated to the towns, or devoted themselves to endless and bitter struggles over local rights and duties with their tenants. Effective power often shifted to those outside the zamindari retinue – especially larger tenants with occupancy rights – who could exercise effective control over production and employment, and over the spreading commodity market network to which profitable production was linked. In ryotwari areas, village-level proprietary rights and productive capacity became closely integrated over the course of the nineteenth century.

The commercialisation of the agricultural economy and the expansion of long-distance trade in primary produce put new demands on the rural credit market. Revenue demands had long had to be paid in cash, which had helped to draw urban moneylenders and traders into local-level economic relations in the 1830s and 1840s. Now the spread of new cash crops for sale outside the locality increased the need for local credit, and also the rewards for its use. Many cultivators needed loans to provide seed, implements and cattle, to dig wells, store grain or simply to obtain food between harvests. Much of this credit was best supplied in kind, and moneylending was closely linked to the grain trade in many parts of the subcontinent. British officials observed the growth of 'peasant indebtedness' with alarm in the last third of the nineteenth century, arguing that it represented yet another threat to the homogeneous character of traditional village communities. The chief evil was thought to be the growth of direct lending by moneylenders to cultivators, who could then be sold up if their debts were not repaid. In many parts of central and western India such moneylenders were often Rajasthani Marwaris, easily identified as alien intruders by villagers and British officials alike. The monument to official concern on this issue was the passing of a series of legislative acts, beginning with the Deccan Agriculturalists Relief Act (1879) and ending with the Punjab Land Alienation Act (1900) and the Bundelkhund Act (1903), that inhibited the sale of land to 'non-agriculturalist castes' and urban interests.

This identification of alien, urban moneylenders as the chief predators of rural enterprise was politically important to British officials, who were trying to fathom the reasons for periodic slumps in agricultural growth and the volatility of political protest in the 1870s and 1890s. However, in most parts of the subcontinent the creation of a credit market for investment and subsistence was not a new phenomenon of the late nineteenth century, and the direct influence of mahajans and other urban capitalists on agriculture was easy to exaggerate. The global extent of land transfers from peasants to mahajans as a result of commercialisation cannot be estimated with any certainty, but in Bombay Presidency, where transfers to non-agriculturalists had to be recorded and monitored under the Deccan Agriculturalist Relief Act, mahajans increased their share of ownership of peasant land from around 6 to about 10 per cent between 1875 and 1910; in 1911 even the Bombay Government was forced to admit that its fears about land transfers had been 'greatly exaggerated'.[26] Where mahajans did have extensive land-holdings their capacity to act as capitalist farmers was often very limited. Social boycotts and exclusions were common, with absentee landowners being unable to hire labour or secure tenants where land was not scarce. Acquiring land by foreclosure or by purchases at debt sales gave scattered holdings that could not be managed as a single entity, so few mahajans obtained viable farms. The sheer inertia of the local legal system produced other problems; holdings were often unregistered, land rights went unrecorded, and many legal loopholes remained to distort the logic of private property rights. As a result, creditors sometimes did not even know where the holdings of their debtors were, and so were unable to take them over had they wished to do so.

As a consequence of such difficulties, indigenous bankers often tried to avoid sinking their capital resources into land. For some, such as the large Nattukottai Chetty bankers of Tamilnad, this meant eschewing investment in local agriculture entirely, and focusing instead on opening up new areas of trade and cultivation in Burma and elsewhere in South-East Asia. When moneylenders were forced to take over land they often re-leased it to its existing cultivators, with the ryot repaying the interest on the old debt as rent. Even so, it was hard for those not directly involved in agriculture themselves to make a profit from the land. Productivity and labour intensity were usually lower on mahajan than on peasant land, and moneylenders, too, could bankrupt themselves in agricultural enterprise. Where mahajans did exercise a pervasive influence on cultivation it was through networks of debt-bondage and hypothecation that determined the cultivating decisions of their debtors, usually requiring them to grow high-value cash crops for export in return for grain-doles for subsistence. Exercising this sort of control was difficult, however, especially in situations where peasants could turn to more than one source of funds. As the history of rural credit in the 1930s was to show, over time the

[26] Quoted in Neil Charlesworth, *Peasants and Imperial Rule: Agriculture and Agrarian Society in the Bombay Presidency 1850–1935*, Cambridge, 1985, p. 196.

mahajans came under increasing challenge from rival sources of rural credit and land management sited within village society.

Once the role of the mahajans has been assessed more carefully, it can be seen that the agricultural enterprise of the years from 1870 to 1929 was largely financed by rurally based entrepreneurs, drawing capital from those who had profited from the export-led expansion of cash-crop farming. This process was not accompanied by any major changes in the pattern of land-holding; indeed the distribution of land-ownership between different social groups and in terms of the sizes of individual holdings remained largely static between the 1850s and the 1940s. Where large-scale alienation of land to commercial interests did occur it typically took place before the 1850s – even before the 1820s in many places – and as a result of institutional rather than economic change. Land-ownership is not the same as the control of production, but the same aura of continuity surrounds this more nebulous but more important category. The picture of a commercially innocent, self-sufficient peasantry falling victim to the capitalist wiles of usurious moneylenders and urban bankers, painted by the colonial government and its nationalist critics alike at the end of the nineteenth century, is a largely inaccurate depiction of the political economy of exchange and production in Indian agriculture in the last century of British rule.

The commercial expansion of the late nineteenth century required new crops, new transport networks and increased market activity. Substantial sums were made by shipping firms and commission agents, and by traders and bankers who moved the crops from market towns up-country to the port-cities on the coast, but some profits remained for the agriculturalists themselves. The distribution of these profits was heavily influenced by the exercise of economic and social power in a rural society that remained stratified throughout the colonial period, giving highly differentiated access to resources, wealth, power and market opportunities. Control of credit, carts, storage facilities and agricultural capital brought advantages to some groups in village society. The protection that the colonial government gave to agriculturalists against non-agricultural moneylenders made it easier for surplus peasants and local landlords to dominate the supply of credit and the power that accompanied it. Tenancy legislation, such as the Bengal Tenancy Act of 1885, which gave occupancy rights on controlled rents to those who had held tenancies for twelve years, with the right to sub-let without hindrances, also bolstered the position of this important stratum of local society.

The extent of market penetration, the character of the markets that operated, and the type of involvement of various economic groups of producers and consumers in them, largely determined production conditions in the rural economy of colonial India. By the end of the nineteenth century those with a privileged position in local society could secure favoured access to credit, product markets and infrastructure, although such access did not necessarily mean great wealth or new opportunities for profit. In over-populated unproductive areas, such as the eastern districts of the United Provinces, for example, widening social divisions were more likely to be the result of 'the slow impoverishment of the mass [rather] than the enrichment of the few'.[27] Connections between rural social stratification and agricultural development were complex and confused: given the reality of cultivating conditions it is hard to identify meaningful divisions in society with particular sizes of land-holding, or to argue that the dominant elites of late-nineteenth-century India represented a new class formation that had resulted from the spread of capitalism to the land. The rural magnates who were best able to take advantage of the new opportunities in cultivation were, for the most part, the same elite that had determined agricultural decision-making since well before the coming of the British: as David Ludden has stressed, 'commercialisation did not break up localities into swarms of individuals related to one another primarily through the market'.[28] However, the spread of market opportunities was not simply a new form of coercion exercised by the old elite over the passive and subordinate ranks of those beneath them.

## MARKET FAILURE AND THE CRISIS IN THE RURAL ECONOMY, 1930–1950[29]

By the 1920s many cultivating decisions were based on market expectations, but such expectations became increasingly unstable and uncertain as the decade wore on. Indian produce was subject to the global pressures of over-production and under-consumption that affected all international trade in primary produce in the 1920s, especially since most of its exports had obvious substitutes and were, in many markets, the marginal source of supply. Inside the country, too, some clear evidence of strain was now surfacing, with the position of the rural elite that had led the expansion of export production in the late nineteenth century coming under pressure. It is likely that the frontier for good-quality land (given the minimal investment in infrastructure)

[27] Eric Stokes, 'Agrarian Relations: Northern and Central India', *CEHI*, 2, p. 65.

[28] Ludden, 'Productive Power in Agriculture', pp. 72–3.

[29] It can be argued that the severe problems of production and distribution that affected the rural economy after 1930 continued until the advent of the 'green revolution' of the 1970s.

began to close after 1900; by the 1920s, population densities were building up in many of the agricultural heartlands, and over-production and credit-supply problems were becoming serious for jute, cotton and other export crops. The 1920s marked the peak of market integration in colonial India, with commodity and credit markets linking all areas of the subcontinent, and unifying port and inland prices everywhere for the first time. The labour market, too, became more flexible and wide-ranging as transport improvements and the spread of information made long-distance temporary migration more practical. At the same time, however, the boom in output was beginning to run out of steam, and it did not take much to tip the rural economy down into a deep depression.

One of the weakest links in the Indian export economy was the supply of credit for trade in agricultural produce. There were some internal mechanisms for credit creation within the Indian monetary systems of the 1920s, but the bulk of rural trade depended on liquidity imported in the form of short-term trading credits by firms hoping to do export business. The increasing liquidity shortage in the international economy from 1928 onwards, as short-term funds moved to the United States and the resulting 'dollar gap' caused transfer problems for the debtor nations of Europe, Latin America and Australasia, reduced India's short-term capital imports. The prices of its export goods turned down decisively in 1928, and its position was damaged further by the onset of world-wide recession in late 1929, and by political uncertainty over the rupee exchange rate that discouraged foreign firms from holding surplus funds in rupees. By 1929–30 the Government of India was also experiencing problems in securing the foreign exchange needed to make its transfer payments to London, and tightened credit in India still further by contracting the money supply to release assets from the currency reserves. It was this liquidity crisis that transmitted the fall in prices in exported goods so speedily to the internal economy. Table 2.3 shows the effect of the depression on export and import prices; in the domestic market, the prices of agricultural produce fell by 44 per cent between 1929 and 1931, by which point they were about half the level they had been at for most of the 1920s.[30]

The onset of the depression was marked by a fundamental shake-out of capital and liquid funds from the agrarian economy. The most striking development of the 1930s was the export of substantial amounts of privately owned gold from India after the rupee accompanied sterling off the gold standard in September 1931, which turned India into a net exporter of precious metals for

[30] McAlpin, 'Price Movements', *CEHI*, 2, appendix table 2.A.

Table 2.3 *Export and import prices in India, 1927–1936*

| | Export price | Import price | Terms of trade |
|---|---|---|---|
| 1927–8 | 100.0 | 100.0 | 100.0 |
| 1928–9 | 97.5 | 96.4 | 100.1 |
| 1929–30 | 90.2 | 93.2 | 96.1 |
| 1930–1 | 71.5 | 80.0 | 89.4 |
| 1931–2 | 59.2 | 71.7 | 82.6 |
| 1932–3 | 55.3 | 65.2 | 84.8 |
| 1933–4 | 53.5 | 63.5 | 84.3 |
| 1934–5 | 54.1 | 63.0 | 85.9 |
| 1935–6 | 56.9 | 62.1 | 91.6 |
| 1936–7 | 57.2 | 62.8 | 91.0 |

*Source:* K. N. Chaudhuri, 'Foreign Trade and Balance of Payments (1757–1947)', *CEHI*, 2, table 10.8.

the rest of the decade. After 1931, gold bullion became India's single most important export commodity, contributing about 30 per cent of the total value of exports from 1931–2 to 1934–5, and between 8 and 19 per cent thereafter.[31] There were large profits to be made from the export of gold, but clearly part of the flow was caused by 'distress' selling by landlords and tenants to meet fixed demands for rent and land revenue, and part by the bankruptcy of traders and indigenous bankers whose business had collapsed in the liquidity crisis. To the extent that gold holdings had been used in the rural economy as security for advances of agrarian and trading credit, bullion exports represented a disinvestment in agriculture and rural trade; but such sales did not diminish, and may even have increased, the total available purchasing power in India, and also served to transfer investment funds from agriculture to other sectors of the economy.

The issue of who benefited and who lost from the impact of the depression in agriculture is again a complex one. During the 1930s the growth of urbanisation, the shifting of terms of trade in favour of urban economies, and the collapse of external demand for a range of primary produce, meant that the balance of advantage in agriculture shifted to those producers who could grow crops for which there was still a buoyant home market. The most obvious beneficiaries here were the sugar producers of northern and western India,

[31] B. R. Tomlinson, *The Political Economy of the Raj, 1914–1947: The Economics of Decolonization in India*, London, 1979, pp. 38–9.

whose production expanded enormously thanks to the creation of a protected domestic market for refined sugar, but they were not alone. Groundnut and tobacco producers, also, received demand stimulation from the closed domestic market and new consumer tastes of the 1930s, while cotton producers still found buyers in the domestic mills.

The existence of new areas of demand that replaced the old, in part at least, ensured that the agricultural sector retained some earning capacity throughout the 1930s. While the acreage under cotton and jute fell slightly, that under wheat rose by 8 per cent over its level the previous decade, that under sugar by 23 per cent and that under groundnuts by 75 per cent.[32] However, the benefits that this brought were skewed, often more so than in the past. Although demand for goods held up, the real cost of capital increased considerably, and so many farmers retrenched on capital-intensive methods, cutting back on irrigation and new seeds. The real cost of labour also rose in many areas, since where labourers were paid in cash their wages were 'sticky' – adjusting only slowly to changes in the price level. Furthermore, with employment opportunities elsewhere in the countryside diminishing, those families that had adequate land-holdings tended to cultivate them with their own resources, rather than hiring labour or borrowing capital from outside. This reduced still further the employment opportunities for deficit agrarians, who were now thrown back on an inadequate family land-holding, or driven off to the city in search of work.

The depression helped to concentrate the power of dominant peasants over the rural economy once more. With the retreat of urban moneylenders, and of alternative sources of credit represented by the agents of an active export trade, peasant families emerged as the controllers of the rural surplus and the social structure based upon it. Their position was not always secure, and at times the tensions caused by the collapse of agricultural networks led to riots and social disorders as tenants and debtors rounded on their landlords and creditors. In areas where demand for new crops diffused resources and opportunity, this process was muted, but in much of the countryside control of capital and employment gave a narrow social group unequal and exploitative access to power and profit. While the propertied classes prospered by the increase in the relative value of capital, those without adequate resources under their own control to ensure social reproduction suffered accordingly. The curtailment of employment, and of windfall opportunities in cash-crop production, threw the deficit producers back still further onto their inadequate resources. The size

[32] Dharm Narain, *Impact of Price Movements on Areas under Selected Crops in India 1900–1939*, Cambridge, 1965, pp. 170 ff.

of this segment of the rural economy cannot be estimated with any precision, but it was certainly large; according to the *Report on the Marketing of Wheat in India* (1937), in the Delhi area 40 per cent of cultivators had no surplus to sell, 33 per cent had to part with all of their surplus to pay their debts, and only the remaining 27 per cent, just over a quarter of the total, were free to market their surplus for profit.[33]

After 1939 the depression of demand and activity in the rural economy was replaced by a sharp expansion fuelled by considerable monetary inflation, which lasted throughout the Second World War and the period of economic reconstruction and political crisis from 1945 to 1950. However, these inflationary demand conditions, coupled to the continued disruptions to employment and vertical networks that had resulted from the depression, further exacerbated the distributional crisis in agriculture, and brought about a severe food crisis in some parts of the country, notably Bengal. The causes of the great Bengal Famine of 1943, in which over a million people died, with a further two million succumbing to delayed mortality effects over the next three years, are still the subject of some debate. While it is likely that the war situation, and adverse weather conditions in 1942, diminished foodgrain availability somewhat, this alone does not explain the severity or widespread nature of the dearth. Differential access to supplies of grain caused by the decline of real wage-rates and other consequences of the wartime inflation skewed distribution networks considerably; equally important was the inability of the government or the market to compel surplus producers to supply rice to the rural poor or the urban areas in conditions of extreme uncertainty. As a result the land-controllers and others in authority inside households, villages, markets and patron–client relationships protected themselves at the expense of their erstwhile clients and dependants.

The subsistence crisis in Bengal revealed what one historian has called 'patterns of abandonment, marked by the snapping of moral and economic bonds upon which rural society had been hitherto erected'.[34] These events were in one sense simply an extreme consequence of the changes in rural social and economic structure that had taken place generally during the 1930s and early 1940s as a result of the depression and the war. Problems of food supply at an acceptable price were widespread across all of India during the war, and attempts to overcome them spawned an intrusive and ineffective system of

[33] Cited in Stokes, 'Agrarian Relations: North and Central India', *CEHI*, 2, p. 85.

[34] Paul R. Greenough, *Prosperity and Misery in Modern Bengal: The Famine of 1943–1944*, New York, 1982, p. 138.

rationing and official procurement. The supply crisis in Bengal was extreme, but elsewhere the moral and market failures of the war years were severe enough to exacerbate political unrest. Cultivators who could be induced or compelled to sell their surplus at harvest time, and who had then to buy grain back at even more inflated prices, formed the backbone of the outbreaks of rural political unrest that gave force to the 'Quit India' movement of 1942 and the Partition riots of 1946–7.

The terms and conditions for supply of agricultural credit was another area of intense market failure during the 1930s. The initial shock of the depression was a liquidity crisis, which was spread through the economy by its impact on internal credit-supply and trading networks. Moneylenders curtailed their activities considerably in these circumstances, for a number of reasons. Many moneylenders were themselves in financial difficulties during the 1930s, especially those who had lent heavily to peasants who could not repay, or who had depended on high profit margins for exportable crops to remain in business. In addition, many pressures quickly built up to discourage further lending; agriculture made low profits, and land had such a low price that repossession was not a viable option. Further, customary and legal barriers to moneylending activities increased, as peasants used violence against their oppressors in some places, and as provincial governments stepped in to mediate.

In response to these problems anti-moneylender legislation was introduced in most provinces during the 1930s, imposing ceilings on interest rates, and drastically reducing the amounts that debtors were required to pay. The only credit suppliers who were able to profit in these circumstances were those who also controlled land in the locality, and so could force debtors to repay their loans in the form of labour services. For this reason sharecropping (the leasing of land on payment of a proportionate crop rent in kind) increased during the 1930s, notably in Bengal, where the debt settlement boards set up by the Agricultural Debtor's Act of 1935 were composed of local *jotedars* (village proprietors, able to supervise cultivation, and accept labour service and payment in kind), who used their position to replace the mahajans (who, as trade-based moneylenders, exchanged cash for cash) as the suppliers of credit. The social tensions that this caused, especially where Hindu landlords and moneylenders were seen to be exploiting Muslim tenants, led to occasionally fierce rural riots, such as those in Kishoreganj in 1930.[35] With the onset of the war, however, the

[35] Omkar Goswami, 'Agriculture in Slump: The Peasant Economy of East and North Bengal in the 1930s', *Indian Economic and Social History Review*, 21, 3, 1984; Sugata Bose, 'The Roots of Communal Violence in Rural Bengal: A Study of the Kishoreganj Riots 1930', *Modern Asian Studies*, 16, 3, 1982.

land market revived, and large traders were prepared to lend again because the land itself was once more an effective security.

The inter-war and immediate post-war years saw little increase in the cultivated area or in the yields of subsistence crops. Both output and acreage for foodgrains lagged well behind rates of population growth from early in the century, with foodgrain acreage only expanding significantly during the war as a result of the 'Grow More Food' campaigns. Between 1900 and 1939, for example, population increased by 36 per cent, while the expansion of the gross cropped area by 13.7 per cent (from 214 million to 244 million acres) was almost entirely as a result of new irrigation. The area under irrigation expanded from 29.1 million acres (13.6 per cent of the total cultivated area) to 53.7 million acres (22 per cent) in the same period.[36] Rural savings and investment were also at a low ebb. Between 1914 and 1946 total net capital formation in agriculture had amounted to Rs 19.58 billion, less than a quarter of this (Rs 4.3 billion) invested in machinery and equipment. The total sum amounted to about 1.7 per cent of agricultural income. Thus, while agriculture provided slightly more than one-half of the national income in the inter-war period, and employed more than two-thirds of the labour-force, private capital formation was only about one-fifth of the national total.[37] In 1951 the total of net rural private investment was the equivalent of Rs 117 per rural household; the total stock of agricultural equipment (excluding livestock) used on Indian farms was worth Rs 5.44 billion (at 1960–1 prices) – Rs 3.86 billion of it in the form of carts, and only Rs 0.49 billion in irrigation equipment, almost all animal-powered.[38]

While such statistical evidence is not always as reliable as it appears to be, it does suggest that agricultural yields were not keeping up with the historically unprecedented rate of population growth after 1920. The population of British India, which stood at about 280 million in 1891, had reached over 380 million by 1941. The total population rose only slowly before 1913, with absolute declines in some regions in most decades from 1891 to 1911, and virtually stagnated between 1911 and 1921 as a result of the plague and influenza epidemics during and after the First World War. From 1921 onwards there was a steady rate of growth, however, averaging over one per cent per year until 1951. This increase was less than half the average annual population growth

[36] Raymond W. Goldsmith, *The Financial Development of India, 1860–1977*, New Haven, 1983, pp. 124–5.

[37] A. K. Bagchi, *Private Investment in India, 1900–1939*, Cambridge, 1972, p. 104.

[38] Raj Krishna and G. S. Raychaudhuri, 'Trends in Rural Savings and Capital Formation in India, 1950–1951 to 1973–1974', *Economic Development and Cultural Change*, 30, 2, 1982, p. 293.

rates of the 1950s, 1960s and 1970s, but nonetheless it represented the first sustained period of consistent expansion of population in the modern period.[39] These rates of population growth were roughly similar in all the main demographic zones of the country after 1921.

The marked population increase of the middle decades of the twentieth century did not signify any significant overall improvements in nutrition, or in public health or welfare systems, except perhaps in malarial areas. It was the result of a striking fall in death rates, which occurred because the main agents of mortality – famine and epidemic disease – were less prevalent than they had been in previous decades as a result of favourable climatic conditions, improvements in the emergency transportation of foodgrains, and the diversification of employment prospects. Even so, the rate of population increase in India remained low in comparison to some South-East Asian countries; Java, for example, sustained an average annual population growth rate of more than 1 per cent throughout the nineteenth and early twentieth centuries.[40] The population of India increased by 30 per cent between 1880 and 1930, while that of Java doubled. Low food availability and the paucity of investment in public health measures such as insect eradication kept death rates in India relatively high throughout the colonial period.

The problems of agricultural production in the inter-war years were having a marked effect on the availability of foodgrains by the 1940s. Estimates of food supply for the first half of the twentieth century, based on fairly optimistic assumptions, suggest that per capita daily availability of foodgrains was between 502 and 613 g in 1921, between 474 and 557 g in 1931, and between 390 and 446 g in 1946. In 1951 per capita foodgrain availability was 395 g, rising to 480 g in 1965.[41] Regional production figures suggest that the potential threat caused by falling foodgrain production and rising rates of population increase was most marked in some parts of eastern India, but a fall in the aggregate supply of grain, coupled to the sharp rise in food prices in the late 1930s and throughout the 1940s, was likely to hit those on low incomes severely everywhere. By the early 1950s enforced hunger was certainly affecting some agricultural labourers and others in the lowest income categories. According to the data collected by the *Rural Credit Survey*, households living

[39] Leela Visaria and Pravin Visaria, 'Population (1757–1947)', *CEHI*, 2, table 5.12.

[40] Anne Booth, *Agricultural Development in Indonesia*, Australian Association for Asian Studies, Sydney, 1988, pp. 28–30.

[41] Heston, 'National Income', *CEHI*, 2, p. 410; Pramit Chaudhuri, *The Indian Economy: Poverty and Development*, London, 1978, table 38.

on Rs 100 a year or less in 1952 consumed only 11 oz (312.5 g) of foodgrains per day, equivalent to a daily diet of 1,100 calories and below the lowest ration level set during the post-war food crisis.[42]

## LAND, LABOUR AND CAPITAL IN INDIAN AGRICULTURE

It is not possible to summarise the pattern of land control or changes in the size of operated land-holdings for the last decades of colonial rule using contemporary data, although the distribution of land-ownership probably remained fairly static across size categories.[43] The first extensive attempts to collect such data by direct surveys were made in the early 1950s, as part of the Indian government's attempts to survey the problems of rural credit and agricultural labour, and the techniques used, especially in the All-India Rural Credit Survey (1955), have often been criticised as too narrow. The best figures based on widespread sampling are for 1954–5, published in the eighth round of the National Sample Survey in 1956. From these sources it is possible to put together a picture of the agricultural situation in the decade after Independence, which can be taken as representative of the whole period after 1930. This suggests that the distribution of land was very uneven, and that the size of the average operated holding in most parts of the country was inadequate for subsistence. The Indian Famine Commission (1946) calculated that 74 per cent of holdings in Madras and 50 per cent of those in Bengal and Bombay produced less than 1 tonne of foodgrains, while half the farms in the United Provinces produced less than 1.5 tonnes of foodgrains.[44] One tonne of foodgrains would supply a subsistence ration of 12 oz per day for 9 people, or a starvation ration of 8 oz per day for 12 people. The Government of India's Agricultural Labour Enquiry (1955) estimated that, in 1951, 17 per cent of land-holdings were less than an acre in area, and 59 per cent were less than 5 acres, which was below the minimum required for a viable independent farm in most parts of the country. For 15 per cent of rural families with land the major activity was supplying labour to others, while about half of the

[42] Cited in Dharm Narain, *Distribution of the Marketed Surplus of Agricultural Produce in Size-level of Holding in India, 1950–51*, Bombay, 1961, pp.36–7.

[43] Dharma Kumar, 'Landownership and Inequality in Madras Presidency, 1853–4 to 1946–7', *Indian Economic and Social History Review*, 12, 3, 1975; Eric Stokes, 'The Structure of Landholding in Uttar Pradesh, 1860–1940', *Indian Economic and Social History Review*, 12, 2, 1975, reprinted in *Peasant and Raj*, Ch. 9.

[44] Cited in Walter C. Neale, *Economic Change in North India: Land Tenure and Reform in the United Provinces, 1800–1955*, New Haven, 1962, p. 153.

agricultural labour-force consisted of poor peasants with some land of their own, who might themselves employ labour at peak seasons.[45]

According to the National Sample Survey data, 23 per cent of rural households owned no land at all in 1954–5, and 75 per cent owned less than 5 acres. The rental market gave most rural households some access to land but, even so, distribution was very uneven. Overall, only 11 per cent of rural households did not cultivate any land at all, but the vast majority could still farm only petty amounts: 31 per cent of operational holdings were 1 acre or less, and 61 per cent 5 acres or less. The amount of land available for rent may have been somewhat limited by the land reform programmes, but even so, about one-quarter of the cultivated land was leased-in at the end of the 1950s, with farmers in north-western India leasing 37 per cent of the land they used on aggregate. Furthermore, the line of demarcation between sharecroppers who were tenants at will and agricultural workers employed on a crop-share basis was rather thin, especially in central and north-western India.[46]

Despite the small size of the units of production, the agricultural system in 1950 was heavily market-oriented. A large volume of agricultural produce was sold, and many cultivators depended on cash sales to maintain themselves. A detailed study of the marketed surplus for 1950–1 indicated that cultivators with small-holdings marketed a disproportionately large share of their output, about one-third on aggregate. As a result, more than one-quarter of the total marketed surplus of Indian agricultural production came from cultivators with operated holdings of 5 acres or less, and a further 20 per cent from those with holdings of 5 to 10 acres.[47] Even for small-holders, cash markets were of crucial importance to service debts; pay rent and land revenue; and buy in necessities such as cloth, kerosene and salt. In addition, there was an extensive non-cash market operating in foodgrains used for barter or as payments for labour. Various estimates from the 1950s suggest that around 40 per cent of the total man-days worked by adult casual agricultural labour were paid for in grain, while up to 20 per cent of rice production was used to pay wages in kind.[48]

[45] Government of India, *Agricultural Labour Enquiry. Volume i: All India*, Delhi, 1955, pp. 3,5.

[46] K. N. Raj, 'Ownership and Distribution of Land', *Indian Economic Review*, New Series, 5, 1, 1970.

[47] Narain, *Distribution of the Marketed Surplus of Agricultural Produce*, p. 35.

[48] *Second Enquiry on Agricultural Labour* (1956–7), cited in A. G. Chandavarkar, 'Money and Credit, 1858–1947', *CEHI*, 2, p. 764; *First Report of the National Income Committee* (April 1951), cited in Daniel Thorner, *The Shaping of Modern India*, New Delhi, 1980, p. 292.

Markets were as important for rural consumers as for rural producers. Data collected in the mid 1950s demonstrated that the consumption of grain among the rural poor rose as market prices fell and declined as market prices increased, which was clear evidence that many poor consumers were dependent on an integrated, cash-based market (often in 'superior' foodgrains such as rice and wheat) for their nutritional requirements. Access to this market depended on cash income, and hence on the employment possibilities for rural labour. The poorest rural consumers obtained a higher than average proportion of their consumption of fruits, vegetables and fuel in kind, but a lower than average proportion of their consumption of cereals, for which consumption in kind rose with income.[49] The poorest members of rural society – those with the most inadequate control over land – were the most dependent on cash earnings and cash markets for foodgrains; this group included some small-holders as well as those who relied entirely on agricultural wages for their income. As the Government of India's Committee on Distribution of Income and Levels of Living reported in 1964, reviewing the evidence of income inequality in the 1950s,

> to a large extent the phenomenon of economic concentration in the Indian economy is the result … of unemployment and under-employment and consequent low productivity per unit of labour, that is to say, of inadequate economic development rather than merely structural inequalities of a distributional character.[50]

The problems of rural production and consumption were bound up with the functioning of coherent labour and capital markets, markets that depended on institutions which were focused at a very local level. Where productivity increased it was often the result of new inputs of agricultural capital – a precise, but variable, mixture of manure, draught animals and water delivered in the right mix and order. In particular, manure was useless without water, and even draught animals were comparatively ineffective without water. So far as consumption was concerned, given man–land ratios, debt-bondage and the highly imperfect nature of market arrangements, most agricultural producers and their families had to secure at least part of their food supplies by selling their labour, rather than simply by growing crops for their own consumption. As we have seen, by the early 1950s between two-thirds and four-fifths of rural households farmed too little land to achieve self-sufficiency, even assuming

[49] Dharma Kumar, 'Changes in Income Distribution and Poverty in India: A Review of the Literature', *World Development*, 1, 1, 1974, p. 35.

[50] Government of India, Planning Commission, *Report of the Committee on Distribution of Income and Levels of Living: Part 1*, Delhi, 1964, (Mahanalobis Committee), p. 28.

they were able to consume all that they produced. As a result, the market for rural labour became the key determinant of the welfare and income of the vast mass of the agrarian population.

Many historians of rural South Asia have pointed out that Indian agriculture was consistently undercapitalised throughout the modern period. In the nineteenth century the most important item of capital equipment was the animal power supplied by bullocks, which were needed to pull carts and ploughs, draw water from wells and down irrigation channels, and supply rich and cheap manure. In much of peninsular India, away from the wet-crop zones of the east and south-east, as many as six bullocks were needed to pull the heavy ploughs, and double that number for carts. Yet early surveys of the Deccan revealed that in the 1840s and 1850s the vast majority of cultivators did not own, or even have access to, enough of this basic capital equipment to farm their lands properly. As a result, land remained unmanured, and was sometimes ploughed only once every three or four years.[51]

The supply of capital goods for the rural economy may have eased somewhat during the second half of the nineteenth century, although the staple items of agricultural equipment remained bullocks, wooden ploughs and unsprung carts right up to the 1950s. By 1860 the rural economy in most of colonial India had recovered from the shocks that accompanied the British conquest and the first phase of punitive revenue extraction. Cultivated acreage grew substantially, and windfall gains in overseas demand, as well as consistent improvements in road and rail transportation networks, all increased the profits to be made from the rural economy. However, such benefits were often skewed, and also fluctuated wildly in time and space. Indian agriculture remained a gamble in rain; when the monsoons failed badly in the nineteenth century famine could still be devastating, especially in the late 1870s and the late 1890s. As we have seen, it is probable that the increased mortality of these years, which was exacerbated in the 1890s by a large-scale outbreak of plague in western India, fell more heavily on those who relied on returns from the labour market to meet their subsistence needs. Famine years also damaged capital equipment, for bullocks starved when the rains failed. In many parts of the Bombay Presidency, for example, cattle numbers fell sharply in the famines of the late 1890s, and had not recovered their former numbers by the late 1920s. Here, and on the plains of Tamilnad as well, the population increase and intensification of land use for arable crops in the 1920s and 1930s were

[51] Charlesworth, *Peasants and Imperial Rule*, p. 78.

leading to pronounced shortages of cattle and fodder and increased pressure on the forest areas and waste land that remained.[52]

By the twentieth century the key to agricultural improvement through capital investment lay in irrigation, but expanding the irrigated acreage was again a difficult matter. Increasing the provision of water for cultivation was a technological problem in part, but one that existed in a distinct socio-economic context. Mechanised irrigation pumps were not available until after 1945; before then the delivery of water from canal schemes and large-scale irrigation systems, or from local dams (*bunds*) and reservoirs (*tanks*) through gravity-fed channels or simple machines of the 'Persian-wheel' type, or even from wells, relied on gravity or animal power. Bullocks required feed and careful breeding; reservoirs, dams and channels needed hard labour for maintenance and repair. Using government irrigation facilities required paying a water rate, and preparing land for irrigation involved considerable work and some prior capital expenditure.

At the micro-distributional level, the sharing of water between rival claimants was in large part a social issue, with water rights and privileges being determined by local power and the ability to exploit common effort for private gain. The link between water, agricultural growth and local power could have the effect of limiting investment in irrigation in some circumstances. In north India in the mid nineteenth century, for example, tenant investment in wells gave a customary claim to occupancy rights; zamindars tended to discourage such improvements because they would disturb the local balance of power. More generally, however, the emergence of local elites of substantial cultivators in the nineteenth century led to increased investment in rural capital goods such as wells, and also other economic and social activities, as an expression and underpinning of their increased power and wealth.[53]

The most spectacular advances in irrigation were those made by large-scale public works in northern, north-western and south-eastern India. By contrast, the small-scale irrigation systems of dams and reservoirs traditionally constructed and maintained by local rulers, patrons and magnates often suffered neglect from a colonial administration incapable or unwilling to co-ordinate the supply of public goods at the village level. The extent of various forms of irrigation at the end of the colonial period is shown in maps 2.5(a) and 2.5(b). The 'canal colonies' of western Punjab used canal irrigation to convert semi-arid scrubland for productive agriculture, beginning with 3 million

[52] *Ibid.*, p. 212; Christopher John Baker, *An Indian Rural Economy, 1880–1955. The Tamilnad Countryside*, Delhi, 1984, pp. 159–61.

[53] Ludden, 'Productive Power in Agriculture', pp. 68, 71.

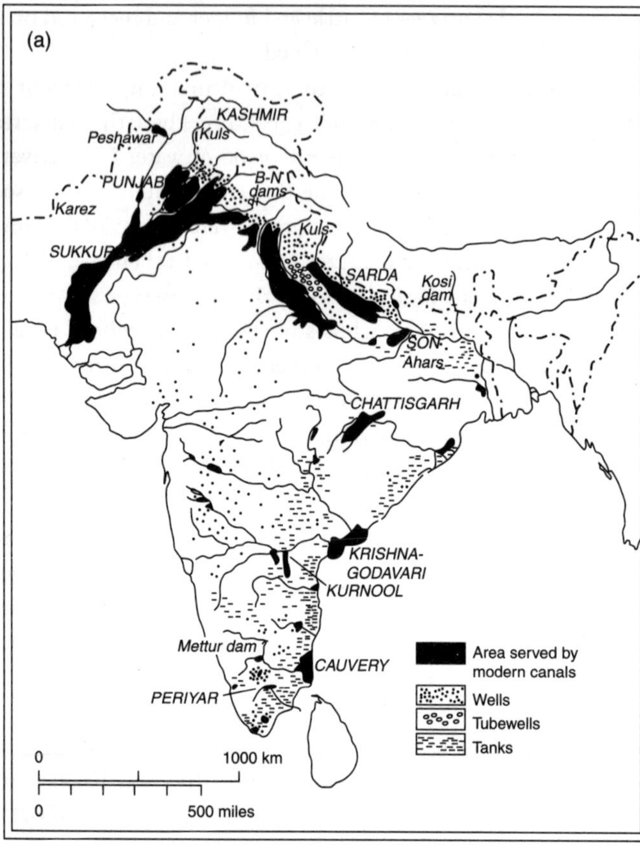


Map 2.5(a) Types of irrigation at work in India, by district, *c.* 1940

acres in 1885 and rising to 14 million in 1947. However, the economic effects of the establishment of these new settlements were somewhat muted, since the Punjab government used the creation of the colonies to indulge in a wide-reaching programme of social engineering, making land grants directly to those it wished to favour for political or social reasons, rather than to those who were necessarily best able to make use of the new resources of land and water for efficient agricultural production. In the western districts of the United Provinces, where large public-works projects resulted in the spread of canal irrigation at a rate of 50,000 acres a year from 1860 to 1920, considerable economic growth took place, but only in those areas where other conditions were favourable. The other major colonial irrigation system, in the

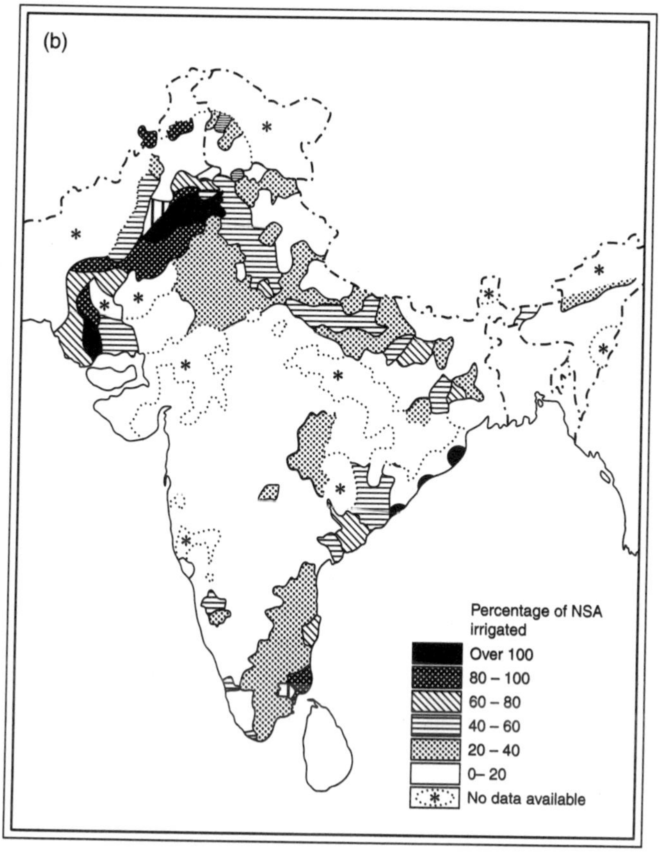


Map 2.5(b) Percentage of agricultural land irrigated, by district, *c.* 1940

Krishna-Godavari delta of south-eastern India, made that part of Andhra into a major exporter of rice for the domestic market.

In 1900, when the Indian Irrigation Commission was set up to consider the future of large-scale public works, about one fifth of the total cultivated area (44 million acres) of British India was served by some form of irrigation works. Private sources, chiefly wells and tanks, supplied 60 per cent of this area; only one-quarter of it was watered by any of the major public-works schemes built in the second half of the nineteenth century. Furthermore, such works were concentrated in a relatively few areas of the subcontinent, with almost half the irrigated area supplied by them being in the Punjab by the end of the colonial period. Nineteenth-century canals had been built with nineteenth-century objectives in mind, mainly the defeat of famine through insurance for dry-land grain cultivation. As ecological, climatic and economic circumstances changed and offered new opportunities for growing different crops, the old system was not always able to adapt very well to the demands made of it.

Agricultural labour in colonial India came from two chief sources of supply. One was the traditional landless groups, or 'menial' (often untouchable or tribal) castes, who were usually bound to dominant cultivators by custom, sometimes on a hereditary basis and often reinforced by debt-bondage. This group of 'farm servants' were clearly defined in many regions before the British conquest, and they probably remained the only major rural group without any access to land at all through the colonial period. The terms on which such labour was employed varied over time, as different systems of agricultural production evolved. Periods of growth provided employment opportunities that gave traditional labourers fresh bargaining power, although, as cultivation became more profitable and prices rose, landlords also had an interest in substituting casual cash employment for fixed obligations to provide grain.

The second source of rural labour came from the large numbers of deficit cultivators, families that did not have enough land to provide employment or subsistence for all their members. This was supplied both directly, through casual employment at harvest and other times of high seasonal demand, and also indirectly, through debt-bondage, sharecropping arrangements and hypothecation. A 2.5 acre plot in a 'dry' region absorbed perhaps 125 labour days a year, most of which could be supplied by women and children, leaving male family members free to seek seasonal employment elsewhere. In one village typical of the arid regions of peninsular India that was studied by H. H. Mann in 1920, 82 per cent of total income came from labour, and only 7 per cent of households (with 19 per cent of the land) could reach a minimum subsistence level without working away from their own holding. Indebtedness and hypothecation produced a further supplementary source of rural labour, as small-holders struggled to retain their nominal independence while working under the instruction of their creditors. Land symbolised sovereignty to the peasant, but the economic opportunities of many tenants and small-holders were almost indistinguishable from the landless. In Tamilnad a report on tenancy in 1947 noted:

> In this province, the prevailing notion of rent among the land-owning classes is that the tenant is merely a wage-earner and is not entitled to any appreciable margin of profit over and above what an ordinary agricultural labourer will get for cultivating the land.

Under the *waram* system of crop-sharing tenancies in Tamilnad the cultivator might get as little as 20 per cent of the output, where the land was especially fertile and the owner supplied the capital for cultivation.[54] This system was widespread, and induced increased effort with diminishing rewards. As a detailed study of 'peasant proletarians' in the Punjab concluded:

> The indebted peasant resisted the process of complete dispossession, striving continuously to produce more and consume less. The property which belonged to him was, in a way, 'sham property'. It had in effect been taken over by the rich peasant or the bania. But to the 'peasant' his hold over the land did not appear to be a sham. He considered it *his* property, the basis or the potential basis of his independence.[55]

Despite some moves towards more flexible hiring arrangements and cash wages over the late nineteenth and early twentieth centuries, the rural labour market was always strongly differentiated, especially for those workers who were paid in kind, either through sharecropping or crop-hypothecation agreements. While the market for cash labour or cash credit did become more competitive at times, this was less marked in the market for labour paid in kind and bound by customary relations. Sharecroppers without capital assets of their own and consumption-debtors usually had less opportunity than independent peasants to switch between landlords or creditors. This could result in a classic monopoly relationship in which dependent cultivators acted as price-takers, 'buying' grain and 'selling' labour as differentiated products in a market with high entry and exit barriers. Despite these structural barriers, however, the rural labour market was unified in certain important respects, even where consumption needs were largely met by non-monetary transactions. Subsistence wage levels were not simply fixed by custom, but responded to the cash market price of grain and commercial crops, and the relationship between them. *Jajmani* payments for services in kind survived into the 1950s in the less commercialised areas of the countryside, yet even traditional relationships of this sort were often linked to market conditions. In one relatively uncommercialised village in the Kannada region of northern Tamilnad in the 1950s, for example, where *jajmani* payments were still being made to artisans, labourers and other dependents, these were clearly calculated to equalise the distribution of resources in bad seasons, but to enable the village leaders to skim off the surplus in good years.[56]

[54] Baker, *Indian Rural Economy*, pp. 172–5.

[55] Neeladri Bhattacharya, 'Agricultural Labour and Production: Central and South-East Punjab, 1870–1940', in K. N. Raj (ed.), *Essays on the Commercialization of Indian Agriculture*, Delhi, 1985, p. 121.

[56] Baker, *Indian Rural Economy*, p. 570.

## COLONIAL INSTITUTIONS AND INDIAN AGRICULTURE

British officials had imported much ideology and many misconceptions to their analysis of the Indian rural economy in the first half of the nineteenth century. Perhaps the most important and lasting of these was the notion that the Indian rural economy was made up of self-sufficient and self-governing village 'republics', which required no exchange economy with the outside world, and were linked to it only by the extraction of political tribute in the form of taxation. This analysis dominated nineteenth-century thinking about rural economic development because it could be adapted to fit a wide range of intellectual prejudices and preconceptions. To paternalists it justified the imposition of British rule and taxation as a more 'civilised' form of traditional government. To radical modernisers in the British administration trained in classical political economy, especially those concerned with land rent and revenue schemes based on Utilitarian principles, it pointed the way forward for releasing the pent-up energies of the Indian people, by transforming institutions, taxing the inefficient out of business, and creating economic incentives for cultivators. It also provided a convenient stick with which to beat the landlords, who could be seen as leeches sucking the surplus out of the peasantry.

The English Utilitarians, who formulated the administrative principles by which the British Raj was governed in the 1830s and 1840s, wanted to transform traditional India from the bottom up. Their greatest critic, Karl Marx, shared their prejudices to a large extent and argued that Company rule in these decades was dissolving 'these small semi-barbarian communities by blowing up their economical basis', and bringing the 'greatest, and to speak the truth, the only *social* revolution ever heard of in Asia'.[57] To Marx the consequences of the social revolution unleashed by British rule were not very happy, a view shared by many later conservative commentators on British policy. This contrast between 'traditional' village India, built around non-material values, self-sufficiency and continuity, and the 'modern' countryside of markets, social differentiation and rural exploitation, continued to haunt analyses of South Asian agriculture throughout the colonial period and beyond, achieving perhaps its most pervasive influence in the selection of community development programmes to secure agricultural growth under the Indian five-year plans of the 1950s and early 1960s. However, the distinction it was built on was largely false, as we have seen, for it misinterpreted or overlooked the large and

[57] These phrases occur in Marx's articles for the *New York Daily Tribune* published in 1853, cited in Stokes, *Peasant and Raj*, p. 24.

significant continuities between 'traditional' and 'modern' economic institutions in the Indian rural economy of the eighteenth and nineteenth centuries.

The staple units of analysis that colonial officials devised to identify and categorise rural systems of production have largely been abandoned by historians of the agrarian economy. Many of those whom the British identified as landowners had the right to raise taxation, rather than the capacity to cultivate the soil; such land-ownership was usually less important in giving access to scarce resources than was land control, which is much harder to identify in the aggregate. Such control was closely bound up with the working of the rural labour and capital markets, especially the supply of credit, but analyses of the structure and workings of these markets must go far beyond simple categories that can be derived from, or applied to, generalised data. Most disconcerting of all, perhaps, is that many individual cultivating households cannot be identified unambiguously by the conventional labels of 'landlord', 'tenant', 'labourer', 'creditor', 'debtor', and so on. Many examples exist of household survival strategies that involved a wide range of economic activities, often combining some ownership with tenancy or sharecropping, and even labour, and with employment in the urban or rural handicraft sector as well as in cultivation.

The persistence of both under-investment and under-consumption in the rural economy was part and parcel of the institutional structures that emerged under colonial rule. In setting up Company rule over the subcontinent, British administrators brought with them a package of policy initiatives that, by the second half of the nineteenth century, had helped to create and sustain a wide band of privileged groups who benefited from state action over land revenue, tenancy and agricultural investment. Favouritism by the state brought some direct economic advantages, the most usual being the provision of privileged land tenures that gave tax-free or tax-favoured status to the *inam* or *sir* land that formed the personal holdings of village officials, local zamindars and proprietary ryots. More important, however, was the control of production that came from manipulation of the scarce resource of land, and the local markets for employment, rural capital and sales of output. Such control was most often derived from social power, reinforced by the privileges of a position in local organs of the state such as the land-revenue hierarchy and village administration.

The direct economic returns from such activities were often remarkably small. In the first half of the twentieth century income obtained directly by rural moneylending possibly contributed no more than 10 per cent of total agricultural income.[58] Buying land for rent was not usually a profitable

[58] Calculated from figures in Goldsmith, *Financial Development of India*, p. 115.

investment in itself, although land had other important advantages as an asset, such as absolute security. Real returns from rent in the 1920s and 1930s have been estimated at 3–4 per cent of the purchase price of the land in western India, and about the same level for the best valley land in Tamilnad, while they were probably below that in zamindari areas. The annual rental paid for land in the United Provinces during the 1930s amounted to less than 1 per cent of total net farm income.[59] By far the biggest share of rural income was derived from the returns from agricultural production and trade, but this remained a risky and uncertain business, especially in the difficult conditions of the inter-war years. Thus farm profits were often used to spread and avoid the risks that resulted from practising under-capitalised agriculture at times of ecological adversity and unstable market conditions. Given the limited and unstable nature of the market opportunities that faced the agricultural sector, maximising security was often more important than maximising output. Consequently, some dominant groups invested the surplus derived from their economic strength in reinforcing their social power, and the dominance of local state agencies, on which their command of scarce resources ultimately depended.

Access to state-granted privilege or the exercise of social power alone did not always ensure a permanent dominance of the rural economy, however. While the colonial state favoured certain groups in the revenue settlements of the nineteenth century, it did not consistently reinforce them thereafter, and those who found their position usurped had little redress. Subsidised entry to land, capital and commodity markets gave certain advantages, but could not resist all challenges. New crops, markets and institutions gave others the opportunity to challenge and overcome the control networks of old elites. Economic growth from below was possible in some circumstances, and such growth was able to trickle down, or bypass, the social hierarchy to a significant extent. The history of wheat in the Punjab, of cotton and tobacco in Gujarat, of jute in Bengal, and of garden crops everywhere, suggests that where the market mechanisms and demand stimuli were the strongest, the influence of social networks on the allocation of factors of production and economic choices was weakest.

Market opportunities that could fundamentally rearrange access to economic reward in rural India occurred most often at times of rising demand,

[59] Sumit Guha, 'Rural Economy in the Deccan', in Raj, *Commercialization of Indian Agriculture*, p. 128; Baker, *Indian Rural Economy*, p. 325; Neale, *Economic Change in North India*, tables 14 and 20. Charlesworth in *Peasants and Imperial Rule*, p. 191 gives an alternative estimate for western India of 5–10 per cent in the 1900s.

either inside or outside the country. Between 1860 and 1930, dependent cultivators had a number of opportunities to produce commercial crops directly on their own account, and thus move partially out of the subsistence and into the cash economy. The peasants of the cotton-growing areas of the Khandesh in western India, for example, were able to control production and marketing of their crop from the 1870s onwards, and got good terms for output and credit from a competitive service economy.[60] In Bengal the jute boom of the 1900s temporarily freed peasants in districts such as Faridpur and Dacca from debt, and enabled them for a time to market their crop independently, without resort to *dadan* (the taking of loans against a standing crop hypothecated at half the market price of the previous season).[61] The opening up of groundnut cultivation on the plains of Tamilnad offered a similar opportunity. In South Arcot in the 1920s the 'exceptionally low' cost of production meant that:

> [i]t is possible for one man with a pair of oxen and a single plough to do all the work necessary – cultivation, manuring, sowing, weeding, reaping etc., for from five to eight acres of groundnuts and other grains, with the exception of some assistance at weeding and harvest. This is not uncommon in this locality.[62]

The benefits of rising demand could help weaken the ties of the social hierarchy in other ways. In boom times the price of land rose faster than interest rates, so that peasants could hope to recover some of their land-holding by selling or mortgaging another part at a higher value. Where agricultural profitability increased, demand for labour also rose, returns to labour increased accordingly and freer wage-labour markets grew up to replace older custom-based systems.

It is important to realise that these market opportunities, where they existed, were mediated through a complex mix of particular local economic, social, political and ecological circumstances, and so did not lead inevitably to a 'pure' form of agrarian capitalism. There was often no clear link between investment and profitability in Indian agriculture, nor were there universal returns to scale or to scope waiting to be captured. Equally, commercialisation did not lead to 'proletarianisation' or to any major changes in the distribution of land-holdings by size. Possession of even a tiny holding of land retained considerable psychic and cultural advantages for Indian villagers, as well as assuring them of a more favourable relationship with the local labour market. Large farms secured no significant advantages over small ones, provided

60 Guha, 'Rural Economy in the Deccan', pp. 216–17.

61 Goswami, 'Agriculture in Slump', pp. 337–8.

62 Quoted in Baker, *Indian Rural Economy*, p. 151.

that small-holders could super-exploit their own labour and obtain off-farm employment. Thus economic growth did not necessarily change the social structure or the factor-mix used to produce the staple crops.

Opportunities for market-based growth in agriculture were always limited, and were only securely based in ecologically balanced areas growing crops for which there was substantial demand. For export crops this stimulus virtually came to an end with the onset of the Great Depression that hit the Indian rural economy in the late 1920s. The collapse of international demand for primary products after 1929 weakened the Indian rural economy considerably and disrupted the capital and labour markets based around export-led production that had grown up since 1900. The most corrosive and lasting effects came from the liquidity crisis that undermined the market for rural labour both in cash and in kind. Dominant cultivators did not retreat from cash-crop production, but they looked for ways of minimising costs, especially labour costs. This was done by switching to less labour-intensive crops, or to less labour-intensive methods of cultivation, and by employing family rather than hired labour on the farm. The Bombay Government estimated that rural wage rates fell by over 20 per cent between 1929 and 1931; family labour was always paid less than even the market rate.[63] Erstwhile labourers were, in turn, thrown back onto their own, inadequate, family plots, or had to migrate to the cities in search of work.

For the rural poor the disruption of the rural labour market was probably the most severe direct consequence of the depression in agriculture, and this also had two serious subsidiary effects. Firstly, sharecropping increased in some areas, most notably in Bengal, and was probably accompanied by a further decrease in agricultural efficiency through a loss of incentives for the cultivator. Secondly, the collapse of cash credit networks from outside the village led to an increase in the prevalence of consumption credit provided in kind by surplus food producers, leading to fragmentation in the rural credit market and its control by village-level surplus cultivators rather than district-level bankers and traders. Decentralised sharecropping gave dominant farmers an alternative method of grain redistribution via the product market once the credit market had slumped.

As a result of all these changes, deficit food producers could no longer earn enough to meet their subsistence, rent, revenue and capital costs by growing commercial crops for market on their own account. In east Bengal, for example, peasant small-holders had switched to jute, a high-value, labour-intensive cash

[63] Charlesworth, *Peasants and Imperial Rule*, p. 230; Guha, 'Rural Economy in the Deccan', p. 220.

crop, after 1900 as a way of solving the subsistence crisis caused by diminishing land-holdings and rapid population growth. When the international market for jute collapsed in the 1930s, this solution was no longer sustainable. During the 1940s urban demand for consumption goods rose sharply, fuelled by the wartime inflation, and the real cost of rent and capital probably fell. Deficit producers did not benefit, however, because these changes pushed up the price of food still further, and meant that entry into various forms of tied labour became a crucial mechanism for securing subsistence goods. The vicious circle of under-consumption of basic wage goods tightened still further once the rural poor had to compete directly with urban demand in the domestic foodgrain market (a food-market severely distorted by procurement, transportation and allocation difficulties throughout the 1940s), and could no longer benefit from windfall gains in international prices for exportable crops. In these two decades it became significantly more difficult for those with inadequate unencumbered holdings of land, or with insufficient access to credit and employment, to obtain surplus produce. Deficit producers who were unable to command consumption from non-market sources suffered considerably, but they were not the only group whose economic opportunities were diminished; labour enforcement problems and the shock to the land market of the 1930s severely damaged the position of non-cultivating landlords, rentiers and urban moneylenders as well.

By 1950 the failings of the rural economy were obvious, but their causes were complex and remain somewhat obscure. Our account has stressed that the institutional networks of the rural economy were an important variable determining performance, since the social mechanisms for allocating capital and credit, and for providing access to land and employment, acted as replacements or substitutes for missing markets. But there was nothing inevitable about the dominance of social structure over economic opportunity in Indian agriculture, nor did the apparent shortage of productive resources and the increase in man:land ratios constitute by themselves an insurmountable barrier to sustained development. It is true that at the end of the colonial period there were severe problems of food supply, and that institutional control had once again become more important than responsiveness to market opportunity in ensuring economic survival and success. However, these phenomena were not the inevitable consequence of either the social formations of colonial capitalism, or an implacable Malthusian crisis – rather they were largely the result of the specific institutional inadequacies and market failures of the last twenty years of British rule. Social mechanisms were strong only because market stimuli were often weak, and state agencies were virtually non-existent. With more favourable and stable market networks, linked to sustained, positive stimuli from the export trades, and coupled to a more diffused and efficient system for allocating capital and labour, the developmental thrust of Indian agriculture could have been stronger, more universal and more consistent in the colonial period.

CHAPTER 3

# TRADE AND MANUFACTURE, 1860–1945: FIRMS, MARKETS AND THE COLONIAL STATE

## THE IMPACT OF THE COLONIAL STATE

Colonial India was a private enterprise economy in the sense that most decisions about the allocation of resources were made by the private sector; the state's annual share of gross national product averaged less than 10 per cent in every decade from 1872 to 1947. However, the history of firms and markets cannot be isolated from an analysis of the activities of the colonial state and its public agents. By its attitude to property and tenancy rights in land, its public expenditure priorities, and its monetary and financial policies, the British regime in Calcutta and New Delhi helped to shape, if not solely to create, a distinctively 'colonial' economy in late nineteenth- and early twentieth-century India, in which its own institutions played a significant role. The social structures, economic opportunities, and cultural and ideological systems in which firms and entrepreneurs operated in India were nourished by, and themselves helped to sustain, the peculiarities of a colonial regime that had a far longer and more complex history than that of any other European administration in Asia.

The structure and performance of firms and markets for trade and manufacture in colonial India after 1860 were heavily influenced by institutional developments that had occurred in the first century of British rule. In the eighteenth century, Indian merchant and service-gentry groups had played a crucial role as intermediaries between the agricultural economy and the state. Such groups were able to organise and finance long-distance trade and remittance for local rulers through a network of trade-bills (*hundis*) and they attained a strong coherence across the urban centres and warrior-states of the Gangetic plain, in the Maratha fiefdoms of western India, in the new mercantilist powers of the south (notably Mysore and Hyderabad), and even in Bengal during the early years of Company rule. Indigenous merchants, revenue farmers and organisers of new settlements were able to use the supply lines of courts and armies in turn, and the state-organised revenue collection and transfer mechanisms, to co-ordinate extensive patterns of inter-regional trade as well as making substantial investments in rural production.

This redeployment of Indian merchant capital suffered a decisive shock as the East India Company spread out to control large parts of the subcontinent after 1760. New definitions of property rights and commercial law were an important part of this process, as was the manipulation of state power by British officials acting as private traders inside the Company's territories. Company servants were barred from private trade in 1788, and the private sector passed into the hands of agency houses, initially often run by ex-officials drawing on capital from both European and Indian sources, who profited further from the removal of the East India Company's monopoly to trade in India in 1813. The position of such agents was insecure, however, and a series of financial crises in 1826 and 1834, following problems in the market for indigo, destroyed the established agency houses. The business failures that resulted, coupled with the ending of the Company's monopoly in the China trade in 1833 and the granting to Europeans of the right to own land in India, opened up the private sector to new interests. By the 1840s British capital and enterprise had moved into tea plantations and a number of small industrial concerns in Bengal. The established Indian trading firms that still dominated the rural economy of the interior played little part in these developments, but an important role was taken by a small group of Bengali entrepreneurs, led by Dwarkanath Tagore, who founded the Bengal Coal Company and the Union Bank, and set up the managing agency house of Carr, Tagore and Co. in the 1840s to expand further. However, Tagore's enterprises, and other fledgling firms, were destroyed by a new wave of financial crises after 1846, caused by unstable trading conditions in Asia and Europe, and British expatriate firms ruled the roost in Calcutta for the next century.

Despite these market-based difficulties that plagued the Indo-British entrepreneurial groups of the first half of the nineteenth century, the main direct destructive effect that the coming of British rule had on trade and finance resulted from the activities of the colonial state acting in and for itself. The East India Company's administrators extensively revised the basis of revenue assessment and collection, and provided new centralised institutions for cash transfer both domestically and internationally. Once the state's own apparatus took over these functions, the scope of the activities of private operators, especially Indian private operators, was considerably reduced. Before the 1850s there was still some room for private enterprise in these activities by Company servants and, once the Company's trading monopoly had been abolished, by formal firms and agencies of expatriate businessmen. Such operators generally required Indian partners, and many of the established native business firms were able to adapt to play this role successfully. However, such operations were largely limited to commodity imports and exports by the 1840s and, as we have seen, the international depression of that decade took a heavy toll of many of the old private business empires, British and Indian alike.

After 1858, the date at which the administration of British India passed formally into the hands of the Crown, the role of private agents in the economic operations of the colonial state was very small. The most significant change was in the financial arrangements that the new regime made for the transfer of government revenues within India and between Calcutta and London. As a direct result of instabilities in the domestic financial system, culminating in the collapse of the Bank of Bombay in 1866 following the boom and bust of the cotton economy during and after the American Civil War, the colonial administration largely withdrew its business from the privately owned Presidency Banks and set up its own treasury institutions to handle, collect, hold and transfer government revenues. At the same time, officials removed monetary flexibility and discretion from the local banking system by withdrawing the note-issuing privileges of the Presidency Banks.

While these changes were being imposed in the domestic monetary system, the international transfer mechanism for Indian revenue and trade surpluses was also fundamentally altered by the growth of the Council Bill system. The colonial administration had heavy administrative costs to meet in Britain for defence expenditure, pensions and the maintenance of the India Office (the Home Charges), and also had to service public borrowing for railway building and other projects. Over the forty years from 1858–9 to 1897–8, service transactions on government account amounted to Rs 5.42 billion, an annual average of Rs 135 million, with the Home Charges alone running at an average of over Rs 100 million per year. To meet this expenditure in Britain the Government of India remitted money by auctioning revenue rupees in its Indian treasuries in return for foreign exchange payable in sterling in London. Between 1872 and 1893 over half of India's accumulated visible trade surplus of £555 million was balanced by the sale of Council Bills.[1] Although alternative methods for transferring trading capital into and out of India still remained, the Council Bill system rapidly became the dominant mode of remittance available to private traders.

By the last quarter of the nineteenth century the colonial state in South Asia had largely created its own institutional mechanisms for sustaining itself through revenue collection, expenditure and transfer. The role of

[1] These figures are taken from A. K. Banerji, *Aspects of Indo-British Economic Relations 1818–1898*, Bombay, 1982, tables 34 and 40A.

private firms as agents of the state in tax-farming, exchange broking and official remittance (common in European-controlled areas elsewhere in Asia) was rare in British India, although some private enterprises, almost always British metropolitan or expatriate ones, were able to participate in the economic institutional structure of the colonial administration to a limited extent. The most obvious were those that provided private inputs to public services – such as defence suppliers and railway contractors, and the owners of shipping lines that secured mail contracts for international and coastal routes. Other private interests were able to force their way into public operations at particular times, as did the London-based exchange banks which, from the late 1890s to the mid 1920s, succeeded in effectively subcontracting the foreign exchange market from the Secretary of State. However, such dominance was limited and temporary. After the First World War new official purchasing policies and the creation of the Imperial Bank of India with quasi-central bank powers over the exchange market again substantially distanced British manufacturers and bankers from the economic infrastructure of the colonial state.

The renting out of public agencies to private interests under monopoly conditions was one hallmark of colonial capitalism in the British Empire, but no such opportunities arose for the vast bulk of British-owned and -operated trading and manufacturing firms in India under the Raj. It has been argued that the colonial regime implemented a less intense form of structural favouritism by discriminating in favour of British interests in tariff policy, in the allocation of licences for mineral extraction, in the provision of public transportation services, and in the creation of trading networks for export crops between the up-country producing areas and the ports, but many of these instances have been contested. When such favouritism did occur, at particular times in particular places, it was usually not strong enough to give British businessmen the power to defeat their Indian or foreign rivals for very long. While large-scale industry, foreign trade and institutional finance in eastern India were all dominated from the 1860s to the 1920s by classic colonial firms, owned and operated by British metropolitan and expatriate businessmen, some of whom had close social relations with colonial officials and imperial political leaders, the connection between race and economic success was short-lived. After the First World War a new breed of Indian entrepreneurs challenged the hold of the expatriates on the institutional structures of the organised economy very effectively, weakened it decisively in the 1930s, and destroyed it almost completely after 1945.

In the nineteenth century, official attitudes often reinforced aspects of Indian economic organisation that were unhelpful to the activities of large-scale traders and manufacturers, British and Indian alike. Firms in the organised business sector were largely passive agents in the process of economic change, able to make substantial profits and undertake considerable expansion, but always limited by the boundaries of political, economic and social markets and institutions designed and constructed by others. In particular, the opportunities presented after 1860 by export-oriented agricultural production were sustained by vertical linkages built on local modes of social power within the subsistence economy, and provided a barren field for 'modern' business operations. In the first half of the twentieth century structural changes in the domestic economy, supplemented by the opportunities offered by the collapse of the established networks of agricultural investment and marketing during the slump of the 1930s, offered more favourable circumstances for import-substituting industrialisation. However, the sluggishness of agricultural output and the stagnant rates of capital utilisation and labour productivity in the inter-war period weakened the dynamics of business growth. Levels of risk and uncertainty remained high, and by the 1940s businessmen had turned to the state as the only agent that could construct a sound institutional base for their operations. It is against this background that studies of the trading and manufacturing economy of colonial India must be set.

## DEINDUSTRIALISATION AND THE FATE OF HANDICRAFTS

The historiography of trade and manufacture in colonial India is dominated by counter-factual questions about the process of industrialisation. The South Asian subcontinent had a large and active trading and manufacturing economy in the seventeenth and eighteenth centuries; its handicraft manufactures supplied a wide range of Asian and European markets for cotton goods, and its businessmen played a full part in a trading world based on the Indian Ocean that rivalled that of any other region. The onset of British rule through the agency of the East India Company was linked closely to political battles over control of production for the export trade, and over the supply of credit and liquidity for local states, and the financial and trading networks that they required, in the second half of the eighteenth century. Throughout the nineteenth century India was host to a large and diverse expatriate business community that created the modern industrial sector of Bengal; from the

Table 3.1 *Share of net output of all large-scale manufacturing production by selected industries, 1913–1947 (per cent of total net output)*

| | Cotton | Jute | Paper | Cement | Woollens | Iron and steel | Matches | Sugar | Other industries | Net value of output* |
|---|---|---|---|---|---|---|---|---|---|---|
| 1913–14 | 36.2 | 15.0 | 0.4 | – | 0.3 | 0.8 | – | 1.6 | 45.7 | 635 |
| 1938–9 | 29.0 | 8.0 | 0.5 | 1.0 | 0.3 | 4.4 | 1.2 | 3.4 | 52.2 | 1701 |
| 1946–7[a] | 23.2 | 5.3 | 0.6 | 1.1 | 0.5 | 3.6 | 0.8 | 4.1 | 60.8 | 2258 |

* Net value of all large-scale manufacturing output (Rs millions in 1938–9 prices).
[a] 1939–40 to 1946–7 (annual average).
*Source:* Morris D. Morris, 'The Growth of Large-Scale Industry to 1947', *CEHI*, 2, table 7.22.

1870s onwards, Indian-born businessmen were instrumental in establishing a mechanised cotton industry, and in the first half of the twentieth century Indian entrepreneurs became the dominant force in most business sectors. Between 1870 and 1947 India was an industrialising country in the sense that manufacturing output was growing as a share of national income, that value added per worker was increasing, and that productivity was higher and rising faster in the secondary sector than in agriculture. In output terms the Indian cotton and jute industries were significant in global terms by 1914, while in 1945 India was the tenth largest producer of manufactured goods in the world.

On closer inspection, however, much of this 'progress' turns out to be illusory. Per-capita output of manufactured goods in India remained well below that in countries such as Mexico or Egypt throughout this period. Mining and manufacturing did contribute about 17 per cent of total output in 1947, but more than half of this was supplied by small-scale, largely unmechanised, industry. The rate of structural change in employment was very slow over the long term; the proportion of the total workforce employed in industry (mining, manufacturing, transport, storage and communications) remained constant at around 12 per cent between 1901 and 1951. Average daily employment in large-scale factories increased nearly five-fold between 1900 and 1947, but at 2.65 million this was still less than 2 per cent of the total labour-force at Independence. As tables 3.1 and 3.2 make clear, there was only a slow diversification of the modern industrial base away from cotton and jute manufactures over the first half of the twentieth century: the textile industries still supplied about 30 per cent of both output

Table 3.2 *Share of particular industries in total manufacturing employment in large perennial factories in India, 1913–1947 (per cent)*

| | Cotton | Jute | Paper | Cement | Woollens | Iron and steel | Matches | Sugar | Other industries | Total manuf. employment (000's) |
|---|---|---|---|---|---|---|---|---|---|---|
| 1913–14 | 28.3 | 23.5 | 0.5 | – | 0.4 | 0.9 | – | n.a. | 44.6 | 918 |
| 1938–9 | 23.8 | 15.9 | 0.5 | 0.7 | 0.6 | 1.1 | 0.9 | n.a. | 56.5 | 1854 |
| 1946–7 | 18.4 | 11.8 | 0.8 | 1.0 | 0.7 | 0.8 | 0.7 | n.a. | 65.8 | 2654 |

*Source:* Morris D. Morris, 'The Growth of Large-Scale Industry to 1947', *CEHI*, 2, table 7.23.

and factory employment in 1947; the rest of the industrial sector comprised a small amount of production across a large range of products. Even in the early 1950s, the bulk of the subcontinent's industrial production came from the two small areas of western and eastern India that had been the predominant industrialised regions since the late nineteenth century, as can be seen in map 3.1. Increases in industrial productivity in India were modest by international standards, and technical changes in the mechanised sector often lagged behind best practices elsewhere. This may well have been inevitable given the plentiful supplies of cheap labour, but that labour itself remained badly educated and poorly trained.

The history of Indian industry across the nineteenth century has often been analysed in terms of deindustrialisation, with British rule seen as destroying handicraft industries and ruining their workforce by commercialising agriculture, promoting imports of manufactured consumer goods, and inhibiting India's established exports of cloth. The Indian handicraft sector was certainly large in absolute terms at the beginning of the colonial period, supplying perhaps a quarter of world production of manufactured goods in 1750, and during the nineteenth century manufacturing activity in India remained almost entirely confined to handicrafts – modern factories employed less than 5 per cent of the manufacturing workforce as late as 1901.[2] Production techniques reflected the availability of cheap manual labour; as Francis Buchanan (the author of a famous set of reports on the domestic economy at the beginning of the nineteenth century) pointed out,

[2] J. Krishnamurty, 'Deindustrialisation in Gangetic Bihar during the Nineteenth Century: Another Look at the Evidence', *Indian Economic and Social History Review*, 22, 4, 1985, p. 399.

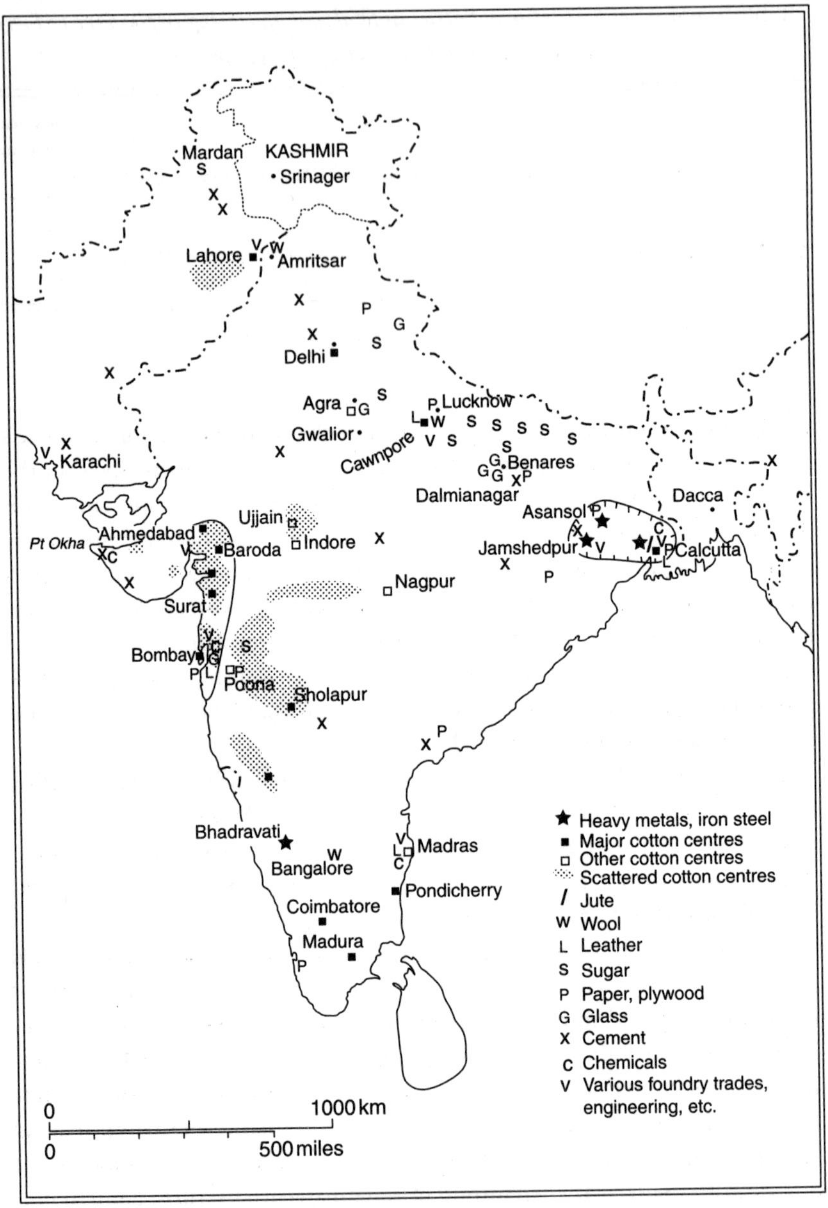


Map 3.1 Industrial location, India and Pakistan, 1947

the processes were such as 'could not be used in any country where manual labour possessed value'.[3] It is plausible to assume that labour productivity remained static throughout the eighteenth century, and little technical change seems to have occurred even where demand conditions were favourable. As with agriculture, these techniques were well suited to the relative factor endowment of the economy, and institutional imperfections were inevitable given the lack of information networks coupled to high risks, large uncertainties and the segregation of markets.

All the main issues in the 'deindustrialisation' debate are ambiguous and difficult to test. While the proportion of the labour-force employed in manufacturing certainly did not rise over the course of the nineteenth century, it is hard to estimate how far it fell since the employment figures cannot be corrected to allow for underemployment and for those following multiple occupations. One careful estimate for textiles has suggested that between 1800 and 1850, over the subcontinent as a whole, the loss of export markets was balanced by a growth in domestic demand, with only a small fall in employment in manufacturing; but that from 1850 to 1880 between two and six million cotton weaving and spinning jobs were lost, enough to have given full-time employment to between 1 and 2 per cent of the population.[4] Production of small-scale industry provided roughly the same share of national output from the late nineteenth century onwards, although the proportion of the labour-force employed full-time in handicrafts probably continued to decline slightly during the first half of the twentieth century.

The handicraft manufacturing sector in eighteenth- and nineteenth-century India was divided into two parts. In most rural areas local craftsmen supplied a basic range of consumer goods, notably cloth, and provided the goods and services essential for agrarian production, including simple ploughs, implements, pots, and so on. This manufacturing sector was largely decentralised, much of it was domestic, and many of its participants worked only part-time as industrial producers, spending the rest of their time in the fields, or having family members who did so. The techniques used in this sector were often fairly primitive, and certainly required little in the way of capital investment

[3] Quoted in M. D. Morris, 'The Growth of Large-Scale Industry to 1947', in Dharma Kumar with Meghnad Desai (ed.), *Cambridge Economic History of India: Volume 2, c.1757–c.1970* (hereafter *CEHI*, 2) Cambridge, 1984, p. 559.

[4] Michael J. Twomey, 'Employment in Nineteenth Century Indian Textiles', *Explorations in Economic History*, 20, 1, 1983, p. 82.

or product development. As Buchanan noted of the *Kol* (iron smelters) of Bhagalpur in the tribal areas of Bihar,

> The heat of the furnace is so trifling, that it cannot vitrify the stony particles of the ore, which consequently must be reduced to a coarse powder to separate these particles by winnowing. Having no means of performing this operation, except by beating ore with a stick, wherever it is found in solid masses, it is considered useless ... The furnace consists of kneaded clay.[5]

Away from the villages, handicraft industries were largely concentrated in specialised communities that supplied the demands of urban, military and luxury consumption. In the eighteenth century, parts of the cloth industry became particularly specialised to meet the demand of the East India Company for exports, especially of fine cloth from Bengal and Madras, while the proliferation of military states and localised markets boosted local centres manufacturing textiles, metal-wares and other artefacts. The urban trades were usually run by self-administering guilds, which often overlapped with caste organisations. The coming of a new pattern of political and administrative control after 1800, and changes in taste following European dominance in India, as well as direct competition from imports, challenged the position of many centres of manufacture. As one colonial official reported in 1890:

> Bengal is very deficient in arts. They formerly flourished in the shadow of the courts of Native Princes and have disappeared with them. Modern Rajas appear more inclined to patronize foreign productions than the arts of the country, and the native artists have not adapted themselves to the times.[6]

The opening-up of the Indian internal market to manufactured consumer goods from Europe benefited some artisans by giving them access to cheaper semi-manufactured imports in industries such as brassware, but how far this outweighed the cost to others of direct competition from these new sources of supply cannot be measured precisely. The existence of home-based domestic systems in a number of crafts makes it difficult to assess the consequences of any structural shift in employment out of manufactures. Furthermore, it is possible that some of the workers displaced from handicrafts were re-employed in agriculture, and may have been better off there since the price of food in

[5] Quoted in Marika Vicziany, 'The Deindustrialization of India in the Nineteenth Century: A Methodological Critique of Amiya Kumar Bagchi', *Indian Economic and Social History Review*, 16, 2, 1979, pp. 30–1. To Dr Vicziany 'the most significant fact about the *Kol* was that they combined iron smelting with cultivation' (p. 31).

[6] E. W. Collin, 'Report on the Existing Arts and Industries of Bengal' (1890), quoted in D. R. Gadgil, *The Industrial Evolution of India in Recent Times, 1860–1939*, 5th edn, Bombay, 1971, p. 43, fn. 8.

terms of manufactured goods rose after 1850. However, underemployment probably also increased, and any narrowing of the range of employment opportunities brought dangers and a loss of security, given the market imperfections and ecological fragility of the rural economy in many regions. As the 1880 Famine Commission pointed out, by the middle decades of the century,

> at the root of much of the poverty of the people of India and of the risks to which they are exposed in seasons of scarcity lies the unfortunate circumstance that agriculture forms almost the sole occupation of the mass of the population, and that no remedy for present evils can be complete which does not include the introduction of a diversity of occupations, through which the surplus population may be drawn from agricultural pursuits and led to find the means of subsistence in manufactures or some such employment.[7]

The developmental effect of the decline of domestic handicrafts is as unclear as the employment and welfare implications outlined above. Deindustrialisation of the type experienced by nineteenth-century India as a result of competition from machine-made imported manufactures does not necessarily represent a movement into economic backwardness, since there is little evidence that the handicraft industries that were destroyed in this process brought about significant changes in labour productivity or the composition of capital. The crisis of domestic manufacture in the first half of the nineteenth century was more significant as a further symptom of the upheaval to the established socio-economic institutions of eighteenth-century India that resulted from the political changes brought by the imposition of British rule. The decline of the Mughal successor states under the domination of the Company, and the assault by British administrators on the semi-autonomous local rulers to whom these states had often sub-contracted their power, weakened the links between elite consumption and urban guild production of manufactured goods, and undermined the privileged position on which many of the Indian trading firms that dealt in handicraft manufacture relied. In the rural areas the pace of change was slower, but here too the political revolution eventually permeated down to disrupt the tied labour and capital markets around which handicraft industries were organised.

## FROM IMPORTS TO INDUSTRIALISATION: COTTON TEXTILES

All the important historical themes that have arisen from the study of Indian industrial capitalism can be illustrated from the example of the cotton trade and industry. Cotton cloth was probably the biggest manufacturing sector of eighteenth-century India, and certainly the most important export commodity.

[7] Government of India, *Report of the Indian Famine Commission, 1880*, Part II, p. 175.

India was the largest supplier of coarse cloth (calico) to world trade from the seventeenth century, much of it exported to Asia from the ports of Gujarat, and also of fine cloth (muslin), chiefly produced on the Coromandel coast and in Bengal and exported by the East India Company to Europe and the Americas in the eighteenth century. Between 1780 and 1830 the export market for muslin and calico was lost, partly because of British tariffs and the disruptions to trade caused by the Napoleonic Wars, but mainly as a result of the competition from the Lancashire cotton industry, which prospered thanks to its access to cheap raw cotton exports from the American South and the introduction of mechanised spinning technology.

The progress of the Lancashire industry was swift in the first half of the nineteenth century. By 1800 Britain had replaced India as the largest supplier of cotton goods to the rest of the world, and the domestic market for Indian yarn and cloth came under threat soon after. India was probably a net importer of yarn by the 1820s, although such yarn was used only for particular products within limited areas. Cloth imports were more directly competitive with the local product, but their penetration was patchy across regions, with handicraft industries in the more remote areas of central India and Rajasthan not feeling the full brunt of competition until the end of the century. Average per capita consumption of cotton cloth in India was around 11–15 yards in the later nineteenth century; per capita imports rose from 1 yard in 1840 to 7 yards in 1880, and to 8 yards in 1913 (falling to 5 yards in 1930).[8] Perhaps the main effect of the imports of Lancashire piece-goods was to help drive down the price of cloth in India after 1850, and to push the remains of the domestic handloom industry into the low-quality end of the market, where demand fluctuated considerably because it depended on the incomes of the poorest consumers. Thus by the late 1890s, in eastern India, the demand for cotton textiles from traditional sources

> was limited to a few specialities, such as the cloths of Dacca, Farashdanga, and Santipur, which still have their admirers, and to very coarse cloth which is still worn by the poorer classes on account of their strength and durability; but even these are in most cases manufactured from machine-made thread, either European or Indian, which is available in almost every market in these Provinces.[9]

Lancashire's success in India rested on the twin foundations of falling prices and favourable market organisation.[10] The steady decline in the price of raw

[8] Twomey, 'Employment', pp. 47–8.

[9] N. N. Banerjei, *Monograph on the Cotton Fabrics of Bengal* (1898), quoted in J. Krishnamurty, 'Deindustrialisation in Gangetic Bihar', p. 408.

[10] This account is largely based on that in D. A. Farnie, *The English Cotton Industry and the World Market, 1815–1896*, Oxford, 1979, Ch. 3.

cotton was especially important in sustaining the competitiveness of the cheap unfinished goods that sold so well in India, since for these products the raw materials were by far the largest input cost. The decline and eventual abolition of the East India Company's monopoly powers to trade with India and China also boosted the competitiveness of British manufacturers. At the beginning of the nineteenth century the East India Company was the greatest competitor of the Lancashire mills in the domestic and European markets, while Lancashire's exports of muslin and calicos could not compete in the Indian market until the abolition of the Company's monopoly of Indian trade in 1813, which meant that goods could be shipped direct from Liverpool to the Indian ports and marketed more effectively once they had arrived. The subsequent collapse of India's export trade in cotton manufactures hit the Company hard and focused the attention of its supporters on the fate of native weavers, especially during the charter-renewal debate in the early 1830s.[11]

Lancashire dominated Asian markets for machine-made yarn and cloth until the 1870s, when the revival of Indian cotton production, in the form of a mechanised spinning and weaving industry, presented a new threat. Despite the rapid penetration of imported yarn after 1815, the handicraft cotton textile industry did manage to survive inside the Indian market throughout the nineteenth century. Yarn imports to India probably never provided more than half of total domestic consumption, and a considerable hand-spun yarn industry survived the first wave of imports quite well, only to succumb to the more intense competition from Indian mills after 1870. Table 3.3 sets out the main sources of supply for the Indian domestic markets in cloth and yarn from the 1880s to the 1920s. In the early 1880s hand-spun yarn probably still supplied about 50 per cent of domestic production by weight, with 36 per cent already coming from domestic mills and 14 per cent from imports; by 1900, imports had fallen to 7 per cent of consumption by weight, while Indian mill-made yarn supplied 68 per cent of the market and hand-spun yarn 25 per cent. The share of domestic consumption supplied by hand-spun yarn fell further thereafter, to 18 per cent before the First World War, and to less than 10 per cent in the late 1920s. In addition to their domestic sales, the mechanised Indian spinning mills developed a substantial export market in China and Japan, with more than 40 per cent of yarn production by weight being sold overseas in the 1890s and early 1900s. Over the whole period between 1880 and 1914

[11] It was in this context that Lord Bentinck, Governor-General in the 1830s, may have made the remark attributed to him by Karl Marx that 'the bones of the weavers are bleaching the plains of India'.

Table 3.3 *Indian cotton textiles, 1880–1930*

| | Total domestic production | | | | Net imports[a] | | Approx. total |
|---|---|---|---|---|---|---|---|
| Year | Hand-spun yarn (m.lb.) | Machine-spun yarn (m.lb.) | Hand-woven cloth[b] (m.yd.) | Machine-made cloth (m.yd.) | Yarn (m.lb.) | Cloth (m.yd.) | Total consumption of cloth (m.yd.) |
| 1880–4 | 150 | 151 | 1000 | 238 | –1 | 1730 | 3000 |
| 1885–9 | 140 | 261 | 1160 | 344 | –41 | 1912 | 3400 |
| 1890–4 | 130 | 381 | 1200 | 429 | –117 | 1847 | 3500 |
| 1895–9 | 120 | 463 | 1292 | 477 | –160 | 1823 | 3600 |
| 1900–4 | 110 | 532 | 1286 | 545 | –206 | 1872 | 3700 |
| 1905–9 | 100 | 652 | 1470 | 801 | –216 | 2055 | 4300 |
| 1910–14 | 90 | 652 | 1405 | 1140 | –148 | 2405 | 5000 |
| 1915–19 | 80 | 663 | 1178 | 1545 | –122 | 1171 | 3900 |
| 1920–4 | 70 | 679 | 1468 | 1742 | –19 | 1192 | 4400 |
| 1925–9 | 60 | 774 | 1721 | 2176 | +3 | 1643 | 5500 |

[a] Minus sign (–) indicates net exports.
[b] Includes hand-woven cloth made from hand-spun and machine-spun yarn. Approximately 46 per cent of hand-woven cloth was made from machine-spun yarn in the 1880s, and over 80 per cent in the 1920s.
*Source:* Michael J. Twomey, 'Employment in Nineteenth Century Indian Textiles', *Explorations in Economic History*, 20, 1983, table 5.

India exported more than 532,000 tonnes (1,172 million pounds) of machine-spun yarn, 38 per cent of production, and imported only 129,000 tonnes (283 million pounds).[12]

The hold on the Indian market of imports of cloth was much stronger throughout the late nineteenth century, but the market share retained by handicrafts held up quite well. Imported cloth supplied 59 per cent of the market by weight in 1880, and 54 per cent in 1900; the market share of hand-woven cloth fell slightly from 33 per cent to 31 per cent during the same period, while that of Indian machine-made cloth rose from 8 per cent to 15 per cent. Imported piece-goods retained just over half the total market for cotton cloth until 1914, but this then declined to about one-third by the late 1920s, and to under 20 per cent for most of the 1930s. Handlooms continued to produce 30–35 per cent of domestic cotton cloth consumption by weight until the mid 1930s, when the proportion dropped to around one-fifth, but the percentage of total cloth output supplied by handlooms in the 1930s (including

[12] Twomey, 'Employment', table 5.

Table 3.4 *Indian textile production, market shares, 1931–1932 to 1937–1938 (percentages)*

| | Quantity | | | | Value | | | |
|---|---|---|---|---|---|---|---|---|
| Year | Mills | Import | Power loom | Handloom | Mills | Import | Power loom | Handloom |
| 1931–2 | 51.6 | 15.2 | – | 33.2 | 35.1 | 16.5 | – | 48.4 |
| 1932–3 | 47.0 | 19.7 | 0.4 | 32.9 | 31.5 | 17.9 | 1.2 | 49.4 |
| 1933–4 | 51.7 | 14.9 | 0.8 | 32.6 | 35.5 | 13.3 | 3.0 | 48.3 |
| 1934–5 | 53.0 | 16.4 | 1.0 | 29.6 | 36.3 | 15.0 | 3.4 | 45.3 |
| 1935–6 | 50.6 | 16.3 | 1.3 | 31.8 | 36.3 | 13.1 | 3.2 | 47.4 |
| 1936–7 | 54.9 | 13.6 | 1.6 | 29.8 | 39.1 | 11.5 | 4.3 | 45.1 |
| 1937–8 | 56.9 | 10.5 | 1.9 | 30.7 | 36.9 | 9.2 | 5.3 | 48.6 |

*Source:* Tirthankar Roy, 'Size and Structure of Handloom Weaving in the Mid-Thirties', *Indian Economic and Social History Review*, 25, 1, 1988, table 11.

higher-value silk and rayon products) was significantly higher at around 30 per cent by volume and 40 per cent by value. The figures given in table 3.4 revise the usual estimates of the market share of the handloom and power-loom sector by including non-cotton textiles in the totals. The Indian mills were the largest suppliers of piece-goods for the domestic market throughout the inter-war period, and had up to two-thirds of the total market by the late 1930s.[13]

The Indian mechanised cotton textile industry was born in 1856 when the first operational steam-powered cotton mill in Asia went into production in Bombay (an unsuccessful steam-driven yarn mill at Bowreah in Bengal had functioned intermittently from the 1820s to the 1850s), and the boom conditions of the next decade encouraged a number of other flotations. Many of these companies were short-lived, however; there were only ten mills at work in 1865, and no new ones were established during the disturbed trading conditions of the late 1860s. The real take-off came in the 1870s, with 47 mills in operation by 1875 and 79 by 1883; although mills were now also built in other parts of western and southern India closer to the handloom weavers and supplies of raw cotton, Bombay continued to dominate the industry, with more than half the looms and spindles in the country located there until after 1900. The initial expansion of the Bombay industry was based on yarn production,

[13] *Ibid.*; A. K. Bagchi, *Private Investment in India, 1900–1999*, Cambridge, 1972, pp. 226–7; Tirthankar Roy, 'Size and Structure of Handloom Weaving in the Mid-Thirties', *Indian Economic and Social History Review*, 25, 1, 1988.

largely for export to other Asian markets, and succeeded in replacing British yarn exports to China in the 1870s and 1880s. Many of the early promoters of the Bombay textile industry had a background in the export trade in raw cotton and opium from western India to China, and were able to build on these contacts in marketing their new product. When they began to run into difficulties in the China market in the 1890s some Indian mill owners adapted by creating integrated mills that could produce both yarn and cloth, and the number of looms in Bombay doubled between 1900 and 1913. Diversification into cloth production provided an additional outlet for yarn factories, but its sale required the development of contacts in the domestic market that were not open to all. Greaves Cotton & Co., a British expatriate firm which controlled seven spinning mills in Bombay and was the largest private industrial employer in the country before 1914, was unable to adapt and had to sell off its mills once the export trade came to an end during the First World War.[14]

Most of the successful industrialists in western India had close links with commodity trade and handicraft production; the origins of the Indian cotton mills lay in changes in market structures in Bombay City or further up-country in the cotton-growing regions of Gujarat and Maharashtra after 1865. By the 1870s, Indian firms were being pushed out of the handling of the trade in raw cotton to Europe and the Far East by the improvements in transportation, communication and market networks that gave a decisive advantage to large purchasing and shipping firms with access to the Liverpool exchange. This led to the decline of a consignment system of shipping cotton out of India (in which the grower, a network of up-country middlemen, and the shipper all took a share of the risk of exporting), and its replacement by a simple purchase and storage system that depended on vertical integration, good information and the consolidation of procurement and supply. The boom and bust of the cotton economy during the 1860s also increased the desire for stable trading arrangements, while the expansion of demand in Europe (and later in Japan) increased the potential for economies of scale. Both in Bombay and elsewhere in western India cotton dealers sought a new form of business to broaden and integrate the basis of their activity. They found it in yarn manufacture, which enabled them to hedge their bets in the commodity market.

The second major centre of the cotton textile industry was in Ahmedabad. This city had long been a centre of the Gujarati weaving industry, and had prospered with the coming of imported yarn in the 1820s which lowered the price of yarn for fine cloth. Established trading and banking groups financed

[14] Morris, 'Large-Scale Industry', p. 579.

and supplied a putting-out system based on imported machine-made yarn, providing weavers with raw materials and marketing the product. These indigenous bankers were also involved in the financing of agriculture and the trade in raw cotton; when these trading and moneylending activities lost some of their profitability in the late 1870s, as a result of increased competition from European trading firms spreading out from Bombay City, the Ahmedabad *shroffs* diversified into cotton yarn production.[15] The Ahmedabad industry grew particularly fast between 1900 and 1913, by which date it had become a major centre of mill-made cloth production as well as yarn. The close integration of trading, moneylending and modern industry within the city's business community, and sometimes even inside the same family groups, gave the Ahmedabad cotton textile industry its distinctive profile and provided the foundation for its eventual success after 1918 as the supplier of better-quality cloth to the domestic market.

Throughout the nineteenth century the Indian market was important to the British cotton industry, and in the second half of the century just under a quarter of Lancashire's total exports was sent to South Asia. Before 1914 almost all India's cloth imports came from Lancashire, but this dominance began to change in the 1920s; by 1929 Lancashire supplied only 65 per cent of imported cotton cloth by weight, and 45 per cent in 1937. Despite this decline, the Indian market remained Lancashire's best customer until 1939. This meant that the spectre of competition from Indian industry obsessed British cotton manufacturers from the late nineteenth century onwards, leading to successive agitations in Lancashire for the adjustment of Indian tariff policy to suit their interests. Indian tariffs were reduced in 1862 and abolished in 1882 in the name of free trade; when fiscal necessity required a new tariff of 5 per cent in 1894, Lancashire insisted that a countervailing excise be imposed on Indian manufacturers to remove any protective effect. In reality, however, the degree of competition between Indian and British machine-made cloth was limited, with the Bombay mills catering for the cheapest end of the market where Lancashire could not follow them.

By 1913 the cotton textile industry, centred in Bombay and Ahmedabad, was well established as the most important manufacturing industry in India. Its output levels made it one of the largest in Asia, and significant in global terms, but it displayed a number of distinctive features that impeded its further development. Firstly, the industry was largely run by firms of managing

[15] Rajat K. Ray, 'Pedhis and Mills: The Historical Integration of the Formal and Informal Sectors of the Economy in Ahmedabad', *Indian Economic and Social History Review*, 19, 3 and 4, 1982.

agents which secured a commission on output rather than profit. Secondly, the output of cotton goods was subject to considerable fluctuations, especially in Bombay, which suffered a series of supply and demand crises associated with famine, plague and increased competition in the China market between 1893 and 1913. Perhaps as a result, the Bombay mills were slow to diffuse innovations in production technology in the late nineteenth century, and in particular stuck to an inappropriate and less productive type of spinning machinery (mules rather than ring spindles) for much longer than their rivals in Japan. Labour supply was never a problem for the cotton industry, but it was sometimes difficult to maintain labour discipline, and the Bombay mill workers were able to mount significant strikes in the early 1890s, 1901 and 1908 in defence of wage levels. The ties between Bombay and Lancashire in technical information and machinery supply remained close; one-third of all technical staff in middle management in the Bombay mills were Europeans down to the 1920s, although the absolute numbers of such staff ceased to rise significantly after 1913, and almost all of the machinery and plant used in the Indian industry was supplied from Britain.[16]

During the 1920s the Bombay industry continued to run into difficulties, which eroded its competitiveness to a serious extent. Although by now the Indian industry was by far the largest supplier of the home market, it was not able to fix its own prices, even after the considerable revenue-tariff increases of the early 1920s. The Bombay mills did not control the market for Indian raw cotton, the price of which formed by far the largest item in the production costs of yarn and cloth. Over half of the Indian crop was exported to Japan, and there was an extensive and unstable petty-commodity dealing system in yarn, cloth and raw cotton for domestic consumption centred in Bombay that was seen by the mill owners as an encouragement to speculation and cornering. Attempts to control the operation of the market by legislation stirred up considerable discontent in the 1920s, while moves to bypass the smaller dealers by direct agencies in the interior ran into the sand during the slump at the end of the decade. Japanese exports of cloth to India were also an important threat to Bombay immediately after the First World War and, although they were held in check for most of the 1920s, they reappeared after 1930 to supply about one-tenth of the market for mill cloth by 1938, despite import tariffs of up to 50 per cent.

The cotton textile industry of western India was the site of the most complex and comprehensive set of industrial labour institutions in modern South Asia.

16 Y. Kiyokawa, 'Technical Adaptations and Managerial Resources in India: A Study of the Experience of the Cotton Textile Industry from a Comparative Perspective', *The Developing Economies*, 20, 2, 1983.

The Bombay mill owners had little trouble recruiting a labour-force, but labour relations in the city were often difficult. Whereas in Ahmedabad and the other up-country centres most of the labour in the mills was drawn from established local spinning and weaving communities, in Bombay the industrial workforce was hired from a number of fairly distant rural areas in the southern Konkan districts of Bombay Presidency and the eastern United Provinces to the north. In 1911 only 11 per cent of the mill-hands had been born in Bombay; by 1931 this figure had risen to 26 per cent, but still over one-third had been born in the Konkan region and another 12 per cent in the United Provinces. The Bombay mills recruited labour and organised casual employment through the brokerage activities of intermediaries (known as 'jobbers'). This system tended to limit management contact with, and control over, the mill-hands significantly, without making the workers fully subservient to the jobbers either. Aided by their rural connections as well as by the development of neighbourhood links within the industrial areas of the city, the mill workforce was able to assert itself quite effectively against the formal and informal management systems in the inter-war years. Eight general strikes of over one month were called in the Bombay mills between 1919 and 1940, one of which lasted for almost eighteen months in 1928–9; over 48 million working days were lost in the Bombay mills between April 1921 and June 1929, almost half of them in 1928.[17]

Indian cotton mills employed a larger percentage of male labour than was common elsewhere in Asia, drawing heavily on displaced handloom weavers. Such workers were highly unionised and better able to defend their working practices than was the young, largely female, workforce living in corporate accommodation that was common in Japan. For whatever reasons, labour productivity was somewhat lower in Bombay than in other centres of textile manufacture. In Indian mills it was rare for a weaver to control more than two looms, whereas the average was four in Britain and six in Japan; an average of 16.5 hands per shift were used to mind 1,000 looms in Japanese spinning mills in 1925–6, as opposed to 23 in Ahmedabad, 24 in Madura and 24.2 in Bombay. Such figures tell us more about working practices than about relative efficiencies, since the cheapness of labour in India made a different usage of machinery appropriate, but there were some discrepancies in real wages and productivity between India and Japan. A comparison of direct labour costs in the late 1920s found that spinners' wages per pound of yarn produced were 8 per cent lower in Japan than in India, while weavers' wages were 40 per cent lower.[18] In Bombay

[17] Bagchi, *Private Investment*, p. 143.
[18] D. H. Buchanan, *The Development of Capitalistic Enterprises in India*, New York, 1934, p. 381.

at the same time new investment in automatic looms was clearly held back by problems of labour discipline, since workers could not be compelled to increase their productivity enough to make such capital equipment pay.[19]

The Bombay capitalists, who had founded their mills on the basis of their contacts and institutional connections in the China trade, could never operate with the same security in the Indian market. Lacking the institutional mechanisms to substitute for missing markets, they were at a disadvantage faced with problems of labour productivity, capital intensity and raw-material supply, and inevitably ran their business in such a way as to minimise risks, limit long-term commitment and maximise immediate returns. Even so, many mills made losses for most of the 1920s, despite some assistance from local and national government, and the effect of the depression of 1928–33 was devastating, with one-quarter of the Bombay mills closing in 1931.[20]

Perhaps the most dramatic change in the structure of the Indian cotton textile industry in the inter-war period was the way in which the Bombay mills lost ground to new rivals from within India. Prominent here was the rise of new up-country centres, such as Coimbatore and Kanpur, which made use of second-hand machinery and new sources of raw cotton supply to enter the yarn market. In cloth, the Bombay mills lost out to a revival of the handloom sector in centres such as Sholapur in Maharashtra and Madurai and Coimbatore in Madras, where local entrepreneurs hired weavers directly to work in semi-mechanised manufacturing centres, producing cloth adapted to particular market requirements, and supplying it to local, national and some foreign markets. Many of these producers were diversifying into higher-value non-cotton textiles, especially silk and art-silk (rayon) products where power looms were beginning to be used quite widely, but even in purely cotton textiles handlooms had a market share of 24 per cent by volume and 36.5 per cent by value in 1937–8.[21] By the 1930s the Government of Madras was arguing, with some justice, that tariffs on yarn imports did more to protect Bombay against domestic handlooms than against Japanese mill-made cloth.[22]

The decline of Bombay was more than matched by a rise of other centres of cotton textile manufacture. Mill piece-good production rose at an annual

[19] Raj Chandavarkar, 'Industrialization in India before 1947: Conventional Approaches and Alternative Perspectives', *Modern Asian Studies*, 19, 3, 1985, pp. 659–60.

[20] A. D. D. Gordon, *Businessmen and Politics: Rising Nationalism and a Modernising Economy in Bombay, 1918–1939*, New Delhi, 1978, pp. 177, 205.

[21] Roy, 'Size and Structure'.

[22] Christopher John Baker, *An Indian Rural Economy, 1880–1955: The Tamilnad Countryside*, Delhi, 1984, p. 407.

rate of almost 5 per cent between 1913 and 1938; in 1938 mill production supplied almost two-thirds of the domestic market for cotton textiles, with imports restricted to about one-tenth. The most successful industrialists in Ahmedabad, and later in Coimbatore and other inland centres, were those who had close links to the local labour and capital markets, and were able to influence supply and distribution networks directly. The development of the cotton textile industry in India can be characterised as a process of 'relentless improvisation in the use of old machinery, the manipulation of raw materials and the exploitation of cheap labour',[23] coupled to the success of emerging groups of industrial entrepreneurs in devising and adapting market-substituting institutions to secure stability in the supply of labour, capital, raw materials and an adequate level of technology. As the number of improvisers increased, and as the institutional networks necessary for their success became more decentralised, so the apparently 'modern' cotton textile industry in Bombay gave way to more 'traditional' ones elsewhere.

## EXPATRIATE ENTERPRISE IN EASTERN INDIA: JUTE, TEA, COAL

In contrast to Bombay, the industrial history of eastern India was heavily influenced by the emergence of managing agency firms run by British expatriates, which represent the classic colonial business sector in India. By the late nineteenth century these networks were widespread, with the commercial and industrial economy of Calcutta the largest single focus of their activity. Through their agency, British businessmen and investors, resident both in the United Kingdom and South Asia, were involved in almost all sectors of the 'organised' economy of the Indian subcontinent from the 1860s until the 1950s. Even in their heyday in the last quarter of the nineteenth century, however, colonial firms were never entirely dominant. In transportation their role was overshadowed by that of the Government of India, which had become the chief manager of railway activity by the 1900s. In banking, too, the position of European private businessmen was a limited one. Their banks financed foreign trade, in conjunction with the official remittance mechanism, but the links between the credit used for this and the domestic capital markets were often tenuous. Indian indigenous bankers were entirely responsible for the financing of agricultural production and cottage industry before 1914, while the public sector played by far the largest role in making the market for foreign

[23] Chandavarkar, 'Industrialization', p. 650.

exchange. Even in trade and manufacture the effective power of the expatriate sector was sometimes less than it appeared to be. Non-Indians had probably secured a controlling influence over the cash-crop marketing process by 1913, and certainly ran almost all the large-scale factory industries except for cotton textiles; however in internal trade and raw material supply the expatriate firms of Calcutta and elsewhere always relied on partnerships and agency agreements with native Indian firms who could establish much better contacts up-country through links with the trading and moneylending networks of the agricultural economy.

The form and shape of the expatriate business sector in the half century before the First World War was influenced by changing opportunities and constraints in the British and international financial and commercial environments. The problems of exchange instability associated with the depreciation of the silver-standard rupee from the 1870s to the 1890s made British-based companies wary of extensive investment in India because of the difficulties of calculating possible exchange losses on the payment of dividends or repatriation of capital. Even those trading and banking firms that expanded their operations in India sought to minimise their risks, and prided themselves on limiting asset holdings and withdrawing balances from South Asia at the end of the trading season. The expatriate firms often found it hard to attract new capital and personnel from the United Kingdom to their operations in India, and increasingly relied on profits generated within the South Asian economy to finance further development. All these difficulties existed in some form before 1914, and worsened considerably as a result of changes in the capital and employment markets in Britain after the First World War. By the 1920s the expatriate sector found it increasingly difficult to respond to new opportunities, and many of its staple activities never recovered from the slump at the end of the decade. Before them now lay the nemesis of the 1940s when many colonial firms found themselves subjected to asset-stripping raids and take-overs by their Indian competitors.

Contrary to what is often supposed, the expatriate firms of Calcutta and elsewhere were not simply managers of other people's money. The classic picture of a managing agent as essentially an agent, however powerful, running companies with the capital of British investors put up through the London Stock Exchange is, at best, somewhat exaggerated. In jute and coal, especially, most public companies were floated in India where the partners in managing-agency houses were themselves major players in the market; even in the sterling tea companies a controlling interest was often held by a group of investors associated with the managing agency itself. The general public, in India or Britain, were usually given access only to debentures or to preference (non-voting) shares, which were sold off through banks in Calcutta or London. Thus there is a real sense in which it can be said that the expatriate business sector in the first half of the twentieth century, if not before, was a self-sustaining, closed world, essentially engaged in recycling the profits that had been made in the great export-led booms of the agricultural economy in the 1880s and 1900s.

Most expatriate business enterprise before 1914 was based around the procurement, processing and shipping of the main export commodities – raw jute, jute manufactures, wheat, tea, hides and skins, oilseeds, and raw cotton. With the exception of tea, all these products were the output of peasant agriculture, and were not subject to direct management by the colonial firms. The export of most primary produce involved some processing, but the jute textile industry was the only one that required extensive industrial investment. However, from the 1860s onwards, small-scale engineering and metal-processing industries, as well as coal mining, were begun or expanded as an adjunct to these enterprises, and to service the river-steamer and rail transport systems that helped to create them. By 1914 colonial firms managed almost all the capital invested in joint-stock companies and private partnerships in Calcutta, with the concentration of ownership being particularly tight in the three staple industries of tea, jute and coal. Large expatriate managing-agency houses were able to integrate their activities in extractive and plantation industries, and light manufacture for export, to some extent, and also usually had extensive connections in foreign trade. The biggest Calcutta trading firms were among the largest importers of Lancashire piece-goods in Asia, while all the major managing agencies handled the export of agricultural products, notably jute from Bengal. On the whole, the Calcutta agency houses did not develop direct business connections with the agricultural economy of the interior, preferring to sub-contract such dealings to Indian agents, or *banias*, who often contributed independently to the trading mechanisms by making capital advances for trade and stocks.

Jute was in many ways the central commodity in the agricultural and industrial economy of Bengal in the second half of the nineteenth century, and became the focus of the manufacturing activity of most of the large colonial firms in Calcutta between 1880 and 1929. Jute fibre was developed as a cheap substitute for flax and other coarse textile materials in Dundee in the 1830s, and its use was spread thanks to the disruption of flax supplies during the Crimean War (1854–6) and the cotton famine of the American Civil War (1861–5). Bengal was the monopoly supplier of raw jute for this industry, and had traditionally sustained a small handloom-manufacturing sector selling in

Indian and Burmese markets. The first mechanised jute mill in Bengal was established in 1855, and drew heavily on the existing handicraft industry for skills and techniques. Progress was slow at first: in the mid 1870s there were still only five mills in operation, mostly aimed at replacing handloom production in the country and coastal markets.

The world trade boom that began in the 1870s and lasted, with some minor interruptions, until 1913, established jute as the premier packing material for bulk shipments of agricultural produce, especially grain. Exports of raw jute from Calcutta (by weight) almost doubled between 1875 and 1913, while the export of jute cloth and bags rose enormously. By the 1880s the Calcutta mills required overseas markets to sustain their activities – the proportion of jute manufactures consumed locally dropped from around 60 per cent in 1885 to about 10 per cent in the 1900s. The door from Calcutta to the global market was opened by a group of Dundee businessmen, headed by Thomas Duff, who founded the Samnuggar Jute Factory Company on the Hooghly in 1874, and then used their Scottish experience to break into the Australasian and American markets. Between the mid 1880s and the First World War the Calcutta mills captured all of the Australian market and a substantial share of the American market for cheap and coarse bags from Dundee, exploiting their access to cheap labour and raw materials and forcing the Scottish industry eventually to move up-market into finer goods such as carpet-backing. In 1913 there were 64 jute mills in Bengal, with 36,050 looms and an average daily employment of 216,288 workers. The First World War, with its phenomenal demand for sand-bags, saw another great spurt in the Indian industry, which recorded net profit rates of over 50 per cent of paid-up capital in the war years, and even higher rates for some years thereafter. As D. H. Buchanan noted in 1934, 'it is doubtful if any other group of factories in the world paid such handsome profits between 1915 and 1929', although he argued that part of these profits were 'required to balance up the poor returns of the "nineties" and the first decade of the twentieth century'.[24] At the peak in 1928–95 jute mills of Calcutta had an average daily employment of 343,868 workers, only a few thousand less than in the cotton mill industry, and provided over a quarter of net income from the manufacturing sector at current prices.

The apparent success of the Indian jute manufacturers in the early twentieth century masked a long-running problem of over-capacity, which was only held in check for so long because of the business organisation of the industry. Despite the absence of competition, the jute trade was subject to considerable

[24] Buchanan, *Capitalistic Enterprises*, p. 253.

fluctuations, reflecting instabilities in demand brought about by cycles in the international trade in grain and other primary produce. Jute machinery was simple and cheap; the temptation to increase capacity in good times was irresistible. The Indian Jute Mills Association (IJMA), to which all the major expatriate managing-agency houses belonged, was founded in 1884 to implement the first of many output restriction schemes, and from then until 1930 continuous attempts were made to limit output through co-operative schemes of short-time working, except for a brief period in 1920–1. Even in the pre-war boom of 1912–14 the Calcutta mills were working no more than half time, while the installed machinery was already enough to meet a higher demand than had ever been known; by the 1930s there were perhaps three times as many mills and four times as much machinery as could ever possibly be required. So long as demand remained largely unaffected by price, and the IJMA could enforce restriction schemes that reduced supply and pushed up prices, the industry continued to prosper, but such conditions could not last forever even in colonial Calcutta. In 1930 the jute industry of Bengal entered a deep and long depression that did profound damage to the medium-term expectations of many expatriate firms. The world-wide slump in trade affected demand for jute bags in the early 1930s, and new competition from substitute forms of packaging depressed returns greatly. The value of jute manufactures exported more than halved between 1929–30 and 1930–1, and did not begin to rise again until 1935–6; net profits as a percentage of paid-up capital fell from 27.4 per cent in 1929–30, to 7.2 per cent in 1930–1, and remained below 10 per cent for most of the rest of the decade.[25]

The greatest threat to the colonial firms came not from external conditions, but from new challenges to expatriate hegemony inside the industry. During the 1920s a number of new mills were set up outside the IJMA, and some member mills increased capacity without permission. The real cost of plant and machinery fell considerably in the 1930s; using second-hand machinery and public electrical supply it was now possible to establish a viable mill for under one-tenth of the cost at the height of the post-war boom. New Indian entrepreneurs, almost all from Marwari firms who had built up a strong position in the jute trade during the First World War, began to enter the industry during the 1920s, partly to give themselves more flexibility in their trading operations. These Marwari companies, the most prominent of which were run by the Birla family, extended their hold in the 1930s, profiting from the

[25] Dipesh Chakrabarty, *Rethinking Working-Class History: Bengal 1890–1940*, Princeton, 1989, pp. 36–7.

collapse of the established arrangements for jute marketing during the depression to establish new networks for securing raw materials from the countryside. By 1934–5 Indian balers shipped 37 per cent of raw jute exports, and had replaced the expatriates as the main suppliers of American, Russian and European demand. As a result, the IJMA restriction scheme collapsed in 1931, a makeshift replacement had to be abandoned in 1935, and a new agreement that included the Indian mills was only arrived at in 1939 after direct intervention by the elected provincial Government of Bengal.

The industrial history of both tea and coal in eastern India demonstrates further the somewhat peculiar features of expatriate enterprise in colonial South Asia. Tea was found growing wild in India in the 1820s, and first cultivated as a garden crop in 1835; the next thirty years saw a gradually accelerating increase in company flotations and garden plantings in Assam, culminating in a sharp and speculative boom in the early 1860s. These early companies produced little tea (only 4 per cent of British imports in 1866 came from India), and were often based on manic optimism, ignorance and fraud; a severe depression in 1866–9 burst many of the bubbles, and allowed a more soundly based industry to emerge and grow at a steady but not spectacular rate for the rest of the nineteenth century. By the early 1900s, when another depression caused a sharp setback in the industry, Indian tea supplied 59 per cent of the British market, with most of the rest coming from Ceylon (Sri Lanka).[26] British planters and expatriate managing-agency houses continued to dominate the industry within India until the 1950s, but their position in the international market came under further pressure in the inter-war period with the continued expansion of rival industries in Ceylon, the Dutch East Indies (Indonesia) and East Africa. The producers in India co-operated with their rivals to create an international Tea Regulation Scheme in 1933, which gave them a quota of 47 per cent of world exports, and tried to expand the internal market as well.[27] Tea was one of the growing consumer industries in India in the 1930s, with per capita consumption rising by about 50 per cent over the decade.[28]

In coal, the expatriates dominated the industry in the nineteenth century, and continued to control the best mines down to Independence. Dwarkanath Tagore's Bengal Coal Company survived its founder's insolvency, but had passed entirely into British hands by 1858. A second Indian-run concern, the

[26] Gadgil, *Industrial Evolution of India*, p. 117.

[27] V. D. Wikisell, *Coffee, Tea and Cocoa: An Economic and Political Analysis*, Stanford, 1951, pp. 194 ff.

[28] See table 3.5 below.

Searsole Coal Company, was started on the same Raniganj coal field in the 1840s, and these companies remained the only serious producers of coal until the coming of the railways and the jute industry pushed up demand. In the 1890s India's imports of coal started to fall off sharply, and the railways were using local supplies almost entirely by the early 1900s. Internal transport costs, and the high ash and moisture content of the local coal which gave a low calorific value, meant that imports provided some competition away from the eastern seaboard – in Karachi, allowing for quality, Welsh coal sold at about the same price as Bengali.

The coalfields depended on demand from the railways and the industrial sector of eastern India, and the big mines were mostly owned by British capital and run by expatriate managing-agency houses. In addition, there were a large number of small, Indian-owned mines, employing small amounts of labour and working under Indian management. None of the coal mines in India used very sophisticated techniques or equipment. Levels of investment in machines and safety equipment were very low, although the large European-run concerns tended to have higher rates of investment, and better profits, than their Indian rivals, who were confined to second-grade coal that sold only to domestic consumers and for brick manufacture, and who suffered discrimination in the supply of transport and other infrastructure. In the inter-war period all coal-owners came under pressure from overproduction and declining demand. As with jute, the government was reluctant to intervene to enforce a restriction scheme to maintain prices, and excess capacity ran along with cost reductions until the surge of demand during the Second World War led to statutory price fixing in 1944.

Labour supply was never a serious problem for the jute industry. The pioneer mills of the 1860s and 1870s largely used local labour, drawn in part from the old weaving groups, and in part from villagers semi-employed in rice cultivation and other agricultural activities. Some companies found that 'skilled' labour (labour that required no further training to work the mill machinery) was not plentiful, although its supply was determined by the wage policy of individual mills to some extent. During the 1880s labour was recruited from further afield, in ever-widening circles that spread out to cover all of Bengal and the neighbouring regions of Bihar and Orissa, and from the predominantly Muslim weaving communities of the eastern districts of the United Provinces by the 1890s. By 1901 the proportion of Calcutta's population speaking Bengali had fallen to 51 per cent, while that speaking Hindustani had risen to 36 per cent, and in 1921 60 per cent of the skilled workers used in the Calcutta jute mills, and 83 per cent of the unskilled, had been born outside Bengal.[29] Relative wage levels and rates of return in agriculture and industry explained much of this shift in labour recruitment, especially before 1914. The expansion of jute cultivation in Bengal and the relative prosperity of the rural economy during the boom years before the First World War made the returns from agriculture higher than the prevailing factory wage rates and so diminished the supply of local labour to the mills.

The other factory industries of the Calcutta industrial area saw a rather different pattern of labour recruitment from that in the jute industry, with the proportion of Bengali hands holding up rather better for some time. In the iron foundries, railway workshops and machinery engineering works set up in Bengal from the 1880s onwards local labour was quite well represented, especially in the skilled workforce, although the proportion of employees coming from marginal groups in the rural economy was quite high, with large numbers of low caste, tribal and untouchable groups, and also of displaced artisans and Muslims. As in the Bombay cotton mills, the rural connections of the workforce imposed important limitations on the culture, control and discipline of the factory labour of eastern India, with the behaviour of industrial relations in Calcutta dominated by the needs of those economically or socially disadvantaged in the countryside. The Calcutta factory workforce was much less unionised than was that of Bombay, no more than 4 per cent of the workers in Bengal jute mills being members of a trade union in the late 1920s, as opposed to 42.5 per cent in the cotton industry of Bombay City. The total number of days lost in industrial disputes in Bengal between 1921 and 1929 was 16.5 million, of which 8.5 million were in the jute industry (3 million of these in the big strike of 1929).[30]

By contrast, both the mining and plantation sectors required some special techniques of labour recruitment and management. The coal mines of eastern India were mostly situated in rural areas of Bihar and Orissa where local tribal peoples provided a good source of labour recruitment. To attract and hold this workforce many of the mining companies bought zamindari rights to the land in which their mines were situated, and rented this out to their workers to grow crops. The zamindari system was widely considered necessary to secure labour, and it also played a significant part in labour control in some mines, with the company and its agents able to influence and discipline

[29] Ranajit Das Gupta, 'Factory Labour in Eastern India: Sources of Supply 1855–1946: Some Preliminary Findings', *Indian Economic and Social History Review*, 13, 3, 1976; and Wolf Mersch, 'Factory Labour during the Early Years of Industrialization: A Comment', *Indian Economic and Social History Review*, 14, 3, 1977.

[30] Bagchi, *Private Investment*, pp. 140, 142.

behaviour through manipulation of tenancy and debt relations. However, as opportunities for agriculture increased and the price of land rose after the First World War, this method of labour management became too expensive and ineffective, since it worked well only when agricultural opportunities were underdeveloped.

In most coal mines, the recruitment and management of the workforce was facilitated by the extensive use of raising contractors (*ticcadars*) to organise gangs of labour, who in turn hired other intermediaries as foremen to supervise the work and clerks to record output so that, as the *Royal Commission on Labour* reported in 1931, a mine manager 'has ordinarily no responsibility for the selection of the workers, the distribution of their work, the payment of their wages or even the number employed'.[31] Since the raising contractors and their associates had no interest in the long-term future of any particular mine, there was an absence of pressure for investment or basic safety precautions, and in large mines the management had little knowledge or control over the production processes. As many coal owners and mine managers discovered in the 1930s, when the collapse of profits turned the spotlight on costs, the *ticcadari* system led to corruption and higher costs, and companies tried to implement direct labour systems as a result.

In contrast to coal, the plantation-based tea industry of Assam depended almost exclusively on imported migrant labour, which came from the upland regions of central and southern India, as well as from Bihar and the United Provinces. Small plots of land at nominal rents were provided for the workforce as a means of meeting subsistence requirements. Despite this inducement, migration to a distant and, as it turned out, often profoundly unhealthy plantation in Assam was a very serious commitment for migrant workers, especially since penal provisions for breach of labour contracts were in force between 1859 and 1926 and workers had no right to repatriation until 1932. Some degree of ignorance or desperation among its intending workforce was probably important for the plantation sector, as the *Report on Labour in Bengal* (1906) commented on the recruitment activities of 'coolie catchers' in the tribal areas of Bihar:

Deficiency of labour is experienced far more by the tea gardens than by any other industry, and it would certainly not be fair to that industry for government to point out to the intending emigrants how silly they were to go away to Assam, when they could earn more

[31] *Royal Commission on Labour*, p. 119, quoted in C. P. Simmons, 'Recruiting and Organizing an Industrial Labour Force in Colonial India: The Case of the Coal Mining Industry, c. 1880–1939', *Indian Economic and Social History Review*, 13, 4, 1976, p. 476.

pay by working half the month in the neighbouring coalfields, from which they could return home whenever they liked.[32]

Economic conditions in the poorer agricultural regions of central and eastern India were the main determinant of labour supply for the tea companies; as an official report pointed out in 1926: 'Tea, offering as it does a low cash wage no larger than that offered locally to the agricultural labourer, is forced to depend on seasons of famine and scarcity for the replenishment of its labour force ... The best recruiting districts have been found to be those with poor communications.'[33]

## THE EMERGENCE OF INDIAN ENTERPRISE: IRON AND STEEL

Throughout the colonial period government officials tried to keep a distance from the textile, mining and plantation industries. Such enterprises could become established and survive without active government assistance, although the issuing of licences to mines and leases to plantations required some official intervention, and attempts were made to regulate labour and market conditions and to control the extremes of economic fluctuation in the inter-war period. India's heavy industries, on the other hand, required a more intense relationship with the colonial state, since the government sector itself was crucially important in generating both supply and demand for them. This was especially true of the railway network, which itself had only been built up so rapidly because of state construction in the 1870s, and subsidy schemes in the 1860s and 1880s by which the government guaranteed a return on private capital. The guarantee system gave government the right to purchase the lines after twenty-five years, and so by the 1920s the state owned about two-thirds of the total mileage, and had some interest in almost all the railways running in India. Half of the publicly owned lines were now operated directly by the state, and the other half leased out to private companies based in London. The railways were of particular importance to the development of the iron and steel industry in India in the first half of the twentieth century.

The manufacture of iron products by traditional methods was a well-established trade in eighteenth-century India, largely practised by groups of hereditary tribal and non-agricultural craftsmen. The methods used were simple, and the iron produced usually impure; however, further forging could

[32] Quoted in *ibid.*, p. 473.

[33] Government of India, Department of Industries and Labour, *Note on the Labour Position in the Assam Tea Gardens* (1926), quoted in Bagchi, *Private Investment*, p. 138, fn. 55.

produce weapons and implements of high quality. Blacksmiths and other craftsmen remained the main suppliers of the rural market for tools and agricultural implements throughout the colonial period, adapting their techniques to make use of manufactured iron and scrap. From the late eighteenth century onwards European entrepreneurs tried to improve local iron-making by splicing in isolated pieces of British technology, such as the use of smelting coal and blast-furnaces. The most substantial enterprise of this type was the iron works at Porto Novo in Madras which was promoted by J. M. Heath, a former East India Company official, with assistance from the Company and the Government of Madras in 1825. This factory was based largely on traditional methods, using charcoal for smelting and animal power for bellows and forging equipment. Lacking economies of scale and the technological capacity to create a new niche in the market, it could compete neither with imports of British coke-produced blast-furnace iron and steel nor with the product of traditional smelters in the villages, and had ceased to be a serious proposition long before it was finally wound up in the 1870s.

The first recognisably modern iron works in India was established by the Bengal Iron Works Company in 1874. This, too, had a chequered and largely unsuccessful career. The company began to produce iron in 1877, but was already heavily in debt and committed to outmoded technology, and closed down two years later. The Government of Bengal, which had offered some support in an attempt to obtain local supplies of railway equipment, bought up the defunct firm, operated it as a public company for a few years, and then sold the assets to a group of British businessmen who re-established the enterprise as the Bengal Iron and Steel Company in 1889. The new Bengal Company was again undercapitalised, and lacked adequate information on input costs or market potentialities. The government refused to provide subsidised loans to weather a crisis in the mid 1890s, but in 1897 agreed to purchase 10,000 tonnes of iron annually (more than half the output of the works) for ten years, at rates 5 per cent below the import price. This agreement was not renewed in 1907, and an attempt to begin steel production at the plant, for which the government had agreed to subsidise a rate of return of 3 per cent for ten years, failed at the same time. In 1910 the Company got access to new and improved supplies of ore and coal, and by the First World War had established itself as a modest producer of iron products, mostly of pig-iron for export; it made good profits during the war, but lacked any clear potential for expansion thereafter except into cast-iron pipes, and ceased large-scale production of pig-iron in 1925.

In 1918 a second iron works was founded in Bengal by the Indian Iron and Steel Company (IISCO), which was linked to the Bengal Company through the managing-agency firm of Martin Burn & Co. IISCO began production of pig-iron, largely for export to the United States and Japan, in the early 1920s. The Bengal Company virtually ceased production in the early 1930s, and the two companies were formally amalgamated in 1936, and made a move to diversify into steel by setting up the Steel Corporation of Bengal (SCOB) in 1937. The SCOB plant began to produce steel from IISCO iron in 1940, and by 1945 supplied about one-fifth of the market; however, managerial and capital difficulties meant that there was incomplete rationalisation of the plant, which consequently had poor integration and was too small to achieve full returns of scale. A further small iron works was set up by the Mysore State government in 1923 (the Mysore Iron and Steel Works), using a charcoal-fuelled blast furnace. Like other iron companies the Mysore works depended heavily on the export market, but their pig-iron was uncompetitive, and diversification into cast-iron pipes and steel production was unsuccessful. The Tariff Board deliberately protected the Mysore works for strategic reasons, but it only survived thanks to a large subsidy from Mysore State; it supplied no more than 5 per cent of total national consumption of pig-iron and 2 per cent of steel in the late 1930s, and by 1935 had already cost the Mysore government over Rs 40 million.[34]

By far the most important firm in the Indian iron and steel industry was the Tata Iron and Steel Company (TISCO). Active preparations for this company were begun by the Parsi entrepreneur J. N. Tata in 1899 and in 1907, two years after his death, the firm was founded to manufacture iron and steel at a large, modern plant at Jamshedpur, in Bihar. TISCO differed from its predecessors in several ways. The Tata family were prominent in the business community of Bombay, and owned cotton mills and other industrial enterprises in central India. They knew the domestic market for metal products very well since their family firm, Tata Sons and Company, was one of the largest iron and steel importers and dealers in India, and had offices in potential export markets in China and Japan. The new plant was thoroughly researched and planned, and care was taken to site it near suitable supplies of coking coal, iron ore and water. Technology transfer was arranged by hiring skilled foreign personnel, rather than using consultants. Attempts to secure finance in London to set up the plant failed, but when the company was registered in Bombay in August 1907, the starting capital of over Rs 23 million (£1.6 million) was subscribed within three weeks. Many small investors bought preference shares, but the

[34] Bagchi, *Private Investment*, p. 328, fn. 128.

bulk of the equity capital was subscribed by a relatively small group of family members, fellow-businessmen and rulers of Princely States.[35]

The TISCO plant produced 155,000 tonnes of pig-iron and 78,000 tonnes of steel in 1913–14, supported by a standing order from the government for 20,000 tonnes of steel rails for the next 10 years at the import price. The outbreak of war boosted demand, and almost all of TISCO's steel output was bought by the government at fixed prices. The Tata management seem to have followed a deliberate policy of buying official goodwill by active co-operation in the war effort, sacrificing immediate profits for medium-term support. This policy began to pay off in 1917, when the Government of India agreed to assist Tatas with a major expansion scheme by giving priority to the import of plant, machinery and equipment for TISCO. The 'Greater Extensions', as this expansion programme was known, were finally put into operation in 1924 and more than tripled the annual output of steel to over 420,000 tonnes. The costs of this expansion were very high, however, and the company was hit hard in 1921–3 by the slump in world trade, which increased pressure from dumped imports from Continental Europe, and the rapid fall in the value of the rupee against the dollar, which pushed up the cost of machinery from the United States. TISCO only survived this crisis thanks to some firm management and the raising of £2 million worth of debentures in London in 1923.

By the mid 1920s TISCO had weathered the storm, and was supplying about 30 per cent of the Indian market for steel, including more than two-thirds of the government's purchases of steel rails. TISCO was also a major producer of pig-iron for export to supplement demand from its protected steel production. India was widely believed to be the cheapest source of pig-iron in the world in the inter-war years – production costs were Rs 25 per tonne (less than £2) in 1926, according to the Indian Tariff Board.[36] Further expansion to the steel plant took place piecemeal during the rest of the inter-war years, and by the late 1930s TISCO was producing over 700,000 tonnes of finished steel annually in India, more than two-thirds of the country's total consumption.

The Tata Iron and Steel Company has been widely regarded as a unique example of a successful large-scale, innovative industrial enterprise in India, and one that was set up and run under Indian leadership, with Indian capital and largely with Indian labour. TISCO had no difficulty in hiring local tribal labour for many of the jobs in initial construction of the steel works, although

[35] William A. Johnson, *The Steel Industry of India*, Cambridge MA, 1966, p. 245.
[36] Cited in Buchanan, *Capitalistic Enterprises*, p. 291.

the company suffered damaging strikes for more pay to meet the high local cost of living at Jamshedpur in 1920 and 1922, and to oppose lay-offs in 1928. Jamshedpur grew from nothing to a town with a population of 218,000 in 1951. Many of these employees had travelled some distance to find work: nearly a third of the new workers hired by the steel company between 1932 and 1937 had been born more than 350 miles away. For skilled workers the Company offered a system of permanent employment and paid a premium over wage levels in other industrial centres in Bihar, and it issued generous covenants to secure stability in its vital workforce of managerial and supervisory staff. The number of foreign specialist workers hired peaked at 229 in the mid 1920s; thereafter Indian personnel were used increasingly and a successful training programme set under way. This gave a considerable saving in labour costs, since foreign technicians had to be paid substantially higher amounts than they could have commanded in their home industries to entice them to India, and their Indian replacements were typically paid only two-thirds of European salaries.[37]

TISCO was more fortunate than most manufacturing companies in its relations with the colonial state. The Government of India was somewhat sympathetic to the ambitions of an Indian iron and steel industry even before 1914 because of the requirements of the railway system, and the supply crisis of 1916–18 made the importance of local manufacture very clear. TISCO needed state support in the 1920s for several reasons. The Government of India was the major purchaser of steel rails and other railway equipment in its own right. Secondly, the entire domestic market had to be protected against the dumping of surplus European production at prices lower than the costs of production. All over the world governments subsidised steel industries in the inter-war years, maintaining prices at home and disposing of the surplus abroad, and thus TISCO needed substantial amounts of protection, and the guarantee of a privileged position as supplier to the public sector, in order to survive. The Indian industry was protected by bounties and tariffs imposed between 1924 and 1927, and in 1934, although the levels were not high; in return the company expanded its production by an average of 8 per cent each year between 1911 and 1939, output per man rising almost seven-fold between 1919 and 1939.

By the early 1930s British steel producers had come to the conclusion that their sales in India would be better protected by incorporating TISCO into the imperial market-sharing cartel agreements than by political pressure for

[37] Morris, 'Large-Scale Industry', p. 652.

greater direct competition. A series of private deals resulted, underpinned by official agreements in 1932 and 1934 that maintained a measure of tariff preference for United Kingdom exports in return for guaranteed British purchases of Indian pig-iron and semi-finished steel. By 1939 TISCO was involved in negotiations to join the International Steel Cartel.

## INDUSTRIAL POLICY: REVENUE TARIFFS AND 'DISCRIMINATING PROTECTION'

Despite its general support for TISCO during and after the First World War, there were strict limits to the Government of India's will and capacity to sponsor a broader process of industrialisation. By 1916 the colonial administration was aware that strategic necessity and public pressure for a new policy to encourage industrial development were building up, and an Industrial Commission was appointed to consider future options. The *Report of the Indian Industrial Commission 1916–18* urged that government play an active part in the industrial development of the country, to make India more self-sufficient in the wide range of manufactured goods. The Commissioners concluded that 'the circumstances of India have made it necessary for us to devise proposals which will bring the State into far more intimate relations with industrial enterprise' than before; their main recommendations were for government to supply technical education suited to practical industrial requirements and technical and scientific information services, and to encourage private agencies to provide industrial finance.[38] However, this initiative was not sustained, and the political reforms of the 1919 Government of India Act devolved industrial policy to the provincial governments, who were given neither the resources nor the incentive to pursue such an ambitious programme. The two central cadres of technical services that survived this change in policy were killed off by local jealousies and financial stringency in 1922.

As a result of these failures government industrial policy became centred on the tariff issue in the 1920s, and here it was overlaid by strong currents of political debate and fiscal necessity. Revenue tariffs became an essential source of income for the Government of India during and after the First World War as expenditure increased and the staple land tax was handed over to provincial administrations under the new constitutional reforms. In 1917 the general tariff rate, including cotton goods, was raised to 7.5 per cent, in return for an

[38] *Report of the Indian Industrial Commission 1916–18*, Volume 1, reprinted edn, Calcutta, 1934, p. 243.

agreement by the Indian authorities to buy up £100 million worth of British War Debt. The general rate of revenue tariffs was further increased to 11 per cent in 1921 and to 15 per cent in 1922, with rates of up to 25 per cent on imports of sugar and luxury goods such as motor vehicles and confectionery. The difficult political and economic conditions of the late 1920s and early 1930s saw further substantial increases in revenue tariffs. The general rate was raised in 1930 and twice in 1931, reaching 31.25 per cent in October 1931, although with a reduction for machinery and railway equipment, while luxuries now paid up to 50 per cent. A special rate of 20 per cent (15 per cent for British goods) was fixed for low-quality cotton textile imports in 1930, this rate being increased to 50 per cent for non-British goods in 1932 and 75 per cent in 1933.[39]

These levels of revenue tariffs protected the domestic market for Indian manufacturers to some extent, but local opinion wanted substantially more than this. As a response, the Government of India initiated a policy of 'discriminating protection' in the early 1920s, based on the proposals of the Indian Fiscal Commission (1922) that local industries be given protection for a fixed period if they could show that they would be able to compete with imports without further assistance thereafter. The policy that was implemented was much weaker than many of its advocates had intended, because officials retained control over it for themselves. While the Fiscal Commission had recommended a permanent and independent Indian Tariff Board, the Government of India decided that the Board should be ad hoc and semi-official, to act as a buffer between itself, the pressure of business interests inside India, and the demands of the British Government and opinion in London. As it was eventually set up, the Tariff Board was an advisory body making proposals that were not binding on government, and it did not even have the power to initiate its own enquiries – a recommendation from the Commerce Department in New Delhi was needed before it could take evidence from any industry.

Between 1923 and 1939 Tariff Boards conducted fifty-one enquiries and granted protection to eleven industries (iron and steel, cotton textiles, sugar, paper, matches, salt, heavy chemicals, plywood and tea-chests, sericulture, magnesium chloride, and gold thread) and, under somewhat different criteria, to rice and wheat producers. The way in which the Boards were set up, and the briefs that they were given, inhibited the formulation of a long-term, integrated protective policy; however the measures that were enacted on their recommendation did give real aid to all the industries concerned except, perhaps, heavy chemicals and plywood. By the early 1930s some protective tariffs had reached

39 Dharma Kumar, 'The Fiscal System', pp. 921–4.

remarkable levels, imported sugar being charged at 190 per cent in 1931 – it is hardly surprising that imports of sugar machinery increased in real terms by 3,000 per cent between 1928 and 1933.[40] Other industries which were set up in this period as a direct result of changes in revenue and protective duties include matches, rubber manufactures, hydrogenated vegetable oils and paper.

Government purchasing policies also stimulated a measure of import-substitution in the inter-war years. Before 1914 tenders for contracts to supply Indian public-sector enterprises had to be submitted to the India Office in London. Quotations were scrutinised in sterling prices, and the 'best' equipment was usually selected irrespective of price. These conditions tended to favour British manufacturers of steel products, railway equipment and machinery for government workshops and mines. In the 1920s control of this expenditure was handed over progressively from London to New Delhi, and, in an atmosphere of financial stringency, the rules were changed to encourage the acceptance of goods of 'adequate' quality, quoted in rupees, with lowest cost the main criterion for selection. By 1930 all railway stores were purchased through the Indian Stores Department, which now also had discretionary powers to favour goods manufactured in India, and those manufactured from Indian raw materials. These arrangements favoured local manufacturers where they existed, and encouraged some British engineering firms to set up subsidiary manufacturing plants in South Asia. The total amount of stores purchased in India was not very great, rising from Rs 16.4 million in 1922–3 to Rs 47.6 million in 1934–5, but such purchases were vitally important for certain sectors of industry, especially for suppliers of railway equipment. In 1939 over a quarter of the value of all railway stores, and almost half the value of such stores for state railways, were bought from firms operating in India.[41]

These changes in central government policy in the 1920s and 1930s created some new opportunities for Indian manufacturers of consumer and intermediate goods. However, the emasculated remains of the new industrial policy, coupled to revenue tariffs, amended stores purchase rules, and discriminating protection did not represent, together or separately, a major new economic strategy. State factories and industrial intelligence had a minimal impact; educational reform was neglected; stores purchase rules affected a very limited area of enterprise; revenue tariffs were imposed to meet fiscal, not developmental, criteria; protective tariffs were subject to stringent tests and stiff conditions. In

[40] Government of India, *The Gazetteer of India, Volume III: Economic Structure and Activities*, Delhi, 1975, pp. 468–9.

[41] B. R. Tomlinson, *The Political Economy of the Raj, 1914–1947*, London, 1979, p. 63.

the important area of monetary policy the government lost control of the rupee exchange and the money supply in 1919–20, and could only re-establish its influence on the money market and financial systems by ruthlessly following its own deflationary policies in the post-war slump. During the depression of the 1930s the Government of India found that any attempt to mitigate local difficulties by an independent exchange and monetary policy was impeded by its weak reserve position, or blocked by the British Treasury in London.

Perhaps equally damaging for all branches of heavy industry were the Government of India's continued fiscal difficulties throughout the inter-war period, which limited public expenditure and public capital formation rigorously. While the overall rate of capital formation in colonial India was very low, perhaps 1 to 1.5 per cent of national income over the whole period 1860–1947, the state's share in this was quite high in the first half of the twentieth century. Central, provincial and local government together accounted for about a quarter of all fixed capital formation between 1914 and 1946, but with considerable annual fluctuations in the total.[42] In railways, by far the largest single item, gross public investment (in current prices) was high immediately after the First World War but fell steadily from Rs 381 in 1920–1 (roughly twice its level just before the war) to Rs 214 million in 1924–5, then rose again to an annual average of Rs 401 million in 1927–8 to 1929–30, only to fall sharply thereafter to Rs 246 million in 1930–1, Rs 150 million in 1931–2, and an annual average of Rs 83 million for the rest of the 1930s.[43] Overall, the capital expenditure of central government was somewhat higher in the 1920s than it had been before 1913, but shrank to almost nothing in the early 1930s and remained at a low level for the rest of the decade. By far the largest item of current expenditure was defence – over 40 per cent of central government's expenditure in peacetime, between 2 and 3 per cent of national income – but this had a minimal effect on the demand for industrial goods since so little of the equipment used by the armed forces in India was manufactured locally.

## INDUSTRIAL DIVERSIFICATION IN THE INTER-WAR YEARS

The constraints on public expenditure limited the opportunities for firms in the nascent engineering industry in colonial India, which had been

[42] Raymond W. Goldsmith, *The Financial Development of India, 1860–1977*, New Haven, 1983, p. 79.

[43] M. J. K. Thavaraj, 'Capital Formation in the Public Sector in India: A Historical Study, 1898–1938', in V. K. R. V. Rao *et al.* (eds.), *Papers on National Income and Allied Topics*, Volume 1, Bombay, 1960, table 7.

stimulated by the First World War and had hoped for considerable expansion after 1918. The success of TISCO during the war led a number of established companies, Tatas and a number of British expatriate firms among them, to consider new ventures in civil and mechanical engineering in the early 1920s. Many of these companies were initially financed by the high profits made during the war, but most of them were abandoned when the slump of the early 1920s triggered a dramatic retrenchment programme in the public sector. Similarly, a number of large British firms abandoned proposals to form a consortium to bid for Indian transport and infrastructure building contracts at the same time, as a result of the cut-backs in government spending plans. By the 1930s some local engineering firms (notably Jessop, Burn, and Balmer Lawrie) revived their plans for construction of steel structures, cranes and railway wagons in India, and this sector was strengthened by the establishment of a number of subsidiary manufacturing companies by British-based multinational firms (such as Braithwaites and GKN) responding to the protection available to Indian products. Diversification in these products was limited, however, and attempts to set up a machine-tool industry moved very slowly until the Second World War. Perhaps the key indicator of the problems of heavy industry in India in the inter-war period is that the country's consumption of steel remained roughly static during the 1920s and 1930s, and only in three years of heavy public investment in railways (1927–8 to 1929–30) did it rise above the pre-war peak of 1.3 million long tonnes in 1913–14.

Despite these constraints on industrial expansion and diversification, some developments in the Indian economy in the 1930s gave a further boost to industrialisation in consumer goods. As table 3.5 suggests, falling wholesale prices for agriculture resulted in cheap food for the cities, and demand for some basic consumption goods continued to expand throughout the 1930s. Tariff policy encouraged some local manufacture as import-substitution, in sugar, paper and matches for example, while the development of new consumer markets in urban areas, and the expansion of urban construction and public utilities, stimulated fresh demand for new products. Falling food prices and the growth of professional employment also created a new urban middle-class market for a wide range of brand-named, packaged consumer goods such as cigarettes, cosmetics, toiletries, electric batteries and processed foodstuffs, while the construction boom stimulated sales of cement, paint and asbestos cement products. In addition, markets for heavy chemicals, industrial gases, rubber products and steel manufactures such as screws were also expanding, and could be supplied by local manufacture more effectively than by imports.

Table 3.5 *Indices of domestic economic activity, 1920–1921 to 1938–1939 (1928–1929 = 100)*

| | 1920–1 | 1923–4 | 1926–7 | 1929–30 | 1932–3 | 1935–6 | 1938–9 |
|---|---|---|---|---|---|---|---|
| Wholesale prices[a] | | | | | | | |
| Calcutta | 123[b] | 118 | 102 | 97 | 63 | 63 | 65 |
| Bombay | 136[b] | 124 | 102 | 99 | 75 | 68 | 69 |
| Retail price of food | 128[b] | 88 | 103 | 106 | 54 | 54 | 55 |
| Railway traffic[c] | 80 | 88 | 99 | 98 | 75 | 93 | 101 |
| Per capita consumption | | | | | | | |
| Cotton[d] | 92 | 88 | 111 | 117 | 121 | 119 | 121 |
| Kerosene | 78 | 98 | 97 | 115 | 94 | 86 | 91 |
| Sugar | n.a. | 56 | 79 | 101 | 76 | 78 | 78 |
| Tea | 82 | 82 | 82 | 112 | 100 | 129 | 159 |

[a] In calendar years (viz. 1920–1 is 1920); 1928 = 100.
[b] 1921.
[c] Quantity of goods carried per mile of track open.
[d] Piece-goods only.
*Note:* 1928–9 has been selected as base as the last pre-depression year.
*Source:* B. R. Tomlinson, *The Political Economy of the Raj, 1914–1947*, London, 1979, table 2.4.

These new industries were built on resources from the rural economy that were now being put to work elsewhere. Before 1929 the profits of agriculture had tended to remain in the countryside. Some expansion of small-scale industry for processing agricultural produce had taken place but, in general, the agrarian surplus was ploughed back into land-owning and rural moneylending. The decline in agricultural profits and the disruption of established capital markets and marketing networks during the depression provided an incentive to diversify investment into new activities. In particular, the liquidity crisis of 1929–30 pushed many rural bankers out of business and forced some peasant families to draw down their savings; the rising rupee price of gold after 1931 gave others a further incentive to liquidate their bullion reserves. From the mid-1930s onwards in Madras, for example, landlords and others began to invest increasingly in industry, especially in sugar and cotton; company flotations in the province boomed and a stock exchange was formed. In the United Provinces and Bihar a number of the rural elite joined forces with urban interests to establish sugar mills and other industries. In the country as a whole between 1931 and 1937 the paid-up capital of joint-stock companies increased by over 10 per cent, while the number of registered companies at work rose by more than one-third. The increase in Indian-owned joint-stock banks (many of them started by bankers moving out of rural trade and money-lending) was particularly impressive: between 1930 and 1939 the number of joint-stock banks operating in India increased from 54 to 154 (with more than 1,000 new branches opening), while the amount of private cash deposited in them increased by 60 per cent.[44] Table 3.6 makes clear the considerable increase in bank deposits in India during the 1930s, as well as the expansion of life insurance business and the Post Office small savings schemes.

The major industrial depression of the early 1930s that caused such severe damage in Europe and North America bypassed India to a great extent. In South Asia the recession of the early 1920s had a sharper impact on manufacturing output than that of the early 1930s. While Indian manufacturing output in the depression years was somewhat below the trend of the previous three decades, it never dipped beneath the average level of 1925–30, and had risen substantially above this by the middle of the 1930s (see table 3.7). By 1938–9 the output of manufacturing industry as a whole was more than 50 per cent above its level in 1929–30. There was a substantial fall in jute output in the five years from 1929–30 to 1933–4, and some decline in coal and wool as well, although this was all made up again in the next five years. Against this, sugar grew strongly in the early 1930s, while cotton, paper, cement, iron and steel, and matches all advanced somewhat, and were consolidated in the second half of the decade.[45] Private-sector machinery imports (a proxy for industrial investment) held up well during the depression.[46] Their real value was lower in the 1930s than it had been in the 1920s, but this was the result of the problems in jute and cotton. The availability of cheap, second-hand machinery being sold off by the depressed industrial sectors of Europe and North America may also distort these figures – the start-up costs for a number of industries were certainly lower in the 1930s than they had been during the boom at the end of the First World War.

Despite some advances in new industries, a number of familiar problems had surfaced by the late 1930s. The liquidation of rural banking, and the search for an alternative medium for savings following the gold exodus after 1931, were unique events, not part of a continuous process. Thus the release of resources from the rural economy was not constant throughout the decade; the available

[44] Reserve Bank of India, *Banking and Monetary Statistics of India*, Bombay, 1954, p. 282.

[45] Colin Simmons, 'The Great Depression and Indian Industry: Changing Interpretations and Changing Perceptions', *Modern Asian Studies*, 21, 3, 1987, p. 612.

[46] Bagchi, *Private Investment*, table 3.2.

Table 3.6 *Partial estimate of allocation of internal savings in India, 1930–1939 (in Rs millions)*

| | 1930 | 1933 | 1936 | 1939 | % rise 1930–9 |
|---|---|---|---|---|---|
| Total private cash deposited with banks: | | | | | |
| Imperial Bank[a] | 766.0 | 741.3 | 788.0 | 878.4 | 14.7 |
| Joint-stock banks | 632.5 | 716.7 | 981.4 | 1007.3 | 59.3 |
| Exchange banks | 681.1 | 707.8 | 752.3 | 740.8 | 8.8 |
| Co-operative banks | 125.7 | 171.2 | 205.7 | 229.4 | 82.5 |
| Paid-up capital of joint-stock companies | 2863.4 | 2864.7 | 3026.3 | 2903.9 | 1.4 |
| Post Office savings bank balances and cash certificates | 721.3 | 990.4 | 1332.3 | 1414.3 | 96.1 |
| Premium income of life insurance companies | 79.6 | 96.3 | 130.2 | 142.6 | 79.1 |
| Government of India funded rupee debt | 4051.1 | 4468.9 | 4261.8 | 4385.3 | 8.2 |
| Net private imports (+) or exports (–) of treasure | +244.3 | –572.3 | –145.0 | –302.8 | – |

[a] Private deposits only.
*Source:* B. R. Tomlinson, *The Political Economy of the Raj, 1914–1942*, London, 1979, table 2.5.

surplus had probably been transferred out of agriculture by the mid 1930s. The very large profits that were made initially in a narrow range of industrial products – notably sugar and cement – encouraged over-investment and the creation of excess capacity. By the end of the 1930s both these industries had evolved output-restriction schemes that ran plant at less than full capacity to maintain prices and share out the market. In addition, the availability of some new supply and demand within the domestic economy did not remove all the barriers to deepening the industrial sector. Output and employment remained heavily concentrated in finished consumer goods, with four-fifths of the industrial workforce in large-scale private industry still employed in that sector in 1937.[47]

[47] D. R. Gadgil *et al.*, 'Notes on the Rise of the Business Communities in India', (mimeo.), Institute of Pacific Relations, New York, 1951, table 5.

Table 3.7 *Index numbers of output by industry, 1930–1931 to 1939–1940 (1925–1926 to 1929–1930 = 100)*

| Year | Minerals | Cotton mills | Jute mills | Sugar | Paper | Cement | Woollen mills | Iron and steel | Matches | Total manufactures |
|---|---|---|---|---|---|---|---|---|---|---|
| 1925–30 | 100.0 | 100.0 | 100.0 | 100.0 | 100.0 | 100.0 | 100.0 | 100.0 | 100.0 | 100 |
| 1930–1 | 100.8 | 100.0 | 77.5 | 113.4 | 138.8 | 122.6 | 72.1 | 120.1 | 128.4 | 101 |
| 1931–2 | 92.6 | 121.2 | 72.6 | 151.2 | 138.8 | 124.5 | 87.2 | 124.3 | 118.3 | 106 |
| 1932–3 | 85.0 | 133.6 | 76.7 | 205.8 | 138.8 | 126.4 | 80.5 | 117.3 | 128.4 | 115 |
| 1933–4 | 86.2 | 117.8 | 76.7 | 231.0 | 145.8 | 137.9 | 78.8 | 145.6 | 123.4 | 109 |
| 1934–5 | 97.3 | 124.9 | 78.3 | 247.8 | 115.0 | 166.6 | 82.2 | 166.1 | 111.9 | 123 |
| 1935–6 | 106.0 | 139.4 | 75.9 | 268.9 | 162.0 | 191.5 | 88.9 | 180.1 | 164.9 | 133 |
| 1936–7 | 107.8 | 134.7 | 100.1 | 394.9 | 162.0 | 212.6 | 97.3 | 185.0 | 163.5 | 143 |
| 1937–8 | 123.5 | 141.7 | 109.0 | 344.5 | 194.4 | 250.9 | 109.0 | 183.5 | 147.0 | 155 |
| 1938–9 | 119.4 | 166.4 | 109.8 | 243.6 | 203.7 | 323.7 | 95.6 | 194.7 | 143.4 | 175 |
| 1939–40 | 123.5 | 157.6 | 96.9 | 453.7 | 266.2 | 371.6 | 95.6 | 211.5 | 149.2 | 181 |

*Source:* Colin Simmons, 'The Great Depression and Indian Industry', *Modern Asian Studies*, 21, 3, 1987, table 3(b).

Perhaps the most significant aspect of the industrial diversification in South Asia in the 1930s and 1940s was the opportunities it gave for particular groups of entrepreneurs to consolidate their position in the manufacturing sector. Several of the new industries that were founded – including electrical engineering, machinery and metal manufactures, food, tobacco and household goods, industrial chemicals and pharmaceuticals, rubber goods, and paints and varnish – were dominated by foreign capital in the form of subsidiary manufacturing plant of multinational companies based in Britain, Europe and North America. By 1947 about half of British private capital in manufacturing in India took the form of direct investment in such companies. These firms often set up in India to take advantage of a new market opportunity or to exploit standardised and integrated production and marketing techniques. Thus Brooke Bond (India) Ltd was the first company to supply the domestic market with branded and widely distributed packet tea even before it produced any tea in India for itself, while ICI's success was due, in part, to the establishment of the largest sales network of any firm in the subcontinent, with 1,500 depots, 15,000 distributors and a staff of 2,500 by the mid 1930s. By 1950 there were 41 British subsidiary companies at work in India with over Rs 500,000 worth of share capital; of these 3 had been set up before 1920, 6 in the 1920s, 21 in the 1930s, 2 between 1939 and 1947, and 9 between

1947 and 1950. More than half the British subsidiary manufacturing companies that were prominent in India in the early 1970s had already made sizeable investments before Independence.[48]

The largest advances in industrial development in the last thirty years of British rule were led by a diffuse group of Indian entrepreneurs from many different communities, of which the Parsis (Tatas), Marwaris (Birla, Dalmia, Sarupchand Hukumchand), Gujarati Banias (Walchand Hirachand, Ambalal Sarabhai, Kasturbhai Lalbhai) and Punjabi Hindu Banias (Lala Shri Ram) were the most prominent, but including also Gujarati Patels and Maratha Brahmins in western India, and Tamil Brahmins and Nattukottai Chettys in the south. Many of these new business groups had their roots in the trading sector, and were focused at first around jute or cotton textiles, exploiting the opportunities presented by the decline of the Calcutta colonial firms and the Bombay cotton mills, and responding to the new patterns of demand and supply brought about by the depression and its aftermath. However, they expanded their activities considerably during the 1930s, moving into import substitution in products such as sugar, cement and paper, and some used the high initial profits in these industries to finance diversification into entirely new areas such as shipping (Hirachand), textile machinery (Birlas), domestic airlines (Tatas) and sewing machines (Shri Ram). Indian firms provided more than 60 per cent of the total employment in large-scale industry by 1937, and over 80 per cent by 1944. Such firms also made the bulk of new private investment in industry in the inter-war period, especially in the 1930s.[49]

During the Second World War supply shortages and a ruthless insistence by government on strategic priorities limited the expansion of local industry, but the Indian industrialists who had established themselves in the colonial economy were well placed to expand their operations after 1945. Indian capitalism was on the offensive in the late 1940s, and bought out many of the expatriate firms of Calcutta, which were facing new uncertainties caused by the radical changes in political and economic conditions in both India and Britain, at bargain prices. All Indian industrialists, and most foreign businessmen as well, were now happy to work in a system in which official agencies shared out markets and capacity through a rigorous licensing system. The only foreign

[48] B. R. Tomlinson, 'Continuities and Discontinuities in Indo-British Economic Relations: British Multinational Corporations in India, 1920–1970', in Wolfgang J. Mommsen and Jürgen Osterhammel (eds.), *Imperialism and After: Continuities and Discontinuities*, German Historical Institute, London, 1986, p. 156.

[49] Gadgil *et al.*, 'Business Communities in India', tables 5 and 8; Rajat K. Ray, *Industrialization in India: Growth and Conflict in the Private Corporate Sector, 1914–47*, Delhi, 1979, pp. 276 ff.

firms which tried to resist cartelisation were those multinationals that thought themselves to have a clear competitive advantage based on technical or organisational superiority. As D. R. Gadgil, frustrated by his failure as a member of the Commodity Prices Board to implement control schemes on industrial output that might encourage efficiency and meet the urgent needs of consumers, gloomily concluded in 1949, 'private enterprise in India is ... far from being free enterprise'.[50] Indian entrepreneurs were not necessarily anxious to increase competition in the post-colonial economy.

## COLONIAL AND NATIONAL FIRMS, AND BUSINESS NETWORKS

Analysing the competition between rival entrepreneurs during the inter-war period raises the role of political factors in Indian business history in a direct way. Colonial firms managed by British expatriates controlled most of the organised business sector, in eastern India at any rate, before the First World War, and retained a considerable presence until Independence; thereafter such firms experienced a rapid decline, and had almost vanished within twenty years. It has often been argued that the dominance of such firms before 1947 was the result of political alliances with the colonial state, and their subsequent decline the consequence of that state's replacement by the nationalist regime, to which rival businessmen had long-standing ties, but such accounts underplay the effect of more subtle economic changes that were undermining the expatriates' business position in the inter-war period. In reality the success of expatriate enterprise depended as much on a particular set of economic circumstances as on the political condition of colonial India. Their position inside the Indian market rested on their ability to draw resources of men, money and markets from outside South Asia, and hence on a specific form of imperial and international economy. The rise of new industries in Britain, changes in the British employment and capital markets, and the difficulties faced by Indian raw material exports in the 1930s, all combined to undermine the foundations of expatriate firms' past success. Their activities were heavily biased towards exports, and the triple foundation of colonial Calcutta – jute, coal and tea – was seriously undermined during the depression. By the 1930s problems of capital, liquidity and profitability were major constraints, and the

[50] D. R. Gadgil, 'The Economic Prospect for India', *Pacific Affairs*, 22, 2, 1949, reprinted in his *Economic Policy and Development*, Gokhale Institute of Economics and Politics, Poona, Publication no. 30, Poona, 1955, p. 114.

expatriates became locked tightly into a set of staple industrial and trading activities that were in serious decline. The very profitability of jute, the key industry for the British-owned managing-agency houses of Calcutta, depended on control over production and prices through cartels and restriction schemes; such control was substantially weakened in the inter-war period by the rise of new industrial and trading groups from within the local economy. In the 1930s, Indian entrepreneurs were able to exclude the expatriates entirely from operating or financing the marketing system for agricultural produce in many parts of India, and to attack their position in the export trade as well.

A second threat to the position of colonial firms in the domestic market came from the activities of British-based multinational companies that set up manufacturing subsidiaries and sales and distribution networks in India in the 1920s and 1930s. As we have seen, these firms invested in products for a new consumer market, such as processed foods and pharmaceutical goods, as well as in intermediate products such as chemicals, industrial gases and some engineering products, in which the expatriate firms had little expertise. Some of their investments were defensive, to protect an existing market threatened by tariffs or by changes in official purchasing policies, but most represented a more positive response to the opportunities of a growing market or improved business techniques. Few of these newcomers to India used the services of British expatriate companies as managers or agents after the initial phase of market penetration was over. Instead, they constructed independent networks to run their Indian operations, often integrating sales and marketing, and providing their own management of production and distribution.

In the difficult and disturbed conditions that were endemic in colonial India it is hardly surprising that business behaviour was dominated by considerations of risk, uncertainty and imperfect knowledge. The fact that British firms tended to have good institutional links to overseas markets, but poor connections to up-country sources of supply and demand, while Indian firms generally knew more about the internal economy than they did about foreign trade, accounts for the decentralised nature of so much of the marketing of imported and exportable goods in the late nineteenth century. Neither the British nor their Indian banias could construct effective internalised networks to replace the imperfections of the existing markets. For many colonial firms there was the further complication that British capitalists were wary of sinking money in private investments in India, especially while the rupee was linked to a declining silver standard from 1873 to the mid 1890s. Once the possible losses on exchange had been minimised by the implementation of a de facto gold-exchange standard after 1900, the forces of foreign and indigenous capitalism were too weak to break the hold of small-scale producers and petty traders on the supply of agricultural goods. In the industrial sector, too, modern enterprises such as the mechanised textile mills of Bombay and Calcutta – even those run by large firms of managing agents – were unable to create effective networks of vertical and horizontal integration to enable them to overcome the risks and uncertainties of dealing with the 'unorganised' sector of the local economy from which most of their supply and demand ultimately came.

Before 1914 the colonial firms were strong enough to prevent local entrepreneurs creating autonomous marketing networks from the bottom up, but were too weak to impose their own from the top down. The result was an uneasy compromise characterised by complex patterns of agency agreements between suppliers and producers at all levels of the supra-local economy. In the inter-war years this position was modified by the creation of new Indian business empires by dynamic and aggressive entrepreneurs whose activities were based on a closer integration between the rural and urban sectors. The switchback of inflation and deflation between 1917 and 1923, and the prolonged price depression of the years from 1928 to 1934, shook out resources from agriculture and local trading, and also hastened the retreat of the expatriate managing-agency houses from up-country markets. A new generation of Indian businessmen captured these resources, replaced the established trading networks dominated by colonial firms, and then followed the expatriates into the foreign trade and manufacturing sectors as well. Thus 'modern' financial and business institutions were created between 1919 and 1939, especially from 1929 to 1936 – a time when the absolute wealth of the economy was probably not increasing. After 1939 these Indian firms went from strength to strength in the private sector, the only sustained business challenge to them coming from the subsidiaries of multinational corporations, which brought similar organisational advantages to bear on their Indian operations.

Formal cartels, informal agreements and the search for political influence were all important parts of business activity in India in the first half of the twentieth century. The desire to control supply and manipulate demand, rather than an obsession with expansion for its own sake, was probably the dominant motive in business activity. Those best able to achieve this profited accordingly. Connections to public institutions were important here, but the vital factor was relations with the vast and potentially very powerful 'unorganised' business sector, especially the up-country merchants, bankers and credit suppliers who controlled so much domestic economic activity, and provided distribution, sales and credit services for the factory sector. The emergence of business groups from this shadowy underworld into the full glare of 'modern' business activity was an important influence on the history of trade and manufacture in India, and probably dictated the fate of the pioneer large-scale industrialists in both Calcutta and Bombay.

In both jute and cotton the links between rising industrial and commercial groups and the decentralised rural economy of petty producers and consumers progressively undermined the ability of established industrialists to influence their environment after 1900. The history of sugar, and the other new import-substituting industries of the 1930s, shows again that the successful firms were those that could control raw material supply and price, which required close contact with the institutional mechanisms and market relations of local moneylenders and landlords in the rural economy. These new links were not always forged very strongly, however, and after Independence Indian entrepreneurs in the 'organised' sector often found difficulty in forcing petty traders, producers and consumers to conform to their vision of economic progress.

## THE POLITICAL ECONOMY OF THE RAJ

By the 1930s all the constituent parts of the private business sector sought some form of state intervention in the economy. Throughout the inter-war period government policy was seen as important in ensuring domestic protection; in creating infrastructure through public investment; and in regulating the internal capital, commodity and labour markets to provide a basis for business expansion. Specific help was also needed to regulate production in industries faced by overcapacity (especially jute, and also cement), and to negotiate international agreements for commodities such as cotton textiles and iron and steel for which the world market was particularly unstable. Many of the Indian businessmen who moved into the industrial sector in the inter-war period had close links to the nationalist movement and, through the Federation of Indian Chambers of Commerce and Industry (FICCI), acted in harness with the leaders of the Indian National Congress to press for alternative fiscal, monetary, exchange, remittance and trade policies. Even within FICCI, however, there was considerable variation in material interests and political commitment, and the Indian capitalist class was not a distinct or unified group in national politics. Between the Ottawa Conference of 1932 and the Indo-British Trade Agreement of 1939, in particular, Indian business leaders played a complex political game to attract both nationalist and government support for a favourable trading relationship with the rest of the imperial system.

The colonial Government of India rarely acted within the domestic economy simply as the agent of metropolitan or expatriate business interests, although officials were even less disposed to assist Indian entrepreneurs or to bring about conditions that would encourage them in dynamic industrial programmes. Officials strove to uphold a particular system of political economy in India – one in which administrative concerns took precedence over developmental initiatives. The advances that were made in business organisation in India, including the slow spread of the mechanised industrial manufacturing sector, were largely achieved in spite of the inertia created by an administration that ruled in economic matters by a mixture of benign and malign neglect. The result, especially in fiscal and financial policy, was to create tensions between British wants and Indian needs, both official and non-official, that eventually compromised the basis of imperial rule as well as the future progress of the South Asian economy.

Colonial bureaucrats did not stop to ask themselves the question, 'what is the purpose of British rule in India?', but the underlying trend of their actions between 1860 and 1947 shows that they had an answer ready. Government policy, at least the 'high policy' made on the telegraph lines between New Delhi and London, was meant to secure a narrow range of objectives of particular interest to government itself, and in the attainment of which the actions of government were all-important. This lowest common denominator of official concern can be termed India's 'imperial commitment', the irreducible minimum that the subcontinent was expected to perform in the imperial cause. This commitment was three-fold: to provide a market for British goods, to pay interest on the sterling debt and other charges that fell due in London, and to maintain a large number of British troops from local revenues and make a part of the Indian army available for imperial garrisons and expeditionary forces from Suez to Hong Kong.

Over the course of the late nineteenth and early twentieth centuries it became clear that the imperial commitment contained contradictions that released a destructive dialectic of their own. The Government of India's ability to meet its imperial obligations depended on the stability of the twin foundations of its rule – political acquiescence and public revenue. Each arm of the imperial commitment cost the Indian treasury money, and sacrificed India's interests to Britain's. Encouraging imports meant forgoing tariffs; maintaining debt repayments and external financial confidence meant deflationary policies and high exchange rates; large military responsibilities meant a big defence budget, much of which was spent overseas. The relative poverty of the Indian economy imposed a further constraint by limiting the amount of revenue that could be

Table 3.8 *Central and provincial tax revenues, selected years 1900–1901 to 1946–1947*

| | | Percentage of total tax revenues | | | | | |
|---|---|---|---|---|---|---|---|
| Year | Total tax revenues[a] | Land revenue | Customs | Excises | Taxes on income | Salt | Others |
| 1900–1 | 575 | 53 | 9 | 10 | 3 | 16 | 9 |
| 1917–18 | 914 | 36 | 18 | 17 | 10 | 9 | 10 |
| 1921–2 | 1269 | 27 | 30 | 14 | 15 | 5 | 10 |
| 1930–1 | 1310 | 23 | 36 | 13 | 12 | 5 | 11 |
| 1940–1 | 1424 | 19 | 28 | 16 | 19 | 5 | 13 |
| 1946–7 | 4420 | 7 | 22 | 22 | 37 | 2 | 9 |

[a] Central and provincial tax revenues, in Rs millions.
*Source:* Dharma Kumar, 'The Fiscal System', *CEHI*, 2, table 12.7.

extracted, and this helped to convince the British bureaucracy that the secret of successful government in India lay in low taxation. As Lord Canning, the first Viceroy to hold office after the Mutiny, pointed out in the early 1860s, 'I would rather govern India with 40,000 British troops without an income tax than govern it with 100,000 British troops with such a tax.'[51] This advice was heeded for the rest of the life of the British Raj, tax revenues amounting to only 5 to 7 per cent of national income except during the First and Second World Wars.[52] The main features of the colonial government's revenue and expenditure policies are summarised in tables 3.8 and 3.9.

From the 1860s onwards the colonial administration steadily devolved some power to local and provincial government bodies, first nominated and then elected, to buy political acquiescence from its Indian subjects. This policy of administrative decentralisation had fiscal as well as political purposes. The local, district and municipal councils established in the late nineteenth century, and the increasingly autonomous provincial administrations created between 1909 and 1935, were all intended to devise and legitimise new sources of revenue. However, as the process of political reform took on a dynamic of its own, the effect was to starve the central administration of cash by transferring existing powers of taxation from the centre to the provinces and localities. By 1919 the central government had surrendered its rights over the staple land

[51] Quoted in Gordon, *Businessmen and Politics*, p.11.
[52] Kumar, 'Fiscal System', p. 905.

Table 3.9 *Breakdown of central and provincial government expenditure for selected years, 1900–1901 to 1946–1947*

| | | Percentage of total expenditure | | | | | | | | |
|---|---|---|---|---|---|---|---|---|---|---|
| | Total government expenditure (Rs millions) | Administration | | | | Social and developmental expenditure | | | | Other |
| Year | | Cost of tax collection | Other | Debt service | Defence | Education | Medical and public health | Capital outlay | Other | |
| 1900–1 | 958 | 12 | 12 | 4 | 22 | 2 | 2 | 17 | 16 | 14 |
| 1913–14 | 1199 | 12 | 15 | 2 | 25 | 4 | 2 | 18 | 15 | 8 |
| 1917–18 | 1335 | 11 | 16 | 8 | 33 | 4 | 2 | 5 | 12 | 9 |
| 1921–2 | 2132 | 8 | 16 | 8 | 33 | 4 | 2 | 12 | 6 | 12 |
| 1931–2 | 1906 | 7 | 21 | 12 | 28 | 7 | 3 | 5 | 7 | 13 |
| 1946–7 | 7973 | 4 | 11 | 6 | 26 | 3 | 2 | 26 | 7 | 15 |

*Source:* Dharma Kumar, 'The Fiscal System', *CEHI*, 2, table 12.8.

revenue to provincial administrations in an attempt to buy the political peace needed to expand the tax base. From this point on the centre was dependent almost entirely on either tariffs or the income tax for any significant increase in revenue. The result was that customs duties were raised repeatedly, despite the protests of British manufacturers, since they were politically more popular and administratively much easier to collect than any form of direct taxation. Thus in the inter-war years local revenue needs severely damaged India's role as a market for British goods. Over the same period the government in New Delhi found it increasingly hard to keep its military establishment up to strength, and curtailed Britain's expansionary ambitions in western Asia and the Caucasus in the early 1920s by refusing to supply men and *matériel* to the imperial cause. In the great crisis of imperial defence from 1939 onwards the British Government was forced to take over financial responsibility for much of India's war effort.

Over the course of the late nineteenth and early twentieth centuries, the Government of India faced an increasingly severe fiscal problem because of implacable competition for scarce resources between imperial and domestic interests. The additional difficulties for financial and monetary policy created by India's sterling debts and payment obligations represented a more intractable economic and political problem in the inter-war years. The Home Charges amounted to more than a quarter of current government revenues

Table 3.10 *Government of India expenditure and liabilities in London, 1899–1900 to 1933–1934 (annual averages in £ million)*

| | Current expenditure | | | |
|---|---|---|---|---|
| Year | Interest payments | Military expenditure | Civil expenditure[b] | Government sterling debt[a] |
| 1899–1900/1913–14 | 9.4 | 4.2 | 4.1 | 177.1 |
| 1914–15/1920–1 | 13.1 | 4.1 | 5.5 | 153.2 |
| 1924–5 | 14.4 | 10.1 | 7.4 | 262.5 |
| 1933–4 | 15.7 | 8.1 | 5.0 | 385.1 |

[a] Total outstanding on 31 March in end year of period (viz 31 March 1914 for 1899–1900/1913–14).
[b] Pensions, furlough, stores and other civil expenditure.
*Note:* 1899–1925, Rs 15 = £1; 1934–5, Rs 13 = £1.
*Source:* Dharma Kumar, 'The Fiscal System', *CEHI*, 2, table 12.10; Reserve Bank of India, *Banking and Monetary Statistics of India*, Bombay, 1954, table 7, p. 881.

by the 1930s, with interest payments on the accumulated sterling public debt of £350 million taking over half the total; the composition of the Home Charges over the first half of the twentieth century is shown in table 3.10. Continuing the payment of interest and principal on loan capital, and the rest of the Home Charges, was an important aim of British policy in India between the wars, especially during the sterling crisis of the early 1930s when the British Government became convinced that it would have to make good these payments should India default. The result was that the London authorities, at the urging of the British Treasury, ensured that New Delhi follow a conservative financial and monetary policy during the slump to retain confidence and convertibility, and insisted on creating 'safeguards' to guarantee that any further constitutional reforms would not lead to a real transfer of authority over external financial policy to an assembly of elected politicians. This was done by creating an independent central bank (the Reserve Bank of India) in 1935, which was to be accountable to the Viceroy rather than to an Indian finance minister. Once the negotiations for the federal centre envisaged in the 1935 Government of India Act ran into difficulties in the late 1930s, these arrangements made it difficult for the colonial authorities to secure further political support in India by new financial or constitutional concessions. No real progress on this issue was possible until 1945, by which time the new system for financing India's participation in the imperial war effort during the Second

World War had reversed the financial relationship between Britain and India. By the end of the war all the Government of India's pre-war sterling debt had been repaid, and was replaced by credits in London (India's sterling balances) amounting to over £1,300 million.

The particular interests of the colonial government required that its economic policy favour the externally oriented sectors of the local economy at the expense of purely domestic activities. This was a plausible position so long as it seemed likely that the international economy's influence on India was benign, or would become so with the evolutionary growth of appropriate domestic economic institutions and markets. In the inter-war years, however, this view became increasingly hard to sustain, yet the colonial government was still inescapably committed to securing its external obligations as a first priority. During the trade depression in the late 1920s, for example, the Government of India had to contract the currency to secure remittance to pay the Home Charges, just at the point that the domestic credit system was undergoing a liquidity crisis associated with the onset of the agricultural depression. Thus the actions of government to fulfil one arm of its imperial commitment caused further dislocations in the domestic economy, leading to economic retardation and to widespread social discontent and political protest in the 1930s.

Once the international open economy of the long trade boom of 1860–1929 had collapsed in the early 1930s, the British Raj ran out of room to manoeuvre. Imperial control of South Asia was conditional on the smooth working of a domestic and international economy that could supply adequate tax revenues from production, and a foreign exchange surplus on private account. Before 1914 the colonial administration provided important linkages, through its Council Bill and domestic treasury system of financial and monetary institutions, among the Indian, British and international economies, and was able to combine the political acquiescence of its subjects with an export-oriented free-trade economy run on laissez-faire principles. After 1929, however, these circumstances changed fundamentally, as global depression and war broke down the established systems of marketing and credit supply within India. In attempting to repair the damage, government was sucked into a new relationship with the domestic economy in the 1930s and, as we will see shortly, by the 1940s it had to improvise new institutions to allocate scarce goods, capital and foreign exchange among competing local interests. Operating a government of this type required a much more sensitive and participatory political system than the colonial administration could provide, and its failure to manage the economy effectively during the war and in the immediate post-war period helped to intensify the nationalist and communal passions pushing inexorably towards independence and partition. In 1947 the British were ready to abdicate their responsibilities in South Asia, hoping that the successor governments of India and Pakistan had enough political skill and legitimacy to run the interventionist economic systems that a century of colonial neglect had made necessary, in the short run at least.

CHAPTER 4

# THE STATE AND THE ECONOMY, 1939–1980

## THE COSTS OF WAR, PARTITION AND RECONSTRUCTION

The Republic of India that came into existence on 15 August 1947 was a large, diverse and poor country that inherited many economic problems from its colonial past. It was operating within novel political boundaries, and the separation of sizeable areas of the north-western and north-eastern areas of British India to create the new state of Pakistan created some important economic difficulties and dislocations, especially in the supply of Punjabi wheat and Bengali jute. The Indian Union had a federal constitution, with power over economic policy split between the central government in New Delhi and the state administrations. In several parts of the country, notably in central and western India, the administrative units were made more unwieldy by the need to incorporate the old Princely States into the new administrative system, and to meet demands for the creation of linguistically based states out of the old provincial administrative units of British India. This process continued throughout the first thirty years of Independence, resulting in the boundaries and units shown on the political map of India in the 1970s, shown at map 4.1. In 1947 the economy remained largely agricultural, with over four-fifths of the population living in rural areas, and only about 10 per cent working in manufacturing. Economic activity was also strongly regionalised: some indicators of this diversity are given in table 4.1, while map 4.2 shows the distribution of the labour-force and per capita income for the whole subcontinent in 1961.

From the early 1940s onwards the Indian economy was subjected to a regime of state-imposed controls: this extensive web of government regulations – disparagingly known as the 'permit-licence-quota raj'[1] – has been widely attacked for both inhibiting growth and distorting distribution, and for establishing a

[1] This phrase has been attributed to C. Rajagopalachari, the veteran Congress leader from Tamil Nadu who became the first Indian head of state in 1948–50, played an active part in government in the 1950s and then established the pro-business Swatantra Party. See Paul Brass, *The Politics of India Since Independence*, Cambridge, 1990, p. 286.

Table 4.1 *Population, area, agricultural labour, foodgrains output and literacy rates: regional distribution, 1951*

| | Population 1951 | | Distribution of area 1951 | Agricultural labour as % of total agricultural population | Foodgrains output average 1949–50 to 1951–2 | | Literacy rates 1951–2 |
|---|---|---|---|---|---|---|---|
| Area | (millions) | % | % | % | ('000 tonnes) | % | % |
| India | 361.9 | 100.0 | 100.0 | 17.8 | 51 748 | 100.0 | – |
| Andhra Pradesh | 31.3 | 8.6 | 8.4 | 7.2 | 4 243 | 8.2 | 18.0 |
| Assam | 9.6 | 2.7 | 6.7 | 2.5 | 1 591 | 3.1 | 18.2 |
| Bihar | 38.8 | 10.7 | 5.2 | 25.8 | 4 751 | 9.2 | 12.1 |
| Bombay[a] | 48.3 | 13.3 | 15.1 | 19.5 | 6 031 | 11.7 | 21.2 |
| Kerala | 13.5 | 3.7 | 1.2 | 39.2 | 684 | 1.3 | 40.5 |
| Madhya Pradesh | 26.1 | 7.2 | 13.6 | 19.4 | 5 433 | 10.5 | 9.8 |
| Madras[b] | 29.2 | 8.3 | 3.9 | 26.6 | 3 070 | 5.9 | 20.8 |
| Mysore[a] | 19.4 | 5.4 | 5.9 | 14.7 | 2 528 | 4.9 | 19.3 |
| Orissa | 14.6 | 4.0 | 4.8 | 15.5 | 2 258 | 4.4 | 15.8 |
| Punjab[c] | 16.1 | 4.4 | 3.7 | 4.5 | 3 336 | 6.4 | 15.2 |
| Rajasthan | 15.9 | 4.4 | 10.5 | 4.2 | 1 313 | 2.5 | 9.0 |
| Uttar Pradesh | 63.2 | 17.5 | 9.0 | 7.7 | 11 187 | 21.6 | 10.8 |
| West Bengal | 26.3 | 7.3 | 2.7 | 20.6 | 4 499 | 8.7 | 24.0 |

[a] Bombay and Mysore were later re-formed into the states of Gujarat, Maharashtra and Karnataka.

[b] Later re-named Tamil Nadu.

[c] Punjab was subsequently divided into the states of Punjab, Haryana and Himachal Pradesh.

*Source:* Pramit Chaudhuri, *The Indian Economy: Poverty and Development*, London, 1978, table 2.

culture of collusion and corruption between politicians, bureaucrats and businessmen during the first three decades of Independence. Official interference in the allocation and pricing of resources has often been seen as an inevitable consequence of the ideological underpinnings of the nationalist movement, and especially of the socialist ideas that were espoused by Jawaharlal Nehru

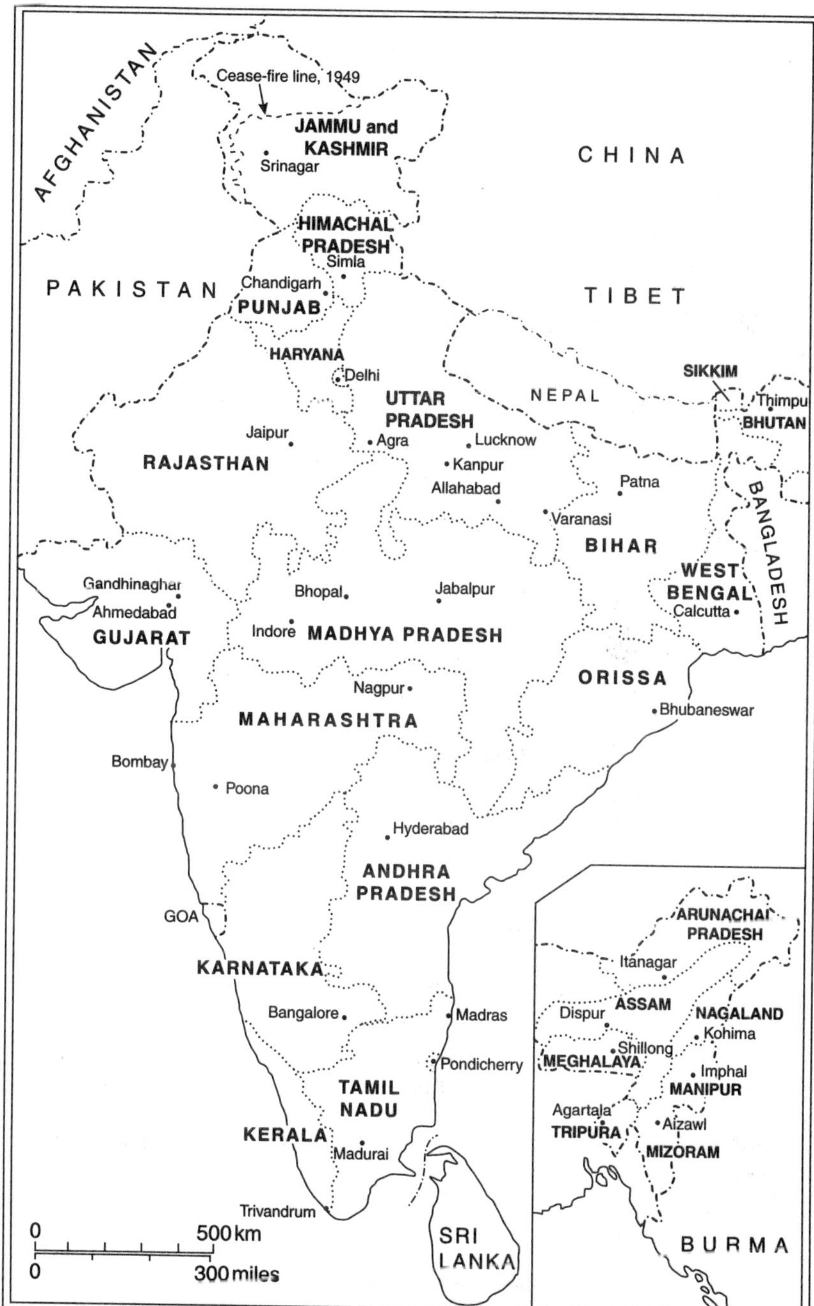


Map 4.1 India: political divisions, 1978

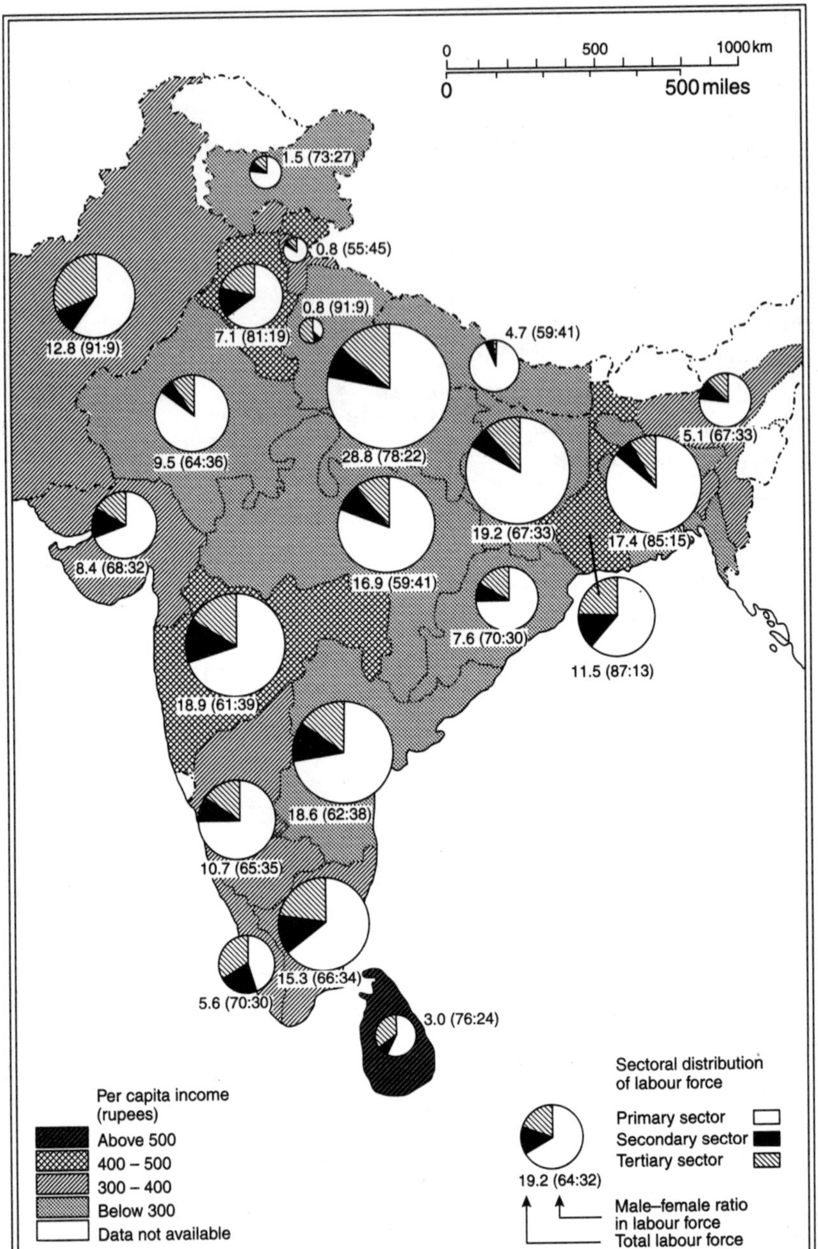


Map 4.2 Sectoral distribution of labour-force and per capita income by states, 1961

and others. However, as we will see, many of the institutions of the managed economy were pragmatic in origin. The circumstances of the late 1940s imposed many constraints on policy-makers: to understand them we must consider the wartime controls and the crucial transition years from 1945 to 1952 in some detail, and evaluate the severe dislocations of economic activity and the intense fluctuations in policy that they caused.[2]

The Second World War had a devastating effect on economic life in India. Between 1939 and 1945 the Indian economy was subjected to enormous strains, which left fundamental imbalances in many areas that lasted long after the coming of peace. The central problem was severe inflation, caused by the financing of military expenditure. Despite the running down of the Indian army during the retrenchment drives of the 1930s, India was still a major British military base and provided a large army paid for by Indian revenues. In 1939 and 1940 the Government of India concluded defence expenditure agreements with the British Government that divided the costs of India's war effort between them. The Indian exchequer was to pay a fixed amount based on the level of effective costs of the army in peacetime, and the extra cost of any war measures taken solely in India's interests. The British Government was to pay for the extra expenses caused by the use of Indian troops outside India, plus, up to 1943, the entire costs of capital outlay needed for industrial expansion for the war effort. As a result Rs 17.40 billion of India's defence expenditure from 1939 to 1946 (almost exactly half the total of Rs 34.83 billion) was recoverable from Britain.[3]

In theory the cost of the war was to be met by taxation in India and reimbursement from Britain. In practice, however, the war could only be financed by inflationary currency issue. Until the Japanese entry into the war in late 1941, the costs of Indian defence for which Britain was responsible were relatively small, and were met by cancelling out India's sterling debt bonds and railway annuities held in London. From 1942 onwards Britain paid for its share of Indian defence expenditure by giving sterling credits (in the form of Treasury Bills lodged with the London branch of the Reserve Bank of India), leaving the Indian authorities to issue currency notes against these reserve assets. The result was inflationary: of the total government expenditure of Rs 39.96 billion incurred during the course of the war, 37 per cent was met

[2] This section is largely drawn from B. R. Tomlinson, *The Political Economy of the Raj, 1914–1947*, London, 1979, pp. 92–100; and 'Historical Roots of Economic Policy', in Subrato Roy and William James (eds.), *Foundations of India's Political Economy: Towards an Agenda for the 1990s*, Delhi, 1992.

[3] Reserve Bank of India figures, cited in R. G. Kulkarni, *Deficit Financing and Economic Development*, London, 1966, p. 144.

by taxation, 36 per cent by borrowing and 27 per cent – Rs 10.78 billion – by increases in the money supply.[4]

The most serious economic effect of India's war effort was to increase purchasing power while limiting the quantity of goods available for the civilian population. The volume of imports fell sharply during the period of hostilities, while industrial production was allowed to expand significantly only in those industries that supplied a strategic need. The result was a savage increase in the price of consumer goods in domestic markets until 1943, and the imposition of rationing schemes and price controls in many commodities after that. The most severe problems arose in food supply, but all consumer goods were affected to some extent. The money supply continued to rise after the end of the war, and inflation was further fuelled by increases in government capital expenditure and the cheap money policy that was launched in 1946. In addition, political uncertainty and battles over economic performance during the lifetime of the Interim Government of 1946–7, an uneasy exercise in power-sharing between the Congress and the Muslim League, weakened the will and ability of government to maintain an effective control regime. As a result the prices of basic commodities again rose sharply, and this caused acute distributional problems, most notably for foodgrains.

The food crisis that emerged during the war did not end in 1945: poor harvests in 1946 and 1947 made the supply situation worse. In 1946 the basic daily food ration was reduced to 12 oz of grain (equivalent to 1,200 calories); by the end of that year about 150 million people were covered by rationing arrangements of some kind, and a full-scale system of official procurement was now in operation, which extracted about one-sixth of the food surplus over the country as a whole. The threat of starvation receded in the winter of 1946–7, but it was replaced with another, more intractable, problem – that of setting appropriate ceiling and floor prices for grain procurement, at a time of increased communal unrest, and the political upheaval and administrative pressure that accompanied the transfer of power and partition of the subcontinent. By early 1947 it was clear that the harvest would be a poor one in many regions of India. Procurement prices were pegged back and, with the anticipation of shortages coupled to the inflationary pressure of cheap money and high government expenditure, farmers hoarded their surplus or turned to the black market.

[4] Total money supply (notes in circulation, bank deposits and cash holdings and deposits with the Reserve Bank) rose from Rs 3.17 billion in August 1939 to Rs 21.9 billion in September 1945.

The rationing system could not cope with these events. Following the advice of a Foodgrains Policy Committee packed with influential businessmen, the new Congress Government of India abolished all controls on foodgrain supply, price and distribution in December 1947. Sugar was decontrolled at the same time, and controls were also abandoned on cotton cloth – the second most important wage good in the internal consumer market. However, decontrol caused more problems than it solved in the chaotic conditions of the late 1940s. The aim of the policy had been to increase supply with only a modest rise in price, yet in practice prices for staple goods rose much faster than availability. By 1949 it was clear that Indian price levels for food and primary produce were considerably higher than those in the outside world, and that an export-based trade policy could not succeed without a reduction in general prices, which was unlikely after the decontrol episode. Thus the result of attempting to free internal markets for food and cotton cloth was to make restrictions on trade all the more necessary.

The post-war history of the control regime over commodity imports and foreign exchange was similar to the case of domestic rationing of consumer goods. Complete controls over imports were in place by January 1942, with licences issued on a qualitative basis, in accordance with strategic requirements and shipping availability rather than the amounts of foreign exchange involved. Once the war had ended, pressure for liberalisation grew, and in January 1946 controls were lifted from trade in a wide range of goods from the sterling area. Where licences were still required these were issued more generously than before, with the only real constraint being the possibility of what was termed 'undue injury' to Indian industry. By September 1946 the authorities allowed free imports of many types of foodstuffs and consumer goods from any source inside or outside the Sterling Area.

This progressively liberal import policy could not be sustained for long. With exports lagging, and large imports of foodgrains needed to supplement the rationing system, opening India's ports to foreign consumer goods had a dramatic effect on its balance-of-payments position. A much more restrictive regime had to be imposed in March 1947, retaining only a small number of essential goods on the open list. With sterling (in which almost all of India's foreign exchange reserves were denominated) due to become convertible in August 1947, the authorities introduced exchange controls and further import restrictions in early July. In the confused monetary conditions of late 1947 following the world-wide run on sterling that caused Britain to abandon convertibility within three weeks, the main object of Indian import trade control became conserving its foreign exchange resources. From July 1947 to June 1948 imports other than food were successfully choked off by the restrictive policy regime. However, restricted supply meant that inflationary pressures became severe, exacerbated by the rise in price of foodgrains following decontrol in December 1947. In response, import controls were liberalised considerably to allow goods that would absorb excess purchasing power to enter the country. The effect of this liberalisation was a new payments crisis early in 1949, exacerbated by a fall-off in exports to the Dollar Area as the American economy moved into recession. Thus by May 1949 policy came full circle again with the cancellation of all Open General Licences, even for soft currency areas, and the exclusion from open licensing of most consumer goods. Licences of imports from dollar and hard currency areas were suspended from the end of June until September. When sterling devalued against the dollar by 31 per cent in September, India followed suit: since Pakistan kept to the old parity, Indo-Pakistani trade was brought almost to a standstill until a formal trade agreement was negotiated in April 1950. As world prices rose in the winter of 1949–50, India's export receipts increased once more, resulting in a much smaller balance-of-trade deficit for the year than had been expected. Licensing policy was accordingly relaxed again, and imports of a wide range of raw materials and intermediate goods went back onto the Open General Licence. The Korean War boom boosted Indian exports still further in 1950 and 1951, but then imports rose again, pushing the whole current account heavily into deficit once more.[5]

The initial phase of Indian import control was dominated by short-term considerations, centred on balance-of-payments problems. Behind these lurked the lingering impact of the wartime inflation, continued into the disturbed conditions of the post-war world. High levels of demand and high domestic prices sucked in imports and deterred exports; international currency arrangements were confused, with sterling moving in and out of convertibility, and with rapid fluctuations in many exchange rates. Despite these difficulties the Indian Government did try consistently to run a liberal import policy in the late 1940s, with as large an Open General Licence and as few quantitative restrictions as possible. When the failure of this strategy led to a more autarchic policy in the early 1950s, it was the result of circumstances, not intention.

## THE PREHISTORY OF PLANNING, 1945–1956

During the war much thought had been given to India's long-term economic development, with wide support for some form of planning. The intellectual

[5] A. K. Banerji, *India's Balance of Payments, 1921–2 to 1938–9*, Bombay, 1963, table L.

origins of planning in Indian policy discussions go back to the 1930s when the impact of the Great Depression of 1929–33 seemed to require some sort of co-ordinated policy response. The coming of war focused attention firmly on industrialisation, and on the rival intellectual traditions (capitalist, socialist and Gandhian) that dominated Indian thinking about economic development. By 1945 a number of non-official schemes had been devised, of which the reports of the Congress National Planning Committee and the 'Bombay Plan' authored by a number of prominent industrialists were the most important.[6]

As the war progressed, even official thinking about post-war planning and industrial development became quite ambitious. The Reconstruction Committee of the Viceroy's Council was formed in 1943, and in 1944 a Department of Planning and Development was set up, with Sir Ardeshir Dalal (who was closely associated with Tatas) as its head, which sounded out business opinion and encouraged other government departments to think about coherent programmes of economic management. By the last months of the war Dalal and his associates on the Reconstruction Committee had produced a wide-ranging report (the *Second Report on Reconstruction Planning*) setting out an overall vision of an industrialised future for India backed by government aid which required considerable state involvement and regulation. The Industrial Policy Statement of 1945 identified twenty industries deemed to be of national importance in which the central government was to regulate operations by licensing any new capacity, and by direct investment in return for a say in management. Ordnance, public utilities and the railways were to be nationalised, and other 'basic industries' put under public ownership if adequate private capital were not forthcoming.[7]

Dalal and his colleagues were very anxious to ensure that the benefits of a more active policy of industrial development should go to Indian, not British, capital. Indian politicians saw the encroachment of British firms as a major threat to the future industrialisation of India, and many businessmen feared that 'India Ltds', the branches and subsidiaries of British multinational companies, were poised to control any new opportunities within the national economy. Indian capitalists realised that they would need foreign assistance to develop their full industrial potential, but were concerned that overseas firms should not be allowed to dominate them. For this reason the Government of

[6] The National Planning Committee was set up in 1938 under the chairmanship of Jawaharlal Nehru; the Bombay Plan, which advocated state intervention to stimulate and protect Indian industry, was published in 1944.

[7] A. H. Hanson, *The Process of Planning: A Study of India's Five Year Plans 1950–1964*, Oxford, 1966, pp. 37–8.

India proposed that foreign capital should only be allowed to hold a minority interest in Indian companies in key sectors such as iron and steel, electrical and heavy engineering, machine tools, heavy chemicals, fertilisers, and pharmaceuticals. Unfortunately, this proposal contravened the 'safeguard' conditions for British business laid down in the 1935 Government of India Act, and caused the British Government to reject New Delhi's proposals for industrial policy in May 1945. The colonial government's Department of Planning and Development was disbanded in 1946, and replaced by an Advisory Planning Board which recommended the creation of a non-political, non-ministerial Planning Commission to play a co-ordinating central role in economic management. Little further could be done until Independence had been achieved and the urgent crises of the Partition period overcome.

Once colonial rule had come to an end in 1947 the independent Indian government was free to make industrial policy in the interests of its subjects, and to proceed with full-blown economic planning if it wished. However, at a time of great political instability, and with an ongoing sense of economic crisis, any government commitment to planning had to take a back seat. As the food decontrol episode had shown, many supporters of the new government favoured the abandonment of wartime controls, or a redirection of them to serve particular interests. Indian businessmen had been prepared to accept state intervention in licensing arrangements and import controls during the war to ensure that scarce resources such as foreign exchange were used to build up future industrial capacity, and out of fear of the inroads that foreign capital would make in an open market. With the establishment of a national government in 1946 and the coming of Independence in 1947, the threat of encroachment by foreign firms seemed more remote. Furthermore, Indian capitalists were now becoming alarmed by the socialist rhetoric coming from some parts of the Congress Party, including calls for wholesale nationalisation. In early 1948 business leaders called for an unequivocal reassurance that the new government had faith in private enterprise.

The first five years of Independence saw a bitter battle between opposed political groupings inside the Indian National Congress. Jawaharlal Nehru, who became the Prime Minister of India in August 1947, was personally committed to secular socialism on the Fabian model. Opposing him was Vallabhbhai Patel, the Home Minister, who had been the dominant organiser and party boss in the Congress before Independence, and who represented the conservative, more traditionally Hindu-oriented wing of the Congress. Both had had close links with Gandhi for many years, but differed strongly on what the Mahatma's legacy should be. While Nehru was interested in creating a modern, socialist nation-state with a strong commitment to equality and democracy, Patel stressed the difficulties of moving a traditional society too rapidly along a reformist path. He was most anxious that strong established and entrenched interests should be respected – notably those of the bureaucracy in administration and of private business in the economy. This rivalry was muted until Independence had been achieved, but by December 1947 the members of the 'Duumvirate' were arguing bitterly about their respective powers inside the government. Gandhi was able to force a reconciliation, but his assassination in January 1948 removed his influence, and his two political heirs clashed decisively over the appointment of the first President of the Indian Republic in September 1949, and over the election of a new Congress President in August 1950. Patel won both of these skirmishes, but his sudden death late in 1950 gave Nehru the decisive advantage and enabled him to reassert his dominance over the party organisation.

As a result of these developments the Government of India's initial approach to industrial policy went less far on the issue of state ownership than had the colonial government's statement in 1945. The Industrial Policy Resolution of April 1948 emphasised that India was to have a mixed economy in which private capital had an important place. Full state ownership was to be imposed only on the railways, ordnance and atomic energy; in six other sectors – coal, iron and steel, aircraft manufacture, shipbuilding, telephone and telegraph materials, and minerals – the government reserved to itself the exclusive right to start new ventures if it so wished. Existing private-sector enterprises would not be nationalised in any circumstances for at least ten years. The aim of any future nationalisation would be to increase production, not to obtain social justice.[8] The 1948 Resolution was moderately encouraging to foreign capital, which it described as valuable to the rapid industrialisation of the country, but ruled that every proposal for new enterprises that involved foreign capital and management would have to be scrutinised and approved by central government. Twelve months later, however, a significant shift took place: in a statement to the Constituent Assembly in April 1949 Nehru argued that foreign capital, and the know-how associated with it, were now essential to India's industrial development, and should be actively encouraged. Strict regulation of foreign capital was no longer thought necessary since the economy was

[8] *Government of India Resolution on Industrial Policy 6th April 1948*, para. 3, reprinted in Government of India, *Report of the Indian Fiscal Commission 1949–50*, Volume 1, New Delhi, 1950, appendix iii. The mechanism of state supervision over industrial development was completed by the Industries (Development and Control) Act in 1951, which required the licensing of all existing industrial units, and of any new ones or substantial expansions, in a wide range of sectors.

now controlled by a national government. Foreign firms were allowed to earn and repatriate profits, and were to be subject to only the same restrictions as Indian firms. When protection was granted to an industry, all units (whether Indian-owned or not) would be entitled to its benefits.[9]

The liberalism of the 1949 statement on foreign capital was striking compared to the government's previous position. In 1947 and 1948 India had held firm to the line that foreign firms could not expect 'national treatment' (equal privileges to those of local firms), and had insisted on the need to prevent foreign control of any major sector of Indian industry. The reason for the policy shift was the foreign exchange crisis of 1949, compounded by the need to import increased amounts of food, the loss of Pakistani markets as a result of the trade war, and the weakness of exports due to the American recession. Negotiations with the World Bank for a loan took place early in 1949. The new policy went further than many Indian industrialists wished, and for the next few years local businessmen campaigned strenuously against the allegedly unfair advantages that overseas companies enjoyed in their Indian operations, especially where a single large foreign firm dominated the domestic market. Government policy was not always consistent in its treatment of foreign capital thereafter, but from 1949 to the mid 1950s government officials were rather more welcoming to foreign firms than were Indian businessmen.

In April 1950 a National Planning Commission of seven members had been set up with Nehru as its Chairman, and this body produced India's First Five Year Plan in December 1952. In theory, the Commission had only an advisory role over policy formulation, but in practice it quickly became a powerful instrument of Nehru's revived political leadership which gradually strengthened during 1951, with the sweeping victories of the Congress in the election campaign of 1951–2 putting him unquestionably in command of both the government and the party. This dominance enabled the Prime Minister to ensure that the Planning Commission had the personnel and the agenda that he favoured. The First Plan was a relatively modest document, based on a number of projects that had already been approved. The total outlay of plan expenditure was to be Rs 14.93 billion, subsequently raised to just over Rs 20 billion. The final Plan document, published in December 1952, went a little further down the road to state-led development by using public-sector outlays to stimulate increased saving and investment in the economy as a whole. This was done with caution, however, with 37 per cent of expenditure targeted

[9] The official text of the statement is reprinted in *ibid.*, appendix iv.

at agriculture and irrigation, 26.5 per cent at transport and communications, and only 2.8 per cent at large-scale industry and mining.[10]

Despite its modest scale, the First Plan did focus attention on the role of the state in economic development more explicitly than had been done before. While accepting that public and private sectors could supplement each other, the Planning Commission saw the need to retain an extensive system of quantitative controls over capital issues, industrial licensing, foreign exchange rationing, imports and exports, and the prices and movement of foodgrains. The authors of the First Plan argued explicitly that increased public-sector activity would lead to greater distributional equality, which meant that the state would have to raise a surplus out of which savings and investments could be made. Overall, however, the planners remained somewhat vague about the physical and financial targets they wished to attain. They eschewed deficit financing because of continued worries about inflation and declined to raise taxation, ignoring the potential resource gap that resulted. In the event, these contradictions did not lead to serious difficulties for the Plan, since the favourable economic circumstances of the mid 1950s, and the relatively small scale of the plan outlays, meant that the impact of government intervention on production and distribution was muted, and their full implications could be ignored.

The new rulers of India after 1947 were nationalist leaders who had come to power to replace a colonial administration. Inevitably, there was a reaction against the laissez-faire policies that the colonial government had followed for most of its life, and great caution at first about continued contact with foreign governments and business interests. Most important of all, perhaps, was an impression that India's evident poverty was the result of the squandering of a fixed store of national resources as a result of the economic exploitation of colonialism. It was tempting to believe that all India's economic ills could be laid at the door of British imperialism, and that the use of scarce national resources needed to be controlled and rationed more carefully in the future. For all these reasons close supervision and control of the economy seemed essential, with only the state and its agents (the inheritors of the moral legitimacy of nationalism) fit to determine and enforce the common interest.

However, the policies of the new Indian government cannot be explained simply in terms of doctrinaire socialism, or economic nationalism. As we have seen, wartime controls were dismantled in some areas (food supply) and loosened in others (import policy) in the late 1940s, having to be re-imposed, and

[10] V. N. Balasubramanyam, *The Economy of India*, London, 1984, p. 80.

set in an overarching framework of planning, because of practical difficulties as much as ideological predilections. The nationalist government inherited an economy in which domestic prices for all major commodities were substantially above world levels and the internal and external values of the rupee were considerably out of line, and the devaluation of 1949 did little to rectify the situation. In the early 1950s the government could not avoid using controls, but it lacked the capacity to implement a sophisticated regulatory regime. The political struggle between left and right, and the uncertainty in the relationship between the Centre and the States, all made fine tuning in economic management too difficult, and encouraged the use of a broad, rhetorical planning framework as an administrative panacea.

At Independence both the public and private sectors in India contained significant organisational weaknesses, which provided a poor foundation for subsequent economic development. The centralisation of power masked institutional fragility and inflexibility, but inhibited the development of sophisticated or subtle policies of economic management. The fundamental imbalances that existed in the Indian economy in the late 1940s made these defects all the harder to rectify. By 1950 the Indian economy was far from any equilibrium, and its internal market mechanisms were so damaged as to be unable to allocate resources effectively. Controls were essential in the short term to shore up this position, and by the time that normal conditions were restored the Indian government was committed to centralised planning for political and administrative reasons as well as for economic ones. Economic management was, in a real sense, inevitable in the 1950s because of the fundamental economic and political changes that had taken place in the decade after 1945. However, to say that the economic control regime that was devised from 1945 to 1951 was inevitable does not mean that it should also have been immortal. The controls of the late 1940s were necessary to cope with serious imperfections in the market networks of the Indian domestic economy. They succeeded in this, but only at a heavy price – that of perpetuating for many years the institutional failure that they were intended to overcome.

## PLANNING, THE STATE AND INDUSTRY, 1956–1965

The First Plan determined the government's economic programme from 1951 to 1956. The growth rates that it achieved were adequate rather than remarkable, with the annual rate of investment averaging 6 per cent of national income, and national income itself rising by 18 per cent (at constant prices) from 1950–1 to

1955–6.[11] Yet its success seemed more substantial than that. The Plan had been conceived at a time of unprecedented institutional instability, and was implemented against the background of considerable economic uncertainty; but by the middle years of the Plan period circumstances seemed to have become a great deal more favourable for the Indian economy. Any sort of sustained growth looked like a considerable achievement after the problems of the 1930s and 1940s.

In the 1950s the rural economy, which still supplied over half of national product, benefited considerably from good monsoons in 1953–4 and 1954–5, and from modest but significant investment in irrigation. The resultant surge in agricultural production, especially in foodgrains, dampened down inflationary pressures in the economy, stimulated demand for manufactured goods, and enabled the government to supplement the resources available for further development by a modest level of borrowing. At the same time, the foreign exchange constraint that had loomed so large in the early years of Independence was removed by the revival of international trade, the securing of international aid packages and drawings on India's sterling balances – the short-term assets held in London against India's wartime expenditure on Britain's behalf, which could be spent with British agreement, and mostly on sterling goods. With the supply of investment matching demand, with inflation minimal and with the balance of payments buoyant, the available resources for growth made the earlier detailed regulation and control of the economy unnecessary.

The easing of economic conditions from 1954 onwards helped to encourage a much more ambitious approach to economic development under the Second Five Year Plan of 1956–61. The most important feature of this was optimism over the ability of the economy to generate savings. At the heart of the Second Plan lay the strategy proposed by Professor P. C. Mahanalobis of the Indian Statistical Institute, Nehru's most trusted adviser on planning, who orchestrated the production of a draft Plan Frame for the Second Plan in March 1955. Mahanalobis argued that investment in capital goods production, by means of a public-sector-dominated 'industry-first' policy, was the key to growth. Depressing consumption would release extra savings for future investment, and by switching resources to the production of capital goods and steel the new Plan could increase the share of investment goods and diminish the share of consumption goods in GNP. Planned expenditure on industry and mining was set at Rs 8.9 billion (18.5 per cent of the total), as compared with Rs 5.68 billion (11.8 per cent of the total) on agriculture and community development. It was proposed that almost two-thirds of the new investment

[11] Hanson, *Process of Planning*, pp. 114–15.

made during the Plan period should come from the public sector, including more than half of such investment in organised industry and mining. Private investment would be dominant only in construction, and possibly in agriculture (excluding irrigation). The outlay of Rs 48 billion was to be raised from taxation, domestic borrowing, other budgetary heads such as the railways and provident funds, and foreign aid, leaving a quarter of the total to be met by deficit financing (including drawings from the sterling balances), and a 'gap' of Rs 4 billion to be covered from additional domestic resources that would become available as a result of the rapid growth brought about by the Plan.[12]

The formulation of the Second Plan coincided with a peak in Nehru's unencumbered personal influence in government and the planning process. A nominal commitment to socialism had by now become the central plank in the Prime Minister's policy on egalitarianism and welfare. In late 1954 Nehru proposed to the chief ministers of all the states meeting in the National Development Council that social and economic policy should be informed by 'a socialistic picture of society', in which 'the means of production should be socially owned and controlled for the benefit of society as a whole', but in which there was 'plenty of room for private enterprise provided the main aim is kept clear'. This position was endorsed by the Lok Sabha in December 1954 and by the Congress Party in its session at Avadi in January 1955, which passed a resolution committing itself to the view that the purpose of planning was 'the establishment of a socialistic pattern of society where the principal means of production are under social ownership and control'.[13]

Mahanalobis and the other drafters of the Second Plan took on this brief with enthusiasm, and a new Industrial Policy Resolution was issued along with the Plan in 1956. This emphasised the importance of the public sector somewhat more strongly than before, and referred explicitly to 'the socialist pattern of society as the objective of social and economic policy'.[14] Industries were allocated between the public and private sector, with 'basic and strategic' industries reserved for public investment. In seventeen strategic industries, including heavy electrical plant, iron and steel, heavy castings, and most mineral extraction and processing, the state was to have a monopoly or an exclusive right to new investment, and existing private plants were given no guarantee against nationalisation. Another twelve basic industries, including machine

[12] Government of India, Planning Commission, *Second Five Year Plan*, Delhi, 1956, pp. 56–7, 77–8.

[13] Quoted in Francine R. Frankel, *India's Political Economy, 1947–1977: The Gradual Revolution*, Princeton, 1978, p. 117.

[14] Government of India, Planning Commission, *Second Five Year Plan*, p. 44.

Table 4.2 *Composition of aggregate investment, India, 1950–1951 to 1968–1969*

| | First Plan (1951–56) | | Second Plan (1956–61) | | Third Plan (1961–66) | | Annual Plans (1966–69) | |
|---|---|---|---|---|---|---|---|---|
| | Rs bill. | % | Rs bill. | % | Rs bill. | % | Rs bill. | % |
| Agriculture | 9.1 | 27 | 12.6 | 19 | 21.2 | 18 | 19.4 | 20 |
| Industry and minerals | 4.4 | 12 | 18.1 | 27 | 29.9 | 25 | 23.8 | 25 |
| Power | 2.7 | 8 | 4.8 | 7 | 12.9 | 11 | 12.0 | 12 |
| Transport | 5.9 | 18 | 14.1 | 21 | 23.5 | 20 | 14.6 | 15 |
| Others | 11.5 | 35 | 17.9 | 26 | 32.0 | 26 | 27.9 | 28 |
| Total | 33.6 | 100 | 67.5 | 100 | 119.5 | 100 | 97.7 | 100 |

*Source:* A. Vaidyanathan, 'The Indian Economy since Independence', *CEHI*, 2, table 13.6.

tools, ferro-alloys and fertilisers, were to be open to both private and public capital, but with the state committed to further advance. Private capital was to be allowed a free hand elsewhere, subject to the targets of the national plan, and the provisions of licensing and import controls.

The late 1950s and early 1960s represented the high-water mark of Indian planning. Some of the distinctive features of this period are demonstrated in tables 4.2, 4.3, 4.4 and 4.5. As table 4.2 makes clear, resources under the Second and Third Plans were concentrated on industry rather than agriculture, with the proportion of total investment in agriculture falling from 27 per cent under the First Plan to about 18 per cent under the Third. Despite significant increases in investment, the growth rate of output in the economy as a whole remained roughly constant until the mid 1960s, and then fell somewhat, suggesting that the capital intensity required for incremental output was rising over the period, especially in the mining and manufacturing sectors. These increased amounts of capital needed to improve production could not come entirely from domestic savings or budgetary resources; as table 4.3 shows, the Plans were heavily dependent on deficit financing and, increasingly, the use of external resources to meet their outlay targets. The growth rates of agriculture, industry and national product that were achieved during and after the period of intensive planning are given in tables 4.4 and 4. 5. These show clearly the rapid strides in industrial development made under the intensive stimulation of the Second and Third Plans, but that the lagging of agriculture pulled down national product to modest levels of growth.

Table 4.3 *Plan outlay and its finance, 1951–1969*

| | 1951–56 | | 1956–61 | | 1961–66 | | 1966–69 | |
|---|---|---|---|---|---|---|---|---|
| | Rs mill. | % | Rs mill. | % | Rs mill. | % | Rs mill. | % |
| Total plan outlay | 19 600 | 100.0 | 46 720 | 100.0 | 85 770 | 100.0 | 67 560 | 100.0 |
| Domestic budgetary requirements | 14 380 | 73.4 | 26 690 | 57.0 | 50 210 | 58.5 | 36 480 | 54.0 |
| Current surpluses | 7 540 | 38.5 | 12 300 | 26.3 | 28 820 | 33.6 | 16 220 | 24.0 |
| Internal borrowings | 6 840 | 34.9 | 14 390 | 30.7 | 21 390 | 24.9 | 20 260 | 30.0 |
| Deficit finance | 3 330 | 17.0 | 9 540 | 20.4 | 11 330 | 13.2 | 6 820 | 10.1 |
| External resources | 1 890 | 9.6 | 10.490 | 22.5 | 24 230 | 28.3 | 24 260 | 35.9 |

*Source:* Pramit Chaudhuri, *The Indian Economy: Poverty and Development*, London, 1978, table 23.

The industrial policy initiated in 1956 stressed 'capital goods as the leading sector and the state as the leading actor'.[15] This maxim remained at the heart of India's policies for industrial development for the next three decades. In part this policy reflected 'export pessimism' – an assessment that world markets for India's primary produce would remain static and unstable, and that domestic rates of accumulation had to be set free from the restraint of sluggish export growth. The relatively high prices of Indian goods, and the discrimination against exports in exchange rate and domestic interest rate policies, compounded the position. This, in turn, gave a rationale for strict import controls and foreign exchange restrictions as a way of easing the weak balance-of-payments position that resulted from the constrictions on exports. Thus planning and the control regime meshed together quite tightly, and each reinforced the other so long as the Indian government pursued its search for 'self-reliance' in both industrial and agricultural production.

The decline of India's export competitiveness in the second half of the 1950s was striking. In 1953, when world trading conditions had stabilised after the Korean War, India supplied about 1.5 per cent of total world exports by value,

[15] Keith Griffin, *Alternative Strategies for Economic Development*, Basingstoke, 1989, p. 118.

Table 4.4 *Rates of growth of agricultural production, industrial production and national product, India, 1950/1951–1971/1972 (three-year moving averages, percentage change)*

| Years | Agricultural production | Industrial production[a] | National product |
|---|---|---|---|
| 1950/1–53/4 | 7.03 | 5.11 | 4.23 |
| 1951/2–54/5 | 6.30 | 8.56 | 4.06 |
| 1952/3–55/6 | 4.32 | 10.51 | 3.45 |
| 1953/4–56/7 | 2.13 | 8.95 | 3.16 |
| 1954/5–57/8 | −0.35 | 5.01 | 1.96 |
| 1955/6–58/9 | 4.66 | 4.89 | 3.67 |
| 1956/7–59/60 | 1.78 | 6.76 | 2.65 |
| 1957/8–60/1 | 7.10 | 8.95 | 3.29 |
| 1958/9–61/2 | 2.04 | 9.62 | 2.20 |
| 1959/60–62/3 | 2.40 | 9.05 | 2.38 |
| 1960/1–63/4 | 0.39 | 8.84 | 3.92 |
| 1961/2–64/5 | 3.89 | 8.85 | 5.30 |
| 1962/3–65/6 | −1.78 | 5.45 | 2.39 |
| 1963/4–66/7 | −2.57 | 2.35 | 1.29 |
| 1964/5–67/8 | 0.59 | 1.57 | 1.92 |
| 1965/6–68/9 | 6.13 | 4.32 | 4.14 |
| 1966/7–69/70 | 8.16 | 6.06 | 5.12 |
| 1967/8–70/1 | 4.15 | 4.84 | 3.55 |
| 1968/9–71/2 | 3.91 | 5.01 | 3.65 |

[a] Calendar years (1950–1 = 1950).

Figures are of percentage change between three-year moving averages (viz. 1968/9–1971/2 = percentage change between averages of 1968/9–1970/1 and 1969/70–1971/2).

*Source:* Walter C. Neale and John Adams, *India: The Search for Unity, Democracy and Progress*, New York, 1976, tables 9–11.

Table 4.5 *Rates of growth of output, India, 1950–1965 and 1965–1972*

| | 1950–65 | 1965–72 |
|---|---|---|
| Agriculture | 5.16 | 1.70 |
| Industry | 7.70 | 3.82 |
| National product | 3.60 | 2.32 |

*Source:* Neale and Adams, *India: The Search for Unity, Democracy*, table 13.

and its market share fell thereafter to 1.4 per cent in 1956, to 1.3 per cent in 1958 and to 1.2 per cent in 1960. The decline was most striking in a range of traditional exports such as tea, cotton and jute manufactures; peanut oil; leather; and manganese ore. To some extent falling world demand for a wide range of primary products was to blame for this, but Indian exports were also less competitive and lost their market share in the trade that did take place. This was particularly marked in peanut oil, where India's share of the volume of world exports fell from 46 per cent in 1955 to 1 per cent in 1960; in jute manufactures (87 per cent in 1954 to 73 per cent in 1960); and in tea (46 per cent in 1956 to 38 per cent in 1960). In all these commodities Indian policy failed to match the export promotion of its rivals, while high taxes, domestic inflation and a desire to stabilise domestic supply sapped the competitiveness of Indian goods. The price of Indian peanut oil doubled against that of its main West African competitor between 1955 and 1960. The much rarer case of an effective export promotion policy occurred in sugar, where a high level of cash subsidy was granted to exports in 1961–2 to relieve a glut in the domestic market without forcing down the return of local producers.[16]

In framing the Second Plan the government had taken an optimistic view of India's foreign exchange requirements in the mid 1950s, since the experience of the First Plan had suggested that the need to secure overseas earnings would not hold development back seriously. In setting their new targets the authorities arranged for a much higher level of foreign assistance, and estimated a level of exports just below that of the earlier quinquennium. As things turned out, this was over-optimistic, and foreign exchange constraints came to have a powerful impact on the implementation of the Second Plan. Rising import costs, especially of food, iron and steel, and capital equipment, led to a severe balance-of-payments crisis in the winter of 1956–7. Over the whole Plan period exports earned Rs 31.1 billion (a little more than the target figure of Rs 29.7 billion), while imports cost Rs 53.7 billion (far in excess of the target of Rs 43.4 billion). The sterling balances, which had cushioned balance-of-payments problems up to now, had all been spent by 1956. In January 1957 stringent new controls had to be imposed to conserve the diminishing resources of foreign exchange for the 'core' areas of steel, coal, transport and power generation. However, agricultural production had also fallen while deficit financing and private-sector borrowing had both increased, and the resulting inflation further undermined the balance of payments, which meant that Plan outlays had to be revised downwards in 1958.

16 B. I. Cohen, 'The Stagnation of Indian Exports, 1951–61', *Quarterly Journal of Economics*, 78, 4, 1964.

One result of this crisis was to increase India's dependence on foreign aid considerably, with the formation in 1958 of the Aid-India Consortium (made up of Canada, Britain, the USA, West Germany and the World Bank). While the quantity of aid supplied to India remained very low on a per capita basis ($1.5 per head in 1961, $2.1 per head in 1963), it did rise sharply over the Second Plan period to Rs 13.11 billion (net), as against only Rs 1.8 billion (net) in 1951–6. While it is not clear precisely how aid contributed directly to capital formation, more aid probably did mean more public investment. Aid receipts net of amortisation and interest payments amounted to 28 per cent of the total Plan outlay for 1956–61, and 19 per cent of total investment, as against 9.1 per cent of outlay and 5.4 per cent of investment under the First Plan.[17] As a consequence India's relations with the major western nations became more complex, especially with the United States, which remained the largest single source of external financial assistance and commodity flows. The vast bulk of foreign aid to India was tied to individual projects, and to particular sources of supply of plant and equipment, which probably diminished its value to the Indian authorities significantly.

Balance-of-payments problems also help to change attitudes to foreign private investment. Foreign firms were an obvious source of foreign exchange and up-to-date technology, and by the mid 1950s Indian entrepreneurs had modified their earlier hostility to them, welcoming partnership ventures that would reinforce the importance of the private sector in the economy as a whole. In addition, since foreign firms usually covered the direct overseas costs of a new venture, collaboration agreements became a way round strict foreign exchange controls. The number of such collaboration agreements, which had run at an annual average of 50 from 1948 to 1958, rose sharply to over 300 from 1958 to 1968, with a peak between 1959 and 1963.[18] Roughly half of these agreements licensed an Indian firm to manufacture a foreign product (the rest transferring production know-how by other means), and almost all involved major imports of technology. At the peak of its influence in the late 1950s, foreign capital controlled about 40 per cent of the total assets in the organised large-scale private sector. One effect of these capital imports was to help the private sector to escape from the rigid guidelines of the planners. In the late 1950s and early 1960s, in particular, lax restrictions on foreign firms encouraged multiple collaborations to manufacture luxury consumer goods

[17] J. N. Bhagwati and Padma Desai, *Planning for Industrialization: Industrialization and Trade Policies since 1951, 1900–1966*, Oxford, 1970, pp. 180, 201, 206; Balasubramanyam, *Economy of India*, pp. 174–6.

[18] Deepak Lal, *Appraising Foreign Investment in Developing Countries*, London, 1975, pp. 96, 106–7.

such as radios, refrigerators, processed food and tailored clothes, which had weak multiplier effects and did little to raise overall living standards.

The industrial policy of the 1950s was based on import-substituting industrialisation and an expansion of basic goods production by the public sector, fuelled by foreign aid, deficit financing and indirect taxation. Total industrial output increased at an annual average rate of 7.4 per cent between 1951 and 1965, with basic goods and capital goods leading the way. However, employment in industry grew much more slowly, at around 3 per cent per year, about the same as the rate of increase of the labour-force. The share of the industrial sector in total employment reached a plateau of about 11 per cent in the early 1960s and did not advance beyond this, while the share of manufacturing in total national product rose from 10 per cent in the early 1950s to almost 16 per cent in the mid 1960s, but then levelled off at about that rate. The public sector provided more than half the total investment in industry during the Second and Third Plans, with almost 50 per cent of large-scale industrial investment going to the iron and steel industry. However, public-sector industries faced considerable problems of overcapacity and underproduction as a result of locational difficulties, inefficient administration and supply shortages, so that in the mid 1960s approximately 80 per cent of output came from the private sector.[19] State industries bolstered the private sector by supplying underpriced inputs of power, steel and other materials, but the quality of these was variable. The predicament of the steel industry, the largest area of public-sector investment, was particularly acute. The major steel plants were bedevilled by poor labour relations and frequent breakdowns, as well as the problems caused at the Bokaro mill by the unsuitability of foreign designs insisted on by aid donors. Indian steel production rose from 1.5 million tonnes in 1951 to 6.2 million tonnes in 1970, but during the 1960s the public-sector manufacturer, Hindustan Steel, made a loss of Rs 1.4 billion on its investment of Rs 11 billion. In 1970 one of its four plants was out of operation and two were using less than half of their capacity.[20]

Indian industry expanded in the early 1950s by replacing imports of consumer goods, but by the time of the Second Plan import-substitution in capital goods and intermediate goods had become more important. The planning and import licensing bureaucracies imposed a rigid test on imports, which became known as the 'in-principle principle' – imports were not permitted in goods that India was capable *in principle* of manufacturing, whether or not it did at

[19] Balasubramanyam, *Economy of India*, pp. 114 ff, especially table 6.4.

[20] Pramit Chaudhuri, *The Indian Economy: Poverty and Development*, London, 1978, pp. 159–60; J. W. Mellor, *The New Economics of Growth: A Strategy for India and the Developing World*, Ithaca, 1976, pp. 120–1.

the time. Rates of effective protection were very high, and thus large sections of Indian industry could remain profitable with low levels of productivity. Such a policy required close monitoring of the industrial sector, both public and private, and the relentless pursuit of a clear and coherent set of goals for rationalising industrial capacity and improving its efficiency. Measures like this helped to bring about sustained industrial growth and structural change elsewhere in Asia, notably in South Korea, but in India the administrators did not oversee the costs and benefits of protection effectively, nor could they implement an informed or rigorous policy on foreign capital and technology.

For the life of the Second Plan relations between government and private business went smoothly. State involvement in the industrial economy was largely confined to investment in public-sector heavy industry and infrastructure – areas in which private business did not, at that time, wish to become involved. The creation of a heavily protected domestic market to which entry was restricted by a complex and time-consuming system of licensing, capital issues control and import restrictions had clear advantages for established entrepreneurs, especially since licences were often issued on a 'first-come-first-served' basis.

Profit rates in the private sector averaged about 8 per cent of net worth (after tax) in the early 1950s, and dipped to under 7 per cent in the drought-affected years of 1957–9, but rose to 10.5 per cent for 1959–60 to 1961–2.[21] Some subsidised finance was available to private industry through the government-run Industrial Finance Corporation, which disbursed Rs 10.2 billion worth of financial assistance in return for shares between 1957 and 1963.[22] The licence and permit system brought some benefits to private businessmen who could pre-empt their rivals and establish barriers to entry. The Birla Group, in particular, was adept at manipulating the licence system by multiple applications and pre-emptive bids. The conduct of the licence and permit systems also gave scope for corruption among businessmen and bureaucrats over access to both imports and supplies from public-sector enterprises.

## LAND REFORM AND CO-OPERATIVES: AGRICULTURE IN THE 1950S

Rural producers were crucial to the success of the government's development plans as consumers, and as suppliers of a surplus in the form of goods, taxation

[21] Mellor, *New Economics*, p. 139.
[22] Hanson, *Process of Planning*, p. 477.

and savings. However, the agrarian sector had many problems of its own, and these focused the planners' attention in the 1950s on major issues of productivity and distribution that seemed to require drastic solutions. The depression of the 1930s had caused severe disruptions in rural commodity, capital and labour markets. The most damaging consequence was the fragmentation of many of the vertical linkages that had bound agrarian operations together in the past. With the drying up of liquidity for trade, and the fall in the price of exportable cash crops, extensive agricultural networks fell on hard times. Rural indebtedness became a problem because of the inability or unwillingness of traditional lenders to commit funds, especially where such funds represented advances for producing crops that would enter inter-regional or international trade.

The experience of the Congress as a political movement in the 1930s suggested to the nationalist leaders that the problems of agriculture were predominantly a consequence of landlordism and the dominance of traders and professional moneylenders in the supply of rural credit. The most potent rural political agitations in the 1930s were those that captured the support of land-controlling peasants threatened by the action of landlords or outside creditors caught up in the crisis of depression. In much of northern and eastern India the issue of tenant eviction for non-payment of rent, and their demotion to non-occupancy or sharecropper status, had been especially powerful. In eastern Uttar Pradesh and in Bihar, in particular, the internal and external politics of the Congress had revolved around this issue, as nationalists of the left and right, landlord politicians and their supporters, and the leaders of the *Kisan Sabhas* (Peasant Leagues) struggled for control. In both the United Provinces and Andhra Pradesh (the northern districts of the Madras Presidency) the Congress governments of the late 1930s produced plans to abolish zamindari, with landlords being restricted to a fixed amount of *sir* (home farm) land for their direct cultivation. The aim of these reforms was to establish hereditary occupancy rights for all tenants who held leases directly from the landlord, and thus to remove the possibility of legal title conflicting with de facto control of the land derived from local social and economic power. The Congress ministries left office in September 1939 before any of this legislation could be passed onto the statute book, but the political response to these proposals had been quite favourable. In Andhra Pradesh, where landlords had no effective levers of control over their tenants other than that of formal tenancy arrangements, such a reform was welcomed by all sides; elsewhere, notably in the United Provinces and Bihar, compromise proposals for tenancy reforms had secured the consent of all but the largest rentiers.

After Independence most Congress State governments continued this approach and quickly produced plans to abolish intermediaries – zamindars and others – who had rights over the land but did not cultivate it directly, and also to regulate rent, establish ceilings for land-holdings, give security to tenant farmers and enable tenants to obtain ownership of the lands they farmed. Such schemes were a product of political necessity and notions of social justice, but their proponents also justified them in terms of economic efficiency. As the United Provinces Zamindari Abolition Committee (1948) argued, a typical zamindar had invested little capital in increasing production and was not 'an organiser of agricultural activities in the sense in which an industrialist or a businessman is'. Cultivators, on the other hand, lacked the incentive to improve the land under a rental system. As a result, the Committee argued, 'the removal of intermediaries between the tiller of the soil and the State will in itself go a good way towards the rehabilitation of agriculture.'[23] The economic assumption behind such reforms was that agriculture could best be organised around peasant families that needed only to be given unfettered access to land and capital in order to flourish.

Land reform was endorsed by the First Five Year Plan in 1952, but within central government there was more concern with other issues – notably those of sustainable farming and the ability of small-holders to survive. The problems revealed by the inflationary wartime crisis of the 1940s had suggested that underemployment and the imperfections of the labour market were the crucial problems of agriculture, and the skewing of general entitlements that culminated in the Bengal Famine rubbed this message home. Congress radicals had been proposing a strong attack on private property rights in land since the early 1930s. The established leaders of the national movement were careful never to commit themselves to this policy unequivocally, but such ideas had had some influence within the party in the 1930s and 1940s. In 1938 the Congress National Planning Commission's report had urged collectivisation as a solution to credit, marketing and purchasing problems. After the war a number of Congress-sponsored enquiries were set up to examine possible schemes for reform, the most influential of which were the Congress Party Economic Programme Committee of 1947–8 and the government Agrarian Reforms Commission set up in November 1947. These bodies, whose proposals fed directly into the early stages of the planning process, argued that the land reform legislation that had been implemented by state governments was

[23] Quoted in Walter C. Neale, *Economic Change in North India: Land Tenure and Reform in the United Provinces, 1800–1955*, New Haven, 1962, p. 217.

merely ameliorative, and provided an inadequate base for the future development of the rural economy. As the Planning Commission put it in 1951:

The problems of Indian agriculture are far more fundamental than is commonly appreciated. This is apparent, for instance, from the fact that, in recent years, in spite of high prices, public investment on a scale never attempted before, and legislation designed to give greater security to the tiller, there have been no marked gains in production ... The bulk of the agricultural producers live on the margin and are unable to invest in the improvement of the land. There is widespread unemployment ... and the economy cannot provide and sustain continuous employment for the available labour.[24]

The authors of the First Five Year Plan saw the productivity issue as crucial to the future of the Indian rural economy. They tried to resolve it by increasing the size of the units of management to create an economically efficient industry that would provide incentives for cultivators and labourers to increase their output. The planners proposed a two-pronged strategy for the immediate future. Following the argument of the Congress Agrarian Reforms Committee report, they identified the concept of an 'economic holding' of between 5 and 10 acres, which would be large enough to provide a reasonable standard of living and to give full employment to a normal-sized family and at least one pair of bullocks. These were to be designated as 'registered' farms and remain as private units of ownership and management which would receive subsidised inputs in return for a commitment to minimum standards in technical progress, agricultural wage rates and the disposal of surplus food production. The vast bulk of smaller holdings, which could not meet these criteria, were to be rehabilitated through a village-based system of corporate cultivation. The planners rejected radical ideas of collective farming, since they thought that 'a system in which individual holdings were pooled was opposed to the instinct and tradition of the Indian peasant and would not be acceptable to him'.[25] Instead, they proposed that small-holders should be encouraged through a process of persuasion and education to create systems of co-operative management at the village level, based on units that would give economically viable holdings. Such co-ops were again to receive preferential treatment from the government over inputs, and their members would not lose their rights in land they did not cultivate directly themselves.

The First Plan proposed a more wide-ranging solution to the problems of Indian agriculture than any of its successors have done, which is perhaps a

[24] Government of India, Planning Commission, *First Five Year Plan – Draft Outline*, New Delhi, 1951, p. 94, quoted in V. M. Dandekar, 'From Agrarian Reorganization to Land Reform', *Artha Vijnana*, 6, 1, 1964, pp. 51–2.

[25] *Ibid.*, p. 54.

tribute to the overwhelming nature of the agrarian crisis that seemed imminent in the late 1940s. At the heart of its proposals lay a concern for the employment prospects of rural labour and deficit land-holders. At this point the aim was not to create a rural economy made up of self-sufficient peasant families, and any land redistributed under ceiling legislation or the *bhoodan* movement (for voluntary land redistribution) was to be put under co-operative control. The preferred solution of joint farming by small-holders and labourers through Co-operative Village Management units was intended to increase productivity and provide additional employment, although the planners recognised that all of the underemployed labour in the rural economy could not be absorbed in this way. The best means for implementing the new programme of joint farming was left vague, however. The system was to be introduced on a voluntary basis – when two-thirds of the owners, or permanent tenants holding at least a half of the lands in the village, supported it. This point could only be reached by 'a process of education and persuasion' that would 'convince the bulk of agriculturists about the value, from their own point of view, of moving towards a system of Co-operative Village Management'.[26]

The crucial task of changing hearts and minds at the grassroots level was assigned to a new community development (CD) programme, formally initiated in 1952, the successor to the Gandhian Constructive Programme of village uplift. A sum of Rs 900 million, more than a quarter of the total budget for agricultural development, was assigned to this programme under the First Plan, with a further Rs 330 million ear-marked for the co-operative programme and other village-level activities. This enlarged programme of uplift was intended to raise the living standards of villages as a whole, in part by supplying limited amounts of technical assistance and improved inputs, but chiefly by unleashing a desire for rural betterment that was to be harnessed by the traditional agent of village self-government, the *panchayat*. This programme was politically useful within the Congress Party, since it allowed the aims of technical improvement, socialist redistribution and Gandhian uplift to be combined. It also conformed to the nationalist myth of a pre-colonial rural India made up of independent, self-sufficient and self-governing village republics, and to the Gandhian ideal of the moral integrity of the vast mass of rural society.

The CD programme was given a high political profile and continued to be well funded, with almost half of the total expenditure on agriculture under the Second Plan devoted to community development and co-ops, but it achieved little either in increasing agricultural output or in minimising social conflict. The

[26] *Ibid.*

effective units of social organisation in most Indian villages were hierarchical in structure, based both vertically on patron–client relationships and interlinked markets for credit and labour, and horizontally on bonds of common social, ritual or economic status. As a result, group-based and interest-based competition for resources within the village undermined the integrative purpose of the CD programme, and also weakened the impact of village-level service co-operatives and the new institutions of *panchayati raj* (village administration) that the planners hoped would be the instruments of a wholesale reorganisation of rural life.

By the mid 1950s the radical proposals for fundamental changes in agricultural management embodied in the First Plan were dead. No legislation enabling the promotion of Co-operative Village Management had yet been passed in any state, no registration system for 'economic' farms had been set up, and fewer than 1,500 co-operatives had been formed by the end of the Plan period. Land reform legislation had been directed at the primary aim of removing intermediaries between the cultivator and the state, but many tenants had not yet achieved security of tenure or regulated rents. In states where there had been a zamindari system in force, the home-farm lands of intermediaries were still let out to tenants-at-will, and cultivators with permanent rights (tenants-in-chief) were also able to lease out to sub-tenants and sharecroppers. Few of these subordinate cultivators acquired security of tenure, and their rents could still be oppressive. Problems of sub-tenancy and sharecropping existed in ryotwari areas, too, where a good deal of the land was also leased out by rent-receivers and superior cultivators to under-tenants who still had no security of tenure or regulated rents in the early 1950s. The prospect of tenants acquiring rights had led to their eviction in many places: in Bombay the introduction of new laws to protect subordinate tenancies in 1948 led to a decline in the number of such tenancies by 20 per cent over the next few years; in Hyderabad the dispossession of tenants on a large scale took place after the passing of protective legislation in 1950 – between 1949 and 1953 the number of protected sub-tenants in the state fell by 57 per cent. Much of the land taken over for personal cultivation by landowners was then leased back to the former tenants on a crop-sharing basis. In some Uttar Pradesh villages as much as one-third of the land held under occupancy tenancies that in theory allowed no sub-letting was in fact cultivated by labourers and sharecroppers who had no tenancy rights in law.[27]

[27] V. M. Dandekar, 'A Review of the Land Reform Studies Sponsored by the Research Programmes Committee of the Planning Commission', *Artha Vijnana*, 4, 4, 1962; Baljit Singh, *Next Step in Village India: A Study of Land Reforms and Group Dynamics*, London, 1961, p. 33.

Despite these difficulties, the creation of a peasant system of production by land redistribution was made the main plank of the government's programme to increase agricultural output and productivity and ensure social justice in the Second Plan. As the Planning Commission's Panel on Land Reforms stressed in 1956:

> It goes without saying that, other things being equal, a personally cultivated holding is likely to yield more than one cultivated through hired labour. The advantages to the State of a hard-working contented and prosperous peasantry working on the land are considerable. It is their purchasing power which will influence increased production of industrial goods, and thus help industrialisation. The ownership of land, besides conferring security and social status on its possession also provides an opportunity for self-employment and it should be an objective of land policy to increase this sector up to the limit where holdings become so small that these advantages begin to be counter-balanced by other disadvantages.[28]

Ceiling legislation was now to be the chief mechanism for spreading access to land. Limits to the size of individual land-holdings had been announced in principle in 1953, but detailed recommendations for legislation were not made until the Second Plan. These proposals were still very vague – the ceiling was to be fixed at about three times the size of a 'family holding', but it was not clear whether this meant an operational holding (a plough unit or work unit for an average family), or a parcel of land giving a certain level of income. Other problems were simply ignored, such as the redistribution of bullocks, seed and manure to the new small-holders, or their supply by a central agency.

The complexity of tenancy arrangements, and the inter-linking of the land market with the markets for agricultural capital and employment, would have made it very difficult, if not impossible, to create an autonomous peasantry in the Indian countryside by land ceiling legislation. Over the country as a whole, a ceiling of 20 acres would have released enough land in aggregate to allow minimum holdings of 2 acres, but with significant regional variations. In eastern India, for example, a ceiling of 7.5 acres would have been needed to provide a minimum holding of 1.5 acres.[29] Given the levels of infrastructure and investment available in the mid 1950s, holdings of around 7.5 to 10 acres were probably the minimum that would allow the efficient utilisation of capital and labour, and provide an adequate level of farm business income of about Rs 1,200

[28] Government of India, Planning Commission, *Second Five Year Plan*, p. 41.

[29] Raj Krishna, 'Agricultural Reform: The Debate on Ceilings', *Economic Development and Cultural Change*, 7, 2, 1959, pp. 305–8.

a year. One careful study concluded that 'at a size less than 5 acres … farms dwindle down to a level … where serious disincentives and disabilities get the better of farming',[30] and most farms fell well below this crucial figure. Various estimates of the time suggested that about 60 per cent of the operated holdings were of less than 5 acres, and a further 10 per cent less than 7.5 acres. More than half of the available land was farmed by those who directly operated holdings of more than 15 acres, which was above the ceiling of what could be worked satisfactorily as a 'peasant' holding with family labour and one pair of bullocks.

The data collected by the National Sample Survey for 1953–4 show that, despite land reform, tenancy arrangements were still widespread in the 1950s with about 20 per cent of cultivated land being rented out, and almost one-third of all the land farmed by those with less than 2.5 acres being held under some form of lease. According to the 1961 Census data, over half of those cultivators who farmed only leased land had holdings of less than 2.5 acres. Informal contracts were common, especially in eastern and central India, while over the country as a whole only about one-third of all tenants paid cash rents. Sharecropping was most widespread in West Bengal, where high population density, intensive labour inputs to agriculture and limited opportunities for substitution were most marked, and so sharecropping significantly reduced risks for both tenants and landlords.[31]

Despite their apparent enthusiasm for land ceilings the planners dodged these issues in the mid 1950s by leaving the details of further land reform to be decided by the states. This put a brake on ceiling legislation, which in most cases was delayed until the early 1960s, and which set initial maximum levels at generous quotas of 30 acres or more. Large land-holders had ample time and opportunity to exploit the many loopholes that remained in the ceiling legislation, especially by distributing nominal ownership of land among different members of the family. The pattern of land ownership and operated holdings in the early 1960s, given in table 4.6, makes clear that the vast bulk of both owned and operated holdings were less than 1 hectare (roughly 2.5 acres) in size. In the early 1970s, despite a further round of land ceiling measures, the 6 per cent of agricultural households with operational holdings of more than 15 acres still controlled 39 per cent of the land.[32]

[30] A. M. Khusro, 'Farm Size and Land Tenure in India', *Indian Economic Review*, New Series, 4, 1969, p. 133.

[31] K. N. Raj, 'Ownership and Distribution of Land', *Indian Economic Review*, New Series, 5, 1970; P. C. Joshi, 'Land Reform and Agrarian Change in India and Pakistan since 1947: II', *Journal of Peasant Studies*, 1, 2, 1974.

[32] Lloyd I. Rudolph and Susanne Hoeber Rudolph, *In Pursuit of Lakshmi: The Political Economy of the Indian State*, Chicago, 1987, pp. 337, 408–10.

Table 4.6 *Size distribution of operational and ownership holdings in India, 1961–1962*

| | Operational holdings | | | | Ownership holdings | | | |
|---|---|---|---|---|---|---|---|---|
| | Number of households | | Area | | Number of households | | Area | |
| Holding size (ha) | ('000s) | (%) | ('000s) | (%) | ('000s) | (%) | ('000s) | (%) |
| below 0.2 | 4 843 | 9.7 | 464 | 0.3 | 19 005 | 29.7 | 701 | 0.5 |
| 0.20–1.0 | 14 042 | 28.7 | 8 545 | 6.4 | 16 058 | 25.1 | 9 063 | 7.0 |
| 1.01–3.0 | 17 356 | 35.5 | 31 261 | 23.6 | 16 991 | 26.5 | 30 831 | 24.0 |
| 3.01–6.0 | 7 366 | 15.1 | 30 571 | 23.0 | 6 995 | 10.9 | 29 509 | 22.9 |
| 6.01–10.0 | 2 958 | 6.1 | 22 291 | 16.8 | 2 887 | 4.5 | 22 201 | 17.3 |
| 10.01–20 | 1 795 | 3.7 | 23 778 | 17.9 | 1 627 | 2.5 | 22 021 | 17.1 |
| above 20 | 514 | 1.1 | 15 776 | 11.9 | 437 | 0.7 | 14 317 | 11.1 |
| Total | 48 874 | 100.0 | 132 686 | 100.0 | 64 000 | 100.0 | 128 643 | 100.0 |

*Source:* Pramit Chaudhuri, *The Indian Economy: Poverty and Development*, London, 1978, table 1.

Throughout the 1950s the planners assumed that the main constraints on agricultural development were distortions in the reward structure for rural enterprise. The existing technology was thought adequate to increase productivity; all that was needed was to widen access to it. By the end of the Second Plan experts on the agrarian economy were coming to the view that Indian peasants were by nature profit-seeking farmers whose crop-patterns and demand for investment were broadly responsive to the prices they were paid for their output. Residual exploitation by intermediaries such as moneylenders, landlords and traders, who stood between the cultivator and the market distorting production by creaming off the profits of farming through high interest rates, rents and price mark-ups, was now seen as the main factor that depressed farm-gate returns, and so diminished cultivators' responsiveness to the opportunities of further investment. The solution to these problems was to create anew the community-based institutions, especially co-operatives, that would secure access to markets, credit and land at much cheaper rates. This was the rationale behind the CD programme, and the advocacy of producer co-ops and service co-ops for credit and marketing.

Co-operatives still had an important place in planning for agriculture, but the Second Plan marked a significant retreat from the proposals for corporate agricultural management that had been set out in 1952. It suggested that co-operative farming with all village lands held in common was still probably the only long-term solution to the problem of deficit cultivators and landless labour, but virtually admitted that this policy could not be implemented in practice. Instead, the planners hoped that land ceiling legislation would redistribute as much land as possible in economic holdings, and thus reveal the amount of residual underemployed rural labour that would still have to be absorbed. The Third Plan, published in 1961, avoided offering any specific solution to the problems of uneconomic holdings. Agricultural development was now to be achieved entirely by the CD programme, by service co-operatives, by the growth of rural industry and by the implementation of existing land reforms. It was now argued simply that land ceiling legislation and tenancy reform would lead to the abolition of landlords and 'bring tenants into direct relation with the State' to establish 'an agrarian economy based predominantly on peasant ownership'. This would 'give the tiller of the soil his rightful place in the agrarian system and … provide him with fuller incentives for increasing agricultural production'.[33]

The issue of collectivisation surfaced for the last time in early 1959, when the annual Congress session at Nagpur passed a resolution declaring that India's 'future agrarian pattern' was to be 'co-operative joint farming'.[34] The resolution proposed that village lands be pooled, although peasant families would retain nominal property rights, and would be paid ownership dividends as well as returns for work done. These arrangements were to be in place within three years. In the meantime service co-operatives in credit, marketing and distribution were to be started and state trading in agricultural produce increased. State governments were required to complete legislation within the year to remove all remaining intermediaries and to fix land ceilings at around 30 acres. The resulting surplus was to be handed over to the village *panchayat* to be administered as joint farms by the landless. Yet, despite its bold rhetoric, the Nagpur resolution had little effect. Although it had been passed unanimously out of deference to Nehru's leadership, the programme it outlined was wildly ambitious, and provoked a major political storm inside the Congress and in Parliament. This coincided with the Chinese suppression of the Tibetan revolt and encroachments on the Indian border, which led to a reaction against the Maoist model on which the joint farming scheme was explicitly based. In March both the Congress Working Committee and the Lok Sabha passed

[33] Government of India, Planning Commission, *Third Five Year Plan*, Delhi, 1961, pp. 177–8.
[34] Quoted in Frankel, *India's Political Economy*, p. 162.

resolutions declaring service co-operatives alone to be the main focus of policy, and removing the strict timetable outlined at Nagpur.

Co-operative societies remained an important feature of the Indian rural economy during the 1950s and early 1960s, but they could never achieve the goals assigned to them by the planners. Nominal membership of primary societies rose from 4.4 million in 1951–2 to about 17 million by 1960–1, and the share of rural credit supplied by co-ops and other government agencies increased from about 6 per cent in 1951 to over 20 per cent by the mid 1960s. By 1971 co-ops and other agencies supplied a quarter of agricultural credit, just over half as much as that supplied by rural moneylenders.[35] However, the co-ops were less effective as instruments for social justice or for increasing capital investment in agriculture than these figures would suggest. The most effective co-ops, such as the Kaira District Milk Co-operative, depended on community activists as leaders, but in their absence members of the local bureaucracy were put in charge in most places. The management provided by officials was often inadequate, especially in enforcing payment, devising loan policies and linking up credit and marketing arrangements. Officials relied extensively on the local elite for advice and assistance, and so in practice most co-ops in the 1950s and 1960s were controlled by the larger farmers who already dominated the private credit market, and who often used the public institutions to subsidise their operations in the private sector. Loan repayment rates were lowest among high-income cultivators who used local influence to bend the rules in their favour.

The credit co-ops were based on the assumption that the bulk of production loans for agricultural investment (as well as consumption loans to deficit producers) were supplied by monopolistic and collusive moneylenders who used their power to exploit farmers, and that alternative sources of credit would increase production because shortage of capital was an important factor in limiting the pace of technological advance. This was not the case. The market for loans to credit-worthy surplus farmers growing crops for market was fairly competitive in most parts of the country – for example, over 40 per cent of the production loans made in 1953–4 in the sample monitored by the Reserve Bank of India's All-India Rural Credit Survey were made at an interest rate of 12.5 per cent or below.[36] Co-ops certainly added to the pool of capital available to the credit-worthy, but they did not undercut the rates charged to

[35] Government of India, Planning Commission, *Third Five Year Plan*, p. 203; J. W. Mellor *et al.*, *Developing Rural India: Plan and Practice*, Ithaca, 1968, p. 35; Inderjit Singh, *The Great Ascent: The Rural Poor in South Asia*, World Bank/Johns Hopkins, Baltimore, 1990, table 4.3.

[36] Cited in Mellor *et al.*, *Developing Rural India*, p. 64.

substantial cultivators to any significant extent. It was the rural poor, including some small-holders, who faced exploitation from moneylenders, traders and surplus farmers, but the co-operatives were not well equipped to meet the needs of such marginal producers.

Where the co-ops of the 1950s did make credit available to surplus cultivators this did not increase investment, since the available technological base was not able to support capital-intensive agriculture. The loans were used to finance local trading and speculation, or were re-lent as consumption loans to poorer farmers at higher interest rates. Officials tried to spread the benefits of co-operative lending to small-holders directly by underwriting societies against possible losses incurred in lending to those with fewer assets, but this had little effect. Consumption loans did not increase the capital employed in agriculture – to change their farming patterns the rural poor needed more income and better access to employment and land rather than simply more credit. Similar problems affected the marketing co-ops as well; farmers with a freely marketable surplus enjoyed good competition, and competitive prices, for their produce from the private sector. The cultivators that private traders could most easily exploit were those that the co-operatives could not reach.

## CREATING THE 'GREEN REVOLUTION': AGRICULTURE IN THE 1960S

The next stage of agricultural policy-making was set against a series of problems in the production and distribution of foodgrains that forced the central government into a series of compromises over procurement and purchasing systems, and helped to confirm official identification of peasant cultivation as the foundation of rural society. Figure 4.1 highlights the problems of per capita foodgrain supply in the mid 1950s and mid 1960s. Agricultural output in 1954–5 and 1955–6 was certainly disappointing, falling by about 2 per cent in each season, and food prices, which had been pushed down by the bumper crop of 1953–4, began to rise once more. A poor monsoon in northern India in April 1957 damaged the wheat crop, which led to a fall of about 8 per cent in foodgrain production, and a further sharp rise in prices. In May 1957 the Planning Commission's Foodgrains Enquiry Committee recommended that the government establish a buffer-stock of foodgrains administered by an official Foodgrains Stabilisation Organisation, which would undertake purchases and sales of rice and wheat at controlled prices, using requisitions if necessary, and building up a state trading system through co-operatives in the process. The Committee counselled against relying on the price mechanism to

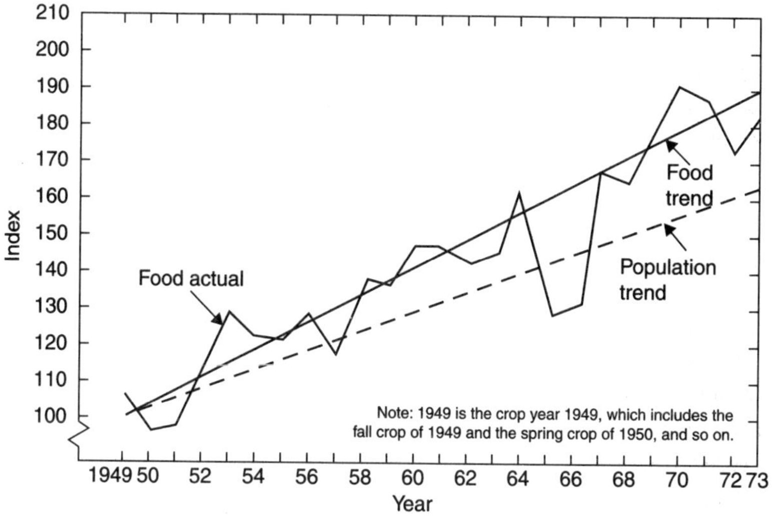


Figure 4.1 Growth of foodgrain output and population, 1949–1973

act as an incentive to farmers for greater food output, suggesting that prices should be determined by the needs of consumers, not producers. The response to this Planning Commission initiative was a spirited rearguard action by the food ministries at the centre and in the states that succeeded in blunting the new policy. In practice, the supply crisis was met by increasing food imports and opening 'fair-price' shops, although limited controls were also imposed to regionalise private trade by dividing up the country into a number of self-sufficient food zones for rice and wheat that matched up contiguous surplus and deficit states, banning private inter-zonal trade in grain and paddy, and leaving the major cities of Calcutta and Bombay to be supplied from overseas.

The success of these arrangements depended on continued food imports, which rose from 700,000 tonnes in 1955, to 1.4 million tonnes in 1956, to 3.7 million tonnes in 1957, and remained at that level, or higher, thereafter. In late 1957, continued rice imports were put in jeopardy by the foreign exchange shortage, and so the Government of India, and a number of state administrations, implemented procurement schemes that imposed maximum controlled prices for wholesale purchases and sales of locally grown rice, and used private traders and co-operatives as the purchasing agents. Some states also imposed a compulsory levy on a fixed proportion of the stocks held by wholesale traders and rice mills. However, this half-hearted attempt to reintroduce controls on foodgrains had little success. The volume of market intervention was small, with less than half a million tonnes of grain being procured through such official channels in 1957–8. Furthermore, the controls imposed were limited, being applied only to wholesale trading and, in some states, only to surplus districts, which left ample room for avoidance and smuggling. Faced by continued shortages in 1958–9 the state governments again licensed wholesale dealers and millers, and procured both rice and wheat through fixed-price offers or a levy: however, these measures were clearly ineffective, especially for wheat in which official dealings were only successful where government prices were favourable. The bumper harvest of 1959–60 changed the situation once again, and ended official attempts at supply through procurement until the much more severe crisis of the mid 1960s.

Despite the flurry of administrative interest in official purchasing schemes, government procurements supplied only 6 per cent of average annual demand for food between 1956 and 1960. Between 1955 and 1963 official purchases exceeded 1 per cent of domestic output only twice – in 1959 (2.34 per cent) and 1960 (1.66 per cent). Most of the food that the government had to distribute came from imports – 90 per cent on average from 1956–60, and 75 per cent for 1961–5 – but, even so, the official agencies had at their disposal less than half the amount of food that they would have needed to provide a basic subsidised ration to the poorest 25 per cent of the population.[37]

The food supply problems of the late 1950s triggered a wider debate about the fundamental principles of agrarian policy in the preparation of the Third Plan. Up to now the planners had treated agriculture as what has been termed a 'bargain sector',[38] which was thought to have large amounts of unexploited potential that could be released by diffusing existing technology and a small amount of capital investment, mostly in infrastructure. The Second Plan used a very low capital–output ratio for agriculture, underlining the point that the rural sector was expected to supply cheap food and cheap labour without technological transformation. These assumptions had been largely borne out by the facts.[39] Foodgrain output increased by about 30 per cent between 1949–50

[37] Raj Krishna, 'Government Operations in Foodgrains', reprinted in Pramit Chaudhuri, *Readings in Indian Agricultural Development*, London, 1972.

[38] Sukhamoy Chakravarty, *Development Planning: The Indian Experience*, Oxford, 1987, p. 94.

[39] The rural savings ratio averaged 2.3 per cent of rural income for 1951–60, and 2.5 per cent for 1961–5. Net capital formation (investment) in agriculture rose from 1.58 per cent of rural income in 1951–5, to 2.89 per cent in 1956–60, and 3.29 per cent in 1961–5, but the absolute amounts involved were small. In 1951 the total of net rural private investment was the equivalent of Rs 17 per rural household; in 1961 the figure was Rs 41 per household. In the early 1960s average annual private investment in agriculture ran at Rs 3 billion, less than half the total of private investment in the economy as a whole. Mellor, *New Economics*, p. 33; Mellor *et al.*, *Developing Rural India*, pp. 98, 111; J. W. Mellor, 'Food Production, Consumption and Development Strategy', in Robert E. B. Lucas and Gustav F. Papanek (eds.), *The Indian Economy: Recent Development and Future Prospects*, Delhi, 1988, p. 69.

and 1960–1, but almost all of this can be attributed to an intensification of labour use and an increase in the cultivated area of unirrigated land. Much of this new land was used to grow less productive but drought-resistant 'inferior' foodgrains such as pulses and millets. In some states, notably Rajasthan, West Bengal and Assam, and to a lesser extent Punjab, there were no yield increases at all, with the rate of growth of area under cultivation being equal to that of output, which suggests that much of the land brought under the plough in the 1950s was marginal. Only 9 per cent of the increased output was due to fertiliser use, and only 17 per cent to the expansion of irrigation. By 1961 less than one-fifth of the cultivated area was irrigated, mostly from publicly funded projects.[40]

The Third Plan paid more attention to agriculture than had its predecessors, although it proposed only a modest increase in public investment, from 11.3 per cent of total outlay to 14 per cent. The actual increase was even lower, from 11.7 per cent of total plan expenditure for 1956–61 to 12.7 per cent for 1961–6, while expenditure on irrigation decreased from 9.2 per cent to 7.8 per cent of the total.[41] The Plan aimed at a 30 per cent increase in agricultural output, almost double the previous rate, to achieve self-sufficiency in food with a daily per capita availability of 17.5 oz (500 g).[42] This was to be achieved by greater capital intensity, particularly in the use of fertilisers and irrigation, to be supplied by private investment. The need to increase private investment in agriculture led to a renewed discussion about agricultural prices. During the Second Plan the authorities had used imports and food aid to keep the price of foodgrains (especially wheat) low in the interests of the consumer. Now, by contrast, the planners accepted that 'the farmer should have the necessary incentive to make these investments and to put in the larger effort', which required that 'the producer of foodgrains must get a reasonable return.' This was to be achieved by buffer stocks which could prevent prices falling below 'a reasonable minimum', and could also protect the consumer at times of shortage.[43] No hint was given as to what this 'reasonable minimum' level of prices might be, but it was not to be determined by market forces. While the Third Plan's discussion of land reform endorsed a peasant structure for rural society more unequivocally than before, price regulation and control still lay at the heart of its proposals for institutional reform to bolster public and co-operative agencies against private operators.

[40] Mellor, *New Economics*, p. 33; Mellor *et al.*, *Developing Rural India*, p. 98.
[41] Chakravarty, *Development Planning*, pp. 94–5; Balasubramanyam, *Economy of India*, p. 80.
[42] Government of India, Planning Commission, *Third Five Year Plan*, pp. 61, 63.
[43] *Ibid.*, pp. 130–1.

In 1959 a more far-reaching scheme to stimulate production had been proposed to the government by a group of foreign and Indian experts organised by the Ford Foundation. The *Report on India's Food Crisis and Steps to Meet It*, which was published in April, argued that 'emergency food production' must be made 'the highest priority ... of Government'. It advocated a range of policy measures to boost production, including price incentives, improved inputs of irrigation and fertiliser, and a selective strategy to concentrate efforts in the most advanced areas.[44] By and large, the *Report* failed to convince Indian planners or academics, and it failed to change the terms of the Third Plan very much. However, at the Ford Foundation's prompting the government agreed to set up an intensive programme in seven districts as a pilot project (the ten-point Intensive Agricultural District Programme, or IADP) in which a package of inputs and techniques would be applied to increase food production. Well-developed, and therefore receptive, districts were selected, and the package was delivered to individual peasants, not village communities, although co-operatives were used to supply subsidised credit and fertiliser. The Ford Foundation met about one-third of the costs for the first five years.

The results of the IADP were far from conclusive. The targeted districts showed some increase in production, but these were little different from neighbouring areas. In practice, the Programme concentrated almost exclusively on chemical fertilisers, and failed to supply either improved seed or pesticides; crucially, the problems of water management were ignored. The package that the IADP managed to deliver was very similar to that which the most productive Indian farmers had already discovered for themselves. The Ford Foundation's own evaluation was that at current prices with expected risks and rates of return, the use of fertiliser was only 'marginally profitable'. Perhaps the most significant effect of the programme was that an influential body of aid suppliers and agricultural economists became persuaded that it had 'established beyond doubt that ... once the Indian farmer is convinced ... that a particular innovation is both useful and within his means, he is as prompt as farmers in any other part of the world to accept it'.[45] This gave the green light for the transformation of traditional agriculture, although it was to take another major food supply crisis, culminating in the Bihar famine of the mid 1960s, before anything much would be done.

[44] Quoted in George Rosen, *Western Economists and Eastern Societies: Agents of Change in South Asia 1950–1970*, New Delhi, 1985, p. 75.

[45] David Hopper (then a staff member of the Ford Foundation programme), quoted in *ibid.*, pp. 78–9.

## THE MANAGED ECONOMY UNDER STRAIN, 1965–1969

The Third Plan pushed the Indian economy along its established path in the early 1960s. Public investment, especially in heavy industry, was stepped up; agriculture was left to look after itself; potential shortages of foreign exchange and domestic resources were made good by foreign aid and deficit financing. The experience of the Second Plan showed that such a programme was feasible only with external support and good weather. In the mid 1960s these were not available. The Third Plan set a new goal of 'self-reliance' for the Indian economy – 'so that the requirements of further industrialisation can be met within a period of ten years or so mainly from the country's own resources'.[46] Ironically, India ended the plan period much more dependent on others than it had been at the beginning.

In the early years of the Plan a fairly high growth rate of 8 to 10 per cent per annum was maintained, but the resource base of food and foreign exchange was put under strain. Food imports, mostly as PL480 aid from the United States, rose from 3.5 million tonnes in 1961 to 7.5 million tonnes in 1965. The monsoon was good in 1964, which led to a spurt in agricultural output, but this was put into reverse the next year. In 1965–6 and 1966–7 there was a severe drought, with the monsoon of 1965–6 being probably the worst of the twentieth century. Foodgrain production fell by 27 per cent (from 89 million tonnes to 65 million tonnes) between 1964–5 and 1965–6, and rose only slightly out of this trough the next year. Food prices started to soar and, even with increased food imports in 1965–6, there were severe shortages. The poor harvest also eroded purchasing power, lowered tax revenue and savings, and pushed up industrial costs significantly. Foodgrain prices rose about 30 per cent relative to industrial prices between 1964–5 and 1967–8; the industrial sector, which had enjoyed an average annual growth rate of 7 per cent for the previous decade, stood still for two years.

These economic problems were exacerbated by a number of other difficulties. The border dispute with China, which led to war in 1962, damaged national confidence and pushed up defence spending. In 1963–4 current defence expenditure was budgeted at about Rs 7 million, more than twice as much as previously, equivalent to 40 per cent of central government expenditure, and defence spending over the rest of the Plan period was increased sharply as tensions with Pakistan escalated, culminating in the destructive war of August–September 1965. Jawaharlal Nehru's authority was seriously

[46] Government of India, Planning Commission, *Third Five Year Plan*, p. 48.

weakened by the China war and, although he was able to hold his rivals inside the Congress Party in check, the succession struggle began in earnest after the Prime Minister's stroke in January 1964. Nehru died, still in office, in May 1964, and was succeeded by Lal Bahadur Shastri, who was acceptable to conservative groups within the states. Shastri was Prime Minister for only twenty months (he died of a heart attack in January 1966), and was succeeded by Indira Gandhi, Nehru's daughter. Mrs Gandhi was brought to power as a compromise candidate who would follow the advice of the party bosses, although she very quickly carved out a much more independent role for herself following the defeat of many of her would-be patrons in the general election of 1967.

The making of economic policy during this period was dominated by the food crisis and by worsening relations with Pakistan, which led to a four-month war in September 1965. These events, in turn, pushed the Indian government into further reliance on outside assistance, especially for food aid, making their policies more vulnerable to American influence. American foreign policy had favoured India after the Sino-Indian war, providing military assistance and cutting off aid to Pakistan during the conflict of 1965–6. The key relationship remained food aid, with the United States shipping 10 million tonnes of surplus grain to India in 1965–6. When the crops failed for a second time in 1966 the Indian government again requested food aid. This time, however, the American administration was less receptive. American grain surpluses were heavily depleted, and the bilateral aid programme to India faced criticism in the US Congress, which refused to renew PL480 beyond June. President Johnson was also concerned by the critical line that the Indian government was taking over increased US involvement in Indo-China. Most importantly, the Johnson administration saw its opportunity to exert pressure on New Delhi to implement new economic policies that would favour private enterprise and foreign investment, especially in agriculture. To achieve this Johnson adopted a 'short-tether' policy, refusing to commit PL480 shipments more than one month in advance, and then only in response to urgent need and the adoption of a policy package of liberal reforms. The new policy was, in the words of John Lewis, the USAID administrator in New Delhi, one of 'specific aid offers contingent upon the institution of particular adjustments in indigenous rural policy'.[47]

The Johnson administration's 'short-tether' policy caused much resentment in New Delhi, and helped to push India into opposing American wants and interests in the region during the next decade. But over agricultural policy

[47] Quoted in Frankel, *India's Political Economy*, p. 286.

the American administration was knocking at a door that was already at least half open. The rise in food prices throughout the Third Plan period, and the crisis of 1965–7, pushed the Indian government down a new path to agricultural development, a path that became a highway with the coming of the 'green revolution' in Indian agriculture in the late 1960s. The food shortages, price increases and stagnant agricultural output of the early 1960s revived the debate inside the central government over the failings of agrarian policy. The Planning Commission argued that price rises and supply difficulties were caused by hoarding by large farmers and traders, and urged an extension of the state trading system, plus strict controls and rationing, to force out the surplus. The Ministry of Agriculture saw the long-term solution in increasing production by investment in fertilisers and other inputs, which required price incentives, a switch in the government's investment priorities, and competition between state and private trading agencies. The result was a compromise arrangement proposed in the *Foodgrains Policy Committee Report* of June 1964, which maintained the procurement scheme based on zoning and support prices, but set the guaranteed minimum price for farmers at a much higher level than previously. The dominant position of the Planning Commission in the making of economic policy was severely undermined by Nehru's death. Shastri distanced himself from extreme centralisation in policy-making, removing the unlimited tenure of Planning Commission members, and establishing a separate Prime Minister's secretariat and an independent National Planning Council to give access to alternative expert advice.

Central government still intended to control the food crisis by increased regulation, but in the winter of 1964–5 Shastri and his new Food and Agriculture Minister, C. Subramaniam, lost control of events. By October 1964 famine seemed likely in Kerala and the Union Government moved to tighten up the procurement system, impose a rigid price-control and rationing system, and give local officials wide powers to police the activities of foodgrain traders. At this point, however, the chief ministers of the state governments rebelled, and informed New Delhi that its procurement prices were unrealistic. Surplus states resisted pressure for stocks to be put into the public distribution system, and the anti-hoarding legislation was broadly ignored. As a result the public distribution system had to rely once more on imports, and throughout the period of scarcity over 70 per cent of the government's food stocks came from overseas. Imports represented 11.5 per cent of total foodgrain availability in India over the 3 years from 1964–5 to 1967–8, with PL480 grain about two-thirds of the total in 1964–5 and 1965–6 and a half of the total in 1967–8.

By the end of 1965 the Indian authorities were aware that future planning faced severe constraints, especially over foreign aid. American aid agencies were already committed to the benefits of new technology for raising food production, and a World Bank report on India in October followed the same line. Foreign experts, and the Indian Ministry of Food and Agriculture, now argued strongly that India's problems could only be solved by the use of new high-yielding varieties of wheat and rice – the 'miracle' plants developed in Mexico and the Philippines that in theory could give yields twice and three times as large as traditional varieties, which were already being tested and adapted to local conditions at research stations in India. This, in turn, required much greater levels of investment in irrigation and in fertilisers and pesticides, which carried a high cost in foreign exchange.

The mid 1960s represented a watershed in the economic history of independent India, with major agricultural and industrial difficulties leading to fundamental changes in policy and the distribution of public investment between agriculture and industry. Government attempts to formulate the next Five Year Plan collapsed late in 1965, although discussions over the content of a Fourth Plan continued until the end of 1966. In its place a series of annual plans – little more than budgetary exercises – were drawn up between 1966 and 1969. The military commitments, economic difficulties and political uncertainties of the mid 1960s made it too difficult to confront the resource constraint of domestic savings and foreign exchange that had appeared by the end of the Third Plan. Any further large-scale public investment in industry and infrastructure would require a broadening of the tax base, with at least a quarter of the new resources to come from agricultural incomes, and a considerable increase in foreign aid. Raising such sums was simply not feasible in the circumstances: instead an IMF loan and new American aid commitments were provided in 1966 and 1967 to fund a programme of capital investment in intensive agricultural techniques. In return, the Indian government had to agree to devalue the rupee, liberalise the import control regime, allow foreign firms to invest in the fertiliser industry on favourable terms and commit itself to new policies on agriculture.

During the 3-year 'plan holiday' of 1965–6 to 1968–9 expenditure on agriculture rose to 25 per cent of the total outlay, with a further 11 per cent being spent on irrigation schemes. Inorganic fertiliser use increased sharply in the late 1960s, doubling from 773,000 tonnes in the boom year of 1964–5 to 1.53 million tonnes in 1967–8, and rising steadily thereafter to around 2.7 million tonnes in the early 1970s. Public expenditure on irrigation averaged Rs 3.32 billion a year between 1965–6 and 1968–9, and Rs 4.82 billion a year under the Fourth Plan of 1969–74, compared to Rs 2.05 billion a year during the Third Plan. Government grants for farmers to implement minor irrigation schemes of their own became particularly important. About one-quarter of all public spending on irrigation was now made in this way and the number of mechanised pump sets quadrupled between 1966 and 1972. By the early 1970s high-yielding varieties (HYVs) of foodgrains were being grown on almost half of the irrigated land in India, with about two-thirds of all farmers with irrigated land making some use of them. The new varieties could increase yields by almost four times for wheat, and more than twice for rice and maize. Over half of the increase in foodgrain output between 1960–1 and 1970–1 was the result of increased fertiliser use, with a further quarter attributable to the expansion in irrigation. The cultivated area of unirrigated land contracted during this decade. By 1972 a third of the total stock of agricultural equipment (valued at Rs 20.72 million at 1960–1 prices) was in irrigation equipment, almost all of it mechanised.[48]

Despite the impression of fundamental change that such figures give, there was at this stage rather less to the green revolution in India than met the eye. The spread of HYVs was inhibited in the 1970s by shortages of credit and irrigation facilities; the higher costs and greater risks attached to the new technology limited its benefits in practice. The new varieties were less drought-tolerant and disease resistant than traditional ones; imported strains of rice adapted poorly in many parts of the country, and hybrid strains of bajra (millet) fell victim to mildew. The world recession, oil-price shock and energy crisis of the early 1970s put up the cost of inputs; the increase in fertiliser consumption slowed markedly in 1972–4, and declined in 1974–5.[49] Credit and irrigation shortages were significant constraints on the use of HYVs, especially for small farmers. In 1970–1 less than 30 per cent of the land cultivated in holdings of up to 7.5 acres was irrigated, and of the irrigated land one-third was unfertilised.[50] At the beginning of the 1970s the green revolution was still, in T. N. Srinivasan's phrase, a 'wheat revolution',[51] and worked

[48] These data are taken from Balasubramanyam, *Economy of India*, pp. 80, 104; Mellor, 'Food Production', table 3.3; S. D. Sawant, 'Irrigation and Water Use', in M. L. Dantwala *et al.*, *Indian Agricultural Development since Independence*, Indian Society for Agricultural Economics, New Delhi, 1986, p. 115; D. S. Sidhu and A. J. Singh, 'Technological Change in Indian Agriculture', in Dantwala *et al.*, *Indian Agricultural Development*, pp. 145, 149; M. Prahladachar, 'Income Distribution Effects of the Green Revolution in India: A Review of the Empirical Evidence', *World Development*, 11, 11, 1983, pp. 931–2; Raj Krishna and G. S. Raychaudhuri, 'Trends in Rural Savings and Capital Formation in India, 1950–51 to 1973–74', *Economic Development and Cultural Change*, 30, 2, 1982, pp. 291–3.

[49] Sidhu and Singh, 'Technological Change in Indian Agriculture', pp.145–7.

[50] Singh, *The Great Ascent*, tables 4–8, 5–7.

[51] Quoted in Chaudhuri, *Indian Economy*, p. 124.

as intended only in the particular conditions of north-western India (Punjab, Haryana and Western Uttar Pradesh). Installing tube wells to provide secure irrigation, the key investment required to raise agricultural output, required operational holdings of about 3 hectares, which were beyond the reach of most cultivators, especially in rice-producing areas. Foodgrain production increased sharply in 1969 and 1971, but this rate was not sustained and output declined in 1971–3 (affected by serious drought) and 1974–5. Over the 1970s annual growth rates in production and yield for all food crops other than wheat were below the levels that had been achieved between 1949–50 and 1964–5.[52]

Perhaps the most significant aspect of the green revolution in India was the new attitude towards rural society and economic development that it signalled. Under Subramaniam's leadership the new strategy took a fresh line on two important issues – pricing policy and selectivity. The prices fixed by the central government procurement system for wheat and rice were well above the costs of production, to encourage investment rather than subsidise. The prices offered by state government agencies were often higher still. In providing inputs the government adopted the strategy of 'betting on the strong' – of concentrating seeds, technology, irrigation and fertilisers in an integrated package in the areas where the returns would be highest. As Pitamber Pant, one of the most influential members of the Planning Commission, admitted in 1969, increasing agricultural growth was more important in the short run than egalitarian reforms such as a radical redistribution of land.[53] The result was to tip the terms of trade between industry and agriculture firmly in favour of the latter by as much as 50 per cent between 1963–4 and 1973–4, at a time when direct agricultural taxes amounted to less than 2 per cent of the value of production.[54] The social effects of these policies were widely discussed: Wolf Ladejinsky, one of the chief architects of US-sponsored land reform programmes in much of East Asia, commented in 1970 on the dangers in India of the 'polarization of income between the rich and the poor farmers and the erosion of the position of the tenantry which has been accentuated by the increases in productivity.'[55]

[52] Mellor, 'Food Production', table 3.1; Balasubramanyam, *Economy of India*, p. 84.

[53] E. A. G. Robinson and M. Kidron (eds.), *Economic Development in South Asia*, London, 1970, p. 150.

[54] Balasubramanyam, *Economy of India*, pp. 97–9; Jagdish N. Bhagwati and Sukhamoy Chakravarty, 'Contributions to Indian Economic Analysis: A Survey', *American Economic Review*, 59, 4, Part 2, Supplement, 1969, pp. 48–9; R. Thamarajakshi, 'Intersectoral Terms of Trade and Marketed Surplus of Agricultural Produce, 1951–2 to 1965–6', reprinted in Chaudhuri, *Readings in Indian Agricultural Development*.

[55] Wolf Ladejinsky, 'Ironies of India's Green Revolution', *Foreign Affairs*, 48, 4 (July 1970), p. 758.

## CONTESTING CENTRAL CONTROL, 1969–1980

In the late 1960s the management of the Indian economy seemed briefly to enter a distinctively different phase. Under pressure from the states, Indira Gandhi disbanded the old-style Planning Commission in August 1966; it was reconstructed a year later with considerably weakened powers, giving much greater decentralised autonomy in economic policy. The National Development Council, made up of the chief ministers of the state governments, was now moved to the apex of the planning process, and in 1968 state governments were given block loans and grants for development that they could then spend virtually as they wished. In the rural sector the states were, in the Planning Commission's words, now 'free to formulate their own plans on the basis of their own appreciation of the local problems, priorities, potentials and past experience'.[56] Liberalisation for industry had begun with the devaluation in 1966, and was extended to the lowering of import barriers and the removal of some licensing restrictions on a number of industries with heavy private-sector investment.

However, this weakness of central control did not last long. Licensing regulations and quantitative restrictions on imports were back in place by the end of the decade. The Congress split of 1969 gave Mrs Gandhi the opportunity to create a new focus for power at the centre around her own office and personality. In 1971 her Congress (R) Party won a decisive majority in the general election thanks to an opportunistic campaign based on the populist slogan of 'Garibi hatao' ('Get rid of poverty'), and this was cemented by a crushing victory in the state elections in 1972 bolstered by success in the war with Pakistan to liberate Bangladesh. Mrs Gandhi's position was now unassailable, and her ability to draw power into the hands of herself and a few favoured allies unchecked. As a consequence the Planning Commission was given a larger role in economic management once more in 1972, and policy shifted to a renewed initiative to force the states to implement distributive land reform. While this was unsuccessful, it signalled that the central government was back in business, and New Delhi continued to play a major interventionist role in the economic system so long as Mrs Gandhi remained Prime Minister.

The short-lived experiment with liberalisation in import licensing and export promotion that had accompanied the devaluation of the rupee in 1966 now ended.[57] In 1970 a new Industrial Licensing Policy was announced that

[56] Planning Commission, 'Preparation of State Plans: An Appraisal of the 4th Plan Experience', quoted in Frankel, *India's Political Economy*, p. 313.

[57] The economic policies of the late 1960s and early 1970s are conveniently summarised in Arvind Panagariya, *India: The Emerging Giant*, Oxford, 2008, pp. 52–5, 59–65, 68–70.

strictly limited the sectors of the economy in which large private companies could invest, restricting them for the most part to heavy industry requiring very substantial amounts of capital. The 'core sector' of industries most necessary for industrial growth was largely reserved for state enterprise; applications for licences for new plant from smaller firms were to be given preference elsewhere in the private sector, and a discrete set of opportunities in labour-intensive industries were reserved for 'small-scale' enterprises. When public-sector financial institutions made a substantial contribution to a new private-sector enterprise, their loans and debentures were to be converted to equity shares so that government could take an active role in the management of the new enterprise. The aim was to ensure joint control of enterprises requiring an investment of more than Rs 50 million.[58] Further restrictions on industrial licensing were introduced in 1973. Industrial licences and access to foreign exchange were now imposed stringently: a list of products that could be imported was issued every six months, with approved users and quantities identified for each permitted commodity. While the entry of new firms into many business sectors was being more tightly regulated, the exit of failing firms was also restricted. The closure of any industrial plant was seen as a social loss, and so changes in the licensing regulations sought to tackle the problem of so-called 'sick' companies, keeping them open by subsidised loans from state agencies, or by takeover by the public sector, or merger with other private firms on preferential terms.[59]

In her approach to economic policy, Indira Gandhi saw a need to assert herself against the old Congress Party bosses from whom she had broken away in 1967, and she took up various populist and left-wing causes to achieve this. Perhaps the most significant of these was the nationalisation of the largest commercial banks by ordinance in July 1969, ratified by the Lok Sabha within two weeks: the immediate result of this move was to force Morarji Desai, Indira Gandhi's most implacable opponent in the Cabinet, to resign as Finance Minister. The rationale of this decision was to extend banking facilities to rural areas, to mobilise savings, extend credit and direct lending to designated 'priority' (under-resourced) sectors.[60] This programme of institutional

[58] The Life Insurance Corporation of India, which had been set up as a nationalised institution by merging a large number of private firms in 1956, was the largest single investor in Indian industry. General insurance business was also nationalised as an effective monopoly in 1972.

[59] A 'sick' company was defined as one that has accumulated losses equal to or exceeding its entire net worth. In 1985 the Sick Industrial Companies (Special Provisions) Act created a Board of Industrial and Financial Restructuring to rescue or close sick companies: by 2004 almost 5,000 private companies and 200 public-sector units were in the care of this board.

[60] The Banking Companies (Acquisition and Transfer of Undertaking) Act nationalised the 14 commercial banks with deposits of more than Rs 500 million. The largest Indian bank, the State Bank

diversification brought some economic benefits over time, but the immediate rewards were political: as one study of the episode has concluded, 'the new banking policy had a great importance in making Indira Gandhi's victory in the 1971 general election possible'.[61]

Indira Gandhi's populist political strategy also led her to attack the apparent monopoly of established domestic and foreign firms over large parts of the economy. A number of government enquiries since the mid 1960s had reported that the licensing system for imports and capital issues restricted competition and created insurmountable barriers to entry for new, smaller firms. This process culminated in the report of the Industrial Licensing Committee (1969), which led on to the Monopolies and Restrictive Trade Practices (MRTP) Act passed the same year to prevent the concentration of economic power to the common detriment and the spread of unfair trade practices. This legislation identified so-called MRTP Companies with gross assets of over Rs 200 million and/or market share of over 33 per cent, which were to be subject to tight scrutiny and regulation over further expansion, acquisition or merger in an atmosphere of official hostility to big business. Controls over foreign capital had tightened during the exchange crisis of the late 1960s, with high-level political approval required for major investment projects in which foreign firms had more than a 40 per cent share of equity, and which limited the product range for which imports of foreign capital and technology could be approved.

In 1973 the Foreign Exchange Regulation Act (FERA) took this policy one stage further by requiring all branches and subsidiaries of multinational companies to dilute their equity share to 40 per cent. Some exceptions were allowed for those in core sectors or with large exports, but such companies were to be subject to additional restrictions. Further foreign acquisitions of Indian companies were banned, and collaborations between Indian and foreign firms were tightly controlled. The FERA regulations caused a considerable shake-out in the remnants of the British expatriate sector that still owned and managed companies in eastern India, especially in tea; those multinationals

of India (formerly Imperial Bank of India) had been nationalised in 1955; after 1969, 84 per cent of bank branches were in the public sector. There was a further round of bank nationalisation in 1980. Panagariya, *Emerging Giant*, pp. 69–70.

[61] Michelguglielmo Torri, 'Factional Politics and Economic Policy: The Case of India's Bank Nationalization', *Asian Survey*, 15, 12, 1975, p. 1095. The immediate rewards of this move were political, but there is evidence that improved access to financial institutions in rural areas contributed to the decisive rise in the savings rate in the late 1970s: Robin Burgess and Rohini Pande, 'Do Rural Banks Matter? Evidence from the Indian Social Banking Experiment', *American Economic Review*, 95, 3, 2005.

that saw a future for their operations in India adapted to the new rules, but the number of new foreign financial collaborations fell drastically over the course of the 1970s.[62]

Internal and external economic circumstances were inexorably pushing the Indian economy into crisis in the early 1970s. The oil-price shock of 1973 coincided with a prolonged drought that affected the output of both agriculture and industry. Production of foodgrains fell by 7.7 per cent in 1972–3 and wheat production fell further in 1973–4; public stocks were used up to meet the needs of the public distribution system; the open market price of foodgrains increased by 20 per cent between January 1972 and January 1973, which fuelled price inflation elsewhere in the economy.[63] The price that the state procurement system paid to farmers was known to be well above the costs of production, but every attempt to lower it was blocked by the chief ministers of the states acting on behalf of powerful rural interests. The official procurement system supplied more than 10 per cent of the demand for grain, and to meet these needs the central government nationalised the wheat trade in February 1973, banning private wholesalers, and authorising the Food Corporation of India to act as the sole agency in the market at the same price – Rs 76 per quintal – paid in previous years. The result was a suppliers' strike: only about 60 per cent of the grain required could be purchased, and surplus wheat changed hands on the black market at up to twice the official price.

As a consequence of these events, food riots in many parts of the country increased political turbulence; corruption and evasion by traders, officials and producers became common-place; smaller farmers, who could not afford to store grain and so had to sell at the official price, protested against compulsory procurement. The outcome has been described as 'the taming of the Indian state':[64] in July the government decided against nationalising the trade in rice; the procurement price for wheat was raised to Rs 105 per quintal in February 1974, and this became the minimum price thereafter. Private wholesale trade in wheat was legalised again early in 1974, although it was still difficult to supply enough food to the poor through fair-price shops; public procurements

[62] The most famous victims of FERA and other controls on foreign companies were IBM and Coca Cola, both of which left India after government pressure in the late 1970s. Arguably these events provided valuable opportunities for local entrepreneurs to expand into the vacant product ranges.

[63] Ashutosh Varneshey, *Democracy, Development and the Countryside: Urban–Rural Struggles in India*, Cambridge, 1995, pp. 93–101. Foodgrain prices rose by a further 29 per cent in 1973–4, and the wholesale price index by 30 per cent.

[64] *Ibid.*, p. 96.

of food had to be supplemented by substantial imports from 1973 to 1976.[65] These problems helped to sustain the protest movement in Gujarat, Bihar and elsewhere that eventually led to the President's declaration of a state of emergency in India in June 1975, allowing Mrs Gandhi to rule by decree and suspending parliamentary democracy and many civil liberties.

## MAINTAINING THE MANAGED ECONOMY, 1939–1980

Between the 1940s and the 1970s a particular type of economy emerged in India in which official planning and government economic management played a crucial part. By 1945 the colonial regime had abandoned all its traditional precepts of laissez-faire and minimal government; in the 1950s and 1960s Indian politicians and bureaucrats saw themselves as the chief agents of economic change and progress. State agencies took on a large role in the running of the economy since markets and private-sector economic institutions could not cope with the disruptions caused by depression, war and food shortages. In addition, both industry and agriculture depended for growth on subsidised inputs in circumstances in which the resources available for subsidisation were never sufficient. With both rural and urban sectors operating inside narrow boundaries drawn by the harsh realities of resource scarcity and market imperfections, economic opportunity became determined by links between systems of political, social and economic power. As the government's role in the economic system increased after 1939 the agencies of the Indian state adopted, with varying degrees of willingness, a mutually supportive alliance with dominant groups in towns and countryside to ensure political and social stability at the cost of structural rigidity and distributional inequality.

Many analysts of this process have focused on the symbiotic alliances that were initiated during the nationalist movement in the 1920s, 1930s and 1940s, and then consolidated in Independent India of the 1950s and 1960s: between the state; the 'dominant' or 'rich' surplus peasants who controlled the rural markets for land, capital and employment; and the urban capitalists in the private corporate industrial sector. The solidarity of rural groups in electoral politics was further cemented by the creation of caste vote-banks in the new universal electorate of the 1950s. The relationship between state power

[65] Mrs Gandhi admitted in April 1974 that the overwhelming need now was that 'grain must reach the people at reasonable prices and it does not matter who supplies the food-grains'; quoted in Wolf Ladejinsky, 'Wheat Procurement in 1974 and Related Matters', *World Development*, 3, 2 and 3, 1975, p. 93.

and the economic and social control of dominant peasants and urban capitalists was not always stable, however, since the interests of rural and urban magnates (known collectively by some analysts as the 'national bourgeoisie') frequently came into conflict with each other, and were rivals for a limited quantity of resources. Such instability limited the scope of economic reform in the 1960s, and encouraged greater centralisation of economic power after 1971, from which grew many of the economic tensions and political crises that overtook India in the 1970s.

While these interconnections between networks of economic, social and political power formed an important element of the political economy of India in the middle decades of the twentieth century, the obstacles to development that emerged in this period had far deeper roots. The economic history of India from the early 1920s to the late 1960s has a striking unity which the political transfer of power in 1947 disrupted only slightly. Over these fifty years or so the managers of the Indian economy were grappling with a coherent and cohesive set of structural problems, including a high sustained rate of population growth, a low level of agricultural growth (caused largely by the failure of productivity in the absence of technical change), a shortage of investment in infrastructure, problems of revenue-raising without regressive taxation, low demand-stimulation for basic wage goods, and endemic foreign exchange constraints (leading to major crises in the early 1920s, early 1930s, late 1940s, mid 1950s and late 1960s). Agricultural output probably grew less fast than population before Independence and not much faster than population afterwards, at least until the coming of new technology and investment policies after 1967. Foodgrain availability fell back to the level of the early 1950s in the difficult years of the mid 1960s and mid 1970s; although industrial output increased as a consequence of import-substitution, the proportion of the total labour-force employed in large-scale industry failed to grow significantly.

After 1947 the Indian government wrestled hard with the meagre inheritance of the colonial past. It adopted a deliberate and active policy of planning for industrial growth based on public-sector enterprises in the 1950s; it tried to create a dynamic peasant agriculture based on new technology and capital investment in the 1960s; it enjoyed a buffer against foreign exchange constraints in the form of the funds available from the sterling balances and international aid receipts. However, these assets and actions were not enough to break free from fundamental constraints. By the late 1960s international pressure, internal dissidence and the administration's incapacity to cope with poor monsoons had cut government policy adrift from its moorings. It seemed that the economy could not develop without active assistance from the state, but the state's ideology, political foundation and technical competence had all been found wanting. The renewed crisis caused by external and internal instability in the 1970s demonstrated the contradictions that lay at the heart of India's political economy, and pushed forward new forces and new solutions.

CHAPTER 5

# BREAKING THE MOULD? ECONOMIC GROWTH SINCE 1980

## INDIA'S GROWTH TRANSITION: WHEN AND WHY?

It is clear that something remarkable has happened to the Indian economy in the last thirty years or so. Economic growth has accelerated dramatically since 1980 and has been sustained without any serious interruptions, from an annual average of 3.4 per cent for 1960–80 to 5.8 per cent for 1980–2004, to 8.6 per cent for 2003–7, to 6.4 per cent for 2007–12. Output per capita and output per worker also accelerated sharply after 1980; total factor productivity, which had increased by about 0.3 per cent per annum between 1960 and 1980, grew at close to 2 per cent per annum in the following two decades.[1] At the same time, the established institutions for managing the economy, based on state regulation, the licensing of capacity and capital, the dominance of the public over the private sector, high barriers to entry and to trade, and strictly controlled interaction with the global business environment, have all changed fundamentally. Increased privatisation and active encouragement of foreign investment have led to a significant increase in private business enterprise, and a much larger share of trade in national income. These events have challenged conventional perceptions of India's economic history across the twentieth century and of its relationship to the international economy. The key data on the growth of GDP are presented in figure 5.1 and table 5.1.

The main outline of India's growth transition since 1980 is well known, but the key questions of why and when a decisive shift occurred have been widely debated, and remain heavily contested. While a number of econometric studies have sought to identify clear trend breaks in growth rates, other accounts have sought to link these to heroic changes in government policy. The sharp fall in GDP in 1979–80 that is apparent in figure 5.1 further complicates the

[1] For a convenient introduction to the key issues and literature, see the special issue of the *Oxford Review of Economic Policy*, 23, 2, 2007; and Barry Bosworth, Susan Collins and Arvind Virmani, 'Sources of Growth in the Indian Economy', *Brookings India Policy Forum*, 2006–07, *Volume 3*, New Delhi, 2007.

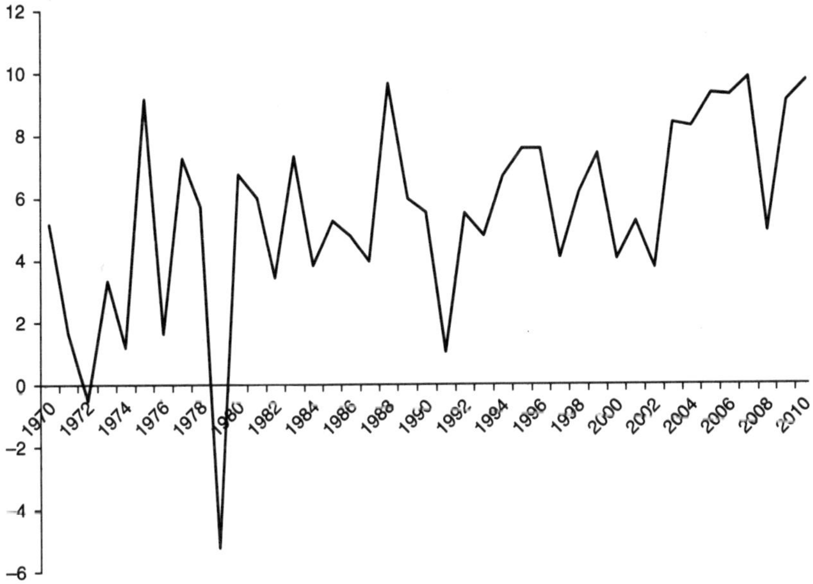


Figure 5.1 GDP percentage annual growth rate, 1970–2010

search for a trend break; the decisive shift to a higher growth rate may have occurred in the mid 1970s, rather than in the early 1980s. The economy had certainly been launched on a higher growth trend well before the liberalisation reforms of 1991, but it can be argued that any such change was not sustainable until the reforms of the 1990s had been implemented, as the instability of growth rates in 1987–91 demonstrated. The timing of any trend break is important for those analysts who seek to attribute sudden economic change to dramatic policies to liberalise the management of the economy by rolling back the state and freeing access to the market (hesitantly in the mid 1970s and mid 1980s, vigorously in the early 1990s, and with fluctuating intensity thereafter); or to a shift in attitudes at the top of the policy-making process in the 1980s that kick-started the growth process by giving incentives to existing large corporations to expand their activities and increase their profits. Given the difficulties in obtaining robust data, especially for the 'unorganised' economy of small-scale, unregulated production units where so much output and employment is generated, it may be unhelpful to expect too much precision in timing and definition here. As one recent study has warned, 'the discussion in the literature about the structural break takes place in the belief that it could offer clues about what policies led to the shift in the economy's growth rate.

Table 5.1 *GDP growth in constant (2004/2005) prices, actual and projected, 2005–2012*

| | 2005–6 | 2006–7 | 2007–8 | 2008–9 | 2009–10 | 2010–11 Revised | 2011–12 Projected |
|---|---|---|---|---|---|---|---|
| GDP at factor cost (Rs trillions) | 32.5 | 35.7 | 39.0 | 41.6 | 44.9 | 48.8 | 52.8 |
| Year-on-year rates of growth (%) | | | | | | | |
| Agriculture | 5.1 | 4.2 | 5.8 | –0.1 | 0.4 | 6.6 | 3.0 |
| Industry | 9.7 | 12.2 | 9.7 | 4.4 | 8.0 | 7.9 | 7.1 |
| Services | 11.0 | 10.1 | 10.3 | 10.1 | 10.1 | 9.4 | 10.0 |
| Annual growth rate of GDP | 7.8 | 7.8 | 7.6 | 5.0 | 6.2 | 6.8 | 6.4 |

*Source:* Advisory Council to the Prime Minister, *Economic Outlook 2011/12*, p. 5.

Such inference is problematic because statistical methods alone are unlikely to provide a precise timing.'[2]

The conventional account of India's 'economic miracle' dated to the 1990s has been neatly summarised by Montek Ahluwalia, who was one of its chief architects:

> India was a latecomer to economic reforms, embarking on the process in earnest only in 1991, in the wake of an exceptionally severe balance of payments crisis. The need for a policy shift had become evident much earlier, as many countries in east Asia achieved high growth and poverty reduction through policies that emphasized greater export orientation and encouragement of the private sector. India took some steps in this direction in the 1980s, but it was not until 1991 that the government signalled a systemic shift to a more open economy with greater reliance upon market forces, a larger role for the private sector including foreign investment, and a restructuring of the role of government.[3]

The stress in this narrative on market-based liberalisation and on encouraging foreign capital, as well as the linked assumption that wealth will trickle down

[2] Ashok Kotwal, Bharat Ramaswami and Wilima Wadhwa, 'Economic Liberalization and Indian Economic Growth: What's the Evidence?', *Journal of Economic Literature*, 49, 4, 2011, p. 1161; also Duke University Bureau for Research and Economic Analysis of Development (BREAD) Working Paper No. 294, May 2010, p. 10, at http://ipl.econ.duke.edu/bread/papers/working/294.pdf. All the internet sources cited in this chapter were accessed between November 2011 and February 2012.

[3] Montek S. Ahluwalia, 'Economic Reforms in India since 1991: Has Gradualism Worked?', *Journal of Economic Perspectives*, 16, 3, 2002, p. 67.

from the advanced sectors of the economy to the rural poor, has clear political implications about the restricted role that the state should play in achieving growth and ensuring economic and social justice in India. Such arguments have led those who see the need to defend continued state intervention to argue that the necessary foundation of India's recent rapid growth was laid in the 1980s, rather than the 1990s, by higher levels of public investment and some deregulation of trade and industrial policies. Some have argued that changes in government policy after 1980 led to a clear attitudinal shift in favour of 'pro-business' (not 'pro-market') policies; others have concluded that such actions were simply the result of personal corruption and political opportunism that inevitably led to unsustainable levels of internal borrowing and overseas debt, creating a new crisis that the reforms of the 1990s had to overcome.[4]

Under the governments of both Indira and Rajiv Gandhi (1980–4; 1984–9), bureaucratic controls on the industrial economy became less intrusive in some areas. Central government gave encouragement and patronage to a small group of established corporations, simplifying licensing legislation and weakening restrictions on monopolies, to allow them to expand operations and move into new areas of production, especially in partnership with foreign firms that provided advanced technology. At the same time, centrifugal political forces led to a decentralisation of economic power and some state-level governments adopted new policies to attract private investment, helped by the gradual dismantling of the old industrial licensing system that had used regional equity as one of the primary criteria guiding industrial investments. A new Industrial Policy Statement in 1980 to accompany the Sixth Five Year Plan

[4] As Atul Kohli put it, 'the recent acceleration of economic growth in India was more a function of the pro-business tilt of the Indian state [in the 1980s], and less a result of the post-1991 economic liberalisation' (Atul Kohli, 'Politics of Economic Growth in India, 1980–2005. Part II: The 1990s and Beyond', *Economic & Political Weekly* (hereafter *EPW*), 41, 14, 2006, p. 1368). Bradford De Long, 'India since Independence: An Analytical Growth Narrative', in Dani Rodrik (ed.), *In Search of Prosperity: Analytic Narratives on Economic Growth*, Princeton, 2003; and Dani Rodrik and Arvind Subramanian, 'From "Hindu Growth" to Productivity Surge: The Mystery of the Indian Growth Transition,' *IMF Staff Papers*, 52, 2, 2005 are two of a number of papers that make the case for the 1980s as the key decade. Arvind Panagariya provides a complex chronology, which labels the period 1981–8 as 'liberalization by stealth', with 1988–2006 as the 'triumph of liberalization' (Arvind Panagariya, *India: The Emerging Giant*, Oxford, 2008, pp. 78, 95). Exponents of the view that the 1991 reforms marked a crucial break include T. N. Srinivasan and S. Tendulkar, *Reintegrating India with the World Economy*, Washington, 2003. See also the debate between Srinivasan and Rodrik and Subramanian in 'From "Hindu Growth"'. Two accounts that see 1975 as the decisive year of attitudinal change are Jessica S. Wallack, 'Structural Breaks in Indian Macroeconomic Data', *EPW*, 38, 41, 2003; and Baldev R. Nayar, 'When Did the "Hindu" Rate of Growth End?', *EPW*, 41, 19, 2006.

(1980–5) stressed the need to promote competition in the domestic market, and encourage foreign investment in high-technology areas.

By the end of the decade this growth-spurt ran out of steam when heavy overseas borrowing and a growing balance-of-payments crisis caused a run on the rupee. The Gulf War of 1990–1 raised oil prices and curtailed remittances; the level of external debt, much of it short-term, was already very high, and reached 39 per cent of GDP in 1991–2. These balance-of-payments problems increased debt-servicing difficulties, and led to a collapse of creditor confidence (especially that of non-resident Indian (NRI) investors) in an economy further weakened by an overvalued rupee. By the end of 1990 India had drawn its permitted tranche of resources from the IMF: in January 1991, at a time of political crisis, a weak and failing government in New Delhi arranged an emergency loan from the IMF and sold reserve gold to raise immediate funds. A general election was called and the leader of the Congress Party, Rajiv Gandhi, was assassinated in May; by June capital flight was serious and the foreign exchange reserves allegedly held only enough cash to finance three weeks' worth of imports. In that month a minority Congress Party government was formed with P. V. Narashima Rao as Prime Minister, and Manmohan Singh, a professional economist and former Governor of the Reserve Bank, as Finance Minister.[5]

The new government immediately devalued the rupee onto a market-determined exchange rate, with a real depreciation of about 30 per cent, and then embarked on negotiations with the IMF to underwrite a very significant programme of economic reform.[6] As at the time of an earlier IMF loan in 1981, senior officials in New Delhi used the threat of an externally imposed structural adjustment programme to argue the case for internally generated economic reforms in advance of outside intervention, and received support from the business community. These events triggered a new, decisive round of liberalisation to eradicate the licence and quota regime that had resulted from the search for economic self-reliance since 1948.[7]

[5] Manmohan Singh had also been an economic adviser to Rajiv Gandhi.

[6] On the details of the 1991 crisis, see Valerie Cerra and Sweta Chaman Saxena, 'What Caused the 1991 Currency Crisis in India?', *IMF Staff Papers*, 49, 3, 2002; and Praveen K. Chaudhry, Vijay L. Kelkar and Vikash Yadav, 'The Evolution of "Homegrown Conditionality" in India: IMF Relations', *Journal of Development Studies*, 40, 6, 2004.

[7] A detailed narrative of the high politics of the reform process in the early 1990s will be found in Gurucharan Das, *India Unbound: A Personal Account of a Social and Economic Revolution*, New York, 2000. Jørgen Dige Petersen, 'Explaining Economic Liberalization in India: State and Society Perspectives', *World Development*, 28, 2, 2000; and Rahul Mukherji, 'India's Economic Transformation', in Sumit Ganguly and Rahul Mukherji (eds.), *India since 1980*, Cambridge, 2011 are two of many attempts to set these events in a wider context.

The 1991 programme was not quite as unprecedented as it seemed at first sight. By the mid 1980s a number of politicians and technocrats had already become convinced that Indian industry needed to be made more competitive and efficient, and that this meant creating genuine competition and limiting direct controls. I. G. Patel, one of the key figures in shaping economic policy in the late 1970s and early 1980s, claimed to speak for a consensus of policy-makers when he argued in 1987 that 'Indian industry must be subjected increasingly to the forces of competition, both internal and international, if it is to become more efficient and this requires that it be made increasingly free from the shackles of industrial licensing, import controls and other forms of control': he also argued for a 'virtual bonfire of the industrial licensing system'.[8] Extensive reforms to the licensing system were proposed in an official Industrial Policy Statement in 1990, but political instability meant that this was not taken forward.

Once the political necessity for reform had become unavoidable in 1991, central government moved quickly to establish a new industrial policy in which 'the bedrock of any such package of measures must be to let the entrepreneurs make investment decisions on the basis of their own commercial judgement ... Government policy and procedures must be geared to assisting entrepreneurs in their efforts.'[9] Lowering the barriers to trade was now a key objective. Tariff levels had begun to be lowered in the 1980s; they were now reduced further, especially for capital goods: by 2007 the peak rate of customs duty on non-agricultural goods had been reduced to 10 per cent. The rate of corporate taxation was lowered consistently from 45 per cent in 1992–3 to 30 per cent by 2005–6. A number of sectors, such as banking and telecommunications, where the public sector had previously had a monopoly, were opened up to private firms. Restrictions on foreign capital were also relaxed, especially in service industries, and in enterprises dedicated to the export market. Most important of all, perhaps, the established licensing policies which had regulated and directed industrial investment and constrained the expansion of established business groups (to combat the possibility of monopolies and restrictive practices, and to reserve activities for small-scale, handicraft producers) were steadily abandoned between 1985 and the early 2000s, and various restrictions on the banking sector were relaxed. About a third of core

[8] I. G. Patel, 'On Taking India into the Twenty-First Century (New Economic Policy in India)', *Modern Asian Studies*, 21, 2, 1987, pp. 215, 217.

[9] Government of India, *Statement on Industrial Policy (1991)*, para. 21: http://dipp.nic.in/English/Policies/Industrial_policy_statement.pdf.

industries were exempted from industrial licensing in the mid 1980s and most of the remainder in 1991.

The progress of the reform process after 1991 was somewhat erratic. The rhetoric of reform has been insistent, but the need to build political consensus and meet the demands of interest-groups have complicated the process of implementation. High inflation and political instability caused a lull in the liberalisation process from 1995 to 1999, but then the BJP-led National Democratic Alliance coalition (1999–2004) implemented further sweeping reforms at the all-India level. Major industries that had been reserved for the public sector since 1956, such as iron and steel, heavy plant and machinery, telecommunications and telecoms equipment, mineral oils, mining, air transport, and electricity generation and distribution, were now opened to private enterprise and foreign investment. The strategy for implementing reforms was characterised as 'gradualist' by its supporters: critics of this slow pace have argued that 'the process of change … was not so much gradualist as fitful and opportunistic'.[10] However, electoral politics in the states at this time were fought by offering tempting menus of public subsidies to powerful vested interests, especially in the countryside.

In 2004 the pace of institutional change slowed as the Congress and its left-wing allies in the United Progressive Alliance (UPA) won a national election campaign on a promise to ensure the economic and social inclusion of underprivileged members of society by defending the interests of '*aam admi*' (the common man). This result suggested that there were political rewards for rhetoric that championed the interests of the rural poor: one consequence was to hamper further privatisation, and to strengthen demands for retaining social protection for organised labour, established farmers and rural labour through regulation of the industrial labour market, rural employment schemes, and subsidies for food and fertiliser. The new government combined commitments to both liberalisation and social justice, with pragmatic decisions about political realities in dealing with its own supporters, and with populist state governments building their own power base. Politically, at any rate, this balancing act was successful: Congress and its allies won another election victory in 2009.

The cumulative effect of the reforms of the 1990s was to move India away from the ideal of self-reliance towards greater integration with the world economy; fewer controls on private business activity, especially in manufacturing; and substantially lower entry barriers to new firms, whether domestic or foreign. It was the combination of these reforms as a package of liberalisation over

[10] Ahluwalia, 'Economic Reforms', pp. 86–7.

twenty years from the mid 1980s to the early 2000s, rather than any single master-stroke of policy or attitudinal change, that created the opportunity for the rapid and sustained growth of recent times. For supporters of market-based reforms, India's current growth transition is still a work in progress, as one review of the data for the mid 2000s concluded:

> Our starting point is that increasing living standards in India will require a combination of increasing employment and raising labor productivity ... India needs to broaden the base of its economic growth through greater efforts to promote the expansion of the industrial sector – especially manufacturing – and to emphasize the creation of jobs as well as gains in TFP [total factor productivity] ... Expansion of both industry and services will draw workers out of agriculture. Thus, reforms should be directed towards making it easier to expand domestic production, and creating a more attractive location for foreign producers.[11]

## DUALISM OR DIVERGENCE? POVERTY, WELFARE AND GROWTH

Economic growth since the 1980s has meant that per capita national income began to rise steadily in the 1980s and 1990s, and took off to unprecedented levels during the first decade of the new millennium. Figure 5.2 presents the aggregate data, but there has been much debate about how the increase in national income has been distributed within the country. In simple terms, the growth of the economy since 1980 has had a beneficial effect on absolute levels of poverty across India. Critics of the reform process argued that the rate of poverty reduction was more rapid in the 1980s than in the 1990s, but best estimates now suggest that the incidence of poverty fell by just under one percentage point per year in both decades. Changes in the way consumption data was collected in 1999–2000 mean that we know relatively little about national poverty trends in the last decade, although it seems clear that the human development indicators have continued to improve somewhat.[12]

The World Bank has estimated that 456 million Indians (42 per cent of the total population) lived under the global poverty line of $1.25 per day (based on purchasing power parity) in 2005–6, down from 60 per cent of the population in 1981. The number of very poor people living below the World Bank's 'deprivation line' of $1 a day also fell – from 296 million in 1981 to 267 million

[11] Bosworth *et al.*, 'Sources of Growth in the Indian Economy', pp. 41–2.

[12] Angus Deaton and Valerie Kozel (eds.), *The Great Indian Poverty Debate*, New Delhi, 2005 contains a number of essays on the problems of measuring poverty in the 1990s, and others interpreting the evidence.

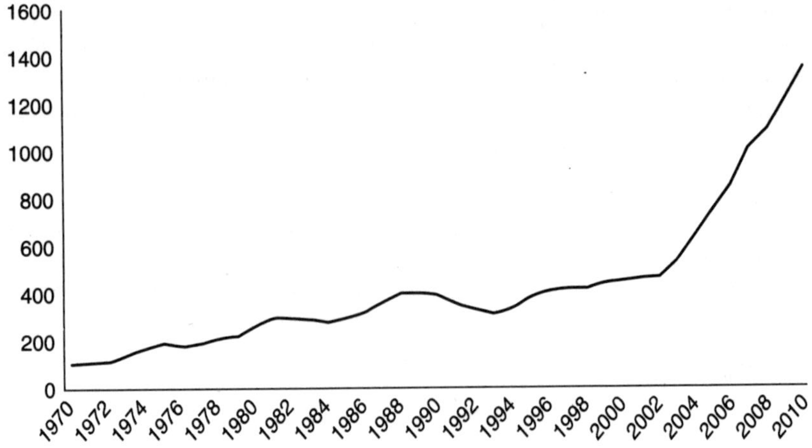


Figure 5.2 Gross national income per capita, 1970–2010

in 2005 – although the number living just above minimum subsistence levels probably increased.[13] The Indian Planning Commission used its own criteria to identify poverty levels, and estimated that 27.5 per cent of the population (301 million people) was living below the poverty line in 2004–5, down from 51.3 per cent in 1977–8, and 36 per cent in 1993–4. In 2009 the Indian authorities introduced a revised methodology for measuring poverty; using this method the official estimate of the number of the poor in India was recalculated at 45.3 per cent in 1993–4 and 37.2 per cent (410 million people) in 2004–5.[14]

An alternative study of the problems of the informal labour market concluded that 31 per cent of the population could be classified as 'extremely poor and poor' in 1993–4, with average daily per capita consumption of less than Rs 12 per day (equivalent to $1.6 PPP), and a further 51 per cent classified as 'marginal and vulnerable', with daily income of less Rs 20 ($2.2); in 2004–5 the equivalent figures were 22 per cent 'very poor and poor' and 58 per cent 'marginal and vulnerable'. Members of the less advantaged communities in the Indian population – Scheduled Castes and Scheduled Tribes, Other Backward Castes, and Muslims – were by far the most likely to find themselves in the poor and vulnerable income

13 World Bank India Country Overview data at www.worldbank.org/india.

14 The revised estimates were based on the recommendations of an Expert Group on Methodology for Estimation of Poverty (Tendulkar Committee). Government of India, Planning Commission, *Databook for Deputy Chairman, Planning Commission*, November 2011, table 31: 'Percentage and Number of Poor in India (73–74 to 04–05)', at http://planningcommission.nic.in/data/datatable/0211/data%2039.pdf.

categories, although between 10 and 20 per cent of these groups were identified as a 'creamy layer' enjoying 'middle to high' incomes.[15] There was also an important spatial dimension to the rate of poverty reduction: initial levels of rural development and human capital formation in any given region were crucial in determining the extent of any improvements in welfare; those parts of the country that were least able to take part in the growth-enhancing effects of the economic reforms were least likely to feel their poverty-reducing effects as well.[16]

India achieved the goal of food security in the 1970s. Since then, concerns have widened to improve economic access through employment creation programmes and providing direct access to food for vulnerable sections of the population. The average per capita availability of basic items of consumption has risen steadily since the 1970s for almost all categories, except coarse foodgrains, as shown by table 5.2. There was a consistent small increase in the supply of foodgrains in both the 1980s and the 1990s; however, wheat supplies increased much more than those of rice. Supply of non-foodgrains rose more rapidly, especially for sugar, edible oils and tea. From 2000 supply of all foodgrains declined, but that of higher value items such as sugar and man-made cloth continued to increase. It is worth noting that supplies of man-made cloth, manufactured from artificial fibres, increased much more rapidly than did the supply of cloth made from locally grown cotton.

The reduction in absolute poverty levels has not necessarily improved health outcomes and long-term nutritional status for the large proportion of the Indian population that suffers from impaired capabilities and poor life-chances, especially women and children. Access to consumption goods in the reforms period was largely determined by purchases in the market-place: returns for labour and the availability of employment have been the crucial means of obtaining subsistence.[17] While average life-expectancy has risen to 64 years, indicators of impaired life-chances such as female adult illiteracy (52 per cent) and child malnutrition (46 per cent of children below 5 years underweight) remain high in the 2000s. Access to public services – especially basic medical and public health facilities – is poor in many rural areas. There is also evidence that

[15] Arjun Sengupta, K. P. Kannan and G. Raveendra, 'India's Common People: Who Are They, How Many Are They and How Do They Live?' *EPW*, 43, 11, 2008, p. 52.

[16] Gaurav Datt and Martin Ravallion, 'Is India's Economic Growth Leaving the Poor Behind?', *Journal of Economic Perspectives*, 16, 3, 2002. There is a useful summary of the evidence in Raghav Jha, 'Economic Reforms and Human Development Indicators in India', *Asian Economic Policy Review*, 3, 2, 2008.

[17] Dipak Mazumdar and Sandip Sarkar, *Globalization, Labor Markets and Inequality in India*, Abingdon, 2008 provides a detailed study of the effects of growth on the labour market, poverty reduction and inequality across the country's major agro-ecological zones.

Table 5.2 *Average per capita availability of foodgrains and other articles of consumption,* 1971–2010

| | Rice (g) | Wheat (g) | Other cereals (g) | Total foodgrains (g) | Edible oil (kg) | Vanaspati (kg) | Sugar (kg) | Cotton cloth (m) | Man-made cloth (m) | Tea (g) |
|---|---|---|---|---|---|---|---|---|---|---|
| 1971–80 | 183.0 | 114.8 | 100.9 | 442.2 | 3.9 | 0.9 | 6.9 | 11.7 | 3.0 | 489.0 |
| 1981–90 | 198.1 | 143.3 | 83.2 | 464.2 | 5.3 | 1.2 | 11.0 | 13.9 | 6.3 | 560.7 |
| 1991–2000 | 209.3 | 162.6 | 67.7 | 470.1 | 7.1 | 1.1 | 14.2 | 15.0 | 12.7 | 653.0 |
| 2001–10 | 194.4 | 151.9 | 58.3 | 444.0 | 9.5 | 1.1 | 15.2 | 14.8 | 18.0 | 662.0 |
| Index numbers (1971–80 = 100) | | | | | | | | | | |
| 1981–90 | 108 | 125 | 82 | 105 | 136 | 129 | 159 | 119 | 210 | 115 |
| 1991–2000 | 114 | 142 | 67 | 106 | 182 | 118 | 206 | 128 | 423 | 134 |
| 2001–10 | 106 | 132 | 58 | 100 | 244 | 122 | 220 | 126 | 600 | 135 |

*Note:* Per capita availability of rice, wheat, other cereals (jower, bajra, maize, ragi, barley, and other cereals and millets) and total foodgrains (including gram and pulses) is the total per day; availability of other items is the total per year; totals include imports. Edible oil includes all vegetable oils, excluding those used in the manufacture of vanaspati.

*Source:* Government of India, Ministry of Agriculture, Department of Agriculture and Cooperation, Directorate of Economics and Statistics, *Agricultural Statistics at a Glance* 2010, tables 10.1, 10.3, at http://eands.dacnet.nic.in/latest_2006.htm.

income inequality increased in the 1990s, especially in rural areas; calculations of income distribution produced by the World Bank for 2005 showed that the bottom 10 per cent of the population secured less than 4 per cent of total income.[18] As the World Bank pointed out in 2011, 'to achieve a higher rate of poverty reduction, India will need to address the inequalities in opportunities that impede poor people from participating in the growth process'.[19]

Aggregate data for such a large and diverse country as India fail to distinguish states such as Kerala, which has rates of development of human resources as high as those in advanced areas in China, from states such as Bihar or Uttar Pradesh, which display gender inequalities in access to life-chances larger than those of most countries in sub-Saharan Africa. The concentrations of tribal populations, which have largely been excluded from the benefits of recent economic growth, within richer states such as Maharashtra and Gujarat pull down their overall aggregates. The degree of diversity between administrative units was increased by the creation of three new states out of the poorer areas of existing units in November 2000 – Chhattisgarh out of eastern Madhya Pradesh, Uttarakhand (known as Uttaranchal from 2000 until 2007) out of north-west Uttar Pradesh and Jharkhand out of the southern districts of Bihar. The new state boundaries, and their populations according to the 2011 Census, are shown on Map 5.1.

Growth rates in some poorer states have increased since the mid 2000s, partly as a result of public investment programmes by populist state governments seeking electoral support from the low income groups who thought themselves excluded from the growth transition. However, as table 5.3 makes clear, the income gap between the richer and the poorer states remains considerable; the seven poorest states – Bihar, Chhattisgarh, Jharkhand, Madhya Pradesh, Orissa, Rajasthan and Uttar Pradesh are still home to more than half of India's poor. Lower levels of labour productivity, education and skill-supply are characteristic of poorer states, regional disparities having widened during the reform period. Poorly performing states, which had lower rates of labour productivity in all sectors in the early 1990s, had failed to catch up by the mid 2000s; even in low-productivity areas of the economy that used predominantly unskilled labour, such as agriculture and hotel and construction services, 'backward' areas failed to make substantial improvements. States with diversified economies provided faster employment growth; laggard states diversified more slowly, and from a lower base.[20]

[18] World Bank, *World Development Indicators*, at http://data.worldbank.org/indicator.

[19] http://go.worldbank.org/51QB3OCFU0.

[20] K.V. Ramaswamy, 'Regional Dimension of Growth and Employment', tables 26.10, 26.11 and 26.12, in Uma Kapila (ed.), *Indian Economy since Independence*, 19th edn, New Delhi, 2008.

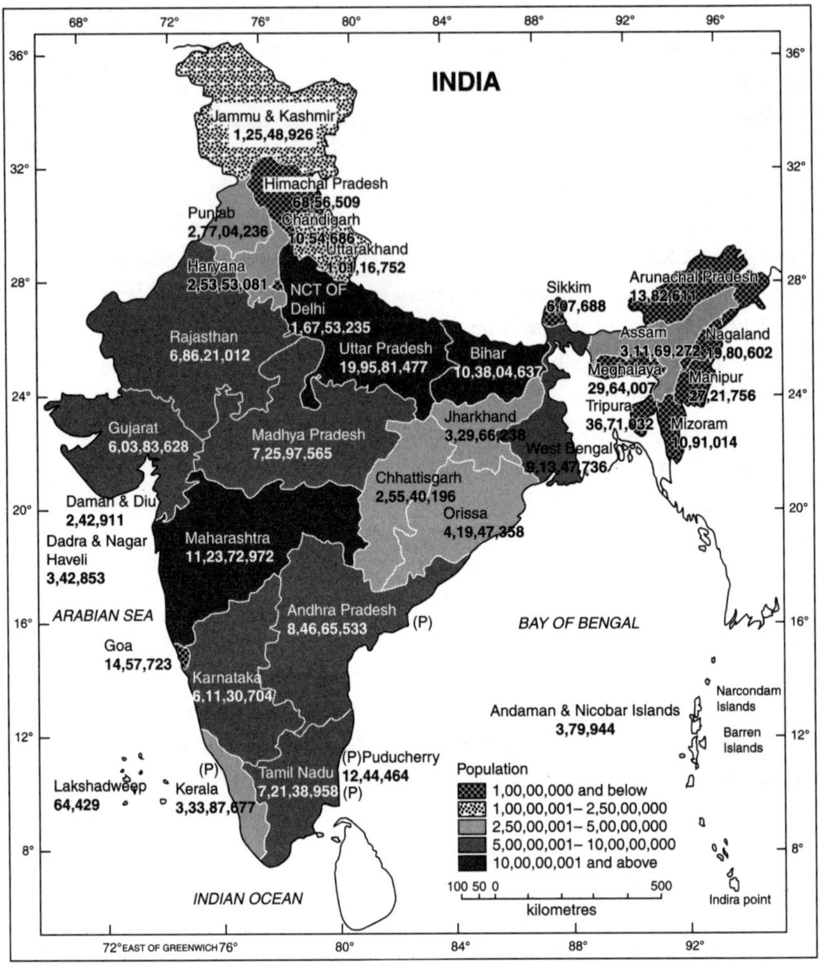


Map 5.1 India: population by states, 2011

## BEYOND SELF-RELIANCE: THE IMPACT OF GLOBALISATION

Increased savings and investment were key features of the Indian growth experience: after 1970 the rate of both savings and investment increased substantially, with public investment picking up in the 1970s, then private corporate investment leading the way from the early 1980s onwards. Gross domestic savings and gross national capital formation both rose substantially,

Table 5.3 *Economic and social indicators by major states, 2004–2005 to 2009–2010*

| 1 | 2 | 3 | 4 | 5 | 6 | 7 | 8 |
|---|---|---|---|---|---|---|---|
| | NDP at current prices (Rs billions), 2006–7 | NDP per capita (Rs),[a] 2006–7 | Average annual % growth in NDP, 2004–5 to 2009–10[b] | Life expectancy at birth, 2002–6 | Literacy rate (%), 2011 | Infant mortality rates (per 1000 live births), 2008 | % of population below poverty line,[c] 2004–5 |
| Punjab | 1 975.9 | 71 322 | 13.9 | 69 | 77 | 41 | 20.9 |
| Haryana | 1 192.9 | 47 050 | 16.9 | 66 | 77 | 54 | 24.1 |
| Maharashtra | 4 446.5 | 39 569 | 16.1 | 67 | 83 | 33 | 38.1 |
| Kerala | 1 268.4 | 37 991 | 14.6 | 74 | 94 | 12 | 19.7 |
| Gujarat | 2 189.0 | 36 251 | 14.7 | 64 | 79 | 50 | 31.8 |
| Tamil Nadu | 2 433.5 | 33 734 | 14.3 | 66 | 80 | 31 | 28.9 |
| Karnataka | 1 796.7 | 29 392 | 15.1 | 65 | 76 | 45 | 33.4 |
| Andhra Pradesh | 2 472.2 | 29 200 | 13.6 | 64 | 68 | 52 | 29.9 |
| West Bengal | 2 393.3 | 26 200 | 13.0 | 65 | 77 | 35 | 34.3 |
| Orissa | 832.6 | 19 348 | 16.4 | 60 | 74 | 69 | 57.2 |
| Rajasthan | 1 334.8 | 19 451 | 11.9 | 62 | 67 | 63 | 34.4 |
| Assam | 583.5 | 18 721 | 10.7 | 59 | 73 | 64 | 34.4 |
| Madhya Pradesh | 1 157.8 | 15 949 | 11.1 | 58 | 71 | 70 | 48.6 |
| Uttar Pradesh | 2 715.3 | 13 605 | 13.5 | 60 | 70 | 67 | 40.9 |
| Bihar | 897.6 | 8 647 | 15.6 | 62 | 70 | 56 | 54.4 |
| All India | 33 423.5 | 27 618 | 14.0 | 64 | 74 | 53 | 37.2 |

[a] Population at 2001 census.

[b] Data for some states incomplete for 2009–10.

[c] Using revised estimates based on recommendations of the Tendulkar Committee for determining poverty.

*Note:* Data for Bihar, Madhya Pradesh and Uttar Pradesh include Jharkhand, Chhattisgarh and Uttarakhand respectively, except for col. 6.

*Source*: Cols. 2–5, 7: *Economic Survey*, *2010–2011*, appendices A12 and A119; col. 6: *Census of India*, *2011*; col. 8: Planning Commission, *Databook for DCH* (2011), table 32, at http://planningcommission.nic.in/data/datatable/0211/data%2039.pdf.

from about 20 per cent of GDP in 1980 to well over 30 per cent in 2010; these are unprecedentedly high percentages for India, but both are well below the levels in China. A large proportion of personal savings – 42 per cent in rural areas and 23 per cent in urban areas – were still held in cash at home in 2010; 45 per cent of rural savings and 63 per cent of urban savings were held in banks. Imports of gold, the traditional rural savings vehicle of choice, and still thought to provide a uniquely secure and liquid asset, have risen sharply as a result of rising incomes and the liberalisation of import policy. By the late 2000s the Indian economy was once again the largest importer of gold in the world, accounting for a fifth of annual global consumption.[21]

One consistent feature of the rhetoric of economic reform in the 1990s and 2000s, both among practitioners and commentators, was the assertion that a closer connection to the international economy through greater liberalisation would lead both to overall growth and to the reduction of poverty.[22] After the 1970s India moved away from its self-imposed autarchy: exports and imports of goods and services both increased as a share of GDP from the 1980s onwards, although exports did not really take off until after the third wave of economic reforms in the late 1990s. The composition of India's imports remained fairly stable with only fuels increasing significantly – from about one-quarter of total imports by value in the mid 1980s to one-third in the early 2000s – balanced by slight falls in agricultural raw materials, food items, manufactured goods, and ores and metals. Within the category of imported manufactures the largest fall was in chemicals, with some increase in information-technology-related equipment. For exports, there was a clear shift from primary produce to manufactured goods; manufactures as a whole increased from 58 per cent of the total in 1985 to 75 per cent in 2002; within this category, chemicals and related products showed the largest increase, rising from 3.6 per cent to 11.1 per cent, while textiles remained stable. In 2000, about 21 per cent of world exports

[21] Government of India, Finance Department, *Economic Survey, 2010–2011*, pp. 24–5; R. Kannan and Sarat Dhal, 'India's Demand for Gold: Some Issues for Economic Development and Macroeconomic Policy', *Indian Journal of Economics and Business*, 7, 1, 2008.

[22] For arguments over the proposition that liberalisation leads to enhanced growth and improved poverty reduction, see David Dollar and Aart Kraay, 'Trade, Growth and Poverty', *Economic Journal*, 114, 2004; Robert Wade, 'Is Globalization Reducing Poverty and Inequality?', *World Development*, 32, 4, 2004; Dani Rodrik, 'Goodbye Washington Consensus, Hello Washington Confusion? A Review of the World Bank's Economic Growth in the 1990s: Learning from a Decade of Reform', *Journal of Economic Literature*, 44, 4, 2006. Local critics of the reform package have argued consistently that closer involvement with the international economy has increased instability in India: see Jayati Ghosh and C. P. Chandrasekhar, 'The Costs of "Coupling": The Global Crisis and the Indian Economy', *Cambridge Journal of Economics*, 33, 4, 2009.

of information technology (IT) services originated in India, which by then had become the largest exporting country of information-technology-enabled services (ITES) and business process outsourcing (BPO) services; this predominance was maintained for the rest of the decade. However, India's overall contribution to the international economy remained modest; in the early 2000s it accounted for only about 1.5 per cent of the global trade in goods and services, with exports of manufactures concentrated in low technology sectors, and high technology manufacturing sectors heavily dependent on imports of crucial inputs.[23]

Another important consequence of trade liberalisation was the increase in foreign direct investment (FDI). In the late 1980s, FDI amounted to about 0.07 per cent of GDP: the Industrial Policy Statement of 1991 lowered the barriers to entry for foreign firms to the domestic economy, setting up a mechanism which allowed investors to bring in funds without prior official permission, and by 2002 the share of FDI had increased to 0.6 per cent of GDP. In an attempt to encourage foreign investment linked to exports, the government abandoned its failed existing Export Processing Zones in 2000 in favour of Special Economic Zones (SEZs) to simplify land acquisitions, administrative procedures and tax exemptions. The legal basis of SEZs was formalised by central government legislation in 2005. The creation of special zones has triggered political conflict in some places, notably at Nandigram in West Bengal, where there was extensive public disorder after the attempt to create an SEZ in 2007.[24] In the six years after 2005–6, cumulative inflows of FDI to India amounted to more than five times the sums that had been invested since 1991, reaching a total of almost $200 million by April 2011.[25]

The sectoral composition of FDI changed significantly during the period of reforms. During the 1980s, about 85 per cent of FDI was concentrated in the secondary sector, with the chemical sector accounting for about one-third, and with only 5 per cent going into the service sector; in the 1990s electrical equipment, including computer software, transportation and telecommunications were the main recipients. By contrast, during the 2000s the services

[23] Michele Alessandrini, Bassam Fattouh and Pasquale Scaramozzino, 'The Changing Pattern of Foreign Trade Specialization in Indian Manufacturing', *Oxford Review of Economic Policy*, 23, 2, 2007, pp. 275, 288.

[24] On the impact of SEZs, see Jona Aravind Dohrmann, 'Special Economic Zones in India – An Introduction', *ASIEN: The German Journal on Contemporary Asia*, 106, January, 2008.

[25] There are convenient statistics on FDI in National Council of Applied Economic Research (NCAER), *FDI in India and Its Growth Linkages*, New Delhi, 2009; and Government of India, Ministry of Commerce and Industry, Department of Industrial Promotion and Policy, 'Fact Sheets on Foreign Direct Investment', at http://dipp.nic.in/English/Publications/FDI_Statistics/FDI_Statistics.aspx.

sector attracted the largest share of new investment, with a large increase from 2007 onwards, mostly in financial and banking services. A small number of coastal states with suitable infrastructure – notably Karnataka, Tamil Nadu, Maharashtra, Gujarat and Andhra Pradesh – have attracted most foreign capital, and hosted the majority of SEZs, 60 out of the total of 114 in 2010. Overseas investment in manufacturing was characterised by greenfield enterprises to a significant extent, in automobiles for example; by contrast, foreign investment in service industries has largely been through mergers and acquisitions.[26]

Tracing the geographical origins of FDI into India is complicated by regional double taxation agreements, which have meant that many foreign institutional investors (FIIs) have channelled their investments through local jurisdictions where corporate and capital gains taxes are much lower than in India. About 35 per cent of overseas equity investment coming to India between 2000 and 2007 may have originated in the United States, and a further 40 per cent in Europe, including the United Kingdom; but much of this capital entered the country via Mauritius, which was the source of 30 to 40 per cent of cumulative inflows after 1991, with Singapore also an important base after 2005.[27] Some of the money apparently invested in India from Mauritius and other offshore financial centres (OFCs) may in reality have been a form of 'round-tripping' of Indian funds to escape capital gains tax. There has also been a concerted effort to attract remittances and investment from Indians living overseas, and since 2001 private inflows from overseas Indians have amounted to more than 3 per cent of GDP. The bulk of these remittances came from the USA and Europe: just over 10 per cent of the Indian diaspora lived in the United States in the early 2000s, but they provided over 40 per cent of remittances.[28]

Another feature of the increased openness of the Indian economy after 2000 was the flow of outward investment by Indian companies. Some large Indian corporations, led by Birla companies, had created overseas subsidiaries in the

[26] On foreign investment inflows see also Ramkishen Rajan, Sasidaran Gopalan and Rabin Hattari, *Crisis, Capital Flows and FDI in Emerging Asia*, New Delhi, 2011, Chs. 3 and 6; and K. S. Chalapati Rao and Biswajit Dhar, *India's FDI Inflows: Trends and Concepts*, New Delhi, 2011.

[27] Sasidaran Gopalan and Ramkishen S. Rajan, 'India's Foreign Direct Investment Flows: Trying to Make Sense of the Numbers', in UNESCAP Asia Pacific Research and Training Network on Trade, *Alerts on Emerging Policy Challenges*, 5, January 2010, at www.unescap.org/tid/artnet/pub/alert5.pdf.

[28] India became one of the leading recipients of remittances in the world after 2005: Reserve Bank of India, 'Invisibles in India's Balance of Payments,' *RBI Bulletin*, November 2006, pp. 1343–4. On the larger role of the Indian diaspora in stimulating economic growth, see Abhishek Pandey, Alok Aggarwal, Richard Devane and Yevgeny Kuznetsov, 'The Indian Diaspora: A Unique Case?', in Yevgeny Kuznetsov (ed.), *Diaspora Networks and the International Migration of Skills: How Countries Can Draw on Their Talent Abroad*, WBI Development Studies, World Bank, Washington, DC, 2006.

1960s and 1970s to exploit foreign markets free from the problems of exporting from India. There were 149 such projects in operation in the early 1980s, and 250 by 1990, but they were on a medium or small scale; only $220 million worth of outward equity investment was approved by the Indian authorities between 1975 and 1990. A second wave of activity began with liberalisation from the mid 1990s; following the implementation of a new Foreign Exchange Management Act (FEMA) in 2000, investment overseas surged to a new peak after 2005; total FDI outflow from India amounted to about $80 million from 2000 to 2010, and there was a further outflow of almost $50 million between April 2010 and May 2011. A number of OFCs, such as the British Virgin Islands, Singapore and Mauritius, were major destinations of Indian outward capital flows.[29]

The main feature of this sudden growth was the purchase by Indian corporations of established manufacturing enterprises in the United Kingdom, Continental Europe and North America. There have been significant acquisitions by Indian firms in developed economies since 2006, such as Tata Steel's purchase of Corus, and Tata Motors' purchase of Jaguar and Land Rover in the UK; and the acquisition by Hindalco (part of the Aditya Birla Group) of the US-based aluminium sheet manufacturer Novelis. Between 2000 and June 2008 companies in the Tata Group acquired at least thirty-five major overseas companies in a wide range of manufacturing activities: this strategy had a number of different objectives, including accessing new markets (in BPO services), integrating the value chain and increased vertical integration (in steel), and implementing brand control and resource leverage strategies (in tea and cars).[30]

The reform process was traumatic for some of the strategic public-sector enterprises created in the 1950s to manufacture and distribute vital goods and services. These state enterprises had been administered by a 'bureaucratic production regime' characterised by state ownership, soft budgetary constraints (with chronic losses repaid by additional assistance from the state)

[29] In June 2011 the Reserve Bank of India began to report Indian OFDI on a monthly basis, and produced detailed statistics going back to 2007: www.rbi.org.in/scripts/BS_PressReleaseDisplay.aspx?prid=24600. On the contemporary history of Indian OFDI, see Nagesh Kumar, 'Emerging TNCs: Trends, Patterns and Determinants of Outward FDI by Indian Enterprises,' *Transnational Corporations*, 16, 1, 2007; Premachandra Athukorala, 'Outward Foreign Direct Investment from India', *Asian Development Review*, 26, 2, 2009; Karl P. Sauvant and Jaya Prakash Pradhan, with Ayesha Chatterjee and Brian Harley (eds.), *The Rise of Indian Multinationals: Perspectives on Indian Outward Foreign Direct Investment*, New York, 2010, especially Ch. 1.

[30] Gopalan and Rajan, 'India's Foreign Direct Investment Flows', table 2. Andrea Goldstein, 'Emerging Economies' Transnational Corporations: The Case of Tata', *Transnational Corporations*, 17, 3, 2008.

and monopoly market power: strategic objectives were determined largely by the administrative bureaucracy (often at state, rather than national, level), and based more on political considerations than on concern for economic efficiency. One damaging consequence was a failure to take the lead in technological innovation, by eschewing major investment in R&D, and using foreign partners to overcome research deficiencies.[31] To take one well-documented case, Indian Telephone Industries (ITI) – the monopoly producer and supplier of telecommunications equipment – had to operate with very limited resources for capital investment, and endured a shot-gun marriage with foreign suppliers of technology; as a result the company had almost no stake in manufacturing for wireless telephony in the 2000s, just as mobile phone networks revolutionised the Indian communications market.[32]

The reforms also had a wider initial impact on the life-histories of Indian companies: a quarter of the private firms that had been registered in 1985 failed between the late 1980s and the mid 2000s, as institutional safety-nets for chronically loss-making firms were removed. The total number of public-sector firms fell very slightly, while the number of newly established private firms nearly tripled and new foreign ventures rose by 50 per cent. Some large business groups operating in new areas of manufacturing emerged in this period: fifteen of the top twenty Indian business groups in 1980 were still in that category in 1990, but by 2000 only six remained; the newcomers included three groups in pharmaceuticals; three in information and communications technology (ICT); two in motor vehicles; and one each in cement, cellular technology, business services and general manufacturing.[33]

Despite such examples, one feature of the modern corporate economy has been the relatively low level of exit by public and private firms. Overall, there was no dramatic transformation in India's corporate structure following liberalisation. The Indian corporate landscape throughout the reforms period remained dominated by incumbent firms, public and private, that were in place at the start of the 1980s, and best able to take advantage of the manufacturing opportunities offered since then, controlling the largest share of sales,

[31] Direct interference by central government bureaucrats and local government politicians explains the behaviour of management and labour in large public-sector firms much better than generalised theories that identify cultural determinants of economic irrationality or strong leisure preferences among Indian factory workers.

[32] Dilip Subramanian, *Telecommunications Industry in India: State Business and Labour in a Global Economy*, New Delhi, 2011. This paragraph is largely based on Subramanian's exhaustive case-history of ITI.

[33] Ben L. Kedia, Debmalya Mukherjee and Somnath Lahiri, 'Indian Business Groups: Evolution and Transformation', *Asia Pacific Journal of Management*, 23, 2006, table 1. This article contains brief case-histories of a number of leading companies.

assets and profits. Only in the services sector, where novel fields of activity have been pioneered, have new entrants been able to take a substantial share. Between 1988 and 2005, new companies made an annual average return on assets of 9.9 per cent, public-sector firms made a return of 9.7 per cent, established private companies made a return of 12.2 per cent and foreign companies made a return of 13.3 per cent. In terms of sectors, the performance of firms in agriculture, mining and extraction, and business, computer and commercial services were consistently above the norm, while financial services and real estate, and utilities, construction and retail, were consistently below.[34]

Despite the rhetoric of liberalisation that accompanied some parts of the reform programme, the public sector's share of economic activity has held up well: public-sector firms commanded 70 per cent of total business assets in 1989–90, and still controlled over 60 per cent in 2005. Successful public-owned enterprises, such as the Indian Oil Corporation and the Steel Authority of India, where management reforms and fresh opportunity created profits and market leadership, have managed to limit penetration of their markets by new entrants, either domestic or foreign. Public-sector firms that have made consistent profits are allowed some discretion in making investment decisions and undertaking external activities.[35] Paid-up capital in private-sector firms did not exceed that in the public sector until the mid 1990s; since then the number of such companies has increased steadily, with surges in capital investment since 2000: total paid-up capital in the private sector increased from Rs 6.8 billion in 2006 to 10.8 billion in 2010, predominantly in the service sector, especially in business services and communications.[36]

## REFORM AND 'MODERNISATION': CONTINUITY AND CHANGE SINCE 1980

The pattern of growth in the Indian economy since 1980 has not followed the orthodox trajectory pioneered by East Asian countries such as China,

[34] Laura Alfaro and Anusha Chauri, 'India Transformed: Insights from the Firm Level 1988–2005', *Brookings India Policy Forum Journal*, 6, 2010, table 5. On changes in business strategies in response to liberalisation, see P. N. Khandwalla, 'Effective Organisational Response by Corporates to India's Liberalisation and Globalisation', *Asia Pacific Journal of Management*, 19, 2002; and Anusha Chauri and Nandini Gupta, 'Incumbents and Protectionism: The Political Economy of Foreign Entry Liberalization', *Journal of Financial Economics*, 88, 3, 2008.

[35] Government of India, Department of Public Enterprises, at http://dpe.nic.in/newsite/navmini.htm. As of November 2011, 88 public-sector enterprises (out of a total of 245 listed as central government enterprises) have received some form of 'Ratna' status which allows them limited management autonomy as a reward for sustained profitability.

[36] Data from www.indiastat.com.

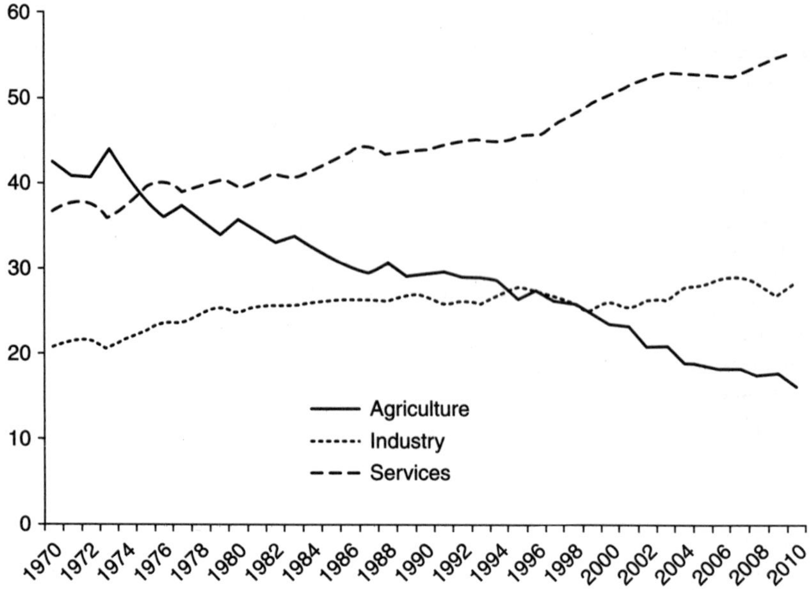


Figure 5.3 Value added by sector (percentage of GDP), 1970–2010

Korea and Taiwan, or the historical model of Japan. The general experience of developing economies in the nineteenth and twentieth centuries has been that only large-scale industrialisation can deliver sustained economic growth, rapid technical change and rising real incomes. By contrast, the Indian economy from the 1980s was driven by the dynamism of the services sector, rather than by increased agricultural output, industrial production or commodity exports. Figure 5.3 shows the value added by the main sectors of the economy since the 1970s; table 5.4 shows the percentage of the workforce employed in the various sectors of the economy between 1993–4 and 2004–5. Agriculture has lagged behind both industry and services, with lower growth rates and a declining share of GNP; however, the share of the workforce employed in agriculture has declined very slowly, and by some estimates the agricultural labour-force has increased slightly in absolute numbers since 1980.[37] Industry, especially manufacturing industry, has enjoyed unprecedented growth rates

[37] According to an alternative sample-based survey in 2009–10, 45.5 per cent of the workforce over the age of 15 was employed in agriculture, forestry and fisheries; 8.9 per cent in manufacturing; 8.8 per cent in the wholesale and retail trade; 8.4 per cent in community services; and 7.5 per cent in construction: Government of India, Ministry of Labour and Employment, Labour Bureau, *Report on Employment & Unemployment Survey*, 2009–10, Chandigarh, 2010, p. iv.

Table 5.4 *Employment, sectoral shares, 1993–1994 to 2004–2005*

| | 1993–94 | | 1999–2000 | | 2004–5 | |
|---|---|---|---|---|---|---|
| | million | % | million | % | million | % |
| Agriculture, forestry and fishing | 242.46 | 64.8 | 237.56 | 59.8 | 267.57 | 58.4 |
| Mining and quarrying | 2.7 | 0.7 | 2.27 | 0.6 | 2.74 | 0.6 |
| Manufacturing | 42.5 | 11.3 | 48.01 | 12.1 | 53.51 | 11.7 |
| Electricity, gas and water supply | 1.35 | 0.4 | 1.28 | 0.3 | 1.37 | 0.3 |
| Construction | 11.68 | 3.1 | 17.62 | 4.4 | 25.61 | 5.6 |
| Trade, hotels and restaurants | 27.78 | 7.4 | 37.32 | 9.4 | 47.11 | 10.3 |
| Transport, storage and communication | 10.33 | 2.8 | 14.69 | 3.7 | 17.38 | 3.8 |
| Financing, insurance, real estate and business services | 3.52 | 0.9 | 5.05 | 1.3 | 6.86 | 1.5 |
| Community, social and personal services | 32.13 | 8.6 | 33.20 | 8.4 | 35.67 | 7.8 |
| Total employment | 374.45 | 100 | 397.00 | 100 | 457.82 | 100 |

*Source:* C. Rangarajan, Padma Iyer Kaul and Seema, 'Revisiting Employment and Growth', *Money and Finance*, 3, 2, 2007, table 3.

since the 1980s, but these have not amounted to a driving force for increased income or employment. The services sector led the way in output growth, especially since the 1990s: the overall share of services in GDP rose from 37 per cent in 1980 to 52 per cent in 2005. Between 1993 and 2004, 45 per cent of India's growth came from services.[38] However, employment in services grew slowly, and mainly in traditional sectors such as trade, hotels and restaurants, and construction.

[38] Barry Bosworth and Susan M. Collins, 'Accounting for Growth: Comparing China and India', *Journal of Economic Perspectives*, 22, 1, 2008.

### *Agriculture*

The rural economy and agriculture show the greatest continuity across the reform period, with continued growth in the 1980s and 1990s building on foundations that were laid down in the first phase of the 'green revolution' after 1965.[39] As table 5.5 shows, total foodgrain production in India rose by about 40 per cent in the 1980s, and by a further 15 per cent in the 1990s; since then it has levelled off at just above the 2000 figure: total non-foodgrain production rose more sharply in the 1980s, by over 50 per cent, then by a further 30 per cent in the 1990s; production dipped briefly in 2003–5, and has recently fluctuated at around 15 per cent above the 2000 figure. Across the sector as a whole, the average annual rate of growth fell from more than 4 per cent per year between 1992–3 and 1996–7 to less than 2 per cent per year between 1997–8 and 2002–3, and has remained low since then. The annual growth rates of yields for both foodgrains and non-foodgrain crops were lower in the 1990s than they had been in the 1980s; foodgrain yields increased even more slowly in the 2000s, but were balanced by a sudden spurt in vegetable oils and cotton. Wheat remained the foodgrain crop most responsive to new investment, with greater increases in yields than for rice throughout the period. Per capita availability of foodgrains has stagnated at around 200 kg per capita per annum since 2000, but this would meet the basic energy needs of the population if it were distributed equally.[40]

Since the 1990s overall consumption patterns have changed away from cereals to high-value agricultural products including fruit, vegetables, milk products, eggs, meat and fish. Some farmers were now able to concentrate on high-value products for the growing urban market. Net per capita availability of foodgrains in the 1990s was a little higher than in the 1980s, but only because of an increase in output of wheat, with rice more or less constant, and coarse cereals declining; availability of other agricultural products did rise in the 1990s, especially vegetable oils, sugar and tea: vanaspati and cotton cloth remained static, while the largest single increase in availability of popular consumer goods was in man-made cloth.[41] However, a number of studies of rural

[39] On the spread and development of improved varieties of foodgrains since the 1920s, see Robert E. Evanson, Carl E. Pray and Mark W. Rosengrant, 'Agricultural Research and Productivity Growth in Indian Agriculture', International Food Policy Research Institute, Research Paper no. 109, Washington, DC, 1999, Ch. 4.

[40] Takashi Kurosaki, 'Long-Term Agricultural Growth and Crop Shifts in India and Pakistan', *Journal of International Economic Studies*, 20, 2006.

[41] See table 5.3 above, and Directorate of Economics and Statistics, New Delhi, *Agricultural Statistics at a Glance: August 2004*, New Delhi, 2004, tables 10:1, 10:3.

Table 5.5 *Indices of agricultural production, 1980–2010*

| | 1980–1 | 1981–2 | 1982–3 | 1983–4 | 1984–5 | 1985–6 | 1986–7 | 1987–8 | 1988–9 | 1989–90 | 1990–1 | 1991–2 | 1992–3 |
|---|---|---|---|---|---|---|---|---|---|---|---|---|---|
| Foodgrains | 105 | 108 | 104 | 123 | 118 | 123 | 117 | 114 | 138 | 139 | 144 | 138 | 144 |
| Non-foodgrains | 97 | 112 | 107 | 112 | 119 | 113 | 113 | 118 | 143 | 150 | 156 | 159 | 164 |
| | 1993–4 | 1994–5 | 1995–6 | 1996–7 | 1997–8 | 1998–9 | 1999–2000 | 2000–1 | 2001–2 | 2002–3 | 2003–4 | 2004–5 | 2005–6 |
| Foodgrains | 135 | 141 | 131 | 145 | 141 | 150 | 153 | 142 | 155 | 127 | 155 | 144 | 153 |
| Non-foodgrains | 111 | 119 | 122 | 130 | 121 | 127 | 128 | 126 | 129 | 121 | 110 | 112 | 130 |
| | 2006–7 | 2007–8 | 2008–9 | 2009–10 | | | | | | | | | |
| Foodgrains | 159 | 169 | 171 | 159 | | | | | | | | | |
| Non-foodgrains | 155 | 158 | 141 | 132 | | | | | | | | | |

*Note:* 1980–1 to 1992–3, triennium ending 1981–2 = 100; 1993–4 to 2009–10, triennium ending 1993–4 = 100.
*Source:* www.indiastat.com.

poverty have shown that nutrition levels fell for those at the margins in the 1990s and 2000s, and that a substantial proportion of rural consumers have failed to maintain appropriate daily intake levels of calories.

Irrigation has been the key feature of Indian agricultural growth since the 1970s, especially the provision of electrically powered pump-sets for tube wells. This form of irrigation became crucially important for wheat production in ecologically favoured areas of north-western India: by 2006–7 over 90 per cent of wheat was grown under managed irrigation systems, as opposed to 57 per cent of rice and 13 per cent of other foodgrains.[42] Although investment rose consistently as a share of GNP since 1980 across the economy as a whole, agricultural investment as a share of total investment fell from 15 per cent of GNP in the early 1980s to 5 per cent twenty years later: public investment in agriculture declined slowly from Rs 80 billion in 1980 to Rs 60 billion in 2001 (at 1993–4 prices). To some extent, this simply reflects a different model of funding agriculture, as public investment has been replaced by direct subsidies of the prices of crucial inputs such as fertiliser and diesel and electric pumps for groundwater irrigation. These subsidies rose sharply in the late 1980s to around Rs 250 billion in 1990–1 and then to Rs 450 billion in 2002–3. By 2000 input subsidies on fertiliser, irrigation and power accounted for more than 2 per cent of GDP; as a share of the value of agricultural output the cost of input subsidies doubled from 6 per cent in 2003–4 to almost 12 per cent in 2009–10.

Fertiliser subsidies began in the late 1970s following political agitations by farmers in areas that had benefited from the green revolution who had been badly affected by the rise in oil and energy prices after 1973. Subsidies were paid to the manufacturers by central government to insulate consumers from the effects of price rises caused by fluctuations in input prices – especially for oil-based products. An attempt was made to change the system in 1992 by decontrolling the production of fertilisers in India, but this led to an increase in price and a concessionary scheme had to be implemented, so that the cost of the subsidy has continued to rise over time. Total subsidies paid by central government on fertilisers and oil products have risen from 1.4 per cent of GDP in 2004–5 to 2.3 per cent of GDP in 2010–11, with an additional 2 per cent of GDP spent on bonds issued in lieu of subsidies. The effective rate of the fertiliser subsidy has increased from 41 per cent of the cost of fertiliser production in 2003–4 to 67 per cent in 2009–10.[43] Charging farmers for electricity

[42] Data from www.indiastat.com.

[43] Ashok Gulati and Sudha Narayanan, *The Subsidy Syndrome in Indian Agriculture*, New Delhi, 2003; Raghbendra Jha, 'Investment and Subsidies in Indian Agriculture', Crawford School Working

also became problematic in the 1970s, as those requiring power for irrigation faced uncertainty and rising input prices. A number of State Electricity Boards (SEBs) started charging a flat monthly tariff not connected to actual usage, partly as a way of economising on metering and billing costs. This brought the price of electrically pumped irrigation water down below that supplied by diesel pumps, but this policy was not sustainable everywhere.

After the financial reforms of 1991, electricity subsidies for agriculture were provided by state governments, and became an important part of the patronage systems of rural politics. Since 2000, following populist campaigns in some southern states, a number of SEBs have provided rural electricity free of cost; this was seen as a way of reducing the cost of power theft and irregular connections. By the 2000s, the cost of power supply has become a major drain on state budgets, and, in some places, had a perverse effect on power availability. Unable to secure enough revenue to provide adequate investment and maintenance, some SEBs neglected their infrastructure in poorer and less developed areas, where irrigation-intensive agriculture was not yet fully established, leading to a hierarchy of electrically privileged and under-privileged districts – the latter including parts of eastern India (eastern Uttar Pradesh, northern Bihar, coastal Orissa and northern Bengal), which combine large volumes of undeveloped groundwater potential with massive concentrations of rural poverty, and have suffered rural de-electrification. In eastern Uttar Pradesh these problems were overcome by a 'dieselisation' scheme to provide subsidised diesel pump-sets for small-holders; but this has not been implemented elsewhere.[44]

Another arena of public investment in the rural economy has been the expansion of social protection programmes, which have sought to provide various forms of welfare safety-net. The midday meals service for primary school children, which was introduced across Tamil Nadu in the 1980s, was extended across the whole country in 1995. In 2005 the central government passed a National Rural Employment Guarantee Act (NREGA; subsequently renamed to commemorate Mahatma Gandhi) which promised 100 days of unskilled

Paper, May 2007, at www.crawford.anu.edu.au/acde/asarc/pdf/papers/2007/WP2007_03.pdf; Nick Grossman and Dylan Carson, 'Agriculture Policy in India: The Role of Input Subsidies', *USITC Executive Briefings on Trade* (March 2011), at www.usitc.gov/publications/332/executive_briefings/EBOT_IndiaAgSubsidies.pdf.

[44] Regina Birner, Surupa Gupta and Neeru Sharma, *The Political Economy of Agricultural Policy Reform in India*, International Food Policy Research Institute, Washington, DC, 2011; N. C. Saxena, 'Wells and Welfare in the Ganga Basin: Essay on Public Policy and Private Initiative', Government of India, Planning Commission, 2001, at http://planningcommission.nic.in/reports/articles/ncsxna/index.php?repts=wells.htm.

manual work to adult members of any rural household at a statutory minimum wage, with the cost split between the union and state governments. The Act was initially applied to 200 of the poorest districts in the country, and then spread more widely. However, most states have not been able to provide a full quota of work to all applicants, and the provision of work to landless labourers has not prevented migration from backward rural areas to urban areas. The effectiveness of the NREGA in individual areas has largely depended on social mobilisation by officials, activists and NGOs to compel political commitment to the scheme by state functionaries and to ensure that the implementation process is properly institutionalised.[45]

There are a number of indications that the agricultural economy entered a cul-de-sac at the beginning of the twenty-first century, as the engines of growth that had powered its progress since the late 1960s ran into difficulties. Agriculture has had significantly lower rates of productivity than the other sectors of the economy, yet the sector has been required to continue to absorb considerable amounts of labour in the countryside, much of it with low levels of skills and only partial employment. Many agricultural holdings have not been able to absorb surplus labour: in the 1990s and 2000s about 60 per cent of agricultural operational holdings were classed as 'marginal' (less than 1 hectare), and a further 20 per cent were classed as 'small' (1 to 2 hectares).[46] The non-farm share of rural employment increased only marginally across the reform period, from 20 per cent in the 1970s to less than 30 per cent in the late 2000s.[47] Initial subsidies in credit, fertiliser and irrigation helped small farmers to adopt new technologies in agriculture: however, the opportunities for continued productivity gains through capital investment in irrigation, fertiliser, pesticides, and new seeds and techniques have narrowed as the costs of subsidies have risen and ecological limitations on technical change have become apparent.

Commercial banks supplied an increasing share of institutional rural credit from the early 2000s (70 per cent in 2005–6), replacing co-operatives;

[45] For analysis of the effects of the NREGA, see National Commission for Enterprise, *The Challenge of Employment in India: An Informal Economy Perspective* [Sengupta Report], New Delhi, 2009, Ch. 9; D. Narasimha Reddy *et al.*, *Institutions and Innovations in the Implementation Process of the Mahatma Gandhi National Rural Employment Guarantee Scheme in India*, Centre for Social Protection (CSP) Research Report 09 (2011); Institute of Applied Manpower Research, 'All-India Report on Evaluation of NREGA: A Survey of Twenty Districts', http://planningcommission.gov.in/reports/genrep/rep_NREGA.pdf.

[46] Data on agricultural holdings from 1995–6 to 2005–6 are available from the Department of Agriculture and Cooperation's agricultural census at http://agcensus.dacnet.nic.in/.

[47] Shenggen Fan, Ashok Gulati and Sukhadeo Thorat, 'Investment, Subsidies, and Pro-Poor Growth in Rural India', International Food Policy Research Institute Discussion Paper 00716, 2007, p. 21, at www.ifpri.org/sites/default/files/publications/ifpridp00716.pdf.

moneylenders still met about a quarter of the borrowing needs of rural households.[48] Individual farmers in some regions have suffered considerably from the consequences of indebtedness caused by participation in capital-intensive agriculture. Elsewhere existing irrigation schemes have depleted groundwater and caused environmental degradation.[49] The green revolution model of agricultural development that produced substantial gains in production for farmers in well-resourced regions during the last decades of the twentieth century will need to be significantly modified and adapted to meet the requirements of the new millennium. Thus lagging areas cannot catch up with advanced regions by following a similar policy of investment and subsidy. It is not clear that a simple reform-based agenda, seeking to free up land and capital markets to increase competition, can provide viable solutions to the problems of production and distribution in the rural economy.[50] The restrictions on agricultural trade across state boundaries, and the ceilings imposed on farm prices by official procurement policies, are further disincentives for productivity-enhancing improvements in the rural economy.[51]

### *Industry*

The development of manufacturing industry in the period of economic reforms was initially shaped by the long years of planning for a self-reliant economy. At the beginning of the 1980s, in contrast to the pattern elsewhere in Asia, medium- and large-scale Indian manufacturing firms operated with relatively generous amounts of capital investment and skilled labour; however, the size of firms and plants was well below the optimum levels needed to achieve economies of scale. The allocation of labour and capital in the private sector was further distorted since large public-sector companies, which were not run as

48 Ramesh Golait, 'Current Issues in Agriculture Credit in India: An Assessment', *Reserve Bank of India Occasional Papers*, 28, 1, 2007, pp. 82–3.

49 On the 'crisis in agriculture' revealed by farmers' suicides and other malign social indicators, see Srijit Mishra, 'Risks, Farmers' Suicides and Agrarian Crisis in India: Is There a Way Out?', *Indian Journal of Agricultural Economics*, 63, 1, 2008, pp. 38–54; and D. Narasimha Reddy and Srijit Mishra, *Agrarian Crisis in India*, New Delhi, 2009.

50 Richard Palmer-Jones and Kunal Sen, 'What Has Luck Got to Do with It? A Regional Analysis of Poverty and Agricultural Growth in Rural India', *Journal of Development Studies*, 40, 1, 2003. Others have argued that measures to reduce poverty in rural society by increasing protection for tenants can inhibit growth: see Timothy Besley and Robin Burgess, 'Land Reform, Poverty Reduction and Growth: Evidence from India', *Quarterly Journal of Economics*, 115, 2, 2000. For a convenient summary of the issues, see World Bank, 'India: Priorities for Agriculture and Rural Development' (2011), at http://go.worldbank.org/8EFXZBL3Y0.

51 On this issue, see Food and Agriculture Organization of the United Nations, Technical Cooperation Department, 'Towards an Indian Common Market: Removal of Restrictions on Internal Trade in Agricultural Commodities', 2005, at www.fao.org/docrep/010/ai566e/ai566e00.htm.

profit-making enterprises, dominated much of the intermediate and capital goods sectors, and provided inputs and infrastructure for key service industries such as telecommunications. As one analysis of India's relative position concluded, 'the paradox of Indian manufacturing in the early 1980s is ... that of a labour-rich, capital-poor economy using too little of the former, and using the latter very inefficiently'.[52]

The reform agenda carried out by Indian governments of all political persuasions sought to increase competition in the industrial sector, largely by lowering tariffs and encouraging greater foreign trade and investment. Import tariffs were reduced from 1985 onwards, and a range of goods were placed on an open general licence; however by 1990 only 12 per cent of manufactured products – all categorised as capital or intermediate goods – could be imported on Open General Licence (OGL), and the average nominal import tariff was still over 80 per cent, and higher than that on manufactured goods. Tariff levels were brought down more sharply in 1991–2 and 1994–7, to an average of about 30 per cent in 2000, much more substantially for capital goods than for intermediate or consumer goods. Some classes of goods, such as fertilisers and pesticides, petroleum products and items relating to national security and defence, remained 'canalised', and could be imported only through public-sector agencies; consumption goods were protected from imports for longer than other parts of the manufacturing sector; and some basic goods, such as leather products, remained under a licensing regime during the 1990s.

These changes had a significant effect on industrial production. Between 1980 and the early 1990s, manufacturing output doubled, with electrical machinery and appliances, rubber and plastic goods, paper products, wood and wood products, and non-metallic mineral products leading the way. The relative importance of chemicals, food products and non-electrical machinery and machine tools increased considerably between 1980–1 and 1993–4, while the relative importance of cotton textiles, and rubber, plastic, petroleum and coal products, fell sharply. Between the early 1990s and 2010, manufacturing output more than tripled, with the highest increases in machinery and machine tools, beverages and tobacco, and transport equipment. The share of chemicals and chemical products in total manufacturing production increased considerably in the 1990s and 2000s, with the Indian pharmaceutical industry becoming a significant player on the global stage, helped by the

[52] Kalpana Kochhar, Utsav Kumar, Raghuram G. Rajan, Arvind Subramanian and Ioannis Tokatlidis, 'India's Pattern of Development: What Happened, What Follows?', *Journal of Monetary Economics*, 53, 5, 2006, p. 998.

availability of skilled labour and by a process-patent regime that enabled local firms to reverse-engineer the manufacture of standard drugs at low cost.[53] In general, however, expanding Indian manufacturing firms in both the private and public sectors relied heavily on imported technology that came from foreign partners.

Most of the detailed information available on the Indian industrial sector relates to firms in the 'organised' or formal sector – those with establishments employing more than ten persons: however, by far the larger number of production units and workers are engaged in the 'unorganised' or informal sector, which is characterised by lower capital intensity and lower productivity.[54] According to the Planning Commission, the unorganised (informal) sector consists of all unincorporated private enterprises owned by individuals or households engaged in the sale and production of goods and services operated on a proprietary or partnership basis and with fewer than ten workers, or fewer than twenty if they are not using power. Other definitions stress the casual or contract nature of employment in the unorganised sector, and the vulnerability of workers there caused by the lack of legal protection.[55]

Small units of production, which include households, have generally used production techniques that relied on lower skill levels and more traditional technologies. Manufacturing employment in the informal sector grew consistently in the 1990s and early 2000s, while employment in the large-scale manufacturing sector declined, except for a small increase in contract workers. Subcontracting work from the organised to the unorganised sector also increased, especially in some labour-intensive industries. Small-scale units did not operate in an organisational vacuum, since many have been based in local clusters specialising in particular fields, where some sharing of knowledge and resources is possible – as in shoe-making in Agra, and in woollen textiles, and bicycle and sewing machine parts in Ludhiana. However, the potential for enhanced productivity in manufacturing was much weaker in the informal sector, and this has blunted the effect of the reforms on industrial growth and productivity.[56]

[53] Indian patent law was changed to a product basis in 2004 to conform to the intellectual property rights regime required by the WTO.

[54] Sean Dougherty, 'Labour Regulation and Employment Dynamics at the State Level in India', *OECD Economics Department Working Papers*, 624, 2008, pp. 5–10; Kotwal *et al.*, 'Economic Liberalization and Indian Economic Growth', pp. 24–7.

[55] For a history of the emergence of a distinct small-scale, unorganised industrial sector since 1950, see Mark Holmström, *Industry and Inequality: The Social Anthropology of Indian Labour*, Cambridge, 1984. On the impact of changes in regulative policy in the 1990s on the informal economy, see Barbara Harris-White and Anushree Sinha, *Trade Liberalization and India's Informal Economy*, New Delhi, 2007.

[56] Vinish Kathuria, S. N. Rajesh Raj and Kunal Sen, 'Organised versus Unorganised Manufacturing Performance in the Post-Reform Period', *EPW*, 45, 24, 2010; S. N. Rajesh Raja and Mihir K.

The unorganised sector has remained a very significant element in all sectors of the Indian economy. In every sector apart from public services and defence, unorganised labour made up more than four-fifths of the total workforce. Table 5.6 provides a snap-shot of the organised and unorganised sectors of manufacturing industry *c.* 2000. At this date, over 85 per cent of manufacturing employment was in the informal sector, which produced less than 20 per cent of output: while wage rates in the informal sector were very much below those in larger firms, the productivity of labour was also much lower, and was falling in the late 1990s and early 2000s. The existence of this large informal sector with low rates of wages and productivity, and for which survey data is not easy to obtain or to process, complicates any general conclusions about the history of Indian manufacturing since the 1980s.

The most dramatic example of the interaction between the organised and unorganised industrial sectors was provided by the history of the textile weaving industry. Textiles have remained one of the most important industries in India – contributing about 14 per cent of industrial production, 4 per cent of GDP and 17 per cent of export earnings, and directly employing more than 35 million workers in 2011. Government licensing policy after 1950 had consistently sought to regulate the number of units in the textile industry, and the volume of their output, to reserve a place for small-scale, semi-mechanised cloth production, and to restrain the organised sector by limiting capacity and removing incentives for technical change. One result was to damage export competitiveness, despite India's comparative advantage in access to cotton, labour and knowledge of textile production. Large- and medium-scale spinning mills have remained the majority suppliers of thread and yarn, still providing more than 50 per cent of production in the 2000s; in weaving, however, organised-sector mills were weakened by the restrictions imposed by government policy, and have been almost entirely replaced by small-scale power-loom units since the 1980s.

A dynamic power-loom sector had developed in the 1930s, but about four-fifths of cloth output was produced in the organised mechanised sector in the early 1950s; this had fallen to just over one-third by the early 1980s. The deregulation of the textile industry in 1985 encouraged investment and technical improvement in spinning, but also removed any constraints on unauthorised power looms, many of which were operating with obsolete and abandoned equipment passed down from the mechanised mills. By the mid 2000s, the

Mahapatra, 'Growth and Productivity Performance of Small Manufacturing Enterprises (SMEs): Insights from Major States in India', *Journal of Indian Business Research*, 1, 1, 2009.

Table 5.6 *Organised and unorganised labour in manufacturing in India, 1999–2000*

| | Organised manufacturing (1999–2000) | Unorganised manufacturing (2000–01) |
|---|---|---|
| Number of enterprises (million) | 0.13 | 17 |
| Number of workers (million) | 6.2 | 37 |
| Average number of workers per enterprise | 52 | 2.2 |
| Annual growth rates in employment (%)[a] | −0.38 | +4.26 |
| Average wages per worker (Rs)[b] | 44 842 | 4 087 |
| Total loans outstanding (Rs billion) | 25 132 | 868 |
| Value of output (Rs billion)[c] | 87 391 | 18 718 |
| Output per worker (Rs million) | 14.1 | 0.51 |
| Value of output per rupee of wage cost (Rs)[d] | 314 | 125 |
| % of total manufacturing workforce[e] | 14 | 86 |
| % of total manufacturing output | 82 | 18 |
| % of total manufacturing wage costs | 65 | 35 |

[a] Annual average, 1993–4 to 2004–05.

[b] Average per capita annual income at current prices in 2001–2 was Rs 17,978. Government of India, Ministry of Finance and Company Affairs, *Economic Survey* 2002–2003, table 1.1.

[c] Output statistics from the unorganised sector suffer from a range of potential errors and biases.

[d] An alternative estimate calculated the labour productivity ratio of informal to formal manufacturing firms at 0.14:1 for 1999–2000, and 0.11:1 for 2004–5: Kapila, *Indian Economy since Independence*, table 26.13.

[e] These figures are based on a national survey on employment, which estimated total employment at 457 million in 2004–5. Of this, organised-sector employment was about 27 million, i.e. about 6 per cent of the total. If agriculture is excluded, organised-sector employment was 17 per cent of all non-farm employment. An alternative survey-based estimate put organised-sector employment across the economy at 54 million in 1999–2000: about 14 per cent of the total (*National Commission for Enterprises in the Unorganised Sector*, 2008).

*Source:* Calculated from Kotwal *et al.*, 'Economic Liberalization and Indian Economic Growth', tables 1 and 7.

large- and medium-scale weaving mill sector was virtually extinct and power looms produced 99 per cent of Indian woven textiles. There were 1.5 million power looms in operation in the late 1990s, and more than 2.2 million 10 years later. The power-loom industry spread out across India, with about half the total number of units operated in Maharashtra, based around a number of major centres with a history of handloom weaving in coarse cloth. The industry has been administered in a decentralised way, with most units containing between 4 and 24 looms, and most weavers employed as piece-workers on a putting-out system dominated by relatively few proprietors.[57]

Decentralised power-loom production was much more prominent in the Indian textile industry than in its rivals across the globe, and the industry suffered from a lack of modern-style marketing and technical support. As a result the rate of technical change in production – such as the introduction of shuttleless power looms – did not keep pace with improvements in rival countries such as China, South Korea and Indonesia, partly because of problems in the supply of textile machinery.[58] Despite these difficulties, India's apparel exports grew consistently from the mid 1980s onwards, and some dynamic firms were able to turn subcontracting to their advantage by co-ordinating the design, production and sales of customised small-batch production for targeted export and domestic markets.[59]

Increased competition stimulated productivity gains in Indian manufacturing in the 1990s by encouraging the substitution of capital for labour, and by lowering the price of inputs.[60] However, there were limitations to this process in many sectors. Industries using simpler manufacturing processes, such as tobacco goods, clothing and apparel, and furniture manufacture, retained more protection and remained more labour-intensive than other sectors.[61] In the machinery industries, labour productivity and total factor productivity

[57] On the recent history of the textile and garment industries, see Tirthankar Roy, 'Economic Reforms and the Textile Industry in India', *EPW*, 33, 32, 1998; Samar Verma, 'Restructuring the Indian Textile Industry', in Ajit Kumar Sinha and S. K. Sasikumar (eds.), *Restructuring of the Textile Sector in India*, New Delhi, 2000; Sharad Chari, *Fraternal Capital: Peasant-Workers, Self-Made Men, and Globalization in Provincial India*, Stanford, 2004; Abhijit Banerjee and Kaivan Munshi, 'How Efficiently is Capital Allocated? Evidence from the Knitted Garment Industry in Tirupur', *Review of Economic Studies*, 71, 1, 2004.

[58] Arif Anjum and D. V. Thakor, 'An Analytical Study of the Functioning and the Problems of the Powerloom Industry in Maharashtra', *International Journal of Trade, Economics and Finance*, 2, 3, 2011.

[59] For examples of increased investment and up-skilling, see M. Tewari, 'Adjustment in India's Textile and Apparel Industry: Reworking Historical Legacies in a Post-MFA World', *Environment and Planning A*, 38, 12, 2006.

[60] On the impact of changes in trade policy on Indian industry, see Petia Topalova and Amit Khandelwa, 'Trade Liberalization and Firm Productivity: The Case of India', *Review of Economics and Statistics*, 93, 3, 2011; Kunal Sen, *Trade Policy, Inequality and Performance in Indian Manufacturing*, London, 2009, pp. 64–78; Shanthi Nataraj, 'The Impact of Trade Liberalization on Productivity: Evidence from India's Formal and Informal Manufacturing Sectors', *Journal of International Economics*, 85, 2, 2011.

[61] Deb Kusum Das, *Trade Liberalization, Employment, Labour Productivity, and Real Wages: A Study of the Organized Manufacturing Industry in India in the 1980s and 1990*, ILO Asia-Pacific Working Paper Series, 2008; Deb Kusum Das, Deepika Wadhwa and Gunajit Kalita, 'The Employment Potential of Labor Intensive Industries in India's Organized Manufacturing', Indian Council for Research on International Economic Relations, Working Paper 236, June 2009. For a number of case-studies around these themes, see also Suresh D. Tendulkar *et al.* (eds.), *India: Industrialisation in a Reforming Economy*, New Delhi, 2006.

(TFP) for larger companies increased through 'spillovers', as technology was transferred successfully from foreign companies to Indian collaborators and suppliers in the organised sector. There was much less change among small firms in the unorganised sector, which provided subcontracted inputs to modern manufacturing processes using labour with craft-based skills. For the most part they competed against imports on the basis of lower prices and lower quality, with many fewer productivity gains: as one analysis of machinery production concluded in 2001, 'as long as market demands low price and low quality products, the unorganised sector can survive'.[62]

The recent history of the automobile industry provides a more positive example of the impact of changes on technologically advanced industries. Modern motor car manufacture was introduced into India by Maruti Udyog (now Maruti Suzuki) in the 1980s, which began life as a pet political project of Sanjay Gandhi, and went into production as a partnership with Suzuki Motor Corporation, which supplied capital, technology and expertise. Maruti was largely protected from foreign competition until the 1990s, but then a number of overseas car manufacturers set up successful factories on greenfield sites, notably Hyundai in Chennai, while Indian corporations such as Mahindra & Mahindra and Tata Motors expanded their range of locally produced vehicles. The investment by Korean firms, and also by US corporations such as GM and Ford, indicated that India was now seen as a regional export hub for vehicles, and a potential world supplier of auto components.

Annual manufacturing wages in India remained well below those in China and South Korea in the 2000s, so the Indian motor industry retained a competitive advantage in labour costs, which partially outweighed relative weaknesses in infrastructure and supply-chains for inputs. One feature of successful firms has been their ability to build up industrial clusters of input suppliers and component manufacturers using both imported and indigenous capital. While Maruti initially used existing local firms to provide supplies, more recent manufacturers have encouraged joint ventures between foreign and Indian capital, and global suppliers of components have also moved manufacturing plant to India. Over time the Indian firms in these clusters have become more technically sophisticated and larger in size, employing increasing numbers of trained technical staff and moving away from the informal economy based on traditional labour skills.[63]

[62] Shuji Uchikawa, 'Linkage between Organised and Unorganised Sectors in Indian Machinery Industry', *EPW*, 46, 1, 2001, p. 33.

[63] John Humphrey, Avinandan Mukherjee, Mauro Zilbovicius and Glauco Arbix, 'Globalisation, Foreign Direct Investment and the Restructuring of Supplier Networks: The Motor Industry in Brazil

The organised manufacturing sector has not expanded its labour-force much since 1991, and has often been described as undergoing a process of 'jobless growth'. By the mid 2000s the economy needed to create approximately 7 million new jobs outside agriculture each year to maintain existing proportional levels of employment. One direct estimate has suggested that employment in private firms in the formal sector grew by only about 500,000 in the 11 years between 1993–4 and 2004–5, increasing in Karnataka, Andhra Pradesh and Gujarat, and falling in Bihar, Uttar Pradesh, Maharashtra and Kerala.[64] Advocates of increased liberalisation have explained the stagnation of industrial employment by identifying India's portfolio of 'restrictive' labour laws – especially the amendments to the Industrial Disputes Act (IDA) in 1976 and 1982 that required government permission for layoffs, retrenchments and closures in establishments employing more than 100 workers – as a major barrier to continued industrial development. Differential growth rates between states have been explained in terms of the 'pro-worker' or 'pro-employer' biases in their labour market institutions.[65] These views received an official endorsement in the Government of India's *Economic Survey* for 2005–6, which argued that

> various studies indicate that Indian labour laws are highly protective of labour, and labour markets are relatively inflexible. These laws ... have restricted labour mobility, have led to capital-intensive methods in the organised sector and adversely affected the sector's long-run demand for labour ... Evidence suggests that States, which have enacted more pro-worker regulations, have lost out on industrial production in general.[66]

Although far-reaching regulations for employment protection have remained on the statute books throughout the reforms process, their universal

and India', in M. Kagami, J. Humphrey and M. Piore (eds.), *Learning, Liberalization and Economic Adjustment*, Tokyo, 1998, pp. 117–87; Jongsoo Park, 'Korean Perspective on FDI in India: Hyundai Motors' Industrial Cluster', *EPW*, 29, 31, 2004; Aya Okada, 'Skills Development and Interfirm Learning Linkages under Globalization: Lessons from the Indian Automobile Industry', *World Development*, 32, 7, 2004; Shuji Uchikawa and Satyaki Roy, *The Development of Auto Component Industry in India*, Institute for Human Development, New Delhi, 2010.

64 Ramaswamy, 'Regional Dimension of Growth and Employment', table 26.9.

65 Philippe Aghion, Robin Burgess, Stephen J. Redding and Fabrizio Zilibotti, 'The Unequal Effects of Liberalization: Evidence from Dismantling the License Raj in India', *American Economic Review*, 98, 4, 2008.

66 Ministry of Finance, *Economic Survey, 2005–06*, p. 209. Very similar views were expressed by the Planning Commission in 2008 (*Eleventh Five Year Plan, 2007–2012 (Inclusive Growth)*, New Delhi, 2008, Volume 1, p. 3). See Peter R. Fallon and Robert E. B. Lucas, 'Job Security Regulations and the Dynamic Demand for Industrial Labor in India and Zimbabwe', *Journal of Development Economics*, 40, 2, 1993; Timothy Besley and Robin Burgess, 'Can Regulation Hinder Economic Performance? Evidence from India', *Quarterly Journal of Economics*, 119, 1, 2004; Ahmad Ahsan and Carmen Pagés, 'Are All Labor Regulations Equal? Evidence from Indian Manufacturing', *Journal of Comparative Economics*, 37, 1, 2009.

effectiveness can be doubted, and many of the apparent constraints on labour flexibility in the organised manufacturing sector have weakened considerably in practice. Some state governments softened their attitude to industrial restructuring in the 1980s and 1990s, and the rights apparently conferred on trades unions and the workforce by labour legislation were not always recognised or upheld. However, one detailed study of recent evidence has concluded that state legislation that increased the costs of labour disputes or retrenchment above the costs stipulated by national legislation has resulted in measureable declines in registered manufacturing employment.[67] There were considerable variations in labour productivity across Indian states at the beginning of the twenty-first century. The best-performing states produced over 60 per cent more value added per worker than the worst-performing states. According to business opinion, these differences were caused by business perceptions, regulatory hassles, customs delays, problems in energy supply and high interest rates.[68] Problems of infrastructure and provision of finance from outside the company probably constrained Indian manufacturing firms at least as much as, or more than, the potential costs of restrictive labour legislation.[69] The use of informal workers within the organised sector – by the practice of larger companies outsourcing or subcontracting work to units within the unorganised sector where labour rights are much weaker, workers are less skilled, and wages and productivity are much lower – has also depressed the growth of employment in large-scale manufacturing industry.[70]

Since international trade has become more important for the Indian economy since the 1990s, the composition of imports and exports can be used to show how much has changed in the structure of manufacturing industry. In export markets, India's low wages provided a competitive advantage for manufacturing industry, but for many commodities this was offset by lower levels

[67] Ahmed Ahsan, Carmen Pagés and Tirthankar Roy, 'Legislation, Enforcement and Adjudication in Indian Labor Markets: Origins, Consequences and the Way Forward', in Mazumdar and Sarkar, *Globalization, Labor Markets and Inequality in India*, Ch. 11.

[68] Omkar Goswami *et al.*, *Competitiveness of Indian Manufacturing: Results from a Firm-Level Survey*, Confederation of Indian Industry and World Bank, New Delhi, 2002.

[69] Poonam Gupta, Rana Hasan and Utsav Kumar, 'What Constrains Indian Manufacturing?', in Barry Eichengreen, Poonam Gupta and Rajiv Kumar (eds.), *Emerging Giants: China and India in the World Economy*, Oxford, 2010, Ch. 10. This study concludes that only detailed investigation of how these variables operate in practice at the state level will properly quantify their relative importance.

[70] Alakh N. Sharma, 'Flexibility, Employment and Labour Market Reforms in India', *EPW*, 41, 21, 2004; K. P. Kannan and G. Raveendran, 'Growth sans Employment: A Quarter Century of Jobless Growth in India's Organised Manufacturing', *EPW*, 44, 10, 2009; Aditya Bhattacharjea, 'The Effects of Employment Protection Legislation on Indian Manufacturing', *EPW*, 44, 22, 2009; Bishwanath Goldar, 'Trade Liberalisation and Labour Demand Elasticity in Indian Manufacturing', *EPW*, 44, 34, 2009.

Table 5.7 *Technology intensity of India's commodity exports, 1980–2000 (percentage of total non-oil exports)*

| | 1980 | 1990 | 2000 |
|---|---|---|---|
| Group I: primary commodities | 40.9 | 26.6 | 18.9 |
| Group II: manufactures based on labour and natural resources | 38.5 | 51.1 | 52.6 |
| Group III: manufactures characterised by low technology intensity | 5.7 | 4.8 | 6.6 |
| Group IV: medium technology intensity | 7.0 | 6.6 | 6.6 |
| Group V: high technology intensity | 5.1 | 9.3 | 11.7 |
| Other manufactures | 2.7 | 1.6 | 3.6 |

Group I: food; non-ferrous metals; other primary commodities.
Group II: textiles; footwear, leather and travel products; wood and paper products; paper, print and publishing; non-metallic mineral products.
Group III: iron and steel; fabricated metal products; simple transport equipment; ships and boats.
Group IV: rubber and plastic products; non-electrical machinery; electrical machinery (excl. semiconductors); road motor vehicles.
Group V: industrial chemicals; pharmaceuticals; computers and office equipment; communication equipment and semiconductors; aircraft; scientific instruments.
Other manufactures include sanitary and plumbing products; toys and sporting goods; office and stationery supplies; works of art; jewellery; musical instruments.
*Source:* www.indiastat.com, compiled from statistics from Reserve Bank of India, *Report on Currency and Finance*, 2002–03.

of productivity than elsewhere in Asia.[71] The composition of India's exports in the late 1990s and early 2000s suggested that, despite the increased availability of capital and imported technology, its international competitiveness in manufactured goods still lay in commodities that reflected its low labour costs, rather than the productive use of advanced techniques. As table 5.7 shows, 80 per cent of Indian exports in 1980 were made up of primary commodities, such as food and non-ferrous metals, and manufactures based on the availability of labour and natural resources, such as textiles, leather products, wood and paper, and non-metallic mineral products. By 2000 these categories had declined slightly in importance, but still provided over 70 per cent of the value of exports; the only significant increase elsewhere was for industrial

[71] L. Lakshmanan, S. Chinngaihlian and Rajesh Raj, 'Competitiveness of India's Manufacturing Sector: An Assessment of Related Issues', RBI Occasional Paper, 28, 1, 2007.

chemicals and pharmaceuticals, which boosted the high-technology groups of exports from 5.1 per cent of the total in 1980 to 11.7 per cent in 2000.

Subsequent changes in the technological intensity of India's exports were obscured by the increase in India's sale of petroleum products, which rose from 5.6 per cent of the total value of exports in 2003–4 to 15.1 per cent in 2006–7. As a percentage of non-oil exports, primary produce and ores and minerals increased slightly in this period. Manufactures as a whole remained roughly constant; within this category the share of chemicals was unchanged at around 15 per cent; while engineering goods increased from 20 to 27 per cent, and more established lines of export commodities, such as textiles, leather goods, handicrafts and gems, and jewellery declined from 44 per cent of total non-oil exports in 2003–4 to 35 per cent in 2006–7.[72] While exports based on increased technological sophistication certainly increased in the 2000s, in manufactured goods as well as in services, a good deal of continuity with the pre-reform economy remained: slightly more than half of the value of India's non-oil commodity exports in the late 2000s was still made up of the categories of low-technology goods that had been its staple items of trade since the 1980s.

### *Services*

The growth of the service sector has been the most distinctive feature of the Indian economy over the last thirty years.[73] The sector's proportion of GDP increased from less than 40 per cent in 1980 to almost 60 per cent in 2010, and there was rapid growth in high technology areas. Table 5.8 shows the growth rates and sectoral shares of different services from the 1980s to 2010. The data have been organised to distinguish three different types of services: first a group of traditional services, then a mixture of traditional and modern services consumed mainly by households, then a set of modern services consumed by both the household and corporate sectors.[74] Service industries also

[72] Calculated from data from www.indiastat.com. The totals for 2006–7 are for the ten months from April to January.

[73] On the history of service industries since 1980, see Jim Gordon and Poonam Gupta, 'Understanding India's Services Revolution', *IMF Working Papers*, WP/04/17 (2004); Barry Eichengreen and Poonam Gupta, 'The Service Sector as India's Road to Economic Growth', *NBER Working Papers*, 16757 (2010); Sunil Jain and T. N. Ninan, 'Servicing India's GDP Growth', in Shankar Acharya and Rakesh Mohan (eds.), *India's Economy Performance and Challenges: Essays in Honour of Montek Singh Ahluwalia*, New Delhi, 2010; Ajitava Raychaudhuri and Prabir De, *International Trade in Services in India: Implications for Growth and Inequality in a Globalizing World*, New Delhi, 2012.

[74] This categorisation is taken from Barry Eichengreen and Poonam Gupta, 'The Two Waves of Service Sector Growth', *NBER Working Papers*, 14968, 2009, p. 16.

Table 5.8 *Sectoral shares of service industries (percentage of GDP), 1980–2008*

| | 1980 | 1990 | 2000 | 2008 |
|---|---|---|---|---|
| Trade (distribution) | 10.6 | 11.2 | 13.1 | 13.9 |
| Railways | 1.6 | 1.5 | 1.2 | 1.2 |
| Other transport | 3.6 | 4.0 | 4.6 | 5.2 |
| Storage | 0.1 | 0.1 | 0.1 | 0.1 |
| Public administration, defence | 5.7 | 6.4 | 6.7 | 6.3 |
| *(Sub-total I* | *21.6* | *23.2* | *25.7* | *26.7)* |
| Hotels and restaurants | 0.8 | 0.9 | 1.3 | 1.4 |
| Personal and other | 2.4 | 1.9 | 1.8 | 1.6 |
| Community services | 4.6 | 5.1 | 6.3 | 6.1 |
| *(Sub-total II* | *7.8* | *7.9* | *9.4* | *9.1)* |
| Communication | 0.7 | 0.7 | 2.0 | 6.8 |
| Banking | 1.9 | 3.3 | 5.0 | 6.3 |
| Insurance | 0.6 | 0.6 | 0.6 | 1.3 |
| Dwellings and real estate | 4.5 | 5.8 | 5.2 | 3.6 |
| Business services | 0.4 | 0.7 | 2.1 | 4.0 |
| *(Sub-total III* | *8.0* | *11.1* | *14.9* | *22.0)* |
| TOTAL | 37.5 | 42.2 | 50.0 | 57.8 |

*Source*: Barry Eichengreen and Poonam Gupta, 'The Service Sector as India's Road to Economic Growth', *NBER Working Papers*, no. 16757 (2010), p. 45, at www.nber.org/papers/w16757.

formed an important part of India's foreign trade. The share of services in the value of total exports increased from 21 per cent in 1990 to 28 per cent in 2002, and to 35 per cent by 2010, while imports also ran at more than 25 per cent of the total during most of this period. India is currently by far the world's largest single supplier of exports of computer and information services.[75]

Within the service sector, traditional services such as trade, transport and public administration retained a substantial share of the total value, and together contributed more than a quarter of GDP in 2010. These industries

[75] World Trade Organization, *International Trade Statistics, 2011*, table III, 29. On the rise of high-tech services in India, see Nirvikar Singh, 'Information Technology and India's Economic Development', in Kaushik Basu (ed.), *India's Emerging Economy: Performance and Prospects in the 1990s and Beyond*, Cambridge MA, 2004. On subsequent events, see Sabeer Ahmend Khan and Pier A. Abetti, 'The Rise and Globalisation of the Indian IT Industry: Dual Case Study of Wipro Technologies and Infosys', *International Journal of Services Technology and Management*, 15, 3–4, 2011; Jay Mitra and Ganesh Natarajan, 'Science, Technology and Regional Entrepreneurial Growth in India: The Case of the Software Industry', in Sarfraz A. Mian (ed.), *Science and Technology Based Regional Entrepreneurship: Global Experience in Policy and Program Development*, Cheltenham, 2011.

also absorb almost all the labour employed in the sector, and contain a large proportion of small firms in the unorganised sector of the economy. The main feature of the 1990s and 2000s was the very rapid rise of knowledge-based services, based around IT, ITES and BPO. The United States was consistently the largest export market for Indian firms in this sector, with a 60 per cent share. The IT-BPO sector's revenues have grown from 1.2 per cent of India's GNP in 1998 to an estimated 6.4 per cent in 2011, employing a workforce of 2 million. The IT sector's share of total Indian exports (merchandise plus services) increased from less than 4 per cent in 1998 to 26 per cent in 2010–11, and then represented more than 50 per cent of exports of services. Global demand for these services held up well during the economic crisis after 2008, which increased their relative share of Indian exports. Domestic markets for IT-BPO services also rose sharply at the end of the 2000s, on the back of strong economic growth, rapid advancement in technology and institutional change.[76] Productivity increases in this sector were mainly the result of technological change in the early 2000s. Across the economy as a whole, knowledge-intensive production as a percentage of total output rose from about 9 per cent in 1999–2000 to 14 per cent in 2005–6, especially in services such as communications, computer-related services and R&D services.[77]

The dramatic success of the IT-BPO sector arose from a particular set of circumstances in which networks of Indian expatriate or immigrant businessmen and IT specialists in the United States in the 1990s were able to connect to specialised skilled labour in India. In turn, IT became a strong career preference for many Indian entrants to tertiary education, and many graduates in these disciplines sought work in the USA and other developed countries. The rapid growth in communications services since 1990 was the result of a similar unique stimulus with the arrival of effective and rapidly evolving mobile telephone and digital information technology. Telecoms liberalisation began in 1994, when the private sector was allowed entry: the consequence was a dramatic rise in communication services, whose share of GDP rose from 0.7 per cent in 1991 to 4.9 per cent in 2006–7. The success or failure of individual players in the telecoms sector has been heavily bound up with relations between large corporations and the state; apparent favouritism to particular firms, such as Reliance, has played

[76] NASSCOM, *The IT-BPO Sector in India: Strategic Review – 2011*, 'Executive Summary', at www.nasscom.org/sites/default/files/researchreports/Exec%20Summary_0.pdf.

[77] Sunil Mani, *The Growth of Knowledge-Intensive Entrepreneurship in India, 1991–2007*, United Nations University, Maastricht: Economic and Social Research and Training Centre on Innovation and Technology Working Paper #2009–051, 2009, table 3, at www.merit.unu.edu/publications/wppdf/2009/wp2009-051.pdf.

an important role in determining opportunity. With the growth of the Indian mobile market, a number of foreign companies set up equipment assembly plants, at low levels of added value, to take advantage of tax incentives.

India has not been uniquely well-endowed in most areas of the 'new technology economy'. In 2010, compared to comparator countries with similar levels of per capita income, India had below-average numbers of internet users, and broadband and mobile telephone subscriptions per head: ICT provided a much higher percentage of India's exports in services than in other low-middle income economies, but was well below the average percentage of the value of total exports.[78] The leading sectors of the high-tech service industries have relied heavily on recruiting adequately qualified skilled labour, with appropriate training in engineering. By the mid 2000s, the supply of such labour was becoming problematic: many of those who had received an appropriate education were unemployable without extensive retraining, much of which had to be done inside the firm. The Government of India's Knowledge Commission reported considerable problems in both the design and delivery of engineering education, requiring extensive further reforms.[79]

As with manufacturing industry, the service sector became divided between a set of very modern, technologically sophisticated and highly skilled industries supplying ITES and communication technologies to domestic and international markets, and a set of conventional industries rooted in established practices, which employ the bulk of labour, but which have much lower levels of productivity and profitability. The rates of growth of the dynamic parts of the service sector have been much greater than has been the case in manufacturing, and India has established a global brand in IT-BPO exports. The relations between the unorganised and organised parts of the services sector are not so clear-cut as in the case of manufacturing industry, although hopes have been expressed that semi-skilled labour outside the big conurbations may find employment in the informal sector at the bottom end of the IT-BPO industry.

## ECONOMIC INSTITUTIONS IN CONTEMPORARY INDIA

Much of the rhetoric surrounding the reform programme in India, and the subsequent analysis of economic change since the 1980s, has stressed the

[78] Data from World Bank, *World Development Indicators*.

[79] National Knowledge Commission, *Report of Working Group on Engineering Education*, New Delhi, 2008. Carl Dahlman and Anuja Utz, *India and the Knowledge Economy*, Washington, DC, 2005 also identified a potentially damaging mismatch between the education system and the labour market.

tension between the state and the market, and has celebrated or contested a narrative concerned with the triumph of liberalisation and the private sector over state agencies and public institutions. However, the Indian state and its agencies retained a crucial role in the economic life of the country after 1991: 71 per cent of total employment in the organised sector was in the public sector in 1991, and 69 per cent in 2000.[80] In the mid 2000s, the public sector was responsible for about one-fifth of domestic GDP, about one-quarter of gross domestic capital formation and about one-sixth of final consumption expenditure, and these proportions held steady through to the end of the decade.[81]

The prevalence of both political and bureaucratic corruption – a violation of law by public officials for private gain – has required all other participants in economic life to deal closely with the apparatus of the state. Typically, corrupt practices have arisen from the need to secure necessary interventions to obtain discriminatory benefits for powerful political groups to maintain social hierarchies, or to award preferential access to resources for emerging capitalists.[82] Such interventions have provided a way of allocating scarce resources when adequate market institutions or legislative frameworks do not exist. However, corruption has been wasteful of common resources and has prevented efficiency-based or equity-based allocations. Corruption and cronyism have also extended into the private sector, where illegal acts for profit and mutual advantage, often contracted within existing networks of association, played an important part in some business activities. According to some estimates, the 'underground economy' of India in the late 2000s accounted for 50 per cent of the official GDP: black money (illicit capital) outflows from India were estimated at $280 billion for the period from 1948 to 2008, and $104 billion for 2000 to 2008.[83]

The elaborate set of official constraints that determined Indian business activity in the 1950s, 1960s and 1970s provided many opportunities for symbiotic alliances between privileged groups and state functionaries. The policy reforms of the 1980s began to roll back the planning bureaucracy, but gave politicians greater direct influence in economic decision-making on a case-by-case basis. This led to the development of 'briefcase politics', in which

[80] Government of India, Planning Commission, *National Human Development Report*, New Delhi, 2001, tables 7.13–14. There was a slight decline in public-sector employment in the 2000s.

[81] 'Performance of Public Sector in India', www.indiastat.com.

[82] Mushtaq H. Khan, 'Corruption and Governance in South Asia', in *Europa South Asia Yearbook*, 2009, London, at www.eprints.soas.ac.uk/11683/.

[83] Dev Kar, *The Drivers and Dynamics of Illicit Financial Flows from India: 1948–2008* (Global Financial Integrity, November 2010), at www.gfintegrity.org/storage/gfip/documents/reports/india/gfi_india.pdf.

political operators financed their activities by demanding contributions for their services.[84] This trend continued despite the rhetoric of liberalisation in the 1990s, with the funding of much politics and many politicians following an increasingly blatant incentive and reward system. The granting of licences for mineral exploitation in states such as Jharkhand, Karnataka and Orissa; the awarding of contracts for prestige events such as the Commonwealth Games in 2010; and the pricing and allocation of 2G and 3G mobile phone networks since 2008 have been obvious recent examples of this process.[85] The campaign in 2011 to establish an ombudsman with real powers to investigate allegations of corruption, building on the public access to information established in the Right to Information Act of 2005, showed the political importance of such high-profile cases.

Securing favours to obtain necessary interventions by the functionaries of the state runs right through the economic life of India. Surveys of business opinion by the World Bank have highlighted India's reputation as a place where it is necessary to give gifts to secure an operating licence, to get an import licence and to obtain a construction permit.[86] India was ranked 87th out of the 178 countries in the *Transparency International Corruption Perception Index* of public-sector corruption in 2010, lower than Brazil (69th) and China (78th), but above Russia (154th).[87] Bureaucratic procedures and the failings of the legal system still made India seem a difficult place to do business: in the World Bank's *Doing Business Survey 2012*, India was ranked in 132nd place out of 183 countries – scoring badly in terms of difficulty of opening a business (166th place), dealing with construction permits (181st place) and enforcing contracts (182nd place).[88] At the bottom of the social hierarchy, perception of corruption was also very widespread, and one in three of 'below poverty line' (BPL) households in a 2008 survey reported paying a bribe or using a favoured contact in matters concerning the police, land records and registration, and housing.[89]

[84] Stanley Kochanek, 'Liberalization and Business Lobbying in India', *Journal of Commonwealth and Comparative Politics*, 34, 3, 1996.

[85] In February 2012 the Indian Supreme Court ruled that 122 mobile phone licences issued to companies after 2008 were invalid and must be cancelled.

[86] However, only a quarter of the firms surveyed in India identified corruption as a major constraint, as opposed to over one-third in the global sample: World Bank, *Enterprise Surveys* (2006), at www.enterprisesurveys.org/Data/ExploreEconomies/2006/india#corruption/.

[87] www.transparency.org/policy_research/surveys_indices/cpi/2010/results.

[88] www.doingbusiness.org/data/exploreeconomies/india/. A more detailed survey ranks seventeen major Indian cities for ease of doing business on a wide sample of indicators: World Bank, *Doing Business in India*, 2009, Washington DC, 2010.

[89] Transparency International India, *India Corruption Study – 2008*, New Delhi, 2008. This study designated the level of corruption faced by BPL households as 'alarming' in Assam, Bihar, Jammu and

The policy reforms of the 1980s and 1990s had their origins in a series of decisions at the highest levels of government to stimulate economic growth as a way of solving the entrenched economic and political problems of the 1970s. As this priority filtered down the political system, it became amalgamated with the need to secure and maintain support among established political and socially dominant groups, and also to meet the needs of upwardly mobile populist movements. The stimulus provided by the economic reforms has found a much stronger response in some Indian states than in others. Given the complexity of Indian reality, these countervailing forces for destabilising change and stagnating stability have had different outcomes in the different social, cultural and political environments of different arenas and areas.

Many accounts of the economic history of the years since 1980 have placed political institutions, and the actions of the state and its agencies, at the heart of the process. One recent study divides Indian state structures into three ideal types based on the manner in which governmental authority interacts with market conditions. In neo-patrimonial states, such as those which rule in Uttar Pradesh, Madhya Pradesh, Orissa and Bihar, the ruling elites use state power for personal gain or for the benefit of a narrow political community, and have little interest in the public good of development; in social-democratic states, such as Kerala, West Bengal and Tamil Nadu, the power of state-level rulers depends on the mobilisation of lower castes or classes, often around issues of regional nationalism, and requires economic growth to meet the needs of these constituents; in developmental states, such as Maharashtra and Gujarat for manufacturing, Karnataka and Andhra Pradesh for service industries, and Haryana and Punjab for agri-business, the local government works closely with business groups to promote economic growth successfully, but at the cost of encouraging exclusionary political and cultural ideologies. In this analysis, states where the private sector was most advanced at the beginning of the reform period were best able to take advantage of the new opportunities after 1991. Their advantages are seen to stretch back into the colonial period, with better-quality bureaucratic control, higher rates of literacy, successful anti-elitist political movements and more equitable distribution of land.[90]

Kashmir, Madhya Pradesh, and Uttar Pradesh; and as 'very high' in Karnataka, Rajasthan and Tamil Nadu. On the impact of corruption and institutionalised violence at a local level, see Andrew Sanchez, 'Capitalism, Violence and the State: Crime, Corruption and Entrepreneurship in an Indian Company Town', *Journal of Legal Anthropology*, 1, 2, 2010; and Jeffrey Witsoe, 'Everyday Corruption and the Political Mediation of the Indian State: An Ethnographic Exploration of Brokers in Bihar', *EPW*, 47, 6, 2012.

[90] Atul Kohli, *Poverty amid Plenty in the New India*, Cambridge, 2012, Ch. 3. For an alternative analysis of contemporary India's strengths and weaknesses as a developmental state, see Jørgen Dige

Political systems in many parts of the country have successfully adapted to the new circumstances brought about by liberalisation. The continued ability of state agencies to provide so much of the institutional mechanism for allocating economic resources has constrained the emergence of effective market mechanisms elsewhere in the economy. A number of recent studies have argued that economic liberalism and rapid growth have also caused serious problems for the operation of India's key public institutions.[91] In these circumstances, the private sector has failed to develop a smoothly integrated set of institutions to maximise productivity and allocate its rewards effectively. The problems of bounded rationality, imperfect knowledge, unequal access to information, principal–agent problems and public goods have continued the problems of market imperfections that independent India inherited from the colonial past, but some continental drift has taken place between the tectonic plates that lie beneath India's political economy.

In parts of northern India since 1980 there has been a social revolution, mirroring what had occurred in the south from the 1960s, which gave access to political power to lower castes through media exposure, literacy and active participation in local, regional and national elections. Economic opportunities for wider social groups have increased as a consequence. Much of the literature on Indian entrepreneurs and companies has been dominated by the conventional issues of family firms, closed business groups, and the continued expansion of the established business communities such as the Parsis, Marwaris and Chettiars who rose to prominence in the first half of the twentieth century. However, the expansion of manufacturing and high-tech service industries has seen the entrance of a large number of 'new capitalists', many from social backgrounds – such as farming, local trading and white-collar professions – which had no previous links to large-scale industry. While much of the large unorganised sector is still run by traditional methods that have their roots in hierarchic relations between labour and capital, industry studies have shown that careful management and co-ordination of clusters of small firms in some instances can create productivity and technologically sophisticated production processes. It can be argued that the economic history of India since the 1990s has allowed a rich, but previously suppressed, business tradition to flower in

Pedersen, *Globalization, Development and the State: The Performance of India and Brazil since 1990*, New York, 2008.

[91] Arvind Subramanian, 'The Evolution of Institutions in India and Its Relationship with Economic Growth', *Oxford Review of Economic Policy*, 23, 2, 2007; Dev Kishore and Pratap Bhanu Mehta, *Public Institutions in India: Performance and Design*, New Delhi, 2005; Pulapre Balakrishnan, *Economic Growth in India: History and Prospect*, New Delhi, 2010.

many parts of society, which has succeeded in 'democratising entrepreneurship' to a considerable extent, although no substantial body of dalit entrepreneurs have emerged from the most marginalised sectors of Indian society as yet.[92]

The increase in private-sector business activity, the growth of profitable firms and the spread of opportunities for enterprise and entrepreneurship created a new spirit of achievement and ambition in the reform period. With the withdrawal of state agencies from the micro-management of business decisions, private corporations have supplied a crucial segment of the economic institutions necessary to enable growth and development to occur. The organisational structure of Indian firms has traditionally been dominated by two models that have roots far back in the colonial past – family firms based on extended kinship, and closely integrated business corporations in which a small core of investors control a large number of diversified companies as a conglomerate group, often with little vertical or horizontal integration. Despite the new opportunities and external stimuli of the last twenty years or so, these structures have remained largely untouched.

Family connections in business organisation have represented an important mechanism for building networks of trust when the external institutional environment is inadequate. Where property rights are seen to be weak, and legal processes are protracted and unreliable, there is little confidence in institutionalised sanctions to regulate interactions between businesses, especially between small firms in the unorganised sector. Kinship connections, sometimes expressed through caste networks, have provided an important institutional foundation for collaborative arrangements, although in practice these are often based on relationships of unequal power as well as on a shared sense of community. Among large companies, family business groups have also remained predominant, since they reduce problems caused by transaction costs and asymmetric access to information. One result has been to enable the core owners of such conglomerates to manipulate the distribution of resources and profits within the group to maximise their returns at the expense of other shareholders.[93]

[92] On these new developments, see Sumit Ganguly and Rahul Mukherji, *India since 1980*, Cambridge, 2011; Harish Damodaran, *India's New Capitalists: Caste, Business, and Industry in a Modern Nation*, Raniket, 2008; Sumit K. Majumdar, *India's Late, Late Industrial Revolution: Democratizing Entrepreneurship*, Cambridge, 2012.

[93] Rajesh Chakrabati, William Megginson and Pradeep Yadav, 'Corporate Governance in India', *Journal of Applied Corporate Finance*, 20, 1, 2002; John Harriss, 'The Great Tradition Globalizes. Reflections on Two Studies of "The Industrial Leaders" of Madras', *Modern Asian Studies*, 37, 2, 2003, and '"Widening the Radius of Trust": Ethnographic Explorations of Trust and Indian Business', *Journal of the Royal Anthropological Institute*, 9, 4, 2003: this article also contains useful case-studies of industrial firms in Ahmedabad and Chennai.

The internal operations of many large Indian corporations have remained opaque; and the reasons for many inter-firm operations within major groups have remained hidden from view. Thus the key problem of corporate governance – how to prevent the privileging of the interests of one group within a company over all others – has been difficult to identify, much less to correct.[94] Reforms that have provided more oversight of corporate finance through the Securities and Exchanges Board of India (set up in 1992), and legal sanctions to protect the position of minority shareholders, may have mitigated these problems somewhat. Some large groups, such as Tatas, underwent significant restructuring in the 1990s in response to the changes brought about by changes in government policy. However, diversified groups maintained their market valuation as against stand-alone firms in the 1990s and 2000s by using the group structure to reallocate profits, and monitor group performance through interlocking directorships.[95] Such internal transfers can provide capital for new ventures from one part of a group to another, but they can also raise barriers to entry and shut out potential innovators. It remains to be seen whether the continued dominance of the conventional structure of diversified family groups will provide an appropriate institutional framework for the Indian corporate sector in the future.

Overall, the most important institutional issue for the continuation of economic growth and development in India concerns access to the opportunities provided by liberalisation. The benefits of this process remain skewed away from Indian citizens with low levels of literacy and poor access to information, and who lack the means of social and political empowerment. The hope must be that the substantially higher rates of growth and investment, co-ordinated through market mechanisms that are currently being created, will provide more opportunities for social and economic upward mobility than did the public-sector institutions of the past. With government social policies now stressing equality of opportunity rather than redistribution of wealth, it has become more important than ever to address the issues of human capital formation and

[94] On the problems of corporate governance, see Jairas Banerji and Gautam Mody, 'Corporate Governance and the Indian Private Sector', Queen Elizabeth House Working Paper 73 (2001) at: www3.qeh.ox.ac.uk/pdf/qehwp/qehwps73.pdf.

[95] Raja Kali and Jayati Sarkar, 'Diversification and Tunneling: Evidence from Indian Business Groups', *Journal of Comparative Economics*, 39, 3, 2011. For other accounts of the recent history of corporate structures, see Tarun Khanna and Krishna Palepu, 'Is Group Affiliation Profitable in Emerging Markets? An Analysis of Diversified Indian Business Groups', *Journal of Finance*, 55, 2, 2000; P. N. Khandwalla, 'Effective Organisational Response by Corporates to India's Liberalisation and Globalization', *Asia Pacific Journal of Management*, 19, 2–3, 2002; Marianne Bertrand, Paras Mehta and Sendhil Mullainathan, 'Ferreting out Tunneling: An Application to Indian Business Groups', *Quarterly Journal of Economics*, 117, 1, 2002.

the improvement of life-chances. Neither the state nor the market can achieve these goals on their own: the creation of a flexible set of political and economic institutions requires a social and cultural commitment to development that can make best use of the legacy of the last thirty years.

# BIBLIOGRAPHICAL ESSAY

## 1 DEVELOPMENT AND UNDERDEVELOPMENT IN COLONIAL INDIA

There is no space here to list all the works that deal with the economic history of modern India, from the mass of official publications by government and government agencies in India and Britain, through the sturdy classics of imperialism and nationalism that have dominated the historiography for most of the last hundred years, to the plethora of articles and specialist monographs that contain the results of painstaking and detailed qualitative, quantitative and theoretical research. A comprehensive five-volume bibliography for material published up to the 1970s is available in V. D. Divekar *et al.* (eds.), *Annotated Bibliography on the Economic History of India, 1500 AD to 1947 AD*, Gokhale Institute of Politics and Economics, Poona, and Indian Council of Social Science Research, New Delhi, 1977–80. Since the publication of this work there has been a spate of surveys and interpretative essays that have tried to summarise, establish, and contest the main lines of argument over the issues of development and underdevelopment in colonial South Asia, many of which have contained bibliographical material and literature summaries of their own. Among the most important of these has been Peter Robb, 'British Rule and Indian "Improvement"', *Economic History Review*, 34, 4, 1981; Dharma Kumar, with Meghnad Desai (eds.), *The Cambridge Economic History of India, Volume 2: c. 1750-c. 1970*, Cambridge, 1982 (*CEHI*, 2); Neil Charlesworth, *British Rule and the Indian Economy 1880–1914*, London, 1983; *Modern Asian Studies*, 19, 3, 1985, special number entitled 'Review of the Cambridge Economic History of India and Beyond', edited by Gordon Johnson; Colin Simmons, '"Arrested Development" in India – Worthwhile Epithet, Hostage to Fortune or Plain Utopianism?', in Clive Dewey (ed.), *Arrested Development in India: The Historical Dimension*, New Delhi, 1988; D. A. Washbrook, 'Progress and Problems: South Asian Economic and Social History c. 1720–1860', and B. R. Tomlinson, 'The Historical Roots of Indian Poverty: Issues in the Economic and Social History of Modern South Asia: 1880–1960', *MAS*, 22, 1, 1988; Hamza Alavi and John Harriss (eds.), *Sociology of 'Developing Societies': South Asia*, Basingstoke, 1989; Sugata Bose (ed.), *South Asia and World Capitalism*, Delhi, 1990; and Robin Jeffery *et al.* (eds.), *India: Rebellion to Republic: Selected Writings, 1857–1990*, Asian Association of Australia, New Delhi, 1990. Dietmar Rothermund, *An Economic History of India From Pre-Colonial Times to 1986*, London, 1988, provides a chronologically based introduction to the subject and a brief annotated bibliography, while his *India in the Great Depression*, Delhi, 1992, gives an overview of the important decade of the 1930s. In addition, a number of general histories, such as Judith M. Brown, *Modern India: The Origins of an Asian Democracy*, Oxford, 1984; Sumit Sarkar, *Modern India, 1880–1947*, Delhi, 1983; and Bipin Chandra *et al.*, *India's Struggle for Independence*, New Delhi, 1988, all also contain some material on economic history.

The history of development economics, and the elaborate refinements of classical, Marxian and dependency theories, have also spawned large bibliographical accounts of their own. A wide-ranging summary is provided in Charles P. Oman and Ganesh Wignaraya, *The Post-War Evolution of Development Thinking*, Basingstoke, 1991. Jeffrey G. Williamson, *Inequality, Poverty and History*, Cambridge MA, 1991, and Pramit Chaudhuri, *Economic Theory of Growth*, Hemel Hempstead, 1989, provide useful theoretical and historical perspectives on the treatment of growth by economists and economic historians. These are usefully reviewed by J. B. Knight, 'The Evolution of Development Economies', in V. N. Balasubramanyam and Sanjaya Lall (eds.), *Current Issues in Development Economics*, Basingstoke, 1991, and Pranab Bardhan, 'Alternative Approaches to Development Economies', in H. Chenery and T. N. Srinivasan (eds.), *Handbook of Development Economics*, Volume 1, Amsterdam, 1988. Lloyd Reynolds, 'The Spread of Economic Growth in the Third World', in *Journal of Economic Literature*, 21, 1983, details aspects of the economic history of growth in the developing countries that economists have thought significant. Interesting use of Indian material and experience in development studies from a variety of standpoints will be found in I. D. M. Little, *Economic Development: Theory, Policy and International Relations*, New York, 1982; John Harriss (ed.), *Rural Development: Theories of Peasant Economy and Agrarian Change*, London, 1982; G. M. Meier and Dudley Seers (eds.), *Pioneers in Development*, Oxford, 1984; John Toye, *Dilemmas of Development: Reflections on the Counter-Revolution in Development Theory and Policy*, Oxford, 1987; and Pranab Bradhan (ed.), *The Economic Theory of Agrarian Institutions*, Oxford, 1989.

The most authoritative single source of national income estimates for colonial South Asia remains S. Sivasubramonian's unpublished Ph.D. thesis, *National Income of India, 1900–01 to 1946–7*, Delhi School of Economics, 1965. This should be supplemented by the material in M. Muherjee, *National Income of India, Trends and Structure*, Calcutta, 1969; A. Maddison, *Class Structure and Economic Growth: India and Pakistan since the Moghuls*, London, 1971 and 'Alternative Estimates of the Real Product of India, 1900–1946', *Indian Economic and Social History Review* (henceforth *IESHR*), 22, 2, 1985; and A. Heston, 'National Income', in *CEHI*, 2, Chapter IV. Heston also discusses the classic statistical exercises of the colonial era, notably W. Digby, *'Prosperous' British India: A Revaluation from Official Records*, London 1901; Dadabhai Naoroji, *Poverty and Un-British Rule*, London, 1901; and F. T. Atkinson, 'A Statistical Review of the Income and Wealth of British India', *Journal of the Royal Statistical Society*, 65, II, 1902. Raymond W. Goldsmith, *The Financial Development of India, 1860–1977*, New Haven, 1983, provides statistical indicators of the financial structure and development of South Asia and the Indian Union for this and subsequent periods, based on a wide range of secondary statistical sources.

The best modern account of the analytical and conceptual complexities of the 'drain' theory will be found in A. K. Banerji, *Aspects of Indo-British Economic Relations, 1858–1898*, Bombay, 1982. The history of India's international accounts in this period is made more complicated by the problems of the silver standard rupee, and monetary and financial issues have always played an important part in the debate over the costs and benefits of imperial rule. For analyses that reflect various approaches and viewpoints, see S. Ambirajan, *Political Economy and Monetary Management. India 1766–1914*, Madras, 1984; James Foreman-Peck, 'Foreign Investment and Imperial

Exploitation: Balance of Payments Reconstruction for Nineteenth-Century Britain and India', *Economic History Review*, 42, 3, 1989; and Sunanda Sen, *Empire and Colonies: India 1890–1914*, Calcutta, 1992. Balance of payments data for the inter-war years has been somewhat neglected. K. N. Chaudhuri, 'Foreign Trade and Balance of Payments (1757 – 1847)', in *CEHI*, 2, contains some information, but the standard, and by far the most detailed, account is that in A. K. Banerji, *India's Balance of Payments – 1921–22 to 1938–39*, Bombay, 1963.

## 2 AGRICULTURE 1860–1950

An enormous crop of monograph and article literature on agrarian history has been produced over the last twenty years, although much of it deals with administrative history, social structure and peasant studies, rather than with the production difficulties caused by the imperfections of interlinked rural commodity, capital and labour markets, and market-replacing institutions that are the main concern of this study. Collections of essays of agrarian history, reflecting the wide diversity of themes, methods, issues and ideological preconceptions, include Asok Sen, Partha Chatterjee and Saugata Mukherji, *Perspectives in Social Sciences 2: Three Studies on the Agrarian Structure of Bengal before Independence*, Delhi, 1982; Meghnad Desai, Susanne Rudolph and Ashok Rudra (eds.), *Agrarian Power and Agricultural Productivity in South Asia*, Berkeley, 1984; K. N. Raj *et al.*, *Essays on the Commercialization of Indian Agriculture*, Delhi, 1985; and *Studies in History*, new series, 1, 2, 1985, special number entitled 'Essays in Agrarian History: India 1850 to 1950', edited by S. Bhattacharya; and Utsa Patnaik (ed.), *Agrarian Relations and Accumulation*, Bombay, 1990.

David Ludden's essay entitled 'Productive Power in Agriculture', in *Agrarian Power and Agricultural Productivity*, is an excellent survey of the literature on the rural economy published in the 1970s, not least because he is sensitive to the study of agriculture as a way of life, and is aware of both the richness and the indigestibility of the vast range of local studies. These concerns also appear in his *Peasant History in South India*, Princeton, 1985. Christopher John Baker, *An Indian Rural Economy, 1880–1955. The Tamilnad Countryside*, Delhi, 1984; Sumit Guha, *The Agrarian Economy of the Bombay Deccan, 1818–1941*, Delhi, 1985; and Sugata Bose, *Agrarian Bengal: Economy, Social Structure and Politics, 1919–1947*, Cambridge 1986, are monographs that consider the problems of agrarian production in very different parts of the subcontinent. The use made by historians of modern theoretical approaches to tenancy issues is summarised and extended in Neeladri Bhattacharya, 'The Logic of Tenancy Cultivation: Central and Southeast Punjab, 1870–1935', *IESHR*, 20, 2, 1983, while Peter Robb, 'Peasants' Choices? Indian Agriculture and the Limits of Commercialization in Nineteenth-Century Bihar', *Economic History Review*, 45, 1, 1992, emphasises the extent and penetration of labour and capital markets even in a 'backward' rural economy. Omkar Goswami and Aseen Shrivastava, 'Commercialisation in Indian Agriculture, 1900–1940: What Do Supply Response Functions Say?', *IESHR*, 28, 3, 1991, provides an exemplary demonstration of both the possibilities and the limitations of applying econometric techniques to the statistical data available on colonial agriculture. Their conclusion that 'not all economic stories can be told or proved by statistically significant coefficients' (p. 252) is an important one for our argument.

For a convenient introduction to colonial perceptions of rural development, see Peter Robb, 'Bihar, the Colonial State and Agricultural Development in India, 1880–1920', *IESHR*, 25, 2, 1988; and Clive J. Dewey's 'Introduction' to Malcolm Lyall Darling, *The Punjab Peasant in Prosperity and Debt*, Delhi, 1977. Dewey's *The Settlement Literature of the Greater Punjab*, Delhi/Boston, 1991, discusses an important source of material on the agrarian economy, while Shahid Amin's commentary in the reissued edition of William Cooke, *A Glossary of North Indian Peasant Life*, Delhi, 1989, discusses British perceptions of Indian realities as colonial discourses. The place of India in a regional economy based on the exchange of food-crops, remittances, labour and capital is sketched out in Christopher J. Baker, 'Economic Reorganization and the Slump in South and Southeast Asia', *Comparative Studies in Society and History*, 23, 3, 1981. The modern literature on ecological change in rural India through the colonial period mostly deals with colonisation, forest policy and the impact of irrigation. It is summarised in J. F. Richards, James E. Hagan and Edward S. Haynes, 'Changing Land Use in Bihar, Punjab and Haryana, 1850–1970', *Modern Asian Studies (MAS)*, 19, 3, 1985, and Marika Vicziany, 'Indian Economic History and the Ecological Dimension', *Asian Studies Review*, 1991.

The data on which almost all the estimates of agricultural production in the colonial period are based were gathered as part of the land revenue assessment process, and so a strong suspicion remains that, as Neil Charlesworth has put it, fluctuations in the output figures 'possibly tell us as much about the shifting authority of local administration as about actual agricultural performance' (*British Rule and the Indian Economy*, p. 22). Such contributions to the debate over agricultural output are reviewed in Heston, 'National Income', *CEHI*, 2; Satish Chandra Mishra, 'On the Reliability of Pre-Independence Agricultural Statistics in Bombay and Punjab', *IESHR*, 20, 2, 1983; and Carl Pray, 'Accuracy of Official Agricultural Statistics', *IESHR*, 21,3, 1984. For a critique and revision of Heston's own estimates in *CEHI*, 2, see Angus Maddison, 'Alternative Estimates of the Real Product of India, 1900–1946', *IESHR*, 22, 2, 1985. Revised figures for eastern India are presented in M. M. Islam, *Bengal Agriculture: A Quantitative Study*, Cambridge, 1978, but see also the review of this by C. J. Baker in *MAS*, 14, 3, 1980, and the debate between Islam, Omkar Goswami and Manoj Kumar Sanyal in *IESHR*, 23, 2, 1986 and 24, 2, 1987.

On the history of irrigation, Elizabeth Whitcombe, *Agrarian Conditions in North India: 1. The United Provinces under British Rule, 1860–1900*, Los Angeles, 1972, and her chapter in *CEHI*, 2, must be supplemented by Ian Stone, *Canal Irrigation in British India, Perspectives on Technological Change in a Peasant Economy*, Cambridge, 1984. On the effect of irrigation in Madras, see G. N. Rao, 'Canal Irrigation and Agrarian Change in Colonial Andhra: a Study of Godaveri District, *c.* 1850–1890', *IESHR*, 25, 1, 1988. James K. Boyce, *Agrarian Impasse in Bengal: Institutional Constraints to Technological Change*, Oxford, 1987, discusses the social context of water supply in contemporary Bengal in a way that has considerable historical relevance. The social and administrative history of the canal colonies of the Punjab is reviewed in Imran Ali, *The Punjab under Imperialism, 1885–1947*, Princeton, 1988. On railways, John M. Hurd's chapter in *CEHI*, 2, summarises the earlier work of himself and others; see also R. O.

Christensen, 'The State and Indian Railway Performance, 1870–1920', Parts I and II, *Journal of Transport History*, 2–3, 1981–2, and I. D. Derbyshire, 'Economic Change and the Railways in North India, 1860–1914', *MAS*, 21, 3, 1987.

Contrasting attitudes to famine and the administrative response to it are presented in Paul R. Greenough, *Prosperity and Misery in Modern Bengal: The Famine of 1943–1944*, New York, 1982; Michelle Burge McAlpin, *Subject To Famine: Food Crises and Economic Change in Western India, 1860–1920*, Princeton, 1983; Amartya Sen, *Poverty and Famines: An Essay on Entitlement and Deprivation*, Oxford, 1981; and Lance Brennan, 'The Development of the Indian Famine Codes: Personalities, Politics and Policies', in B. Curray and G. Hugo (eds.), *Famine as a Geographical Phenomenon*, Dordrecht, 1984. The demographic history of the period is reviewed in Leela Visaria and Pravin Visaria, 'Population', in *CEHI*, 2, and interpreted in Michelle B. McAlpin, 'Famines, Epidemics and Population Growth: The Case of India', *Journal of Interdisciplinary History*, 14, 2, 1983; Ira Klein, 'When the Rains Failed: Famine, Relief and Mortality in British India', *IESHR*, 21, 2, 1984, and 'Population Growth and Mortality in British India: The Demographic Revolution', *IESHR*, 27, 1, 1990.

Modern work on the first century of British rule is summarised, analysed and discussed in C. J. Bayly, *Indian Society and the Making of the British Empire*, and P. J. Marshall, *Bengal: The British Bridgehead: Eastern India, 1750–1828*, New Cambridge History of India, vols. II.1 and II.2, Cambridge, 1988; D. A. Washbrook, 'Progress and Problems', *MAS*, 1988; and Tapan Raychaudhuri, 'The Mid-Eighteenth-Century Background', *CEHI*, 2. There is, as yet, little modern work on the rural economy of the 1950s that sets it in a historical context. The best introductory study of the condition of Indian agriculture in 1950, and of the first wave of literature written about it, remains T. J. Byres, 'Land Reform, Industrialization and the Marketed Surplus in India: An Essay on the Power of Rural Bias', in David Lehmann (ed.), *Agricultural Reform and Agricultural Reformism: Studies of Peru, Chile, China and India*, London, 1974.

## 3 TRADE AND MANUFACTURE, 1860–1939

The standard statistical series on the value of output of the secondary sector comes from Sivasubramonian's work noted above, some of which is available in his 'Income from the Secondary Sector in India, 1900–1947', *IESHR*, 14, 4, 1977. These have not been supplanted, and form the basis of the estimates in Heston's 'National Income', *CEHI*, 2, and Colin Simmons, 'The Great Depression and Indian Industry: Changing Interpretations and Changing Perceptions', *MAS*, 21, 3, 1987.

The deindustrialisation debate was revived in spectacular fashion in the 1970s by A. K. Bagchi, 'Deindustrialisation in India and the Nineteenth Century: Some Theoretical Implications', *Journal of Development Studies*, 12, 2, 1976, and 'Deindustrialisation in Gangetic Bihar 1809–1901', in Barun De (ed.), *Essays in Honour of Professor Susobhan Chandra Sarkar*, New Delhi, 1976; Marika Vicziany, 'The Deindustrialization of India in the Nineteenth Century: A Methodological Critique of Amiya Kumar Bagchi', *IESHR*, 16,2, 1979, and Bagchi's 'Reply' in the same volume. A further account of changes in output and employment in that region was provided by J. Krishnamurty, 'Deindustrialisation in Gangetic Bihar During the Nineteenth Century: Another Look at the Evidence', *IESHR*, 11, 4, 1985; his chapter on 'The Occupational Structure', *CEHI*, 2, gives an idea of the regional variation in employment changes in the nineteenth century. On north India, see also G. Pandey, 'Economic Dislocation in Nineteenth Century Uttar Pradesh: Some Implications of the Decline of Artisanal Industry in Colonial India', in Peter Robb (ed.), *Rural South Asia: Linkages, Changes and Development*, London, 1983. Michael J. Twomey, 'Employment in Nineteenth Century Indian Texiles', *Explorations in Economic History*, 20, 1983, provides the most complete and sophisticated set of statistical estimates for the most important sector of handicraft manufactures, although the implications of these have been contested from a regional perspective by Konrad Specker, '"Deindustrialisation" in Nineteenth Century India: The Textile Industry in the Madras Presidency, 1810–1870', in Dewey, *Arrested Development in India.* A different approach to the whole question, seeing occupational and structural change in nineteenth-century India in terms of the destruction of local merchant capitalism rather than direct employment or output effects, is provided in Frank Perlin's important and wide-ranging article, 'Proto-Industrialization and Pre-Colonial South Asia', *Past and Present*, 98, 1983, which is one of the most suggestive analyses of the eighteenth-century manufacturing economy.

The destructive effects of colonial trading and financial arrangements on indigenous business groups are discussed in Marika Vicziany, 'Bombay Merchants and Structural Changes in the Export Community, 1850–1880', in K. N. Chaudhuri and C. J. Dewey (eds.), *Economy and Society: Studies in Indian Economic and Social History*, New Delhi, 1978; Blair B. Kling, *Partner in Empire: Dwarkarnath Tagore and the Age of Enterprise in Eastern India*, Berkeley, 1979; A. Siddiqi, 'The Business World of Jamshethji Jejeebhoy', *IESHR*, 19, 3–4, 1982; C. J. Bayly, *Rulers, Townsmen and Bazaars: North Indian Society in the Age of British Expansion*, Cambridge, 1983; Amiya Kumar Bagchi, 'Transition from Indian Banking in British India: From the Paper Pound to the Gold Standard', *Journal of Imperial and Commonwealth History*, 13, 1985; and Laxmi Subramanian, 'Banias and the British: The Role of Indigenous Credit in the Process of Imperial Expansion in Western India in the Second Half of the Eighteenth Century', *MAS*, 21, 3, 1987. Some of this material is summarised and extended in Bayly, *Indian Society and the Making of the British Empire.* For studies of the continuities between 'traditional' and 'modern' business organisations in the late nineteenth and early twentieth centuries, see Thomas Timberg, *The Marwaris: From Traders to Industrialists*, Delhi, 1978; Dwijendra Tripathi, *Kasturbhai Lalbhai and his Entrepreneurship*, New Delhi, 1981; and Rajat K. Ray, 'Pedhis and Mills: the Historical Integration of the Formal and Informal Sectors in the Economy of Ahmedabad', *IESHR*, 19, 3–4, 1982.

The standard modern accounts of the emergence of factory-based, mechanised industry in colonial India are Amiya Kumar Bagchi, *Private Investment in India, 1900–1939*, Cambridge, 1972 (which contains an excellent bibliography), and Morris D. Morris, 'The Growth of Large-Scale Industry to 1947', *CEHI*, 2, Chapter VII. Rajat K. Ray, *Industrialization in India: Growth and Conflict in the Private Corporate Sector, 1914–1947*, Delhi, 1979, tries to mediate between conflicting interpretations based on supply and demand factors, and provides a useful sketch of government policy and business response. I. M. D. Little, 'Indian Industrialization Before 1945', in M. Gersovitz *et al.* (eds.), *The Theory and Experience of Economic Development*, London, 1982, gives a strong revisionist account of the effects of protection on industrial growth in the inter-war period, while Tom Kemp, *Industrialization in the Non-Western World*, London, 1983, Chapter 6, concludes that the unbalanced distribution of political and economic power in India has made industrialisation only a limited success – 'one more example of growth without development' (p. 98). This literature is reviewed in C. P. Simmons, 'De-industrialization, Industrialization and the Indian Economy *c.* 1850–1947', *MAS*, 19, 3, 1985, and is extended in his 'The Great Depression and Indian Industry', and in Rajnarayan Chandavarkar, 'Industrialization in India before 1947; Conventional Approaches and Alternative Perspectives', *MAS*, 19, 3, 1985.

The cotton industry still holds the centre stage in expositions and explanations of India's industrial progress, or the lack of it, under British rule. Studies of this include M. J. Mehta, *The Ahmedabad Cotton Textile Industry: Genesis and Growth*, Ahmedabad, 1982; Yukihiko Kiyokawa, 'Technical Adaptations and Managerial Resources in India: A Study of the Experience of the Cotton Textile Industry from a Comparative Viewpoint', *The Developing Economics*, 21, 2, 1983; R. Kirk and C. P. Simmons, 'Lancashire and the Equipping of Indian Cotton Mills: A Study of Textile Machinery and Supply', in K. Ballhatchet and D. Taylor (eds.), *Changing South Asia: Economy and Society*, London, 1984; and Jim Matson, 'Deindustrialization or Peripheralization?: The Case of Cotton Textiles in India, 1750–1950', in Bose, *South Asia and World Capitalism.* On the cotton handloom sector, see Konrad Specker, 'Madras Handlooms in the Nineteenth Century', *IESHR*, 26, 2, 1989; and Tirthankar Roy, 'Size and Structure of Handloom Weaving in the Mid-Thirties', *IESHR*, 25, 1, 1988. There have been few monographs or articles on the industrial history of the rest of the mechanised factory sector, but for the rural background to the emergence of the sugar industry, one of the archetypal new consumer goods industries of the 1930s, see Shahid Amin, *Sugarcane and Sugar in Gorakhpur: An Inquiry into Peasant Production for Capital Enterprise in Colonial India*, Delhi, 1984.

Morris David Morris's classic study, *The Emergence of an Industrial Labour-force in India*, Berkeley, 1965, can now be supplemented by a number of studies of labour history in the major industrial centres. On Bombay, see Rajnarayan Chandavarkar, *Between Work and Politics: Workplace, Neighbourhood and Social Organization in Bombay City, 1900–1940*, Cambridge, 1992, and 'Workers' Politics in the Mill Districts in Bombay between the Wars', *MAS*, 15, 3, 1981; R. K. Newman, *Workers and Unions in Bombay, 1918–1929*, Canberra, 1981; and Dick Kooiman, *Bombay Textile Labour: Managers, Trade Unionists and Officials, 1918–1939*, Delhi, 1989. Salim Lakha, *Capitalism and Class in Colonial India: the Case of Ahmedabad*, Asian Studies Association of Australia, Bombay, 1988 and Sujata Patel, *The Making of Industrial Relations: The Ahemedabad Textile Industry, 1918–1939*, Delhi, 1987, both deal with some of the same themes for a different industrial centre, as does Eamon Murphy, *Unions in Conflict: A Comparative Study of Four South Indian Textile Centres, 1918–1939*, Canberra, 1981. Dipesh Chakrabarty's study of the Calcutta proletariat, *Rethinking Working-Class History: Bengal, 1980–1940*, Princeton, 1989, seeks to relate the Indian experience to thematic treatments of working-class history developed in the West (as does Chandavarkar's work), and also includes a convenient summary of the history of the jute industry. The rural roots of the industrial workforce are investigated in Lalit Chakravarty, 'Emergence of an Industrial Labour Force in a Dual Economy – British India, 1880–1920', *IESHR*, 15, 3, 1978, and Prabhu Prasad Mohapatra, 'Coolies and Colliers: A Study of the Agrarian Context of Labour Migration from Chotanagpur, 1880–1920', *Studies in History*, new series,

1, 2, 1985. Ralph Shlomowitz and Lance Brennan, 'Mortality and Migrant Labour in Assam, 1865–1921', *IESHR*, 27, 1, 1990, and 'Mortality and Migrant Labour en route to Assam, 1865–1924', *IESHR*, 27, 3 1990, consider some of the human costs of migration.

A number of detailed historical studies of the industrial, fiscal and monetary policies of the colonial government in India, and the interaction of business influence, imperial requirements, nationalist ideology and political necessity, based on archival research in London and New Delhi, have appeared in the last twenty years. The first such account was of trade and tariff policy in an imperial context, in I. M. Drummond, *British Economic Policy and the Empire*, London, 1972, Chapter IV. Subsequent work includes C. J. Dewey, 'The Government of India's "New Industrial Policy", 1900–1925: Formation and Failure', in K. N. Chaudhuri and C. J. Dewey (eds.), *Economy and Society: Studies in Indian Economic and Social History*, New Delhi, 1978, and 'The End of the Imperialism of Free Trade: The Eclipse of the Lancashire Lobby and the Concession of Free Trade to India', in Clive Dewey and A. G. Hopkins (eds.), *The Imperial Impact: Studies in the Imperial History of Africa and India*, London, 1978; A. D. D. Gordon, *Businessmen and Politics: Rising Nationalism and a Modernising Economy in Bombay, 1918–1933*, Delhi, 1978; G. G. Jones, 'The State and Economic Development in India, 1890–1947: The Case of Oil', *MAS*, 13, 1, 1979; B. R. Tomlinson, *The Political Economy of the Raj, 1914–1947: The Economics of Decolonization in India*, London, 1979; Aditya Mukherjee, 'The Indian Capitalist Class and Foreign Capital, 1927–47', *Studies in History*, 1, 1, 1979; D. M. Wagle, 'Imperial Preference and the Indian Steel Industry, 1925–39', *Economic History Review*, 34, 1, 1981; Dietmar Rothermund, 'The Great Depression and British Financial Policy in India, 1929–1934', *IESHR*, 18, 1, 1981, and 'British Foreign Trade Policy in India During the Great Depression, 1929–1939', *IESHR*, 18, 3–4, 1981; Basudev Chatterji, 'Business and Politics in the 1920s: Lancashire and the Making of the Indo-British Trade Agreement', *MAS*, 15, 3, 1981, and 'The Political Economy of Discriminating Protections: The Case of Textiles in the 1920s', *IESHR*, 20, 3, 1983; Claude Markovits, *Indian Business and Nationalist Politics, 1919–1939*, Cambridge, 1985; Dwijendra Tripathi (ed.), *State and Business in India*, Delhi, 1986; Rajul Mathur, 'The Delay in the Formation of the Reserve Bank of India: the India Office Perspective', *IESHR*, 25, 2, 1988; G. Balachandran, 'The Sterling Crisis and the Managed Float Regime in India, 1921–1924', *IESHR*, 27, 1, 1990, and 'Gold and Empire: Britain and India in the Great Depression', *Journal of European Economic History*, 20, 2, 1991; and Dwijendra Tripathi (ed.), *Business and Politics in India: A Historical Perspective*, New Delhi, 1991.

Business history remains a neglected subject in the study of modern South Asia, with the main centre of empirical work confined to the Indian Institute of Management, Ahmedabad. The general constraints and determinants of business activity, especially the political context of business development, are dealt with in several of the works already listed, notably those of T. A. Timberg, A. D. D. Gordon, Claude Markovits and Aditya Mukherjee. The important case of the rise of the Marwari industrialists in Bengal is further considered in Omkar Goswami, 'Collaboration and Conflict: European and Indian Capitalists and the Jute Economy of Bengal, 1919–1939', *IESHR*, 19, 2, 1982, and 'Then Came the Marwaris: Some Aspects of the Changes in the Pattern of Industrial Control in Eastern India', *IESHR*, 22, 3, 1985. A broader explanation of the behaviour of different types of firms, in terms of the differential impact of risk, uncertainty and imperfect knowledge, is given in Morris David Morris, 'South Asian Entrepreneurship and the Rashomon Effect, 1889 – 1947', *Explorations in Economic History*, 16, 1979. A general discussion of the effect of political and economic change on the organisation and activities of British firms will be found in B. R. Tomlinson, 'British Business in India, 1860–1970', in R. P. T. Davenport-Hines and Geoffrey Jones (eds.), *British Business in Asia since 1860*, Cambridge, 1989, which also reviews the sources for statistical estimates of British business activity in South Asia.

Accounts of business history based on case-studies of single firms or small groups of firms are rare: work in this field includes B. R. Tomlinson, 'Colonial Firms and the Decline of Colonialism in Eastern India, 1914–1947', *MAS*, 15, 3, 1981 (based on the experience of Bird-Heilgers); Colin Simmons *et al.*, 'Machine Manufacture in a Colonial Economy: the Pioneering Role of George Hattersley and Sons Ltd. in India, 1919–43', *IESHR*, 20, 3, 1983; Shyam Rungta, 'Bowreah Cotton and Fort Gloster Jute Mills, 1872–1900', *IESHR*, 22, 2, 1985; Stephanie Jones, *Two Centuries of Overseas Trading: The Origins and Growth of the Inchcape Group*, London, 1986; Howard Cox, 'International Business, the State and Industrialisation in India: Early Growth in the Indian Cigarette Industry', *IESHR*, 27, 3, 1990; and Anna-Maria Misra, 'Politics and Expatriate Enterprise in India: The Inter-War Years', in Tripathi, *Business and Politics in India*. Howard John Andersen, 'The British Iron and Steel Industry and India, 1919–1939', Ph.D. thesis, University of Birmingham, 1989, contains case-studies of the Indian operations of Dorman Long, Stewarts and Lloyds, and Braithwaite plc. In banking history, the problems of access to source material have constrained scholars severely. The only works that have been able to overcome this barrier are Dwijendra Tripathi and Priti Misra, *Towards a New Frontier: History of the Bank of Baroda, 1908–1983*, New Delhi, 1985; and the products of a long-term project, headed by Amiya Kumar Bagchi, to write the official history of the State Bank of India and its predecessors – the Imperial Bank of India and the Presidency Banks of Bengal, Bombay and Madras. The first volumes of this have appeared as Amiya Kumar Bagchi, *The Evolution of the State Bank of India: The Roots, 1806–1876*, Parts I and II, Bombay, 1987, and *The Presidency Banks and the Indian Economy, 1816–1914*, Bombay, 1990.

## 4 STATE AND ECONOMY SINCE 1947

The literature on the management and progress of the Indian economy since 1947 is vast, and much of it is not relevant to our purpose here. Pramit Chaudhuri, *The Indian Economy*, London, 1978, provides a good summary of the main concerns of the literature to that date, and can be supplemented by B. L. C. Johnson, *Development in South Asia*, Harmondsworth, 1983; A. Vaidyanathan, 'The Indian Economy Since Independence (1947–1970)', *CEHI*, 2, and V. N. Balasubramanyam, *The Economy of India*, London 1984.

Analytical work on the progress of industry includes Isher Judge Ahluwalia, *Industrial Growth in India: Stagnation Since the Mid-Sixties*, Delhi, 1985, and Ruchira Chatterji, *The Behaviour of Industrial Prices in India*, Delhi, 1989. On agriculture, the literature has been dominated by accounts of the Green Revolution and its aftermath. There is a good bibliographic essay on the main lines of agricultural policy in developing countries in John M. Staatz and Carl K. Eicher, 'Agricultural Development Ideas in Historical Perspective', in Eicher and Staatz (eds.), *Agricultural Development in the Third World*, Baltimore, 1984, while B. H. Farmer, 'The "Green Revolution" in South Asia', *MAS*, 20, 1, 1986, provides an informed commentary on issues in our region. Randolph Barker and Rudolph W. Herdt, with Beth Rose, *The Rice Economy of Asia*, Washington DC, 1985, is a useful source of the usual critiques of the failures of implementation of the new technologies in South Asia, but see the review of this book by Farmer in *MAS*, 21, 1, 1987. Research on technological change, social differentiation and labour employment and productivity is discussed fully, from a variety of perspectives, in M. Lipton, with R. Longhurst, *New Seeds and Poor People*, London, 1989; Inderjit Singh, *The Great Ascent: The Rural Poor in South Asia*, World Bank/Johns Hopkins, Baltimore, 1990; and John Harriss, 'Does the "Depressor" Still Work? Agrarian Structure and Development in India – A Review of Evidence and Argument', *Journal of Peasant Studies*, 19, 2, 1992. On poverty and the problems of food supply, V. M. Dandekar, 'Agriculture, Employment and Poverty', in Robert E. Lucas and Gustav F. Papanek (eds.), *The Indian Economy: Recent Development and Future Prospects*, Delhi, 1988, and Jean Drèze, 'Famine Prevention in India', in Jean Drèze and Amartya Sen (eds.), *The Political Economy of Hunger, Volume 2: Famine Prevention*, Oxford, 1990, review the main issues and policies, while Amartya Sen, 'Food and Freedom', *World Development*, 17, 6, 1989, reflects on the capacity of the Indian economy to provide subsistence for its poorest members in a comparative context.

Historians have not yet got to grips with the events of the 1940s, 1950s and 1960s; government records and other official sources dry up after about 1945, despite the nominal existence of a thirty-year rule in Indian archives. For this reason, the established standard accounts of the planning process and the emergence of economic management down to 1970 that were written at the time still dominate the field. The most important of these are A. H. Hanson, *The Process of Planning: A Study of India's Five Year Plans, 1950–1964*, Oxford, 1966; Paul Streeten and Michael Lipton (eds.), *The Crisis of Indian Planning: Economic Policy in the 1960's*, Oxford, 1968; Jagdish N. Bhagwati and Sukhamoy Chakravarty, 'Contributions to Indian Economic Analysis: A Survey', *American Economic Review*, 59, 4, Part 2, Supplement, 1969; Jagdish N. Bhagwati and Padma Desai, *Planning for Industrialization: Industrialization and Trade Policies since 1951*, Oxford, 1970; E. A. G. Robinson and M. Kidron (eds.), *Economic Development in South Asia*, London, 1970; and Jagdish N. Bhagwati and T. N. Srinivasan, *Foreign Trade Regimes and Economic Development, India*, Amsterdam, 1975. Baldev Raj Nayar, *The Modernization Imperative and Indian Planning*, Delhi, 1972, and Francine R. Frankel, *India's Political Economy, 1947–1977: The Gradual Revolution*, Princeton, 1978, are two attempts by political scientists to analyse these events – Frankel gives a particularly thorough account of policy towards agriculture and food supply. Sukhomoy Chakravarty's posthumous article, 'Development Planning: A Reappraisal', *Cambridge Journal of Economics*, 15, 1, 1991, serves as an epitaph to the classic period of Indian planning and its foremost practitioner.

Following the work of political scientists in the last two decades or so, the 'standard' accounts of economic policy-making can be brought up to date by a number of studies of the political system of contemporary India that contain some discussion of economic policy-making and planning since 1970. These include Robert L. Hardgrave Jr. and Stanley A. Kochanek, *India: Government and Politics in a Developing Nation*, 4th edn, San Diego, 1986; Lloyd I. Rudolph and Susanne Hoeber Rudolph, *In Pursuit of Lakshmi: The Political Economy of the Indian State*, Chicago, 1987; Atul Kohli, *Democracy and Dissent: India's Growing Crisis of Governability*, Cambridge, 1991; Francine R. Frankel and M. S. A. Rao (eds.), *Dominance and State Power in Modern India: Decline of a Social Order*, Volumes 1 & 2, Delhi, 1989/90; and Paul R. Brass, *The Politics of India Since Independence*, New Cambridge History of India, IV.1., Cambridge, 1990. On the process of liberalisation and the possibility of economic 'miracles' in the 1980s, see Atul Kohli, 'Politics of Economic Liberalization in India', *World Development*, 17, 3, 1989, and for the most credulous approach, Lawrence Veit and Catherine Gwin, 'The Indian Miracle', *Foreign Policy*, 58, 1985. Subroto Roy and William E. James (eds.), *Foundations of India's Political Economy: Towards an Agenda for the 1990s*, Delhi, 1992, contains a number of essays that make the case for economic liberalism forcefully, linked in some cases explicitly to a Friedmanite critique of past Indian economic management.

There is little written on India that deals with the context of economic policy-making, and the whole problematic of a 'developmental state' in South Asia, in ways that compare with studies of other Asian countries such as Chalmers Johnson, *MITI and the Japanese Miracle: The Growth of Industrial Policy, 1925–1975*, Stanford, 1982, or Robert Wade, *Governing the Market: Economic Theory and the Role of Government in East Asian Industrialization*, Princeton, 1990. The literature on India is still dominated by polemical critiques of past performance based either on 'rent-seeking' concepts (such as Deepak Lai, 'Ideology and Industrialization in India and East Asia', in Helen Hughes (ed.), *Achieving Industrialization in East Asia*, Cambridge, 1988; his *Hindu Equilibrium: Cultural Stability and Economic Stagnation, India 1500 BC–1980 AD*, Oxford, 1984; and Subroto Roy, *Pricing, Planning and Politics: A Study of Economic Distortions in India*, Institute of Economic Affairs, Occasional Paper no. 69, London, 1984), on the identification of India as an 'intermediate regime' (in Prem Shankar Jha, *India: A Political Economic of Stagnation*, Bombay, 1980; and Baldev Raj Nayar, *India's Mixed Economy: The Role of Ideology and Interest in Development*, Bombay, 1988), or on a functional analysis of class formations in a post-colonial political economy (provided by T. J. Byres, 'India: Capitalist Industrialization or Structural Stasis?', in M. Bienefeld and M. Godfrey, *The Struggle for Development: National Strategies in an International Context*, London, 1982; Anupam Sen, *The State, Industrialization and Class Formations in India: A Neo-Marxist Perspective on Colonialism, Underdevelopment and Development*, London, 1982; and Pranab Bradhan, *The Political Economy of Development in India*, Oxford, 1984). Interesting work that does directly address the questions that dominate the East Asian literature will be found in Robert Wade, 'The Market for Public Office: Why the Indian State is not Better At Development', *World Development*, 13, 4, 1985; and Mrinal Datta-Chaudhuri, 'Market Failure and Government Failure', *Journal of Economic Perspectives*, 4, 3, 1990, which contains an explicit analysis of India's weakness as a developmental regime in a comparative context. It is here, perhaps, that economic historians should begin to reclaim the study of the middle decades of the twentieth century as a whole, linking pre- and post-Independence events and policies explicitly, and searching out the colonial roots of other areas of policy-making and practice, such as education, that have profoundly affected human capital formation, the capacity for economic growth, and the development of the personal capabilities of the citizens of independent India.

# SUPPLEMENTARY BIBLIOGRAPHY

During the 1990s and 2000s a number of very useful general volumes were published on the colonial economy as a whole, or on important segments of it, which tie together a number of the strands of specialist research. These include Tirthankar Roy, *The Economic History of India, 1857–1947*, 3rd edn, New Delhi, 2011; Binay Bhushan Chaudhury, *Peasant History of Late Pre-colonial and Colonial India*, Delhi, 2008; David Ludden, *An Agrarian History of South Asia*, New Cambridge History of India vol. IV.4, Cambridge, 1999 (with an extensive bibliographic essay); and Dwijendra Tripathi, *Oxford History of Indian Business*, New Delhi, 2004. In addition, a number of classic essays have been reissued with a fresh introduction in Amiya Kumar Bagchi, *Colonialism and Indian Economy*, New Delhi, 2010.

The changes that have taken place in the Indian economy since the 1980s have stimulated a new interest in colonial economic history: much of this work has tried to relate events across the modern period to recent developments, and to integrate analysis of the colonial past with the core concerns of economic and business historians of other regions across the modern world. India can now be taught more easily as a part of comparative and global history courses in universities across the world. Interpretations have broadened as well: the revisionism first exhibited at length by the *Cambridge Economic History of India Volume 2* (1982), which presented an analysis of the colonial economy that did not simply focus on the actions of British imperialism resulting in Indian underdevelopment, has been carried forward, chiefly in the work of Tirthankar Roy. In three important books – his *Economic History; Rethinking Economic Change in India: Labour and Livelihood*, London, 2007; and *Company of Kinsmen: Enterprise and Community in South Asian History 1700–1940*, New Delhi, 2010 – Roy has set out a wide-ranging account of the Indian colonial economy in which poverty was associated with exhaustion of natural resources and diminishing returns to labour; in which handicraft-based industrial production survived to become a significant employer of surplus labour and source of national income; in which the spread of markets for goods and labour provided new opportunities that were embraced by significant proportions of the population; and in which kinship and community networks provided the essential institutions for organising capital investment, labour migration, technological diffusion and entrepreneurial innovation. Roy has self-consciously opposed the dominant 'leftist-nationalist' interpretation of Indian history, which sees the colonial state as the chief author of India's tribulations and a socialistic independent state as the best hope for its redemption, suggesting that 'until the 1980s the principal use for economic history in India was to supply a critique of colonialism, which formed the ideological basis for an economic policy of "self-reliance"' ('Economic History and Modern India: Redefining the Link', *Journal of Economic Perspectives*, 16, 2002, p. 128). Critics have argued that the economic history of a colony necessarily requires a political explanation, and that the structure of markets and other co-ordinating institutions in

India masked unequal power relations which limited opportunities and skewed benefits. There are resounding restatements of the orthodox view in Irfan Habib, *Indian Economy, 1858–1914*, New Delhi, 2006; Aditya Mukherjee, 'Empire: How Colonial India Made Modern Britain', *Economic and Political Weekly*, XLV, 50, 2010; and Amiya Kumar Bagchi, 'Review Article: Indian Business History', *Indian Historical Review*, 39, 1, 2012.

The mutation of comparative economic history into a distinct sub-discipline of global history in the late 1990s stimulated a wide-ranging debate about relative levels of development and standards of living in Europe and Asia before colonialism in the seventeenth and eighteenth centuries, and the circumstances that enabled an industrial revolution to take place much earlier in some parts of Eurasia than in others. Much of this discussion has been focused on China, epitomised by Ken Pomeranz, *The Great Divergence: China, Europe, and the Making of the Modern World Economy*, Princeton, 2000. However, there have been a number of important studies within this tradition on the Indian economy. Prasannan Parthasarathi has argued strongly that living standards and real grain wages for weavers were higher in South India than in England in the mid eighteenth century, because competition for labour required those in command of the local economy to invest in agricultural productivity to provide cheap food. Others have been more sceptical, with Stephen Broadberry and Bishnupriya Gupta suggesting that the most dynamic parts of Europe were already substantially more advanced than anywhere in Asia by 1800, and that an important element of structural change in England was the transfer of labour out of agriculture which had not happened elsewhere: thus the 'great divergence' between levels of development in the West and the East was already well under way before 1800 (see Prasannan Parthasarathi, *Why Europe Grew Rich and Asia Did Not: Global Economic Divergence, 1600–1850*, Cambridge, 2011; S. N. Broadberry and B. Gupta, 'The Early Modern Great Divergence: Wages, Prices and Economic Development in Europe and Asia, 1500–1800', *Economic History Review*, 59, 1, 2006). A study of these issues for Bengal has concluded that local incomes were well below European levels, with no clear evidence of either consistent increase or decline across the eighteenth century: Tirthankar Roy, 'Economic Conditions in Early Modern Bengal: A Contribution to the Divergence Debate', *Journal of Economic History*, 70, 1, 2010. There are brief re-statements of the issues in S. N. Broadberry and Steve Hindle, 'Asia in the Great Divergence: Editors' Introduction', *Economic History Review*, 64, 1, 2011; and Patrick O'Brien, 'A Conjuncture in Global History or an Anglo-American Construct: The British Industrial Revolution, 1700–1850, *Journal of Global History*, 5, 3, 2010. Angus Maddison's final account of the global history of economic growth and change appeared as *Contours of the World Economy: Essays in Macro-Economic History, 1 – 2030 AD*, Oxford, 2007.

For colonial India, the publication of S. Sivasubramonian, *National Income of India in the Twentieth Century*, New Delhi, 2000, provides a wealth of detail on aggregate output and rates of growth. These data confirm the impression given by earlier material that per capita national income rose significantly between 1900 and 1913, rose very slowly until the late 1920s and then stagnated, and in some years declined slightly, until 1947. Agricultural production grew very slowly between 1920 and 1947, the largest depressor being low productivity in eastern India, where foodgrain output fell behind population growth in the inter-war years. Suggested causes for this state of affairs include an ecological crisis – Tirthankar Roy, 'A Delayed Revolution: Environment and Agrarian Change in India', *Oxford Review of Economic Policy*, 23, 2, 2007, and a lack of investment in technical change caused by very low levels of return – Sumit Guha, 'Weak States and Strong Markets in South Asian Development, *c.* 1700–1970', *IESHR*, 36, 3, 1999. A case history of southern India provides a detailed narrative on living standards: Peter Mayer, 'Trends of Real Income in Tiruchirapalli and the Upper Kaveri Delta, 1819–1980: A Footnote in Honour of Dharma Kumar', *IESHR*, 43, 3, 2006, found that income for rural labourers increased rapidly from the middle of the nineteenth century until the First World War as employment opportunities expanded, then entered a fifty-year decline after 1931, until the Green Revolution of the 1980s raised demand for labour and restored real wages to the level they had reached in 1916.

There have been a number of significant publications on the Indian famines, possibly stimulated by the reception of Mike Davis's highly contentious *Late Victorian Holocausts: El Niño Famines and the Making of the Third World*, London, 2000. Recent work, such as David Hall-Matthews, *Peasants, Famine and the State in Colonial Western India*, Basingstoke, 2005; and Mufakhurul M. Islam, 'The Great Bengal Famine and the Question of FAD Yet Again', *Modern Asian Studies* 41, 2, 2007, has argued over whether crop failures were more important than market failures in causing dearth, and over the effectiveness and ideology of government relief programmes. These themes, and much more, are considered in Cormac Ó Gráda, *Famine: A Brief History*, Princeton, 2009, which concludes that 'the recognition that inadequate relief was responsible for much of the excess mortality in the late 1870s concentrated policy-makers' minds on the need to focus primarily on saving lives' (p. 206). A broad approach to the environmental effects of colonial rule is presented in the essays collected in Deepak Kumar, Vinita Damodaran and Rohn D'Souza (eds.), *The British Empire and the Natural World: Environmental Encounters in South Asia*, New Delhi, 2011. Several of these essays highlight the rejection of local knowledge by colonial science, and the contradictory impulses of conservationism, timber production and agricultural expansion that were themes of Richard Grove's seminal *Green Imperialism: Colonial Expansion, Tropical Island Edens and the Origins of Environmentalism, 1600–1815*, Cambridge, 1995.

Two areas in which recent literature has developed the subject concern the history of the unorganised sector of unmechanised and semi-mechanised craft-based production that remains such a large employer of labour and producer of manufactures in contemporary India, and the history of firms and business institutions in the modernised economy that now provide a crucial part of the network of economic life. Tirthankar Roy, *Traditional Industry in Colonial India*, Cambridge, 1999, and 'Acceptance of Innovations in Early Twentieth Century Indian Weaving', *Economic History Review*, 55, 3, 2002, make it clear that craft industries extended their operations despite manufactured imports in the colonial period. This sector had a dynamic history; craft industries became progressively centralised during the late-colonial period, moving from family to wage labour, and using extended marketing and transport networks to supply both domestic and foreign markets. Douglas E. Haynes, in 'Artisan Cloth Producers and the Emergence of Powerloom Manufacture in Western India 1920–1950', *Past and Present*, 172, Aug., 2001, and *Small Town Capitalism in Western India: Artisans, Merchants, and the Making of the Informal Economy, 1870–1960*, Cambridge, 2012, provides a means of understanding the economy of western India through the history of the very large body of artisan cloth producers: this work also stresses the role of conflict between labour and capital in shaping the relations of production and the form in which the industry has developed. *Towards a History of Consumption in South Asia*, New Delhi, 2010, edited by Douglas E. Haynes, Abigail McGowan, Tirthankar Roy and Haruka Yanagisawa, contains a number of essays that open up novel perspectives on the material history of everyday life. David Arnold, 'Global Goods and Local Usages: the Small World of the Indian Sewing Machine, 1875–1952', *Journal of Global History*, 6, 3, 2011, provides a case-study of the interplay of foreign technology and local agency that established an important domestic industry in late-colonial India.

The history of firms and business institutions, and the communities and networks from which they emerged in the late-colonial period, has been opened up by Tripathi's *Oxford History of Indian Business*. Medha M. Kudaisya, *The Oxford India Anthology of Business History*, New Delhi, 2011, mixes reprinted academic articles with other testimony from practitioners and commentators, and a new Penguin India popular monograph series 'The Story of Indian Business', edited by Gurcharan Das, began to appear in January 2012. Other work that investigates particular communities or business groups includes Ritu Birla, *Stages of Capital: Law, Culture, and Market Governance in Late Colonial India*, Durham, NC, 2009, which provides a history of the Marwari community in the nineteenth century that shows how 'vernacular' capitalists interacted with and contested colonial attempts to regulate corporate governance and market relations; and Claude Markovits, *The Global World of Indian Merchants, 1750–1947: Traders of Sind from Bukhara to Panama*, Cambridge, 2000, and in his essays reproduced in *Merchants, Traders, Entrepreneurs: Indian Business in the Colonial Era*, Basingstoke, 2008, which explore the process of 'circulation', or the building of business networks, by which a small number of communities of indigenous traders established dominance over a wide area of economic activity. On the industrial economy, Bishnupriya Gupta, 'Wages, Unions and Labour Productivity: Evidence from the Bombay Mills', *Economic History Review*, 64, 1, 2010, shows that low wages and low productivity in the early twentieth century were the result of surplus labour, rather than any cultural preference for low effort; while Chikayoshi Nomura, 'Selling Steel in the 1920s: TISCO in a Period of Transition', *IESHR*, 48, 1, 2011, demonstrates the success of the company in integrating an internal sales network with production. This last is one of the few research projects to make use of the TISCO archives at Jamshedpur: the Tata Group has now opened its central archive located in Pune, which should provide an invaluable resource to business historians.

Finally, any attempt to write the history of state policy and economic management in India remains hampered by the failure of the Government of India to make any useful records of the late 1940s, 1950s or 1960s available to scholars, despite nominally having a thirty-year rule for access to historical documents. G. Balachandran, *History of the Reserve Bank of India, 1951–1967*, Delhi, 1998, provides a history of some aspects of economic decision-making, as the Bank's own archives are available to scholars. However, as things stand, an archival history of Indian economic management and development policy and practice can only be written from American documents – as in works such as Corinna R. Unger, 'Towards Global Equilibrium: American Foundations and Indian Modernization', *Journal of Global History*, 6, 1, 2011; and Jason A. Kirk, *India and the World Bank: The Politics of Aid and Influence*, London, 2011. Post-colonial historians tell us that these are the methodological circumstances in which subalterns lose their voice and 'otherness' is constructed: the Government of India has only itself to blame for any misinterpretations of its history that may result.

# INDEX

# THE NEW CAMBRIDGE HISTORY OF INDIA

## I The Mughals and Their Contemporaries

†* M. N. Pearson, *The Portuguese in India*
†* Burton Stein, *Vijayanagara*
* Milo Cleveland Beach, *Mughal and Rajput Painting*
* Catherine Asher, *Architecture of Mughal India*
†* John F. Richards, *The Mughal Empire*
* George Michell, *Architecture and Art of Southern India*
* George Michell and Mark Zebrowski, *Architecture and Art of the Deccan Sultanates*
†* Richard M. Eaton, *A Social History of the Deccan, 1300–1761: Eight Indian Lives*

## II Indian states and the Transition to Colonialism

†* C. A. Bayly, *Indian Society and the Making of the British Empire*
†* P. J. Marshall, *Bengal: The British Bridgehead: Eastern India 1740–1828*
†* J. S. Grewal, *The Sikhs of the Punjab*
†* Stewart Gordon, *The Marathas, 1600–1818*
* Om Prakash, *European Commercial Enterprise in Pre-Colonial India*

## III The Indian Empire and the Beginnings of Modern Society

†* Kenneth W. Jones, *Socio-Religious Reform Movements in British India*
†* Sugata Bose, *Peasant Labour and Colonial Capital: Rural Bengal since 1770*
†* B. R. Tomlinson, *The Economy of Modern India: From 1860 to the Twenty-First Century*, second edition
†* Thomas R. Metcalf, *Ideologies of the Raj*
†* David Arnold, *Science, Technology and Medicine in Colonial India*
†* B. N. Ramusack, *The Indian Princes and Their States*
Gordon Johnson, *Government and Politics in India*

## IV The Evolution of Contemporary South Asia

†* Paul R. Brass, *The Politics of India since Independence*, second edition
†* Geraldine Forbes, *Women in Modern India*
†* Susan Bayly, *Caste, Society and Politics in India from the Eighteenth Century to the Modern Age*
†* David Ludden, *An Agrarian History of South Asia*
Francis Robinson, *Islam in South Asia*
Anil Seal, *The Transfer of Power and the Partition of India*

**Already published*
*† Available in paperback*